On Love and Charity

THOMAS AQUINAS IN TRANSLATION

ST. THOMAS AQUINAS

On Love and Charity

Readings from the
Commentary on the Sentences
of Peter Lombard

Translated by
Peter A. Kwasniewski,
Thomas Bolin, O.S.B.,
and Joseph Bolin

With introduction and notes by
Peter A. Kwasniewski

The Catholic University of America Press
Washington, D.C.

BX
1749
.P373
T4613
2008

Library of Congress Cataloging-in-Publication Data
Thomas, Aquinas, Saint, 1225?–1274.
[Scriptum super IV libros Sententiarum. English. Selections. 2008]
On love and charity : readings from the commentary on the sentences of
Peter Lombard / Thomas Aquinas ; translated by Peter A. Kwasniewski,
Thomas Bolin, and Joseph Bolin ; with introduction and notes by Peter A.
Kwasniewski.
p. cm — (Thomas Aquinas in translation)
Includes bibliographical references and index.
ISBN 978-0-8132-1525-9 (pbk. : alk. paper) 1. Peter Lombard,
Bishop of Paris, ca. 1100–1160. Sententiarum libri IV. 2. Catholic
Church — Doctrines. 3. Theology, Doctrinal—History—Middle Ages,
600–1500. 4. God—Love. 5. Love—Religious aspects—Christianity.
6. Charity. I. Title
BX1749.P373T4613 2008
230'.2—dc22 2008003949

NOTICE TO THE READER

The Full Introduction (a fuller version of the one published herein), extensive commentary in the form of "webnotes," and a bibliography are all available for downloading and printing at the website of the Catholic University of America Press (http://cuapress.cua.edu). This printed volume contains an abbreviated introduction and brief notes on the text.

CONTENTS

ACKNOWLEDGMENTS

This translation had its origin in 1999 while David Bolin—now Brother Thomas, OSB, of the Monastero di San Benedetto in Norcia, Italy—was a licentiate student at the International Theological Institute in Gaming, Austria. After we had completed a draft translation of most of the contents of the present volume, we learned from the Leonine Commission that it would be possible to consult a provisional critical edition of texts from Books II and III. The critical edition was made available to me toward the end of 2003, after Mr. Bolin had already completed his degree and moved on. I then entered upon the laborious but worthwhile task of comparing the draft translation made from the Mandonnet-Moos edition against the provisional critical edition, adding explanatory notes along the way. Shortly after, David's brother Joseph, a perceptive reader of St. Thomas and a Latinist of marvelous skill, matriculated in the same Institute. During 2005, Joseph and I completed a review of the entire translation and its commentary. Moreover, John Boyle allowed us to use, prior to publication, the critical edition of an important text on charity from St. Thomas's rediscovered second commentary on the *Sentences,* the *Lectura romana,* a text we were thus able to include in our translation.

My thanks therefore go, first of all, to the Leonine Commission for its permission to consult and cite the provisional critical text of generous portions of the *Scriptum.* I thank the Commission's current president, Fr. Adriano Oliva, OP, and two of its members, Fr. James Hinnebusch, OP, and Fr. Kenneth Harkins, OP.[†] Thanks are due also to Fr. Basil Cole, OP, and Fr. Louis Bataillon, OP. In the same line I am grateful to John Boyle for supplying me with a critical edition of Distinction 17 of the *Lectura romana.*

I cannot find words enough with which to thank Brother Thomas Bolin and Joseph Bolin for their countless hours of help in producing and improving this translation and its notes. In the Spring of 2005, four students at the International Theological Institute, Joseph among

---

† While the final published critical edition is expected to differ very little, if at all, from the provisional text we saw, the intensive research that goes into compiling and reviewing the source apparatus can, at times, dictate alterations in wording.

them, participated in a seminar on "Perfection in Charity," for which a draft of the present volume served as course text. I thank them for animated classroom discussions, patience in using a work-in-progress, and friendly suggestions along the way.

It gives me only pleasure to recall the courses I took between 1994 and 1997 at the Catholic University of America with David Gallagher, who kindled in me an admiration for St. Thomas's moral theology and, in particular, a keen interest in his teaching on love and charity, subjects on which Gallagher has contributed some of the best modern studies.

My thanks go also to Kevin White, editor of the "Thomas Aquinas in Translation" series, and to David McGonagle and Theresa Walker of the Catholic University of America Press. The series is a happy venture with which I am proud to see the present volume associated. I am especially grateful to Susan Needham Barnes for her extraordinary attentiveness and precision in copyediting the manuscript.

Many people have helped me with particular questions about this or that passage in the *Scriptum*. Deserving of special thanks for such help are Fr. Lawrence Dewan, OP, Gregory Doolan, Jeremy Holmes, Andrei Gotia, Walter J. Thompson, and Michael Waldstein.

Finally, I owe an enormous debt of gratitude to my wife, who bore with the late nights, distracted thoughts, and fretful brow that inevitably accompany a project of this magnitude.

Peter A. Kwasniewski
October 7, 2006
Our Lady of the Rosary

BRIEF INTRODUCTION

This volume makes available a translation of a sizable portion of St. Thomas's first overview of the whole of sacred theology, the *Commentary on the Sentences of Peter Lombard* (in its Latin title, *Scriptum super libros Sententiarum Petri Lombardi* or *Scriptum super Sententiis*, hereafter *Scriptum*), most of which has never appeared in English before. The translators hope that the availability of the text will encourage the use of the *Scriptum* in the classroom as a supplement to more commonly read texts from the *Summa theologiae*.[1] However much St. Thomas improved in pedagogical focus and the articulation of certain concepts, his "youthful" commentary remains an astonishing *tour de force*, bearing everywhere the stamp of profound reflection. Those who go deeply into this work discover it to be an invaluable, even indispensable source of knowledge and wisdom, one that has been sadly neglected in the modern English-speaking milieu.

It was with an awareness of the riches to be found in the *Scriptum* that I enlisted the aid of two graduate students to undertake with me the project of translating the *Scriptum*'s most important passages on love and charity. The project took a decisive step forward when, thanks to the generosity of the Leonine Commission, a provisional critical edition of the relevant distinctions in Books II and III was placed at our disposal. This made it possible to review and correct the translation line by line against the critical text. In addition, we had the privilege of consulting, prior to *its* publication, the critical edition of the second (Roman) version or *Lectura romana* of Book I, Distinction 17, a translation of which is included so as to make possible a fascinating comparison with the original (Paris) version. We also did not hesitate to include in the webnotes[2] shorter translations of texts from other distinctions whenever these could throw valuable light on the topics at hand.

---

1. To facilitate this use I have provided a chart (see Appendix I) in which the *Summa* articles on love and charity in general are correlated to their parallels in the *Scriptum*. This chart makes immediately apparent some interesting features of the *Scriptum*, such as the sheer breadth of the first article of *In III Sent.* d. 27, q. 1, which does the work, so to speak, of six articles in the *Summa* (I-II, q. 28).

2. These notes may be found on the website of the Catholic University of America Press (http://cuapress.cua.edu).

The result is the present volume, which contains by far the most extensive English translation from the *Scriptum* to date.[3] Finally, to enhance
the value of the translation to those who are interested in the historical development of Thomas's thinking and his methods of working,
we made a point of including the more doctrinally interesting "drafts"
from the autograph manuscript of Book III, as edited by P.-M. Gils.[4]
Here we see the author laboring hard on his materials, emending, canceling out, taking different points of departure. All in all, the inclusion
of draft material, of the finished Parisian product, and of the bold Roman attempt at a second *Scriptum* offers an incomparable window into
the first phase of St. Thomas's career as a theologian.

Our single goal was to produce a translation both accurate and
readable—the former, by sticking to the text as it stands, not pretending that the original is more literary and filled-out than it really is (for
scholastic Latin does at times have the characteristics of an abbreviated code language), the latter by supplying those words or phrases
of which an English speaker would naturally avail himself simply to
make his meaning plain, but that a Latin author, above all a scholastic author, can so easily omit, trusting to inflections, to context, and
to his immediate audience's considerable skill in dialectic. Brackets [ ]
indicate editorial interpolations. Wherever Thomas's condensed Latin
permitted of a non-interpretive expansion to help the English reader—
an example would be a place where Thomas simply writes *hoc,* "This,"
but where the translation supplies the noun or phrase intended, which
might have been three or four lines back—we have expanded it without further notice. We sought to avoid at all costs any smoothing-out
or rewriting of phrases that would intrude our own thoughts into
the text of a master who is perfectly capable of speaking for himself.
Hence, at times, a certain awkwardness was allowed to stand, which
could have been avoided only at the expense of giving the reader a
quite different impression of what the original says. On the many occasions when a sentence or argument seemed to cry out for paraphrase
or commentary, we have strictly confined our paraphrase to the notes,
never imposing it on the translation as such.

So the two general principles of our translation are (1) maximal fidelity to Thomas's text, the attempt to say things *as* he says them, with
the weight and balance of his own statements; and (2) maximal clarity

---

3. See Appendix II for a list of published English translations from the *Scriptum.*
4. See P.-M. Gils, "Textes inédits de S. Thomas: Les premières rédactions du
Scriptum super Tertio Sententiarum," *Revue des Sciences philosophiques et théologiques* 45
(1961): 201–28; 46 (1962): 445–62 and 609–28.

in English, often by preferring phrasings more familiar to our ears and closer to the Latin's *meaning*.[5] Sometimes "at work" or "working" is used instead of "operating," and "activity" instead of "operation"; "has its term in" rather than "terminates in"; "in the manner of" rather than "through the mode of"; and so on. It is often impossible, or absurdly artificial, to find everyday English for the technical vocabulary of Latin scholasticism, nor should one overlook the longstanding, honorable tradition of English-language scholasticism that has always borrowed heavily from the Latin (e.g., "actuality" and "potency"). The resulting policy for us has been a sort of pragmatism that keeps the translation as close to spoken English as possible, but does not go out of its way to avoid technicalities, especially those hallowed by custom.

Throughout the book, the footnotes, which are called out by *lowercase letters*, generally concern textual matters such as the Latin edition consulted, the structure or meaning of a given question or article, parallels in other writings of St. Thomas, and citations of sources. More detailed commentary is available in notes called out by *arabic numerals*, the text of which is to be found on the website of The Catholic University of America Press. These "webnotes," numbered consecutively from 1 to 518, are contained in a single document, permitting easy access. A reader in search of information about the biographical background to St. Thomas's *Commentary on the Sentences*, the peculiar features of this work, its subsequent history, the *Lectura romana* (Aquinas's second attempt at producing a *Sentences* commentary), how to think about and benefit from *loca parallela*, and some of the more philosophically interesting translation issues is advised to go to the Full Introduction available at the same website, where a comprehensive bibliography may also be found.

A few words are in order about unfamiliar features of the *Scriptum*. As with the *Summa contra gentiles*, the *Scriptum* is divided into four books.[6] The main unit of division is not the question or chapter, but the "Distinction."[7] Each Distinction in the *Scriptum* opens with a *divisio*

---

5. And this for no ideological reason (such as "Anglo-Saxon derivatives are always better than Latin derivatives"), but simply looking to how people speak, what comes naturally to their lips. Yet there is no getting around *some* technical terms; no discipline is without them.

6. On the complex structure of Lombard's *Sentences*, see the references to secondary literature provided in the Full Introduction and Bibliography.

7. The division of Lombard's text into Distinctions appears to have been the work of Alexander of Hales (see Jean-Pierre Torrell, *Saint Thomas Aquinas, vol. 1: The Person and His Work*, trans. Robert Royal [Washington, DC: The Catholic University of America Press, 1996], 40).

textus of Peter Lombard's text, leading the reader to the points Thomas wishes to discuss.[8] The Distinction concludes with an *expositio textus*, a set of clarifications on phrases in the Lombard's text that might give rise to misunderstandings. We have called this section "Notes on the Text," because it is by no means an "exposition" of a text in the way that a commentary of Thomas's on Aristotle or Dionysius or Proclus is.

St. Thomas subdivides the Distinctions in various ways. In some cases, a Distinction simply consists of a series of articles.[9] In other cases, it will contain several questions, subdivided into articles. One curious aspect of the *Scriptum* for a reader new to it is the proliferation of *quaestiunculae*—literally "little questions," called herein "subquestions"—beneath the familiar question and article levels. This generates famously lengthy citations such as: "*In III Sent.* d. 27, q. 2, a. 4, qa. 3, ad 1." According to the convention he followed, Thomas does not solve the subquestions in succession; they are organized in such a way that first, *all* the objections and sed contras of *all* the subquestions are presented, and only afterwards, all the solutions and replies, point by point. This happens to be an awkward way of proceeding; it is the more odd for being most of the time unnecessary. The text's readability is improved when the main response and the replies to objections are placed in company with their matching objections and sed contras. This was also the advice of students who used a draft of this translation in a course. Hence, in all cases but one I have brought together all the elements of each subquestion so that it reads like a regular article.[10]

The final determination of which texts to include in this volume took place over a long period of time. My ongoing research into Thomas's understanding of *amor, dilectio, caritas,* and *amicitia* had me frequently turning to discussions in Book III of the *Scriptum,* where he

8. It bears emphasizing, for those unfamiliar with it, that the *Scriptum* is not by any stretch of the imagination a commentary, strictly speaking, on another author's text. As a finished product it bears more likeness to Aquinas's disputed questions or the commentaries on Boethius.

9. Readers should be aware that at times Thomas or his editors introduce a heading styled "Question 1" which is then divided into articles, but after which no further question appears, rendering the "Question" heading entirely superfluous. Citations in secondary literature have waffled between keeping and dropping the "Question 1" in such cases. Here we mention "q." only if there is more than a single question; otherwise the citation will read: *In III Sent.* d. 28, a. 3. There are also a few other numbering confusions in the *Scriptum,* but in most cases the problem is easily spotted and solved.

10. The one exception is a place (*In III Sent.* d. 31, q. 1, a. 4) where Thomas deliberately builds one set of objections upon another and then answers all the sets in the reply to the first subquestion.

explores these themes in great detail. Discussions of the objects, order, commandment, and duration of charity,[11] while less orderly than their parallels in the *Secunda secundae,* examine certain points more finely. Thomas's manner of placing *caritas* squarely within his metaphysical understanding of *amor* and his adaptation of Aristotelian *amicitia* sheds much light on a theme that will become a leitmotif in his works— namely, charity as a purely gratuitous supernatural friendship between God and man which is nevertheless rooted deep within the ontology of man himself. From Book III, I was led by a natural progression to the discussion in Book I of the Holy Spirit as the love poured into the hearts of the faithful (where we witness first-hand Thomas's famous disagreement with Peter Lombard over whether the charity given to Christians is the very uncreated charity that is the Holy Spirit), as well as the opening article of Distinction 1 on *fruitio.* I incorporated crucial discussions in Book II of the love of God above self[12] and of the orientation of right wills toward a single end, which can be variously described as God, beatitude, and charity.[13] Near the end of Book IV, I found much enlightening material in the treatment of beatitude as man's ultimate end, linked inextricably to the possession and exercise of charity.[14] All these texts proved to be mutually illuminating and stand well together.

An overview of the contents may thus be given, with an asterisk indicating that only *part* of that Distinction or question has been translated: *In I Sententiarum* (Paris version), d. 1, q. 1* and d. 17, qq. 1–2 [**Mand.**]; *In I Sententiarum* (Roman version), d. 17, qq. 1–2 [**Boyle**]; *In II Sententiarum,* d. 3, q. 4 and d. 38* [**Leon.**]; *In III Sententiarum,* d. 23*, dd. 27–32, and d. 36* [**Leon.**]; *Deleta Super III Sent.* [**Gils**]; *In IV Sententiarum,* d. 49, q. 1* [**Parm.**]. The Latin editions on which the translations are based: **Leon.** = provisional critical edition of the Leonine Commission; **Boyle** = *Lectura romana in primum Sententiarum Petri Lombardi,* ed. †Leonard E. Boyle and John F. Boyle (Toronto: Pontifical Institute of Mediaeval Studies, 2006), 190–201; **Mand.** = *Scriptum super libros Sententiarum,* vols. 1 and 2 (containing Books I and II), ed. P. Mandonnet (Paris: Lethielleux, 1929); **Moos** = *Scriptum super libros Sententiarum,* vols. 3 and 4 (containing Book III and Book IV, dd. 1–22), ed. Maria Fabianus Moos (Paris: Lethielleux, 1933 and 1947); **Gils** = P.-M. Gils, "Textes inédits de S. Thomas: Les premières rédactions du *Scriptum su-*

---

11. *In III Sent.* dd. 28, 29, 30, and 31; in addition, d. 36, a. 6 takes up the relationship between commandments and the "mode of charity."

12. *In II Sent.* d. 3, q. 4.   13. *In II Sent.* d. 38, aa. 1–2.

14. *In IV Sent.* d. 49, q. 1.

per Tertio Sententiarum," Revue des Sciences philosophiques et théologiques 45 (1961): 201–28; 46 (1962): 445–62 and 609–28; **Parm.** (for Book IV, dd. 23–50) = *Sancti Thomae Aquinatis Opera omnia*, vol. 7/2: *Commentum in quartum librum Sententiarum magistri Petri Lombardi* (Parma: Typis Petri Fiaccadori, 1858), pp. 872–1259. Within the translation, references to page numbers from the above editions are provided in a note placed at the start of each new Distinction. (Note that the titles of the Distinctions are not Thomas's but those of later editors, usually Mandonnet and Moos, and for this reason they are bracketed. Although the provisional critical edition bears no such titles, they have been retained here for ease of orientation.) When Latin phrases are given in the notes, the orthography follows the edition that served as the basis of the translation; so, for Books II and III we take the Leonine edition's spelling, while for Book I we take that of Mandonnet, and so forth.[15] Texts translated from Thomas's handwritten revisions to Book III [**Gils**] reproduce the author's strikethroughs and rewordings. Comparison of the provisional Leonine critical edition of texts from Books II and III with the edition of Mandonnet-Moos disclosed a fair number of minor differences but rather few significant ones. The latter sort, and at times the former, have been indicated in the notes. With the prospect of a critical text with full apparatus being released soon to the public, we do not call attention to every instance of divergence between the Mandonnet-Moos text and the provisional text of the Leonine Commission that was shared with us; to do so would far surpass the ordinary functions of a translation.

For Aquinas's references to a host of authors, we have provided citations detailed enough to enable the reader to locate the texts in modern editions. CCSL critical editions of Patristic authors have been used whenever possible. We have made no effort to be comprehensive in this regard, for when the Leonine edition soon appears, it will include, as always, detailed references to the source-texts and versions from which St. Thomas draws his quotations. All quotations from authorities, especially from Scripture, have been translated directly from Aquinas's text. Because he is citing from memory, the quotations are not always exact; he will at times elide different texts or ascribe to one author or book what is to be found in another. Such discrepancies are duly noted. Usually Thomas cites Scripture by book and chapter; we

15. The Leonine editors of Books II and III, as do the editors of several more recent volumes in the *Opera omnia*, adopt orthographical conventions such as *uis cogitatiua, uirtus caritatis, Vnde amor amicitie* (instead of *vis cogitativa, virtus charitatis, Unde amor amicitiae*).

take the liberty of inserting verse numbers. When he refers to psalms by number, he follows the numbering of the Vulgate; most modern translations, on the other hand, follow the Hebrew numbering, which is, in most cases, one ahead of the Vulgate's. For simplicity's sake, I have followed the Hebrew psalm and verse numbers as given in the RSV, although the translation is directly from the Latin and is more akin to what one would get in the Douay-Rheims version.

A related issue is the expansion of quotations wherever it seems clear that Thomas is quoting only a few words not so as to *limit* himself to them, but rather to call to mind a familiar authority that a listener or reader could be counted on to know. In his commentary on Aristotle's *On the Soul*, Thomas makes the point that Aristotle mentions only the beginning of a verse from Homer, expecting his readers to supply the rest. Boethius had supplied the whole verse for his Latin readership.[16] We will imitate Boethius in this regard. A good example is the abbreviated reference system employed in the *divisio textus* that opens each Distinction of Aquinas's *Scriptum*. By means of this *divisio,* the teacher places before his student the argumentative structure, the topical outline, of some portion of the *Sentences,* to help the student more effectively work his way through the details of the text and to provide an aid to memory. In the medieval manner, Thomas economically writes down only a few words from the start of a paragraph (*"Consequenter modum* etc."), expecting the reader to know just what part of the text he is referring to. To make for smoother reading we have always expanded these abbreviated citations to the extent of forming a complete sentence.

❖⊃❖

Some of the most important translation issues that faced us in our project had to do, not surprisingly, with the vocabulary of love, appetite, and desire.

Amor, dilectio, caritas. At *Summa theologiae* I-II, q. 26, a. 3, St. Thomas poses the question: "Is love (*amor*) the same as dilection (*dilectio*)?" In the response he states that love, dilection, charity, and friendship (*amor, dilectio, caritas, amicitia*) are "four words that refer, in a way, to the same thing." The basic difference is that *amicitia* is like a habit, whereas *amor* and *dilectio* are actions or passions, and *caritas* can be taken either way. Of the latter trio, the most general is *amor,* which signifies any first principle of appetitive motion, whether sensitive or rational. *Dilectio* adds something, namely that a choice[17] of the good is

---

16. See *Sent. II De anima,* ch. 28 (ed. Leon. 45.1:189).
17. This is familiar Thomasian (or Isidorean) word-play: *dilectio* comes from

made, and for this reason it is found only in the will, not in the concupiscible power. *Caritas* denotes a certain perfection of love, because
the beloved is held to be of great price.[18] One should not overlook the
remark Thomas makes regarding the sed contra quotation from Dionysius ("some holy men have held that *amor* means something more
godlike than *dilectio*"): "*Amor* denotes a passion . . . whereas *dilectio* presupposes the judgment of reason. But it is possible for man to tend to
God by love (*amor*), being as it were passively drawn by Him, more
than he can possibly be drawn thereto by his reason, which pertains to
the nature of *dilectio*."[19]

For a translator wishing to be clear, **caritas** presents no difficulty:
it must be translated "charity." The fact that for some people "charity"
has come to mean nothing other than tossing a coin into a beggar's cup
is no reason to throw it out of theology where it occupies the queen-
liest of places; like many another beautiful but endangered species in
the English language, it rather needs to be rescued and bred in captiv-
ity. For the scholastics, charity means nothing less than the very love
which is God's essence, the love that Christ manifested in his death on
the cross. The reductionism that makes "charity" equivalent to almsgiv-
ing or other works of mercy—which are really charity's *effects*[20]—must
be resisted in the name of both sound English and sound theology.

The translator's trouble begins with **amor/amare** and **dilectio/
diligere**. As we saw, St. Thomas finds it useful to draw *some* distinction between them—but not an absolute and exclusive one. He never
shows the slightest hesitation in using *amor/amare* for *all* loves, supernatural and natural, intellectual and sensual (the prologues to *Prima
Pars* questions 59 and 60, announcing the treatment of will and love
in the angels, speak of "*amor sive dilectio*").[21] In actual practice, when
speaking of *caritas* he readily uses *dilectio* and *amor* (with their verbs)

electio. "Addit enim dilectio supra amorem, electionem praecedentem, ut ipsum
nomen sonat" (ibid.).

18. Again, arguing from the word: *carus* means dear, so *caritas* means love of
what is (most) dear to one. See *ST* I-II, q. 26, a. 3.

19. *ST* I-II, q. 26, a. 3, ad 4. Earlier in his career Thomas had given a similar
evaluation of the terms in the Notes on the Text at the end of *In I Sent.* d. 10, a
text translated in webnote 230.

20. See *ST* II-II, q. 30 on mercy or pity, q. 31 on good deeds, q. 32 on alms-
giving.

21. Similarly, at *ST* II-II, q. 27, a. 2, where Thomas writes near the end of
the response: "Sic igitur in dilectione, secundum quod est actus caritatis, includitur quidem benevolentia, sed *dilectio sive amor* addit unionem affectus" (emphasis added).

as synonyms, quite interchangeably. That he does not worry too much about this can be seen in many texts. For example, an objection is phrased as follows: "'Loved' [*dilectum*] is named by a word taken from 'love' [*dilectio*]. Therefore love is not loved [*dilectio non diligitur*], nor is charity loved by charity [*charitas charitate amatur*]."[22] To make the linguistic parallel exact, Thomas would have needed a verb for *caritas*, but he had none, so he substituted the present passive indicative of *amare*—not, as one might have expected, of *diligere*. In another objection of the same article, he writes: "Everything that is loved [*diligitur*] is loved by some love [*dilectione diligitur*]. If therefore the act of charity itself is loved [*actus caritatis amatur*], it must be loved [*ametur*] by some other act, and for the same reason, that act will also be something to be loved [*erit diligendus*]."[23] Here we see the whole gamut of terms.

Such texts indicate a fluidity of usage with *dilectio/diligere, amor/amare,* and *caritas.* It is relevant to point out that since Peter Lombard uses *amor, caritas,* and *dilectio* synonymously,[24] it is hardly surprising that the young author of a commentary on the *Sentences* follows suit, even when, in the interests of greater precision, he sees fit to invest each with a peculiar note or shade of meaning. All this suggests that one ought not to be troubled about using English "love" for Latin *dilectio/diligere* (and we will see more evidence, in a moment, that Thomas would not mind). This is an obvious strategy, especially when one considers that "dilection" is a rare and rather dry latinism that does not at all convey what *dilectio* is supposed to convey, and hence seems useless.[25] (It would be like referring to yawning as "pandiculation," or bread-making as "panification.") Even if one wanted to use "dilection" out of a sense of obligation, there has never been a special English word for *diligere.* Such worries are misplaced, since most of the time there is no problem in translating both *amor/amare* and *dilectio/diligere* as "love/to love." When Thomas speaks of "the charity by which God loves us" (*de caritate qua Deus diligit nos*) or of the Christian's "love of charity" (*dilectio caritatis*), no confusion is possible, since we are manifestly speaking of an intellectual or rational love, just as in the sentence "an empty stomach loves the food that a full stomach abhors,"[26] the reader easily infers that "loves" translates *amat,* for a stomach is

22. *In I Sent.,* d. 17 (Paris version), q. 1, a. 5, obj. 3.

23. *In I Sent.,* d. 17 (Paris version), q. 1, a. 5, obj. 4.

24. See Philipp W. Rosemann, *Peter Lombard* (Oxford: Oxford University Press, 2004), 85.

25. Having sensed this, translators of Thomas's works into English have, as a matter of fact, tended to avoid using "dilection" for *dilectio.*

26. *In III Sent.* d. 27, q. 1, a. 1, obj. 3.

incapable of *dilectio*. Put differently, because *amor/amare* readily refer to *every* kind of love and *dilectio/diligere* are employed where there can be no doubt that the love is the activity of a rational being, there is no reason to employ stiff latinisms or awkward conventions to distinguish them.[27] On the rare occasions when an argument hinges on the words as such, the underlying Latin has been indicated.

Amans, amatum. Many discussions of love in the *Scriptum* are cast in the framework of friendship between two persons, "the lover and the beloved," which exemplifies love at its height. It is customary for Thomas to speak of the agent as *amans* and the object of his love as *amatum*, a neuter word that stands for any object of *amor* or *dilectio*. There is every reason to translate *amans* "lover," though we shall have to purge this word of any narrowly erotic connotations it may have.

The real question is this: How shall we translate *amatum* in the nominative case, with its neuter gender? The same question can be raised about analogous formulae, as when Thomas writes (translating as literally as possible): "That love [of concupiscence] . . . does not have its ultimate term in the thing that is said to be loved, but is bent toward that thing for whom that thing's good is desired. In another way, love is borne to the good of something such that it has its term in that very thing, inasmuch as the lover is pleased that the object of his love has whatever good it [*or* he] has, and desires for it [*or* him] the good it [*or* he] as yet lacks."[28] Or this statement: "But toward that one [*ad illud*] for whom the lover wishes good, he has the love of friendship."[29] In a study on Aquinas's "personalism," David Gallagher, having cited this

---

27. As a matter of fact, such a procedure would have its distinct disadvantages, for although Thomas is consistent in using *diligere* for rational love (arguing at *In III Sent.* d. 27, q. 2, a. 1 that *amor* is transferable from lower to higher levels of appetite or affection, but *dilectio* is never transferable from the spiritual level to the sensual), the Vulgate is not. One of his favorite verses to cite in speaking about likeness as a cause of love is Sirach 13:19: "Every animal loves one like itself"—in the Vulgate, *omne animal diligit simile sibi.*

28. *In III Sent.* d. 29, a. 3, from the response: "Amor autem iste [scil., amor concupiscentie] non terminatur ad rem que dicitur amari, set reflectitur ad rem illam cui optatur bonum illius rei. Alio modo amor fertur in bonum alicuius rei ita quod ad rem ipsam terminatur, in quantum bonum quod habet complacet quod habeat, et bonum quod non habet optatur ei." Thomas is speaking of the contrast between what, in the end, he will fixedly call *amor concupiscentiae* and *amor amicitiae,* which mean: "the love of *things* (goods) intended for persons" and "the love of a person, the love characteristic of a friend." In the translation of this passage contained later in the volume, the reader will notice that some slight modifications have been made, in accordance with the argument about to be made here.

29. *ST* I-II, q. 26, a. 4. The love of friendship is here directed toward a (grammatically) neuter object.

last text, suggests what Thomas's use of the neuter gender in such passages indicates, and what it does not:

> Thomas describes the structure of *amor amicitiae/amor concupiscentiae* using neuter pronouns (here, *illud*) to refer to that for which the goods are willed, i.e., that which is the object of the love of friendship. In my opinion, he does so in order to highlight the fact that we are dealing with a formal structure pertaining to the very nature of this love: a love which has as its object *both* that for which goods are willed and those goods which are willed for that thing. We should not take this to mean, however, that any kind of being at all could fit into this structure and so be the object of *amor amicitiae*. Rather, it is clear that for Thomas only *rational beings* can be loved in this way. Indeed, in other texts we find Thomas using the masculine pronoun to refer to the object of this love.[30] In his general teaching, Thomas holds that the objects of *amor amicitiae* are only beings capable of friendship, an activity he considers proper to rational beings. Thus he consistently maintains that all beings inferior to human beings, whether animals, plants, or non-living beings, can be loved on the level of *dilectio* only with the *amor concupiscentiae* component and only in order to some rational being(s).[31]

What we are seeing in such texts is, in short, a verification of Cajetan's famous dictum *Sanctus Thomas semper loquitur formaliter.*[32] In the texts cited, the thrust of the argument demands that the *illud*, the *rem illam* or *rem ipsam*, is no mere "thing," but always a person.

So much for philosophical preliminaries; the question of English wording remains. "Are we to translate *amatum* 'the beloved' or 'the thing loved'?" asks translator Eric D'Arcy. "The trouble with the former is that, in modern English, it is normally applied to love of a person, and indeed a person loved romantically; the trouble with the latter is that it would exclude persons."[33] Not without hesitations, D'Arcy

30. Gallagher lists as examples *ST* I, q. 20, a. 1 ad 3; *Quaestiones quodlibetales* I, q. 4, a. 3.

31. "Person and Ethics in Thomas Aquinas," *Acta Philosophica* 4 (1995), 57. Friendship is proper to rational beings and thus inextensible to the subrational: *ST* II-II, q. 25, a. 3; *De uirt.* q. 2, a. 7; *In III Sent.* d. 28, a. 2 (translated in this volume). Regarding the neuter gender, one notices that a baby is often referred to as "it," the idiom asserting nothing against the humanity or sex of the child. More noteworthy is the extensive application in certain languages of neuter nouns to children or youths; cf. German *das Mädchen, das Fräulein*. In modern languages, the use of the neuter gender for an *adult* would be offensive.

32. For judicious thoughts on this idea, see M.-D. Chenu, *Toward Understanding St. Thomas*, trans. Albert M. Landry and Dominic Hughes (Chicago: Regnery, 1964), 117–23.

33. *The Emotions* [translation of and commentary on *ST* I-II.22–30] (New York: McGraw-Hill, 1967), 75, note b.

chooses "the object loved," noting that this is broad enough to include things or persons, and that "loving" can include that lesser degree of attachment we call "liking" (thus *amatum* can mean "something liked," "something one is fond of").

Reasonable enough, but a uniform translation has problems of its own. The Latin word *amatum* is a neutral place-holder for a writer accustomed to thinking *formaliter,* whereas to our post-Romantic ears, "object loved" sounds impersonal, smearing a dull brown over the colorful places where Thomas is speaking of personal, even passionate, love.[34] When Thomas asks whether *amans* and *amatum* "dwell within each other" (as he does in *Summa theologiae* I-II, question 28, article 2), he has persons in mind—so much so that the "on the contrary" argument is about the dwelling of Father and Son in the God-loving soul.[35] In many instances, the use of the time-honored pairing "lover and beloved" is not only the most appropriate translation of *amans* and *amatum* but also the most profound. Such a translation does not imply that the discussion pertains only to what has come to be called "romantic love." The "beloved" in question is anything that a moral agent can love for its own sake—parent, sibling, spouse, child, friend, confrere, neighbor, citizen, or, more generally, any community or group which can be styled a moral person.[36] Hence, although the terminology is at times poorly suited, we consider "lover and beloved" applicable to *all* relationships predicated upon a common good, such as a family, a local community, a nation, a team of sportsmen, or an army going to war.

---

34. This claim will become self-evident to anyone who reads *In III Sent.* d. 27, q. 1, a. 1, which contains wording that some have even considered immature because too amorous, too "romantic" in our sense of the word. In reality, however, one may easily find in *all* of St. Thomas's treatments of love those luminous indications of the intensity of personal attachment, of burning devotion and ecstatic self-abandonment, that he takes to be characteristic of charity as it grows in perfection. There are echoes of these qualities in his treatments of virtuous friendship in general—even taken at a "natural" level, prescinding from the gift of charity.

35. D'Arcy himself renders the ubiquitous *amatum* in *ST* I-II, q. 28, a. 2 as "the person loved" or "the person he [the lover] loves," adding in a note: "This article makes sense only if it is taken as applying to the love of one *person* for another" (*The Emotions,* 93, note a).

36. While Thomas usually has individual relationships in mind when speaking of *amans* and *amatum*—parents and children, brothers, neighbors, friends— the structure of his arguments, combined with his teaching on justice and the common good, admits of extension to what have been called "moral persons." On *amor amicitiae* for collectivities, see David M. Gallagher, "Desire for Beatitude and Love of Friendship in Thomas Aquinas," *Mediaeval Studies* 58 (1996), 34–35; idem, "Person and Ethics," 63.

Beloved family, beloved country, beloved team—these are phrases still heard and certainly meaningful. As for the problem that "lover" and "beloved" used just by themselves seem to be *exclusively* romantic in tone, we respond that it is easy enough to conceive of a wider extension of their meaning. There are, moreover, good Thomistic reasons for allowing the "erotic" connotations (in the Platonic sense of the word *eros*) to stand and to be heard in the language, uncontaminated by the contemporary reduction of the erotic to the carnal.

Hence, admitting with D'Arcy that the rendering of *amatum* (or, for that matter, any other neuter term that stands formally for the object of love) is a delicate business, we have taken a different route than he. There is no single solution that works across the board, so our translation varies according to context; and for the reasons just explained, we give precedence to the personal *meaning* over the impersonal *grammar*. English is, at any rate, ill equipped to track the abstract formality of Latin; the moment one writes "beloved" or even "loved one," *a fortiori* if one uses masculine or feminine pronouns, the personal note is so strong as to marginalize other possibilities (such as a miser's love of money, a ruler's love of honor, a sportsman's love of sport, a priest's love of the Church or of his parish, a citizen's love of his country), even when it makes good sense philosophically to include them. On the other hand, if one speaks of "what is loved," "the thing loved," "the object of love," or similar turns of phrase, the *im*personal note is so strong as nearly to cancel out personal applications. We never refer to our friends as *what*s, only as *who*s; to our sensibilities, they are never *things*, they are *people*. All this makes for a bewildering situation in regard to some of the texts of St. Thomas. There is no question that throughout these passages he intends to speak principally of love as it concerns human beings, and even more, love as it concerns human beings divinized by grace. At the same time, in his usual manner, Thomas comes at these intensely personal realities from the vantage of a speculative philosopher, and he treats of them in a language metaphysical, neutral, and abstract. He speaks of "the lover" in the sense of an agent exercising a certain kind of activity, and "the thing loved," in the sense of the object, the target or goal, of this activity.

These things being so, it seemed better to vary the translation according to context—to employ "what is loved" or "the thing loved" in more abstract analyses, but to say "beloved" in discussions that are more concrete. Of course, since all that Thomas writes has both metaphysical depth and personal application, there is something a little arbitrary about such an approach. Still, it is better on the whole to vary the vocabulary in this way, provided the reader remains sensitive to the fact that "beloved" could *also* have been rendered "what is loved," and vice versa.

Affectus, affective, secundum affectum. In modern English, "affection" and "affective" suggest emotional attachment or sentimental love; the words refer to how someone *feels* and, in particular, to the concupiscible passions. St. Thomas uses *affectus* and related words or phrases, like *affective* and *per affectum,* to refer broadly not only to all passions, irascible as well as concupiscible, but to all appetitive acts, whether sensitive or spiritual. In a context like that of *Summa theologiae* II-II, question 175, article 2, where contemplative souls are said to be carried up into the heights *per affectum,* Thomas is using the term with a meaning as broad and deep as the word "heart" or the philosophical term *appetitus.*[37] The contemporary meaning of "affection" does little justice to what Thomas means by the phrase "affective union," *unio secundum affectum,* or to the ways he contrasts such a union with a "real union," *unio secundum rem.* By "affective union" he does not mean an emotional surge or fantasy, but a coming-together, *within* the appetitive power, of the appetite and the object loved, a kind of conforming of the power to its object such that it moves the whole animal to pursuit of the object itself, in its own proper being and goodness. An affective union is thus eminently true, to be sure, but it is not *existential,* it is not yet the actual uniting of the lover with the object loved, so that the lover possesses it most fully—either by absorbing the good it has to offer (if it is an instrumental good) or by rejoicing in its very presence and inherent qualities (if it is a person loved with love of friendship). This being said, we can see why "real union" does not mean a true connection as opposed to a false or imaginary one; it means an existential rather than an intentional union, a union of *having* (and, in the best case, of being had), not a union in the heart that gives rise to longing, waiting, hoping, striving for union "in person." Furthermore, real union, though it always signifies the *presence* of what is loved, does not always indicate a *physical* union, even if the examples that come readily to mind, such as friends enjoying one another's company, do involve bodily presence. For Thomas, a far greater real union is possible at the spiritual level (the domain of truly common goods) than at the

---

37. Walter Principe has written a study, "Affectivity and the Heart in Thomas Aquinas's Spirituality" (in *Spiritualities of the Heart,* ed. Annice Callahan [New York: Paulist Press, 1990]: 45–63), gathering up the varied meanings of *affectus* and *cor* and using them to shed light on more familiar elements of Thomas's thought.

physical (the domain of private goods); and the most real of all unions, the most intimate and the most ecstatic, is the intellectual union of God and the soul in the beatific vision.

Appetitus and **appetibilis** have, for accuracy's sake, been rendered by their clunky cognates "appetite, appetible." While the appetible is also the desirable, there is an important difference between appetite, which is a power, and desire, which more commonly names a passion or affection, and similarly between the appetible, which can refer to the objects of any passion or affection, and the desirable, which *could* suggest too close an association with the specific concupiscible passion of *desiderium*. (It is clear that here, as in many other instances, Thomas is investing a term whose literal meaning is simply "seeking after," *adpetere*, with a broader, more philosophical meaning.) As there is no English cognate of the verb *appetere*, we must be contented with "have appetite for." This has the added benefit of forcing a reader to think about the issue at a metaphysical level, not limiting *appetere* to the emotional response suggested by the term "desire," for which there are other more specific Latin terms.

Ea quae sunt ad finem. This oft-used phrase admits of several translational approaches, one of which should be excluded (and generally has been in this volume): the stark single word "means," which ignores the utter concreteness of the original phrasing and thus evacuates the phrase of its philosophical density: "things that are toward/for an end," "things directed to an end," "things that stand in order to an end." The phrase highlights the end-focused directionality of steps or goods chosen so as to attain that end. "End" is here understood either relatively or absolutely: relatively, as the particular goal or aim of any series of things to be chosen and executed with a view to it; absolutely, as the intellectual creature's ultimate end, beatitude, which is naturally willed and cannot be an object of choice, in contrast with everything else that leads to it or away from it, the realm of choosable goods. The reader may mentally supply such glosses as "actions that contribute to bringing about the end," "steps involved in reaching the end."

A final translation note. The word **ratio** can mean a great variety of things: not only reason (in the sense of the power of reason), but also argument or claim; reckoning; discourse; logical account, definition, or notion; intelligible note or aspect; form, character, or nature. In fact, in many cases several of these meanings appear to be intended by the author. For this reason, and being dissatisfied with the alternatives, we decided to leave *ratio* for the most part untranslated and italicized. The reader is thus left free to pull out the meaning from the context: where it says "The *ratio* of virtue is . . .," one may think: "The definition of virtue . . ." or "The nature of virtue . . ." or "The notion of virtue . . ."—and all of these would be correct, each in its way.

The translations of a number of other words or phrases—*absolute, simpliciter, augere, diminuere, dicendum quod,* the construction gerund + *est, gradus, honestum, nomen, operatio, operare, opus, participatio, participare, in patria, in via, potentiae* (and *vires*), *praecepta,* and *secundum rem*—are discussed in the Full Introduction (see pp. 29–31).

ABBREVIATIONS

Works of Aquinas

Comp. theol.	*Compendium theologiae*
Contra impugn.	*Contra impugnantes Dei cultum et religionem*
De anima	*Quaestiones disputatae De anima*
De caritate	*Quaestiones disputatae De caritate*
De duobus praeceptis	from the *Collationes in decem precepta*
De malo	*Quaestiones disputatae De malo*
De perfectione	*De perfectione spiritualis uitae*
De potentia	*Quaestiones disputatae De potentia Dei*
De spe	*Quaestiones disputatae De spe*
De ueritate	*Quaestiones disputatae De ueritate*
De uirt. card.	*Quaestio disputata De uirtutibus cardinalibus*
De uirt. in comm.	*Quaestio disputata De uirtutibus in communi*
In De div. nom.	*In librum Beati Dionysii De divinis nominibus expositio*
In Metaphys.	*In duodecim libros Metaphysicorum Aristotelis expositio*
In Physic.	*Commentaria in octo libros Physicorum Aristotelis*
Quodl.	*Quaestiones De quodlibet*
SCG	*Summa contra gentiles*
Scriptum	*Scriptum super Sententiarum,* referred to as a whole
Sent.	*Scriptum super Sententiarum,* referring to a particular text

Sent. De anima	*Sententia Libri De anima*
Sent. Eth.	*Sententia Libri Ethicorum*
ST	*Summa theologiae*
Super Ioan.	*Super Evangelium S. Ioannis lectura*
	(in like manner for other scriptural commentaries)

Other works

CCCM	*Corpus Christianorum, Continuatio Mediaevalis*
CCSL	*Corpus Christianorum, Series Latina*
PG	Migne, *Patrologiae Cursus Completus, Series Graeca*
PL	Migne, *Patrologia Cursus Completus, Series Latina*
SC	*Sources Chrétiennes*

Abbreviations of the books of Scripture follow those of the Revised Standard Version (RSV).

IN I SENTENTIARUM

�֎c꜔֎

DISTINCTION 1ᵃ

QUESTION 1ᵃ   On enjoyment and use

ARTICLE 1ᵇ   Whether to enjoy is an act of intellect

Objections:

Proceeding to the first. [A variety of arguments can be put forward, concerning both the power and the habit to which the act of enjoying belongs.]

To what power the act belongs:

1. It seems that to enjoy is an act of *intellect*. For the noblest act belongs to the noblest power. But the highest power in man is intellect. Therefore, since to enjoy is the most perfect of man's acts, because it places man in his last end, it seems that it is an act of intellect.

2. Further, as Augustine says, "vision is the whole reward."ᶜ But the reward of all merit consists in enjoyment of God. Therefore enjoyment is essentially vision. But vision is an act of intellect; therefore so is enjoyment.

3. But it seems that it is an act of *will*. For an act is determined by its object. But the object of enjoyment is the enjoyable, which is [nothing other than] the last end. Now the end, since it has the *ratio* of good, is the object of will. Therefore, too, enjoying is an act of will.

4. Further, Augustine defines enjoyment in reference to the will, saying: "We enjoy what we know, when the delighted will is at rest in it for its own sake."ᵈ Therefore it seems to be rather an act of will than an act of intellect.

5. Further, it seems that it is an act of *all powers*. For recompense

a. The very first Distinction of the *Scriptum* consists of a number of articles (organized loosely into questions) on Augustine's famous *uti/frui* distinction, a key principle of organization for Lombard's *Sentences*. In the *Scriptum* treatment, the first two articles concern whether enjoying (*frui*) is an act of the intellect, and whether use (*uti*) is an act of reason. The former is translated. Latin text: Mandonnet, 32–35.

b. Parallel: *ST* I-II, q. 11, aa. 1–2.

c. Augustine, *Expositions of the Psalms*, Ps. 90, v. 16, n. 13 (CCSL 39:1277).

d. Augustine, *On the Trinity* X, ch. 10 (CCSL 50:327).

3

corresponds to merit. But man merits through [the right use of] all his powers. Therefore he shall be recompensed in all his powers. But the recompense is enjoyment itself; therefore enjoyment belongs to all powers.

6. Augustine says that a man will find inner pastures in the Savior's divinity, and outer pastures in the Savior's humanity.[a] Therefore it seems that man will enjoy as much with his outer powers as with his inner ones.

7. But it seems that it belongs to *no power*. For every act is named from the power to which it belongs, as "understanding" is named from "the understanding."[b] But "enjoying" is not named from any power. Therefore [it belongs to no power].

To what habit the act belongs:

8. Hence it is further sought, to which habit this act belongs; and it seems that it is an act of *charity only*. For as is said in 1 Corinthians 13, charity is a perfect virtue. But, according to the Philosopher, happiness[c] is an activity of perfect virtue.[d] Therefore enjoyment, in which our whole happiness consists, is an act of charity.

9. The same appears from the definition of Augustine brought forward in the text: "To enjoy is to cling by love to something for its own sake."[e]

10. But it seems that it is *not only an act of charity*. For there are three things that come together in enjoyment: perfect vision, full embracing, and the clinging of consummated love.[f] [1] Therefore it seems that it is also an act of the things that succeed faith and hope, [namely, perfect vision and full embracing].

11. Further, it is by enjoyment that we are conjoined to God. But *every virtue* conjoins us to God, since virtue is a disposition of the perfect to the best, as is said in *Physics* VII.[g] Therefore enjoyment is an act according to every virtue.

---

a. Pseudo-Augustine [Alcher of Clairvaux], *On the Spirit and the Soul,* ch. 9 (PL 40:785).

b. *sicut intelligere ab intellectu*

c. Throughout the article, "happiness" translates *felicitas* and "beatitude" *beatitudo.*

d. Aristotle, *Ethics* X, ch. 7 (1177a12).

e. Augustine, *On Christian Doctrine* I, ch. 4 (CCSL 32:8).

f. *perfecta visio, plena comprehensio, et inhaesio amoris consummati*

g. Aristotle, *Physics* VII, ch. 3 (246b8), as found in the Latin version with which Thomas was familiar; the statement does not appear in the Greek text. There are other statements like it in the Aristotelian corpus.

Response:

It should be said that enjoyment consists in man's best activity, since enjoyment is man's ultimate happiness. Now happiness does not consist in habit but in activity, according to the Philosopher. Man's best activity, however, is the activity of his highest power, namely intellect, in regard to the noblest object, which is God; hence that vision of the godhead is set down as the whole substance of our beatitude: "This is eternal life, that they may *know you*, the only true God" (Jn. 17:3). Now owing to the vision, the very thing seen, since it is not seen by way of a likeness but essentially, is in a certain way made to be *within* the seer; and that is the embracing that succeeds hope, following upon the vision that succeeds faith, just as hope is, in a way, generated by faith. But owing to the fact that the very one seen is received into the seer, he unites the very seer to himself, that there may take place a sort of mutual penetration through love.[a, 2] For thus it says in 1 John 4:16: "He who abides in charity, abides in God and God in him." Upon this union of what is maximally fitting follows the highest delight; and in this our happiness is brought to completion. Now enjoyment names happiness more from its completion than from its beginning, since enjoyment implies in itself[b] a certain delight. And therefore we say that it is an act of will, and according to the habit of charity, albeit having some order to preceding powers and habits.

Replies to objections:

1. To the first, therefore, it should be said that appetite always follows upon knowledge. Hence, even as the inferior part [of the soul] has sense and appetite, which is divided into the irascible and concupiscible [powers], so does the superior part have intellect and will, of which intellect is higher according to origin, and will according to perfection. And a like order is found in habits, and also in acts—namely, acts of vision and of love. Enjoyment, however, names the activity that is highest with respect to perfection.[c]

2. And likewise, too, the solution to the second is clear; for vision does not have the perfect *ratio* of happiness except insofar as it is an activity perfected by the things that follow upon it. For delight perfects activity as beauty does youth, as is said in *Ethics* X.[d]

a. *ut fiat quasi quaedam mutua penetratio per amorem*
b. *in se includat*—that is, not just the reality referred to but the very word *fruitio* includes, or implies, delight, since it calls to mind the sweet fruit in which one takes delight.
c. *quantum ad sui perfectionem*
d. Aristotle, *Ethics* X, ch. 4 (1174b31–33).

3–4. These two arguments we concede.

5. To the argument [on behalf of all powers], it should be said that enjoyment, properly speaking, cannot belong to the lower powers, for they do not have an activity concerning the last end, which they do not apprehend, since they are material powers; but as now the intellect is perfected in taking from lower powers, so in the fatherland will the opposite be the case—the perfection and joy of the higher part will redound into the lower powers. Hence Augustine says: "Sensation will be turned into reason, inasmuch as its reward and joy will emanate from reason."[a]

6. To the other argument, it should be said that Christ's humanity is not the last end; hence in the beholding of it there will not be enjoyment, properly speaking, but a kind of accidental joy, and not the substance of beatitude.[b, 3]

7. To the argument [on behalf of no power] it should be said that when some act is absolutely of some power, it is named from it, as the act of understanding is named from the power of understanding;[c] but when there is an act of one power with an order to another, it is named from no one of them, as knowing[d] is an act of reason with an order to the power of understanding, inasmuch as it draws conclusions from principles; and likewise enjoying is an act of will following upon an act of intellect, namely the manifest vision of God.

8–10. To the next set of arguments, the solution is clear from what has already been said, since, although three things run together in enjoyment, still it is perfected in love, as was said in the response.

11. To the last argument, it should be said that other virtues conjoin one to God in the manner of merit and disposition, but charity alone in the manner of perfect union.

a. Pseudo-Augustine [Alcher of Clairvaux], *On the Spirit and the Soul,* ch. 12 (PL 40:788).

b. *non substantialis beatitudo*   c. *intelligere ab intellectu*
d. *scire*

DISTINCTION 17 (PARIS VERSION)[a, 4]

QUESTION 1   On charity as something created in the soul

Division of the first part of the text

After he [the Master] has determined[5] about the visible mission of the Holy Spirit, he determines here about his invisible mission.

And this inquiry is divided into two parts. In the first, he determines the truth, according to his own opinion; in the second, he responds to objections made against it, where he says: "Here the following is sought: if charity *is* the Holy Spirit, then, since charity may be increased and diminished in man, should it be conceded that the Holy Spirit can be increased or diminished in man?"[6]

Concerning the first, he does three things. First, he announces his intention; second, he proposes the truth, where he says: "In order that this might be more intelligibly taught and more fully known, something very necessary to this should be set down first"; third, he brings forward proof, where he says: "However, so that we might not seem to be pouring some private opinion of ours into the thing we are talking about, we corroborate what has been said by appeal to holy authorities."

This is further divided into two parts, according to the two things he proves.[7] He first proves that charity is the Holy Spirit himself, and second proves that the Holy Spirit is given to us precisely when the Holy Spirit makes us to love God, where the text says: "For he is said to be sent or to be given, when he is in us in such a way that he makes us to love God."

The former is again divided into two parts. In the first, he proves that charity is the Holy Spirit himself; in the second, he excludes a certain response to his own position, where he says: "But in order that someone might not perhaps say that the assertion 'God is charity' is intended merely to express the cause[8] . . . [the authority of] Augustine stands in the way."

Concerning the former, he does two things. First, he shows that

a. Latin text: Mandonnet, 390–429.

charity is God; second, that, in a special way, charity is the Holy Spirit, where he says: "Now since fraternal love is God, it is neither the Father nor the Son but only the Holy Spirit, who is properly called love or charity in the Trinity."[a]

In order to understand this part of the text, we will inquire into five things: (1) Whether charity is something created in the soul; (2) whether it is a substance or an accident; (3) according to what measure it is given; (4) whether he who has charity can know for certain that he has it; (5) whether charity itself is to be loved from charity.

ARTICLE 1[b]   Whether charity is something created in the soul

Objections:

Proceeding to the first, it seems that charity is not something created in the soul.

1. An agent that operates without any means is more perfect than one that does not act except by some means.[c] But in our meritorious acts, the Holy Spirit works within us both to will them and to bring them to perfection, according to the Apostle: "For they who are moved by the Spirit of God, these are the sons of God" (Rom. 8:14). Since therefore he is the most perfect agent, it seems that he does not move [us] to this operation by means of some created habit.

2. Again, as the soul is the life of the body, so God is the life of the soul, as Augustine says in *On the Apostle's Words,* sermons 18 and 28.[d] But the soul does not give life to the body by means of some form [since it is itself the body's form]; therefore neither does the Holy Spirit give life to the soul by means of a habit.[e]

3. Further, the being of grace is more immediately from God and closer to him than the being of nature.[f] But God, in creating, did not

---

a. "fraternal love . . . love or charity": *fraterna dilectio . . . dilectio vel caritas*

b. Parallels: *In I Sent.* (*Lectura romana*) d. 17, aa. 1–2 (see below); *ST* II-II, q. 23, a. 2; *De caritate,* a. 1.

c. *sine medio . . . per medium*

d. In fact, Augustine, *Sermon* 161, ch. 6 (PL 38:881) and *Sermon* 180, ch. 7 (PL 38:976).

e. *per aliquam formam mediam . . . per habitum medium.* One could also render this: "But the soul does not give life to the body through some in-between form; therefore neither does the Holy Spirit give life to the soul through a habit in between [the Spirit and the soul]."

f. *esse gratiae immediatius est a Deo et propinquius, quam esse naturae:* the be-ing,

make use of any means when he instituted nature; therefore neither in re-creating does he use any means when he infuses grace.

4. This is also shown from the dignity of charity. For every creature is vanity. If therefore charity is a creature,[a] it will be vanity. But vanity does not conjoin us to the truth, nor does it confirm us in the truth. Therefore charity would not conjoin us to God, which is false.

5. Further, nothing finite is of infinite power. For, since power flows from essence, and every creature is [essentially] finite, infinite power belongs to no creature. But the power of charity is infinite, because it moves over an infinite distance, conjoining the creature to the Creator and making a just man out of a sinner. Therefore it seems that it is not a creature.

6. Again, no creature is worthier than the soul of Christ. But charity is worthier than the soul of Christ, because it is owing to charity that the very soul of Christ is good. Therefore charity is not a creature.

7. Further, a greater love is owed to a greater good. But God is an infinite good and has done infinite things for us. Therefore we owe him an infinite love. But the love by which we love God is charity. Therefore charity is something infinite, and hence is not a creature.

8. Further, every created thing is in one of the predicaments.[b] But whatever is contained in the ten genera of predicaments is some nature. If therefore charity is something created, it will be a certain nature. But one nature coming to another nature makes nothing except nature.[9] Consequently, the soul having charity, if charity is something created, will not have anything except the being of nature. But it is through charity that one is able to merit. Therefore according to this position, some nature, just by itself, will be able to accomplish meritorious acts—which is the Pelagian heresy. Therefore it seems that charity is not something created.

---

i.e., actuality of being, that follows from and belongs to grace, as compared with the same that follows from and belongs to nature. Throughout the present article and in much of what follows, "being" translates not *ens,* but *esse.* One might visualize the word as "be-ing," to keep in focus its *verb*-character, its energetic connotation.

a. *creatura.* In English "creature" is often synonymous with "animal" or "living thing," but its original meaning is much broader: anything God has created. The whole of reality and every aspect thereof (not just substances, but also accidents; not just bodies and souls but thoughts, volitions, habits, powers, etc.) is *creatum* and *creatura.*

b. Or "categories."

On the contrary:

1. Whatever is received into a thing is received into it according to the recipient's mode. But uncreated love, which is the Holy Spirit, is participated in by the creature; therefore he must be participated in according to the creature's mode. But the creature's mode is finite; thus what is received into the creature must be some finite love. But every finite thing is created. Therefore in the soul having the Holy Spirit, there is a created charity.[10]

2. Again, every assimilation [of one thing to another] comes about through some form. But it is through charity that we are made conformed to God himself, and when charity is lost, the soul is said to be deformed. Therefore it seems that charity is a certain created form remaining in the soul.

3. Further, it is obvious that God is present in the saints in some way in which he is not present in [mere] creatures. But that diversity cannot be placed on the side of God himself, who stands uniformly to all things.[a, 11] Therefore it seems that it is on the side of the creature—namely, that the creature itself has something that the others do not have. Consequently, either it has the divine being itself—and if this were so, all the just would be assumed by the Holy Spirit into unity of Person, as the human nature was assumed by Christ into the very Son of God's unity of Person, which cannot be the case; or it is necessary that that creature, in which God is said to be present in a special way, have *in itself* some effect of God that the others do not have. But that effect cannot be merely some *action*, because if it were that [alone], God would not be present in the just who are asleep in a manner different from that in which he is present in other creatures.[b, 12] Therefore, it must be some *habit*. Accordingly, it is necessary that there be some habit of charity created in the soul, according to which the Holy Spirit is said to dwell in the soul itself.

Response:

It should be said that the soul's entire goodness is from charity. Hence, the greater the charity a soul possesses, the greater is its goodness;[c] and if it does not have charity, it is nothing, as is said in

---

a. Or "is related to all things in the same way," *eodem modo se habet ad omnia.*

b. *non esset alio modo quam in aliis creaturis:* literally, "he [God] would not be in them in another mode than [that by which he is] in other creatures"

c. *quantum bona est tantum habet de charitate*

1 Corinthians 13. Now it is clear that a soul does not have less goodness in the being of grace owing to charity than it has in political being owing to acquired virtue. Political virtue, however, does two things: it makes the one who has it good, and it makes his work good.[13] Much more therefore does charity do this. Yet neither of these things will be able to be done unless charity is a created habit. For it is clear that all being is from some inhering form, as being white is from whiteness and substantial being from substantial form. Therefore, just as a wall's being white cannot be understood apart from the whiteness inhering [in the surface], so the soul's being good in the freely given being of grace[a] cannot be understood apart from the charity and grace informing it. In like manner, too, since an act is proportioned to an operative power as an effect is proportioned to a proper cause, it is impossible to understand that an act perfect in goodness should come from a power not perfected by a habit, just as heating cannot come from fire except by means of hotness.[14] And therefore, since an act of charity has a certain perfection from the fact that it is meritorious in all ways, it is necessary to posit that charity is a habit created in the soul, which habit is indeed from the whole Trinity as efficient cause, but flows from love, which is the Holy Spirit, as exemplar cause:[b, 15] and therefore it is frequently found [written] that the Holy Spirit is the love by which we love God and neighbor, just as Dionysius in chapter 4 of *The Celestial Hierarchy*[c] also says that "the divine being is the being of all things"—namely, insofar as all being is led forth exemplarily from him.[16]

The Master, nevertheless, would have it that charity is not some habit created in the soul, but is only an act that is from free will moved by the Holy Spirit, whom he calls charity. In order to explain this position, certain men have said that, just as light can be considered in two ways—either as it is in itself, and from that vantage it is called light; or as it is in the extremity of a limited diaphanous, and from that vantage light is called color (since light is the hypostasis of color, and color is nothing other than embodied light)—so the Holy Spirit, considered in himself, is called Holy Spirit and God, but considered as existing in the soul that he moves to the act of charity, he is called charity. For they say that just as the Son united human nature to himself alone, although in this uniting there was the operation of the whole Trinity, so the Holy Spirit unites the will to himself alone, although in this uniting

a. *in esse gratuito*

b. *quae quidem efficienter est a tota Trinitate, sed exemplariter manat ab amore, qui est Spiritus sanctus*

c. Pseudo-Dionysius, *The Celestial Hierarchy*, ch. 4, n. 1 (PG 3:178).

there is the operation of the whole Trinity. But this cannot stand. For the union of human nature in Christ has its term in the one being of the divine Person, and therefore an act numerically the same belongs at once to a divine Person and to the human nature assumed. In contrast, the will of a saint is not assumed into unity of suppositum with the Holy Spirit. Hence, because operation has unity and diversity from the suppositum, there cannot be understood to be one operation of the will and of the Holy Spirit except in the way in which God works in anything whatsoever. But that way is not enough for the perfection of operation, since in regard to necessity and contingency and perfection and things of this sort, operation follows the conditions of the proximate cause and not the conditions of the first cause. Hence one cannot understand that there is a perfect operation of the will through which it is united to the Holy Spirit unless one also understands that there is also a habit perfecting the operative power itself; nor can there be a likeness of the will's act to the Holy Spirit unless there is a likeness of the soul to the Holy Spirit through some form, which is the principle of the act by which we are conformed to the Holy Spirit. Hence it is necessary to posit in the soul some form through which it is conformed to the Holy Spirit, since an act is not enough for this conformity, as was said.

Replies to objections:

1. To the first, therefore, it should be said that in the engracing of the soul[a] a twofold operation of the Holy Spirit is to be considered: one operation that has its term in being according to first actuality, which, in the one having the habit of charity, is to be pleasing to God, and another operation, according to which is wrought the second actuality, which is the operation moving the will to the work of love; and in each way it is necessary for a means to be involved, not on account of any weakness or defect on the part of the Holy Spirit at work, but on account of a necessity on the part of the receiving soul. Yet [this means is involved] in different ways. For as regards the first effect, which is the being of grace, charity is a means after the manner of a formal cause, since no being can be received in the creature except through some form. As regards the second effect, which is operation, however, charity is a means under the *ratio* of an efficient cause, insofar as the power that is the principle of operating is traced back to the agent cause, since it is also impossible for some perfect operation to go forth

---

a. *gratificatione animae*

from a creature unless the principle of that operation be a perfection of the power of the one at work, in the sense in which we say that the habit that elicits an act is its principle.

2. To the second, it should be said that the soul is compared to the body not only as an agent cause, according to which it is the body's mover, but also as the form; hence, it itself formally makes the body to live, in the sense in which "to live" means "to be alive."[17] God, however, is not the form of the soul itself or of the will, by which it is formally able to live; he is called "the life of the soul" rather as the exemplar principle, pouring the life of grace into it.[18] Something similar should be said about light, which one can consider in two ways: either as light is in the shining body itself, and so considered, it stands to the illumination of air as the *efficient* principle, nor does it illuminate it except through the form of light poured into the illuminated diaphanous; or as light is in the illuminated diaphanous, and so considered, it is the *form* thereof, by which the diaphanous is formally shining. Now God is said to be "illuminating light" after the manner of the light which is in the very body of that which is shining *per se* [e.g., the sun], and not after the manner by which an illuminated body is formally illuminated by the form of light received into itself. To that received light, on the other hand, are likened the charity and grace received into the soul.

3. To the third, it should be said that creation and re-creation are altogether similar. For just as God through creation bestowed the being of nature upon things, and that being is formally from the form received in the created thing itself, which is the term, as it were, of the operation of the agent himself; and again, just as that form is the principle of the natural operations God works in things: so too in re-creation, God bestows the being of grace upon the soul, and the formal principle of that being is a created habit, by which the meritorious operation God works in us is also perfected; and thus, that created habit stands to the operation of the Holy Spirit partly as a term, and partly as a means.[19]

4. To the fourth, it should be said that charity, insofar as it is from nothing, has the characteristic of being vanity; but insofar as it proceeds from God as his very likeness, it does not have the *ratio* of vanity but, quite to the contrary, the *ratio* of conjoining a person to God himself.

5. To the fifth, it should be said that something is said "to make" in two ways: either in the manner of an efficient cause, as a painter makes the wall white, or in the manner of form, as whiteness makes the wall white. The making of a sinner to be just or conjoined to God,

then, is from God himself as from an efficient cause, and from charity as from a form. Hence, it cannot be concluded that charity is of infinite power, but only that it is the effect of infinite power.

6. To the sixth, it should be said that the nobility of anything[a] can be looked at in two ways: either simply or in a certain respect. Now something seems to be worthier simply when it is nobler according to its being; and in this way the soul of Christ, and the soul of any just man whatsoever, is nobler than created charity, which has the being of an accident;[b] but in a certain respect, created charity is nobler than the soul of Christ. For in any genus, act is nobler than potency, as far as that genus is concerned. Hence, just as the whiteness of the body of Christ is nobler than the body of Christ precisely with respect to being white, so too his created knowledge[c] is nobler than his soul precisely with respect to being knowing, which is being in a certain respect. And in like manner, his charity is nobler than his soul precisely with respect to such [accidental] being, because in being that [perfection], it is related to the soul of Christ as act to potency.

7. To the seventh, it should be said that, according to the Philosopher in *Ethics* VIII,[d] in some friendships it happens that an equivalent return is never made, but still it suffices for the equity of friendship that whatever return is possible be made, even as a son can never return to his natural father[e] something equivalent to what he receives from him, namely, being and education and nourishment. Much less is it possible for us to return a love equivalent to the divine benefits and to God's goodness. Hence it does not follow that the love by which we love God is infinite with respect to the substance of the act, although it has infinity from the fact that the object of this love is set before all others.[20] But it suffices that we should love with a love commensurate to us.[21]

8. To the last, it should be said that "nature" is said in many ways,

---

a. *aliquorum,* literally, "of any things"

b. The Parma ed. adds here: "while something seems to be worthier in a certain respect when it is worthier according to something [some feature it has], and in this way created charity . . ."

c. In this translation, both *scientia* and *cognitio* are usually rendered "knowledge," since "science" would now be misleading in many cases, and "cognition" is too esoteric for the plain meaning of its Latin original. The only regular exceptions are when Thomas uses the plural or the phrase *habitus scientiae,* since "sciences" is more idiomatic than "knowledges," and "habit of science" is a more technical phrase.

d. Aristotle, *Ethics* VIII, ch. 8 (1163b12–18).

e. *patri carnali*

according to chapter 1 of Boethius's *On the Two Natures*.[a] For in one way, nature bespeaks all that exists, whether substance or accident; and in this way grace is a certain nature. In another way, nature bespeaks that which is the principle of motion and rest in that in which it is;[b] hence on this understanding, something is said to be "natural" that either is caused by natural principles or is able to be so caused. And in this way charity is *not* nature, since it cannot be caused by the natural principles of a creature; and Pelagius speaks according to this latter sense when he says that man can accomplish meritorious acts by natural principles alone.

ARTICLE 2[c]   Whether charity is an accident

Objections:

Proceeding to the second, it seems that charity is not an accident.

1. For no accident extends beyond its subject. But charity extends beyond its subject, because by charity we also love others. Therefore it seems that charity is not an accident.

2. Again, every accident is caused by substance, since, according to Avicenna's *Metaphysics* (tract II, chapter 1), a subject is what is complete in itself, offering to another an occasion for being. But charity is not caused by the principles of the soul in which it is. Therefore it seems that it is not an accident.

3. Further, no accident is better and nobler than its subject. But charity is better than the soul. Therefore it is not in the soul as an accident in a subject. Proof of the middle: that on account of which anything is such, is more such;[d] but the soul is good on account of charity; therefore charity is better than the soul.

4. Again, the agent is always more honorable than the patient, according to the Philosopher in *On the Soul* III.[e] But charity acts in the soul, cleansing it from sins. Therefore it is more honorable than the soul [upon which it acts], and so the same conclusion follows as before.

a. Boethius, *On the Two Natures*, ch. 1 (PL 64:1341–42).
b. See Aristotle, *Physics* II, ch. 1.
c. Parallel: *In I Sent.* (*Lectura romana*) d. 17, a. 3 (see below).
d. See Aristotle, *Posterior Analytics* I, ch. 2 (72b29).
e. Aristotle, *On the Soul* III, ch. 5 (430a18–19).

On the contrary:

Whatever can arrive and depart without entailing the corruption of the subject is an accident. But charity is this kind of thing. Therefore, charity is an accident.

Response:

It should be said that everything that comes to something after complete being comes to it accidentally, unless perhaps it is assumed into participation of substantial being itself,[a] as was said above, in treating of the soul.[b] Nevertheless, the fact that it comes after complete being is not enough [of a reason] for calling it an accident in itself, for something can be a substance in itself and come to another accidentally, as garments when placed upon a body; but if it should come to a thing as an inhering form after that thing's complete being, it is necessarily an accident. And since it is after the soul's natural being that charity comes to it as a form perfecting it in regard to the being of grace, as was said in the preceding article, therefore it must be an accident.

Replies to objections:

1. To the first, therefore, it should be said that an accident one in number "never extends beyond its subject" in such a way that it would be in another as in a subject,[22] but it can very well extend outside of its subject as to the object of operation. Yet this takes place in different ways in an active and in a passive operation. In an active one, the accident extends to an extrinsic object, impressing the likeness of its form upon it, as it is evident that the heat of fire actively heats another body and is an active operation. Similarly, when there is a passive operation, the accident extends to another extrinsic object, too, [yet with this difference:] the likeness of that object is received into *it*.[23] And in this way the soul, through the habit of science, knows those things which are outside of it, and through the habit of love, loves the same things.

2. To the second, it should be said that a subject is related differently to different accidents. Now certain accidents are natural—namely, those that are created out of the principles of the subject—and this [occurs] in two ways: because they are caused either by the principles of the species, and in this way they are proper passions that follow upon the whole species,[24] or by individual principles, and in this way they are common things following upon [= resulting from] natural individ-

a. *esse completum . . . esse substantialis*
b. See *In I Sent.* d. 8, q. 5, a. 2 (Mandonnet mistakenly says q. 4, a. 2).

ual principles. There are also certain accidents induced through violence, like heat in water, and these are repugnant to the principles of the subject.[25] But there are certain accidents which are indeed caused by something outside the subject, yet are not repugnant to the subject's principles but rather perfective of them, like light in the air: and it is in this manner too that charity in the soul comes from something outside the soul. Nevertheless, it should be known that for all accidents, generally speaking, the subject is the cause in a certain way, namely insofar as the accidents are given their concrete reality in the being of the subject,[a, 26] but not in such a way that all the accidents are derived out of the principles of the subject.

3. To the third, it should be said that by the same argument one could just as well prove that *no* perfection of soul or body is an accident, since any perfectible thing whatsoever has goodness from its perfection.[27] It should therefore be said that, simply speaking, the soul is better than charity, and for that matter, any subject than its accident; but in a certain respect it is the converse. The reason is that, according to Dionysius in chapter 5 of *On the Divine Names,* being is nobler than everything else following after it; hence to be is nobler, simply speaking, than to understand, *if* it were possible to understand understanding apart from being.[b] Hence, that which exceeds in being is nobler, simply speaking, than everything which exceeds in some one of the things that follow after being, although in another respect, being can be less noble.[28] And since the soul, and any substance, has a nobler being than an accident does, therefore it is simply nobler. But with respect to some being, according to some aspect,[c] an accident can be nobler, since it stands to substance as act to potency; and this consequent goodness the substance has from its accidents, but not the first goodness of being.

4. To the fourth, it should be said that charity is not said to act in the soul in the manner of an efficient cause, but only formally; and according to what the form is, it is nobler with respect to second being.[d]

a. *accidentia in esse subjecti substantificantur*
b. Pseudo-Dionysius, *On the Divine Names,* ch. 5 (PG 3:819).
c. *quantum ad aliquod esse, secundum aliquod*
d. First being (*esse primum*) is existence; second being (*esse secundum*) is activity.

ARTICLE 3[a]   Whether charity is given according
to natural capacity[b, 29]

Objections:

Proceeding to the third, it seems that charity is given according to
natural capacity.

1. For it says so in Matthew 25:15: "He gave to each according to his
own power,"[c] upon which the gloss of Jerome says: "Not on account of
liberality or frugality do different men receive more or less, but according to the power of the recipients."[d] But prior to the advent of charity,
no other power is understood to be in a man except that which is according to natural endowments. Therefore it seems that charity is infused according to natural capacity.

2. Again, as substantial form stands to the being of nature, so charity
stands to the being of grace. But substantial form is given according to
the capacity of matter, as Plato says in *On the Soul of the World* II.[e] Therefore charity too is given according to the capacity of nature, which is
perfected by it.[30]

3. Further, as glory presupposes grace, so grace presupposes nature.
But glory is given according to the measure of grace, so that he who
has the greater capacity also receives more glory.[31] Therefore it seems
that charity too is given according to the capacity of nature, so that
a greater charity is infused into him who has better natural endowments.

a. Parallels: *In II Sent.* d. 3, Notes on the Text (translated in webnote 41); *In III
Sent.* d. 31, q. 1, a. 4, qa. 1; *ST* I, q. 62, a. 6; II-II, q. 24, a. 3; III, q. 69, a. 8, ad 3;
Super Matth. 25; *De caritate,* a. 7, ad 9.

b. *capacitas naturalium:* literally, "capacity of/for natural things"; *naturalium* by
itself has been rendered "natural endowments."

c. *Dedit unicuique secundum propriam virtutem. Virtus* here could also be rendered "ability, capacity."

d. Jerome actually writes: "Not giving more to one and less to another on account of his liberality or frugality, but rather on account of the capacities [*viribus*]
of the recipients." See *Commentary on Matthew,* Bk. IV, on Mt. 25:14–15 (CCSL
77:239).

e. The Parma ed. has merely *ut dicit Plato,* while the Mandonnet ed. has *ut dicit
Plato, II De anima mundi.* This work was a collection of Latin fragments of the *Timaeus* available in Thomas's day (see John Tomarchio, "Computer Linguistics and
Philosophical Interpretation," note 7, published by the Paideia Project Online,
www.bu.edu/wcp/Papers/Meth/MethToma.htm, accessed September 25, 2006).
Nowhere else does Thomas refer to this collection, although in his commentary
on Aristotle's *On the Soul* he mentions Plato's views on the *anima mundi* as given
in the *Timaeus* (*Sent. I De anima,* ch. 7, ed. Leon. 45.1:32–36).

4. Again, in anything whatsoever in which a perfection of the same *ratio* is found, there would seem to be the same mode of attaining that perfection, since each thing has its proper mode. But charity is found in men and angels according to the same *ratio*, as is evident from the act and the end [of charity, which is the same for both]. Since therefore angels attain a greater charity and better gratuitous endowments according to the level of their natural endowments,[a] it seems that it would be the same in men.

On the contrary:

Angelic nature is higher and more sublime than human nature. But some men, according to the level of grace, are taken up to a more sublime reward than angels are, since some men are taken up into each of the angelic orders, as Gregory says in *Homilies on the Gospels,* Homily 34.[b] Therefore it seems that the perfections of grace and glory are not given according to the measure of natural endowments. The same thing may also be seen through what is said in Proverbs 30:28: "The stellio advances by hands,"[c] in explaining which Gregory says that "a greater grace is infused insofar as someone exerts himself more to have grace."[d, 32]

Response:

It should be said that, since God stands equally to all things,[e, 33] the diversity of gifts received from him must be viewed according to the diversity of their recipients.[34] Now, this diversity of recipients is viewed in terms of the extent to which something is more apt and prepared for receiving than another. But as we see among natural forms that matter is rendered more or less disposed to receiving form by accidental dispositions like heat and cold and things of this sort, so too in regard to perfections of soul, the soul is made more or less capable of attaining its perfection by the soul's very operations. The soul's opera-

a. *majorem charitatem et meliora gratuita, secundum gradum naturalium*

b. Gregory the Great, *Homilies on the Gospels,* Homily 34, n. 11 (CCSL 141:309).

c. *stellio manibus nititur.* The *stellio* is a lizard marked with star-like spots on its back. See Cornelius a Lapide, *Commentaria in Scripturam Sacram,* ed. Augustine Crampon, 9th ed. (Paris: Vivès, 1868), 6:459.

d. *gratia major infunditur, secundum quod ad habendum gratiam aliquis magis nititur,* which could also be rendered "a greater grace is infused insofar as someone strives/labors more to have grace." The quotation could not be traced exactly; the basic idea is expressed well in Gregory the Great's *Morals on the Book of Job* VI, ch. 10 (CCSL 143:292).

e. *cum Deus habeat se aequaliter ad omnia*

tions, however, are related in different ways to infused and acquired perfections. For acquired perfections are in potency in the nature of the soul itself, not in a purely material way but also actively, as something is in potency in its seminal causes—just as it is evident that all acquired knowledge is in potency in the knowledge of naturally known first principles,[a] which function as active principles from which further knowledge can be deduced; and similarly, moral virtues exist in potency in the rectitude and order of reason as in a certain seminal principle. This is why the Philosopher says that there are certain natural virtues which are the seeds, as it were, of the moral virtues.[b] Consequently, the soul's operations stand to acquired perfections not only in the manner of a disposition to them, but also as their active principles. Infused perfections, on the other hand, are in the nature of the soul itself as in a potency that is material only and in no way active, since they elevate the soul above all of its natural action. Hence the soul's operations stand to infused perfections as dispositions only.[35]

It should be said, therefore, that the measure according to which charity is given is the capacity of the soul itself, which is at once from nature and from the disposition that comes through the effort of works.[c, 36] And because a better nature is more disposed for one and the same effort than an inferior nature, it follows that the one who has better natural endowments, when there is an equal effort of works, will receive a greater share of infused perfections than the one who has inferior natural endowments, and the one who has inferior natural endowments, if there be a greater effort in the work, will

a. *omnis scientia acquisita est in cognitione primorum principiorum, quae naturaliter nota sunt*

b. The Parma ed. contains no reference; the Mandonnet cites *Ethics* VII, ch. 5, but this cannot be correct. More likely candidates are *Ethics* II, ch. 1 (1103a23–25: "Neither by nature, then, nor contrary to nature do virtues arise in us; rather we are adapted by nature to receive them, and are made perfect by habit") and *Ethics* VI, ch. 13 (1144b3–5: "All men think that each type of character belongs to its possessor in some sense by nature; for from the very moment of birth we are just or fitted for self-control or brave or have the other moral qualities"). Aquinas develops the idea of "seeds of virtue" much beyond what can be explicitly found in Aristotle. In many texts he does not even refer to Aristotle or any source. At *III Sent.* d. 33, a. 2, qa. 2, the idea is attributed to Cicero; at *ST* I-II, q. 63, a. 3, arg. 3, he derives it from a gloss on Hebrews.

c. *per conatum operum* (not *operationum*). *Conatus,* used several times in this passage, could also be rendered "exertion" or "endeavor," but cannot be rendered "impulse," since impulse is nothing other than the inclination toward working that arises from a nature, and so could not be condivided against nature. (Human nature and its natural inclination pertains to first actuality; the free exertion of the will toward the good pertains to second actuality.)

sometimes receive more than the one who has better natural endowments.[a, 37]

Replies to objections:

1 and 2. To the first, it should be said that the recipient's power is not to be considered according to nature alone, but also according to the disposition of the effort added to nature;[b, 38] and so it is too in substantial forms with respect to matter.[39] From this, the solution to the second is evident.

3. To the third, it should be said that grace itself is a disposition of nature to glory. Hence, it is not required that yet another disposition between charity and glory should intervene.[40] But between nature and grace there does fall an intermediary effort,[c] which is, as it were, a disposition [of nature to grace].

4. To the fourth, it should be said that in angels there is nothing that, fighting against the intellectual nature's motion, slows down nature's effort, as in man's nature there is the sensitive nature which tends, of itself, to what is contrary to the aim of the intellective nature's motion (namely, the pleasurable according to sense), unless the former nature is compelled and ruled by the latter. And as a result, in angels there is diversity [of gratuitous endowments] according to diversity of *nature.* Nevertheless this point will be explained better in Book II.[41]

ARTICLE 4[d]   Whether he who has charity can know
for certain that he has it[e]

Objections:

Proceeding to the fourth, it seems that he who has charity can know for certain that he has it.

1. For so it is said in the text of Lombard: "Someone knows the love by which he loves more than he knows the brother whom he loves."[f]

a. "Inferior" translates *pejora,* which in this context is not meant to have a pejorative connotation.

b. *secundum dispositionem conatus advenientem naturae*

c. *conatus medius*

d. Parallels: *In I Sent.* (*Lectura romana*) d. 17, q. 1, a. 4 (see below); *In III Sent.* d. 23, q. 1, a. 2, ad 1 (translated in webnote 48); *De ueritate,* q. 10, aa. 9–10; *Super II Cor.,* ch. 12, lec. 1 and ch. 13, lec. 2; *Quodl.* VIII, q. 2, a. 2 [4]; *ST* I, q. 87, a. 2 and I-II, q. 112, a. 5.

e. *Utrum charitas certitudinaliter* (here translated "for certain") *ab habente cognoscatur*

f. *magis novit quis dilectionem qua diligit, quam fratrem quem diligit.*—The Lom-

But for certain, he knows his brother. Therefore much more does he know for certain the charity by which he loves him.

2. Again, in *Posterior Analytics* II, the Philosopher says, against Plato, that it is unfitting for us to have the most noble habits and yet for them to be hidden to us. But charity is the most noble habit. Therefore it seems that it is known for certain by the one having it.

3. Further, whoever has faith knows that he has faith. But faith is not more present to the soul than charity is. Therefore he who has charity, too, knows that he has it.

4. Again, the soul knows whatever it knows by way of the object's likeness made present to the soul.[a] But that which is in the soul *essentially* is more present to the soul than that which is in the soul by way of its likeness. Therefore, since charity is in the soul essentially, it seems that it would be more certainly known by the one who has it than exterior things that are known by way of their likenesses.[42]

5. Further, charity is a certain spiritual light, as can be gathered from 1 John 2:10: "He who loves his brother remains in the light." But light is seen in virtue of itself. Therefore it seems that charity in like manner is seen in virtue of itself; and so its presence is known more certainly than other things.

On the contrary:

1. It is by the charity within him that someone is made worthy of the love of God. But as is said in Ecclesiastes 9:1, no one knows whether he is worthy of love or hatred.[43] Therefore it seems that no one knows for certain that he has charity.

2. Further, the Apostle says in 1 Corinthians 4:4: "I am not aware of anything against myself, but I am not thereby acquitted."[44] Since therefore no greater sign of charity can be had than not to have mortal sin on one's conscience, and yet having a clean conscience is not enough to be sure of acquittal, it seems that it is not possible through *any* sign for someone to know for certain that he has charity.

Response:

It should be said that, as the Philosopher explains in *Metaphysics* II, something is said to be "difficult to know" in two ways: either in it-

---

bard is citing Augustine, *On the Trinity* VIII, ch. 8 (CCSL 50:286). The word *quis* is omitted in the CCSL edition.

a. *quidquid cognoscitur ab anima, cognoscitur ab ea per hoc quod praesens sibi efficitur per sui similitudinem*

self or in regard to us.[a] Those things which, in their very being, are not in matter, are—so far as their own nature is concerned[b]—most of all knowable, but in regard to us they are the most difficult to know, on account of which the Philosopher says in the same passage that our intellect stands to the most manifest things of nature as the eye of the bat to the light of the sun. The reason is this: our potential intellect is in potency to all intelligible things, and before understanding takes place, none of these intelligibles are actually[c, 45] in our intellect. It follows, that in order for our intellect actually to understand, it has to be brought into act by species taken from the senses, illuminated by the light of the agent intellect—for, as the Philosopher says in *On the Soul* III, as colors stand to sight, so phantasms stand to the potential intellect. Hence, since it is natural for us to proceed from sensible things to intelligible things, from effects to causes, and from subsequent things to prior things (at least according to the wayfaring state, since in the fatherland there will be another way of understanding), the consequence is that we cannot know the soul's powers and habits except by their acts, and the acts in turn by their objects.

Now in an act of the soul there are many things to consider: namely, the species of the act itself (which is from the object), the manner, and the effect. If therefore we take the *act* of charity, which is to love God and neighbor, then merely from the *species* of the act it cannot be discerned whether a given act of love comes from an imperfect power or a power perfected by a habit, since power and habit are ordered to the same object, just as knowledge and the possible intellect are both ordered to knowing a thing.[46] Next, the *manner* that habit places in a work is ease and pleasure; accordingly the Philosopher says in *Ethics* II[d] that a sign of habit is when pleasure is taken in the carrying out of some work. Yet it cannot be discerned, by the mere fact of someone's having such a manner in his works, whether it comes from the habit of infused charity or from an acquired habit.[47] Finally, love's proper *effect*, insofar as it comes from charity, consists in the power of meriting. But this—i.e., that we have merited something—does not in any way fall into our knowledge, unless it is specially revealed to us by God. And therefore no one can know with certainty that he has charity, but he can make a conjecture from some probable signs.[48]

a. See Aristotle, *Metaphysics* II, ch. 1 (993a27–b11).
b. *quantum in se est*
c. *in actu*
d. Aristotle, *Ethics* II, ch. 3 (1104b4–5).

Also, as long as we are living in this life, we do not see uncreated charity, which is God, in his essence,[a] as is said in 1 Corinthians 13:12. Certain ones, however, hold another opinion, saying that we see within ourselves the very charity which is God, but that the sight is so poor that it cannot even be called sight, nor does anyone perceive that he is seeing God, because the sight of God himself is confused and mingled, as it were, with the knowledge of other things—just as the same ones also say that the soul always understands itself, but nevertheless does not always think about itself.[b] Now, in what way this may be understood to be true was already discussed above.[c]

Replies to objections:

1. To the first, therefore, it should be said that the authoritative quotations from Augustine set down in the text are speaking of knowledge on the part of the knowable thing itself, and not on the part of the knower.[49]

2. To the second, it should be said that the Philosopher is speaking there about the most noble habits of the *cognitive* part of the soul. But the acts of those habits perfectly express their habits with respect to what is proper to them, as in the act of the habit of science there is certitude through the cause, in which knowledge is expressly shown forth;[50] and this holds even more when it comes to the understanding of principles. Accordingly, the one who has knowledge knows that he has it, although not the converse, because some men believe that they have it, who in fact do not have it. For the oblique is always measured by the right, and therefore, according to the Philosopher in *Ethics* III,[d] the virtuous man is the measure in human works, because that is good which the virtuous man desires; and it is similar with rightness of intellect, since that is true which seems so to the one who has right understanding, not what seems so to just anyone.

3. And through this response, the solution to the third is also evident. For the act of faith is distinguished by its object—that which is believed—from the acts of other habits or of an imperfect power that cannot be directed *per se* to such an object; and therefore the one who has faith knows that he has it.[51]

a. *per speciem*—as he really is, in his proper nature. In the text cited, St. Paul says: "videmus nunc per speculum in enigmate, tunc autem facie ad faciem."

b. The Mandonnet ed. (last line of p. 403 and first line of p. 404) has a typographical error here: "non semper de cogitat," which the Parma rightly gives as "non semper de *se* cogitat."

c. See *In I Sent.* d. 3, q. 1, a. 2.

d. Aristotle, *Ethics* III, ch. 4 (1113a22–33).

4. To the fourth, it should be said that in order for something to be known by the soul, it is not enough that it should be present to it in any way whatsoever; rather, it must be present to it in accord with the *ratio* of the object. Now, in our state as wayfarers, nothing is present as an object to our intellect except by means of some likeness of it, taken perhaps from its effect,[a] since we arrive at causes through their effects. For this reason, we do not know the soul itself and its powers and habits except through their acts, which are known in turn by their objects—unless we wish to speak of "knowledge" in the broader sense Augustine is using, according to which "to understand" is nothing other than for something to be present to the intellect in any way whatsoever.

5. To the fifth, it should be said that when we say that created or uncreated charity is "light," this shows that in itself it is something knowable; but in itself it is not known by our intellect except by means of its effect, the reason for which was just given in the body of the article.

ARTICLE 5[b]   Whether charity is to be loved from charity[c]

Objections:

Proceeding to the fifth, it seems that charity is not to be loved from charity.

1. For there are only four things to be loved from charity, as will be said in Book III[d]—namely, God, the neighbor, the soul, and the body. But charity is none of these. Therefore, charity is not to be loved from charity.

2. Again, nothing is denominated by its own name,[e] since "white-

---

a. *per aliquam similitudinem ipsius, vel suo effectu acceptam.* Although it is rare in Thomas, in earlier and later authors one can find *vel* meaning "even, possibly, perhaps." Alternatively, one might surmise that a bit of text is missing here, and read: "by means of some likeness of it, taken [either from it] or from its effect."

b. Parallels: *ST* II-II, q. 25, a. 2 (Mandonnet, p. 405, mistakenly refers the reader to a. 1); *Super Rom.* 12, lec. 2.

c. *ex caritate* is rendered here and throughout as "from charity," but could also have been translated "out of charity," i.e., from the habit of charity. The question at hand is: Should one love the very habit of charity with the habit of charity? See *In III Sent.* d. 28 (below) for further questions about what should or should not be loved *ex caritate.*

d. Mandonnet gives as the intended *locus* d. 27, a. 5, but no such citation exists (d. 27 is divided into three questions, none of which has more than four articles). On the other hand, Thomas expressly limits the objects of charity to these four in d. 28, a. 7.

e. *nulla res denominat seipsam,* literally "no thing denominates itself"

ness" is not called "white." But "loved" is named by a word taken from "love."[a] Therefore love is not loved, nor is charity loved by charity.[52]

3. Further, as a sense-power stands to sensing, so an affective power stands to loving.[b] But a proper sense-power does not sense itself sensing;[c, 53] therefore neither does an affective power love its own love. But charity is in an affective power. Therefore charity is not loved from charity.

4. Further, everything which is loved is loved by some love. If therefore the act of charity itself is loved, it must be loved by some other act, and for the same reason, that act will also be something to be loved. Therefore in this way one is led into an infinite regress, which cannot be posited. Therefore it seems that charity is not to be loved from charity.

On the contrary:

1. Against this is what is given in the text from the words of Augustine: "If a man loves his neighbor, it follows that he chiefly loves love itself."[d] But the neighbor is to be loved from charity; therefore also charity.

2. Again, the neighbor is not to be loved from charity except insofar as he has the image of God. But charity represents God more expressly than the natural image of God that is in the soul. Therefore it seems that it is to be loved from charity even more than the neighbor.

Response:

It should be said that something is lovable in two ways: either as the *ratio* of love or as the object of love, as, to give a parallel example, color is seen as the object of sight, and light is seen as the *ratio* by which color is actually visible. But just as color and light are seen in the same act of seeing, so too what is loved as the object and what is loved as the *ratio* of the object are loved in the same act of loving. It should be known therefore that "charity" can be taken in a threefold sense: for uncreated charity, which is the Holy Spirit, or for habitual charity, or for the act of charity. Now each of these things is a *ratio* for loving and

a. *dilectum denominatur a dilectione*

b. *sicut se habet sensus ad sentire, ita se habet affectus ad diligere. Affectus* could be translated either "affective power" or "affective part of the soul." This should be borne in mind for the penultimate sentence of the objection: *Charitas autem est in affectu.*

c. *sensus proprius non sentit se sentire*

d. *Qui proximum diligit, consequens est ut ipsam praecipue dilectionem diligat.*—Augustine, *On the Trinity* VIII, ch. 7 (CCSL 50:285).

can also be an object of love—even as we love the neighbor insofar as God dwells in him and he has the habit of charity and exercises its act (and thus, each of these is loved as the *ratio* of what is lovable), and, moreover, if they be considered in themselves, they are loved as the object of love. However, the habit of charity or its act are not so loved by a love of friendship or of benevolence, which cannot be had toward inanimate things, as the Philosopher says in *Ethics* VIII;[a] rather, they are loved by a love of *complacentia*,[b, 54] according to which we are said to love that which we approve and wish to exist.

Replies to objections:

1. To the first, therefore, it should be said that charity is, in a certain way, a mean between God and neighbor, because it is a likeness of God and also the *ratio* for loving the neighbor himself; and therefore it accompanies the love of both.[c]

2. To the second, it should be said that denomination, properly speaking, is according to the relationship of an accident to a subject. But "loved" is not denominated from "love" in this way, but rather is given its name as the *object* of love; and therefore the argument does not follow.

3. To the third, it should be said that the fact that in material powers the power is not turned back upon its own act is because such a power is determined according to the organ's complexion.[d] For sight of the particular cannot know anything except that of which the species can be spiritually received into the pupil,[e, 55] and therefore sight cannot comprehend its own act. Now if it were necessary in all cases that the act of any power whatever could not be known by the proper power but only by a superior one, then it would follow of necessity either that one would go into an infinite regress in the powers of the soul, or that some act of the soul would remain imperceptible. And therefore it should be said that immaterial powers are turned back upon their own objects, because the intellect understands itself to understand,

a. Aristotle, *Ethics* VIII, ch. 2 (1155b27–28).

b. *dilectione cujusdam complacentiae.* The last word is left untranslated because there is no close English equivalent; "complacency" strikes the wrong note. Generally, *complacentia* names the affective reaction to a good that is found, felt, or "taken" to be suitable, right, worthy of acceptance.

c. *consequitur ad dilectionem utriusque,* i.e., is implied in the love of both objects.

d. *secundum complexionem organi,* where *complexio* seems to refer to the make-up and corresponding limitations of the organ. The Parma ed. reads, less plausibly, *compilatio,* which in this case would mean the organ's material disposition.

e. *spiritualiter in pupilla potest recipi*

and likewise, the will wills its willing and loves its loving.[a] The reason for this is that the act of an immaterial power is not excluded from the *ratio* of that power's object, for the will's object is the good, and since it is under this *ratio* that the will loves everything it loves, it can therefore love its own act insofar as it is good; and it is similar on the part of the intellect. And on account of this, it is said in Proposition 15 of the *Book of Causes* that of anything in which the action returns into the essence of the agent through a certain reflection, it is necessary for its essence to return into itself, i.e., for it to be subsistent in itself, and not be based upon another, i.e., not dependent on matter.[b, 56]

4. To the fourth, it should be said that it is clearly the case that the act of love, insofar as it tends toward another, differs in number from that act of love which is loved in another, whether it is loved as the object or as the *ratio* of loving. But seeing that someone can love his own soul from charity, he can also love his own act of charity from charity. And then one must make a distinction. Either love is borne toward the proper act of love as toward the *ratio* of loving only, and in this way it is clear that both the one loving and his act are loved by an act the same in number, and so the same act is loved by the act which is itself; or love is loved as the object of love, and in this way the act of love which is loved, and the act of love *by* which it is loved, are acts different in number[57]—as is evident more plainly in the act of the intellect. For since acts are distinguished by objects, it is necessary to say that acts having their terms in different objects are themselves different. Hence, just as the acts by which the intellect understands horse and man are different, so the acts by which it understands horse and by which it understands that very act of understanding horse under the *ratio* of act are different in number; nor is it unfitting that in acts of the soul one might go to the *potentially* infinite, as long as the acts be not *actually* infinite in number, [as this is impossible].[58] Hence, Avicenna, too, concedes (*Metaphysics* tract III, chapter 10) that it is not impossible that relations following upon an act of the soul might be multiplied to infinity.

---

a. *voluntas vult se velle et diligit se diligere*

b. *cujuscumque actio redit in essentiam agentis per quamdam reflexionem, oportet essentiam ejus ad seipsam redire, id est in se subsistentem esse, non super aliud delatam, id est non dependentem a materia*

Notes on the text of Lombard

"It follows that he chiefly loves love itself."

This may be understood about created as well as uncreated love. For the one who loves someone wishes to love him, and thus he loves his own act of love;[59] and in this very act of love, uncreated love itself is loved as the exemplar in that which is patterned after it, since nothing is good or lovable except insofar as the likeness of the uncreated good is in it.

"Someone knows the love by which he loves more than [he knows] the brother whom he loves."

The whole passage that follows after these words, concerning the certainty of knowing that one has love (whether love here be understood in reference to the created habit or to the uncreated love), may be explained in terms of the way something is called "certain in itself" as opposed to being certain on the part of the knower. But the act of love is known [not only in itself, but] also on the part of the knower, yet whether it proceeds from such a habit remains uncertain.[60]

"And by whom is the one who is filled by love filled, except by God?"

This statement is made because, along with the gift of charity, the Holy Spirit himself is also given, inasmuch as he is said to dwell in the creature in a new way by a new likeness of himself being in it.[61]

"He who loves his brother remains in the light."

Light is compared to charity not as regards a power of manifestation—because in this way [the metaphor of] light would pertain more to the gifts of intellect—but as regards a power of action, for even as light is a form that is universally motive in the whole of nature because it is a quality of the first altering body, so charity moves and informs all gifts insofar as it is a likeness of the first gift, which is the Holy Spirit.[62]

"That text declares openly enough that the opinion that the very same fraternal love is not only from God but also is God, is proclaimed with great authority."

(The other phrase found in that place, "for fraternal love is that by which we love each other," is parenthetical.) Now fraternal love is said to be God by a causal predication, in the manner in which Dionysius says, in chapter 4 of *The Celestial Hierarchy*,[a] that "the divine being is the being of all things," because every being is drawn forth from him and patterned after him.

"Nor are we to say that charity is not to be called God owing to the fact that charity itself is not a substance worthy of the name 'God', but rather we are to say that it is a gift of God."[63]

According to Augustine's authorial intention, charity differs from other virtues in this way: other virtues which in themselves imply some imperfection in the one who has them, such as faith, patience, and things of this sort,[64] are *from* God but are not *in* God essentially, whereas charity, which has nothing of imperfection, both is predicated of God essentially and is in us from him. Nevertheless it does not follow that that charity which is the form of our mind is the same in number with that which is said of God essentially—even as being, too, is said of God properly, yet nonetheless that being is not the same in number with our being.

"For there is nothing more excellent than that gift of God [namely, charity]."

This seems to be false, because wisdom is set down as the most excellent of the gifts.[b] In response, it should be said that (1) insofar as the gifts are distinguished from[65] the virtues, wisdom is called the most dignified of the gifts,[66] and this dignity it has from the charity to which it is always conjoined, inasmuch as wisdom *tastes* divine truth.[67] (2) If, however, "gift" is taken universally for everything we possess from God's giving, then in this way charity, which conjoins us to the divine end itself, is, simply speaking, the most powerful of all gifts.[68]

---

a. Pseudo-Dionysius, *The Celestial Hierarchy*, ch. 4, n. 1 (PG 3:178).
b. Namely, of the gifts of the Holy Spirit.

QUESTION 2 On charity's increase and decrease[a]

Division of the second part of the text

"Here we will inquire into the following: If charity *is* the Holy Spirit, then since charity may increase and decrease in man, should it be conceded that the Holy Spirit can increase or decrease in man?" In this part, the Master raises objections against matters already [to his mind] determined, and this portion is divided into two parts.

In the first, he objects with arguments drawn from reason; in the second, he objects with arguments drawn from authorities, where he says: "It was said above that the Holy Spirit is the charity of the Father and the Son."

The first is handled in three parts: first, he sets down an objection; second, he sets down the response, where he says: "And so we respond to these things, saying that the Holy Spirit or charity is altogether immutable"; third, he offers confirmation of the response, where he says: "That what we have said might become still more certain, we confirm it by authority." Now the objection as well as the solution is twofold, as is evident in the text.

"It was said above that the Holy Spirit is the charity of the Father and the Son." Here he raises objections from authorities; and this portion is divided into three parts, according to the three things that are gathered from the authorities against the Master's position. The first is this: the love by which we love God is other than the love by which God loves us; but the love by which God loves us is the Holy Spirit; therefore the love by which we love God is other than the Holy Spirit. The second is this: charity is said to be from God, just as faith is said to be from him; but faith is from God in such a way that it is not God; therefore charity is also from God in such a way that it is not God. (He speaks of this at the words: "But there is another point, they say, that is more pressing.") The third is this: charity is called an affection or motion of the mind; but the Holy Spirit is not this sort of thing; therefore, charity is not the Holy Spirit. (He speaks of this at the words: "They also bring forward other reasons to show the same thing.") Each of these parts is divided into the objection and its solution.

In order to understand this part of the text, we will inquire into five things: (1) whether charity admits of increase; (2) the manner of its increase; (3) whether it increases by any act [of charity]; (4) whether there is any limit to the increase; (5) whether it admits of decrease.

a. The terms are *augmentatio/augere* and *(di)minutio/(di)minuere.*

ARTICLE 1ᵃ   Whether charity admits of increaseᵇ⁶⁹

Objections:

Proceeding to the first, it seems that charity does not admit of increase.

1. For only a quantity increases. But since every quantity is divisible, nothing simple is a quantity. Now charity is a simple habit, and thus it is not a quantity, either *per se* or *per accidens*, since its subject, the soul, is also indivisible. Therefore it does not increase.

2. If you should say that it *is* a quantity, not of mass but of power, against this I remind you that quantity of power is classified by the objects toward which the power can be directed. But any charity, no matter how small, can be directed toward all the objects of charity. Therefore it does not increase according to quantity of power.⁷⁰

3. Again, since increase is a species of motion, whatever increases is moved, and that which essentially increases is essentially moved. But whatever is moved is a body, as the Philosopher proves in *Physics* VI; and what is naturally moved is corrupted. Since therefore charity is not corrupted, because "charity is never cut out" (1 Cor. 13:8), nor is it a mobile body, it seems that it does not essentially increase.

4. Again, a thing is neither increased nor diminished nor in any way varied if its cause always exists in the same way.ᶜ But the immediate cause of charity is God, who always exists in the same way. Therefore charity is not varied through increase.

5. Further, it is certain that the increase of a quality cannot be reduced to any species of motion except alteration. But as the Philosopher proves in *Physics* VII, alteration does not take place in the soul except in regard to the soul's sensitive part and its objects. Since therefore charity is a quality and is in the intellective part (for otherwise it would not be in the angels, who lack the sensitive part), it seems that it cannot be increased.

---

a. Parallels: *In I Sent.* d. 17 (*Lectura romana*), q. 2, a. 1 (see below); *ST* I-II, q. 52, a. 1; q. 66, a. 1; II-II, q. 24, a. 4; *Quodl.* IX, q. 6; *De uirt. in comm.*, a. 11; *De uirt. card.*, a. 3; *De malo*, q. 7, a. 2; *Sent. Eth.* X, lec. 3.

b. *utrum caritas augeatur,* literally "whether charity is increased," but the first and fundamental question asked is: Is charity the sort of thing that admits of, or allows for, increase? Hence, the phrase has often been rendered this way.

c. *semper se habet eodem modo;* the same phrase is repeated in the next premise concerning God.

On the contrary:

1. Stands the authority of Augustine in the fifth of the *Tractates on the First Epistle of John:*[a] "Once it has been born, charity then receives nourishment; when it has been strengthened, it reaches perfection." But everything in which one can take note of advancement according to different degrees, is [a thing that permits of being] increased. Therefore, charity admits of increase.

2. Further, we arrive at knowledge of a habit through knowledge of the act that comes from it. But it can happen that the act of charity becomes more intense. Therefore the habit of charity, too, can increase.

Response:

It should be said that certain ones posited that charity does not essentially increase, and among them there were four different explanations.

(1) For certain ones said, as the Master does in the text, that charity *in itself* does not increase, but is said to increase in us insofar as *we* make progress in charity; and he advanced this view because he had already stated that charity was the Holy Spirit, in whom variation can have no place. But this view cannot stand, since it is not intelligible to say that we would be making *progress* in charity, which is the [unchanging] Holy Spirit, unless something should come to be within us which was not within us before; and this new thing cannot be merely an act, since every act comes from some power, and a perfect act—the kind by which we are united to the Holy Spirit—comes from a power perfected by a habit.[71]

(2) Others said that charity does not essentially increase, but is said to increase insofar as it is more firmly established[b] in its subject, according to its rootedness in that subject. But from this, too, it follows that it *does* essentially increase. For no form can be understood to be "more firmly established" in its subject except by having a greater victory over its subject. But an increase of victory redounds into an increase of power, and consequently into an increase of essence: because if the power is not the essence itself, it must be *from* the essence and commensurate with it, as an effect is commensurate with its proximate cause.[72]

(3) Others said that charity does not essentially increase, but that the lesser charity that was present is destroyed by the arrival of a greater charity. This view also cannot stand, because form is destroyed in

---

a. Augustine, *Tractates on the First Epistle of John,* Tractate 5, n. 4 (PL 35:2014).
b. *magis firmatur*

two ways only: *per se* by a contrary agent, or *per accidens* by the corruption of the subject. Since therefore the subject of charity remains, and the arriving charity is not contrary to the charity already found there, it cannot be the case that it is destroyed either *per se* or *per accidens*, in the way that a small fire can be destroyed *per accidens* by a great fire, on account of the consumption of matter.[73]

(4) Others said that charity does not increase except with respect to its fervor.[a] But this view also cannot stand. For the phrase "fervor of charity" may be taken in two ways: properly and metaphorically. Metaphorically, we say that charity is "heat," and metaphorically we call the intensity of the act of charity "fervor"; this is how Dionysius is speaking when, in chapter 7 of *The Celestial Hierarchy*,[b] he attributes "fervent" to the love of the angels. But fervor taken in this sense follows *per se* upon the essence of charity; hence an increase cannot come to be in such fervor unless charity itself is essentially increased, since whenever a thing is varied, all the things that follow upon it *per se* are simultaneously varied. In the other way [taking "fervor" properly], we may speak of fervor as we find it in the sensitive part, for just as the lower powers follow the motion of the higher if that motion is more intense (as we see that a man's whole body is inflamed and set in motion at the sight of a woman he loves),[c] so too, when the higher affection is moved unto God, a certain impression follows even in the sensitive powers, according to which they are spurred on to obeying divine love. But the intensity of such fervor is not enough to bring about an increase of charity, because the quantity of merit is not looked at according to an increase of such fervor, since it consists in a disposition of the body.[74] Hence, the more fervent [in this sense] do not always merit more. But the man who is said to grow in charity grows also in merit, if he is in a condition that allows for meriting.[75]

And therefore in response to the question, it should be said that charity *is* essentially increased.[76] Nevertheless it should be known that "to be increased" is nothing other than to take on a greater quantity;

a. *Fervor* means literally "burning," a meaning required by the argument that follows. "Fervor" has for us become a spiritualized word, but for Thomas it still retains its concreteness; hence in this passage he compares the fervor of charity to a man's body being inflamed at the sight of a woman especially loved (cf. the phrase *fervor coitus*, used at *In II Sent.* d. 31, q. 1, a. 1, ad 3 [Mandonnet, 806]).

b. Pseudo-Dionysius, *The Celestial Hierarchy*, ch. 7 (PG 3:206).

c. In the phrase *sicut videmus quod ad apprehensionem mulieris dilectae totum corpus exardescit et movetur*, the *apprehensio* is either catching a glimpse of the beloved (the more likely meaning) or grasping hold of the beloved. The point is that awareness of a "charged" object, which involves a number of cognitive acts, has its consequences in the appetitive part of the soul.

hence, as something stands in relation to quantity, so it stands in relation to increase. Now "quantity" is said in two ways: virtual (i.e., concerning power) and dimensive (i.e., concerning size). Virtual quantity is not quantity from its genus, because it is not divided by the division of its essence;[77] its magnitude is looked at rather in terms of something divisible or multipliable outside of it, which is either a power's object or its act. But of its genus,[78] it [viz., virtual quantity] is either an accidental form in the genus of quality, or a substantial form, which cannot be greater or lesser. And therefore an increase in quantity of power does not pertain to the species of motion called "increase," but rather to the species called "alteration." And it is in this way that charity increases, and other qualities as well.

Dimensive quantity, on the other hand, belongs to certain things *per accidens,* as it may be said to belong to whiteness, which is called a quantity according to the quantity of the surface in which the whiteness exists, as is said in the *Categories*[a] (hence, it increases only *per accidens*); whereas it is found *per se* in bodies that increase *per se.* Now this *per se* increase occurs in two ways. For sometimes that which takes on a greater quantity itself moves from a lesser quantity into a greater.[79] But sometimes the increase occurs without any motion in that which is said to increase, and in this case no part whatsoever increases, in contrast to the way that any and every part of a thing being moved moves *per se.*[80] And this occurs when a quantity is made greater through the addition of quantity, as when a piece of wood is added to a piece of wood, or a line to a line, so that there *is* an increase, but not a *motion* of increase.

Now, it happens in two ways that something *moves* to a greater quantity: either in such a way that the greater quantity is *per se* the term of motion, or in such a way that it follows upon the term of motion. Whenever quantity *per se* is the term of motion, one necessarily finds in that case an addition being made to the whole as well as to any and all parts, so that the whole and every part of it will be increased, as one sees in the growth of animals and plants; and in such a case there is the *motion* of increase, properly speaking. Hence, the motion of increase belongs only to things that have the nutritive power. On the other hand, quantity follows upon the term of motion when the motion is toward some form upon which some quantity follows, for [in the physical domain] a determinate quantity is owed[b, 81] to any

---

a. Aristotle, *Categories,* ch. 6 (5b1–10).

b. *debetur:* in this context, it means a certain quantity naturally belongs to or is destined for a definite kind of thing.

and every form. And since motion does not derive its species except from that which is the *per se* term of motion, such a motion is therefore not called a *per se* motion of increase, but is called either generation, if the form in question is a substantial form, as when fire comes to be from air; or alteration, when the form in question is an accidental form, as is evident in the rarefaction of air.

Replies to objections:

1. To the first, therefore, it should be said that although charity does not have dimensive quantity either *per se* or *per accidens* because its subject, too, is not a quantity, it nevertheless has quantity of power in it, by reason of which it is said to increase, just as whiteness and heat are said to increase.

2. To the second, it should be said that quantity of power may be looked at in two ways: either with respect to the number of objects (and this is in the manner of discrete quantity), or with respect to the intensity of an act directed toward the same object (and this is like continuous quantity); and it is thus [in the latter sense] that the virtue of charity grows.[a]

3. To the third, it should be said that charity is not said to increase as if *it* were the subject of increase, since it is an accident,[82] but rather because increase is considered in reference to it, just as quantity is said to be increased and whiteness is said to be varied when some *thing* is varied through whiteness.[b, 83] Nor does it necessarily follow that it [the former charity] would be destroyed, if it essentially increases. For something is said to move "according to its essence" in two ways: either (1) because its essence is the *per se* term of motion, and in this way to be moved in essence[c] is to lose essence and to be corrupted; or (2) because the motion occurs in reference to something *conjoined to* the essence, which conjoined something is the *per se* term of motion, even as something moving from place to place is said to be moving essentially, since according to its essence it is *in* a place.[d, 84] And under-

---

a. *et ita excrescit virtus charitatis*—i.e., it is precisely owing to the second quantitative aspect of virtual power that the virtue of charity can increase (and, as we will see below, diminish).

b. *sicut etiam quantitas augeri dicitur, et albedo variari, quando aliquid per albedinem variatur*

c. *per essentiam*

d. *vel quia est motus secundum aliquid conjunctum essentiae, quod est per se terminus motus, sicut dicitur aliquid moveri essentialiter dum secundum locum movetur, quia secundum suam essentiam in loco est.* (The Mandonnet ed. has a typographical error here: *assentiam* for *essentiam* on p. 413, line 12; the word is correct in the Parma ed.)

stood in this way, an increase that occurs in reference to the quantity following upon the essence, while the essence remains one and the same under a different quantity, can be called an "essential increase." [And this holds true] whether (A) the quantity [that follows upon the essence as something conjoined to it] is the thing's very essence, as the quantity of a power is the same as the power itself, and yet it can nonetheless be [said to] move *per se,* speaking in reference to quantity, according as the power is of greater and lesser perfection, nor does it then move *per se* according to essence, seeing that it retains its own being; or (B) the quantity is other than the essence, as is evident in bodily increase.[85] Nor is it necessary that everything which is moving be a body, unless "motion" is understood in terms of physical motion;[a, 86] and the motion of the soul is not of this sort.

4. To the fourth, it should be said that although the efficient cause of charity is unchangeable in himself, he can nonetheless bestow a greater charity upon someone by the good pleasure of his will, according to the order of his wisdom, and according to the different ways in which a man—who, in some sense, stands in relation to charity as a material cause receiving it—prepares himself for the reception of charity; such a difference in the recipient also brings about variation in the effect.[87]

5. To the fifth, it should be said that passive alteration includes passion in its very concept;[b] thus, as passion is twofold, alteration is twofold as well. For in one way, all reception is generally spoken of as a passion or a being-affected[c] (according to which one can even say that to understand is to be affected);[d] and so, according to that common meaning of passion or being-affected, alteration consists in any variation whatsoever concerning the reception of some quality; and understood in this way, there can be alteration even in purely intellectual substances. And it is thus that alteration can take place in charity. In another way, passion or being-affected is said properly whenever something is lost from a substance, owing to the action of a contrary bringing about a change in the subject; and according to that proper meaning of passion, nothing is called alteration *per se* unless it has to do with sensible

a. *de motu naturali,* i.e., the change of a body or bodily condition.

b. *in intellectu*

c. *passio.* To say merely "passion" here, though the path of least resistance, would be misleading for most readers. In Latin, *pati* means to suffer, undergo, be formed or affected, and *passio* means not only passion in the familiar sense (emotion, feeling, something to do with bodily appetites), but also any process of undergoing, suffering, being formed or affected. In this sentence, the term has to be understood as broadly as possible. Our solution: use a double phrase.

d. *secundum etiam quod intelligere pati dicitur*

things and the sensible part of the soul; if it has to do with the intellect, it is called alteration *per accidens,* i.e., with respect to those qualities that arise in the intellective part from the activity of the senses, such as are all of our acquired habits; and charity is not among these.

ARTICLE 2[a]   Whether charity increases by way of addition

Objections:

Proceeding to the second, it seems that charity increases by way of addition.

1. For the Philosopher says in *On Generation and Corruption* I: "Increase is something added to a preexisting quantity."[b] If therefore charity increases, it is necessary for this increase that another charity be added to the preexisting charity.

2. Again, nothing can bring about an increase in charity except God who gives it. But God does not newly bring about anything in the soul except by means of a new influx. Now a new influx cannot be understood to occur unless something is newly infused. Therefore it seems that charity increases in this manner—namely, that another charity, newly infused, is added to the present charity.

3. Again, if charity does not increase by the addition of new charity from God, the only other way it would seem capable of increasing is by receding from what is contrary to charity. But against this view, an increase of charity can occur in those in whom there is nothing contrary to charity, as in an angel, or man in the state of innocence. Therefore it seems that charity does not increase in that manner, but in the aforesaid manner.

4. Further, according to this [viz., that an increase of charity can occur by a man's receding from what is contrary to it], it seems that God is not the cause of an increase of charity, but rather the man, by holding himself back from what is contrary to charity, e.g., from concupiscence; and this is unfitting. Therefore it seems that it increases only by way of addition.

On the contrary:

1. One simple thing added to another simple thing does not produce anything greater, as the Philosopher proves in *On Generation and*

---

a. Parallels: *In I Sent.* d. 17 (*Lectura romana*), q. 2, a. 3 (see below); *ST* I-II, q. 52, a. 2; II-II, q. 24, a. 5; *De uirt. in comm.,* a. 11.

b. Aristotle, *On Generation and Corruption* I, ch. 5 (320b30).

Corruption I.[a] But charity is something simple. Therefore a greater charity is not produced by the addition of charity to charity.

2. Further, according to Dionysius in chapter 5 of *On the Divine
Names,*[b] so great is the distance between the participations of God and
the ones participating, that the participation is nobler to the extent that
it is simpler, whereas the one participating is nobler to the extent that
he has a greater composition of participated gifts, just as being is nobler
than living, and living than understanding (if one be understood in
isolation from the other, for being would be preferred to all of them),
yet that which has more of these is better. Now charity is a certain participation of divine goodness. Therefore, to the extent that charity is
more composite owing to the addition of charity to charity, it will be
less powerful.[c] [88] Hence, if charity is increased by addition, then to the
extent that it increases, it will be less choiceworthy. This, however, is
ridiculous. Therefore it is not increased by way of addition.

Response:

It should be said that among those who hold that charity is essentially increased, what is said about this comes down to two opinions.
One is that it is increased by an addition of charity to charity; the other, that it is increased in intensity according to approach to a terminus.
And what certain others say—that charity is increased by its multiplication in the soul just as light is increased by its multiplication in the
air—also comes down to this latter opinion, for light, like other qualities, is increased only in regard to its intensity.

Now I find it impossible to understand the first position, because
in every addition one must understand that there are two different
things, one of which is added to the other. If, then, one conceives of
two charities, they are conceived as either different in species or different in number. But it is certain that they are not different in species,
seeing that all charities belong to the same species of virtue. Difference
in number, on the other hand, results from difference of matter, even
as *this* whiteness differs in number from *that* whiteness because it is in
a different subject. Hence, quality cannot be added to quality except
by one subject being added to another subject.[89] But the charity which
[supposedly] can be added was never in another subject before being
in the one in which it comes to be; and owing to the fact that it is *in*

a. See Aristotle, *On Generation and Corruption* I, ch. 2 (316a30–35); ch. 5
(320a32–17).
b. Pseudo-Dionysius, *On the Divine Names*, ch. 5, n. 3ff. (PG 3:818ff.).
c. *minus valebit*

this subject,[a] it does not differ in number from another charity existing in the same subject, as was proved in this Distinction.[b] Hence there is no way to conceive of addition happening there. But such a view arises from a false imagination, because the increase of charity is imagined to occur in the manner of bodily increase, in which there comes to be addition of quantity to quantity.

And therefore I say that when charity is increased, nothing is *added* there; for just as the Philosopher explains in *Physics* IV, something is made whiter or hotter not by the addition of some other whiteness or hotness, but rather because the same quality which was in it before is intensified according to nearness to a term. Now this intensification occurs differently in simple qualities and in composite ones, in primary qualities and in secondary ones. For composite or secondary qualities are intensified according to the intensification of primary qualities, as taste and health and other things of this sort are intensified according to the intensification of hotness and coldness, wetness and dryness. Primary and simple qualities, on the other hand, are intensified from their [immediate] causes, namely from the agent and from the recipient. For the agent intends to lead the patient along from potency into the actuality of its own likeness, to the extent that it can. Now just as the non-hot is hot in potency, so the less hot is in potency with respect to a greater degree of heat.[c] Hence, just as what is non-hot is made hot through the power of what is actually hot, not because some hotness is placed there, but rather because the hotness that is in potency in the non-hot is brought into actuality, so also the less hot comes to be hotter through the action of what is hot, insofar as the hotness which was already in the former in the manner of an imperfect act is brought into a greater perfection and a greater likening to the agent. And this occurs to the extent that the potency subject to actuality—a potency which, as far as what is in it [is concerned], stands open to many things—finds its term more and more in that actuality,[d, 90] either because the power of the agent is increased, as from a bringing together of many lights illumination is intensified, or on the part of matter itself, insofar as it is made more receptive of that act, as air, when more rarefied, is made more receptive of light.

Now an intensification of charity does not occur because the power

a. *et secundum hoc quod est in isto*   b. See q. 1, a. 1.

c. *Sicut autem non calidum est potentia caloris; ita minus calidum est potentia respectu magis calidi*

d. *magis ac magis terminatur sub actu illo.* This could also be rendered: "is determined more and more by that act." The Parma ed. reads *ab* instead of *sub.* Either is plausible.

of the agent is strengthened, but only because the nature receiving—which, in regard to what is in it, has a certain disposition according to which it is in potency to many things—is more and more prepared for the reception of grace, insofar as it is gathered from the aforesaid multitude (the confusion of potentiality) into one, through those operations by which someone is prepared for receiving charity, as was said before.[a] And therefore Dionysius always describes the perfection of holiness as characterized by a rising up from a divided life into a unified one.[b] And thus it is evident that the increase of charity is similar to the increase of natural qualities, although its origin differs from their origin. The reason for this difference is that natural qualities, certain beginnings[c] of which God imparted to matter in the work of creation, are led out from matter's potency; and therefore, when they proceed into actuality, there is a going-out from the imperfect to the perfect [all on the level of the nature itself]. Gratuitous gifts, by contrast, are not led forth as if from the potency of nature, because nothing that cannot be led out by a natural agent is in natural potency.[91] And therefore grace has its origin through a new infusion, whereas its increase occurs when an already infused actuality is brought from imperfection to perfection.

Replies to objections:

1. To the first, therefore, it should be said that that proposition of the Philosopher, since it is proposed by him in this material,[d] is to be understood as concerning bodily increase, which always comes about by the addition of quantity.

2. To the second, it should be said that in all the things that exist, God acts by one and the same operation, although perhaps that operation differs only according to *ratio*, insofar as it [may be said to] go out from the *ratio* of different divine attributes or different divine ideas.[e] Hence, I say that by one and the same operation grace is both infused and increased; nor is there any difference except on the recipi-

---

a. See above, q. 1, a. 3; q. 2, a. 1, ad 4.

b. Leaving the referent of the last word deliberately vague: *Dionysius perfectum sanctitatis semper designat per hoc quod est ex partita vita in unitam consurgere.* The Parma ed. reads: *ex sparsa vita in unicam consurgere,* "to rise up from a dispersed life into a single one." Thomas does not say *semper* unadvisedly; among many texts that could be cited, cf. *The Ecclesiastical Hierarchy,* ch. 2, n. 5; ch. 3, n. 1; ch. 6, n. 3 (PG 3:402, 423ff., 532ff.).

c. *inchoationes*

d. *quia in hac materia ab ipso proponitur,* i.e., in the context of a treatise on natural philosophy.

e. Thomas writes "attributes and ideas," but clearly he is referring to divine ones.

ent's part, because he receives more or less from that operation according as he is differently prepared for it—just as by the same rays of the sun[a] the air is made bright and still brighter, when foggy vapors that impede the reception of light are banished, so that there need not be two different brightnesses there.[b] Further, even if there were two operations, they need not have their terms in two things that differ in substance, but the first would have its term in the being of imperfect charity, and the second, in the same charity according to perfection, insofar as something one and the same is brought from imperfection to perfection.

3. To the third, it should be said that it does not belong to the *ratio* of any quality's intensification that it should occur through moving away from its contrary, but this [way of intensification] may happen to a quality insofar as it is in a subject that participates its contrary. What does belong of necessity to intensification is that the quality be brought from imperfect to perfect, as is evident in the case of the diaphanous in which there is nothing contrary to light, where the light can be intensified according to an increase[c] of the power of the illuminating source. Now this imperfection [of a quality] is due to the potentiality of the very nature that is subjected to perfection and actuality.[d] For since every potency stands receptive to *many,* it is—precisely because of that multitude in it [of determinations it can receive]—dissimilar to the acting principle, which has its term in *one* act; and insofar as that confusion of potentiality is more subjected to actuality, the actuality is more completely perfected, and that which is perfected is made still more one, and is further likened to the acting principle. Now this confusion of potentiality exists in any created nature whatsoever, insofar as it is not yet perfected by actuality. Hence, too, with this understanding in mind, Dionysius in chapter 3 of *The Celestial Hierarchy*[e] asserts a process of "purgation" among the angels—namely, according as they are removed from the confusion of unlikeness.

4. To the fourth, it should be said that we are the cause of an increase of grace in the same way that we are the cause of grace itself, namely, in the manner of a disposition only; whereas the efficient cause of both [grace and its increase] is on the side of God himself, as is evident from what was said above in the body of the article.[92]

a. *irradiatione solis*
b. *non oportet quod sit ibi alia et alia claritas*
c. here, *incrementum*
d. *ex potentialitate ipsius naturae, quae subjicitur perfectioni et actui*
e. Pseudo-Dionysius, *The Celestial Hierarchy,* ch. 3, n. 2 (PG 3:166).

ARTICLE 3[a]   Whether charity is increased by any act of charity[b]

Objections:

Proceeding to the third, it seems that charity may be increased by any act of charity.

1. For where the cause is the same, the effect is also the same. But all acts of charity belong to the same species with respect to moral being,[c] just as all acts of fortitude belong to the same species. Therefore since *some* act of charity increases charity, it seems that *any* act would do so as well.

2. Again, that which can do something greater, can also do something lesser. But someone merits eternal life by any act of charity; therefore by any act of charity he can also merit an increase thereof.[93]

3. Further, as far as the being of grace is concerned, any act of charity is much more powerful than acts that come from natural abilities[d] only. But by acts that come from natural abilities only, man is prepared, in the manner of a disposition, for receiving grace. Therefore much more is he disposed toward an increase of charity by any act of charity.

On the contrary:

4. Something is increased owing to the same principles as those from which it was born. But one act is not enough to dispose someone in such a way that charity should be infused into him; therefore neither is one act enough to dispose him in such a way that charity should be increased. Proof of the middle term: an act of ours has a greater causality in regard to acquired virtue than it has in regard to infused virtue. But one act is not enough for the generation of an acquired virtue; rather, a man comes to be good from acting well fre-

a. Parallels: *In II Sent.* d. 27, a. 5, ad 2; *In I Sent.* (*Lectura romana*) d. 17, q. 2, a. 3, ad 4 (see below); *ST* I-II, q. 52, a. 3; q. 114, a. 8, ad 3; II-II, q. 24, a. 6.

b. It is clear from the solution to the question that Thomas is asking whether any act *of charity* increases the habit of charity. Thus, I have supplied "of charity" wherever it is understood (in the third objection, Thomas spells it out himself: *per quemlibet actum charitatis*). Of course, any act whatsoever, if it be good in kind and circumstance and performed in a state of grace, will be an act of charity at least in the sense that it can be elicited by charity and performed for the love of God. At *ST* II-II, q. 24, a. 6, the question is formulated more precisely, as found in the lead-in to the objections: *Videtur quod quolibet actu caritatis caritas augeatur.*

c. *esse morale*

d. *ex naturalibus*

quently, according to the Philosopher in *Ethics* II.[a] Therefore much less is one act enough to dispose someone to charity.

5. Again, to the extent that charity is increased, the substantial reward is also increased. But the substantial reward is not increased by any and every act of charity, for it is commonly said that by many works done in charity, a man does not merit more with respect to an increase of the substantial reward than he merits from one act done out of an equal charity. Therefore charity is not increased by any and every act of charity.

Response:

It should be said that the way an act informed by charity stands in relation to an increase of charity already possessed is not the same as the way an act preceding the having of charity stands to the having of charity in the first place.[b] For an act that comes *from* charity is ordered to an increase of charity both in the manner of a disposition and in the manner of merit,[94] but an act preceding the having of charity is ordered to the obtaining of charity in the manner of a disposition alone, as was said in the preceding article,[c] and not in the manner of merit, since nothing can be meritorious before charity is had.[95] Neither act, however, is ordered to the having or increasing of charity in the manner of something *efficient,* in contrast to the way that an act of ours stands to the having of acquired habits.[96]

It should be known, therefore, that of acts preceding the having of charity, at times one act alone is able to dispose someone in such a way that he has the last disposition required in order that charity be infused, according to the unchangeableness of the divine goodness, by which gifts are given to each one insofar as he is prepared to receive them. Sometimes, however, one act disposes someone to the infusion of grace only by a remote disposition, and the following act disposes him still more, and so on, so that the last disposition is attained out of many good acts,[97] insofar as a subsequent act always acts in virtue of all the preceding ones[98]—as is evident in drops of water hollowing out a stone, where it is not each and every drop that takes away something from the stone, but rather, all the preceding ones are disposing

a. In this case reference is made to the whole of Book II of the *Ethics,* a book that concerns the acquisition of good habits by repeated good actions.

b. *non eodem modo se habet actus informatus charitate ad augmentum charitatis, et actus praecedens charitatem ad habendam charitatem.* Phrases have been expanded in accordance with their evident meaning.

c. In the preceding article see esp. ad 4; cf. q. 1, a. 3.

the stone to be hollowed out, and one last agent, in virtue of all the preceding ones (insofar, that is, as it finds a matter disposed through the preceding drops), completes the hollowing out.[99] Now what I have described happens precisely because man is lord of his acts. Hence he is able to act either according to the whole power of his nature or according to part of that power, which does not happen in things that act out of a necessity of nature, for such things always act by their whole power.[100] When therefore it so happens that a man who does not have charity is moved to charity from the whole power of the natural goodness imparted to him, then this one act disposes him by the last disposition required in order that charity be given him. When, on the contrary, a man is prepared for receiving charity not according to his whole power but only according to some part of it, then the act he does is not as the last disposition, but as a remote one, and it is through many such acts that he will be able to arrive at the last disposition. Similarly, I say in response to the other side [of the question] that when an act of charity proceeds from its possessor's whole power—with respect to both the power of nature and the power of the infused habit—then this one act disposes to and merits an immediate increase of charity. When, on the contrary, that act does not proceed according to the possessor's whole power, then it is as a remote disposition, and it is through many such acts that he will then be able to arrive at an increase of charity. Nevertheless, it does not happen of necessity that he *will* arrive at an increase, because man, no matter how he is disposed, is able not to act in accordance with the *ratio* of that disposition, which is something that does not happen in non-voluntary dispositions, for the reason given above.

Replies to objections:

1. To the first, therefore, it should be said that not every act of charity is done in the same manner, because one act can be more intense than another, and even just one act can dispose to an increase of charity with the cumulative power of many preceding ones, as was said in the response; and therefore the same effect does not follow from each act of charity.

2. To the second, it should be said that the substantial reward of eternal life is ordained to be an end for the act of charity, and the one is commensurate with the other, not according to equalization[a] but according to proportion. Thus, the substantial reward is owed to an act

---

a. *secundum aequiparantiam*

of charity, and a greater reward to an act of greater charity. Hence, any act of charity, insofar as it is informed by such a habit, is ordered[a] to the substantial reward—not, however, to an *increase* of reward, as neither to an *increase* of charity, inasmuch as charity remains the first principle of meriting, but only inasmuch as an increase of charity pertains to the reward's perfection.[b, 101]

3. The response to the third is now evident from what was said, since an act of charity surpasses an act preceding the having of charity precisely in its having the power of meriting, and thus it comes closer to the proper causality of charity than an act preceding the having of charity.

4. To the fourth, it should be said that in order for some perfection to be introduced, two things are required: one on the part of the one introducing it, namely that his operation should be commensurate in terms of equality[c] to the perfection to be introduced—for the heat of fire is not induced by a meagre heating, but from a heating that has power equal (at least in its source) to the heat of fire; another on the part of the recipient, namely that his disposition should be proportioned in the same way to the perfection that is to be induced. Now it happens sometimes, as in works of the soul, that something is disposed and receives perfection from itself, as is evident in the case of demonstrative knowledge[d] and virtue. Hence, to be perfectly disposed in such cases, it is enough that the soul work according to a power proportioned to the perfection that is to be induced. And since the whole capacity of the soul is barely enough to receive a perfection as great as charity is, unless God supply of his liberality whatever is wanting, therefore in order that the last disposition to receiving charity be in the soul, there is required an act done according to the soul's whole power, and that is enough as concerns what it is within our power to do;[e, 102] whereas an act less than this is not enough to constitute such a disposition. Further, in those perfections in which, by the soul's own act, there is not only a disposition but also the perfection itself, it is required that that very act of the soul should be proportionate and equal

a. To catch the different nuance in each sentence, *ordinatur* is translated "ordained" just above, and "ordered" here.

b. *Unde quilibet actus charitatis, inquantum est informatus tali habitu, ordinatur ad praemium substantiale; non tamen ad augmentum praemii, sicut nec ad augmentum charitatis, secundum quod charitas remanet primum principium merendi, sed solum secundum quod augmentum charitatis pertinet ad perfectionem praemii*

c. *secundum aequalitatem*

d. *scientia,* repeated below where the same translation is given.

e. *et iste sufficit quantum in nobis est*

in power to the perfection to be introduced. Now it belongs to the *ratio* of every habit that it be difficult to change, i.e., that it have a certain firmness. Hence when a single action of the soul has the requisite firmness, of itself it induces a habit, as it is evident that one demonstration, owing to its certitude and firmness, produces a habit of demonstrative knowledge, whereas when a single act does not have this firmness, the one act is not enough, but there have to be many acts. Hence, opinion is generated not from one dialectical argument but from many brought together.[103] In the same way, too, because an act of the human will does not by itself have firmness (since the will stands indeterminately to many things), the habits of political virtues, which are acquired through acts of the will, cannot be acquired by one act alone, but many such acts must come together. The habit of charity, however, does not get its firmness from any act of the soul, but only from its cause, which is God; and therefore one act of the will can be enough to dispose one in such a way that charity should be infused, and likewise that it should be increased.

5. To the fifth, it should be said that when an act of charity is of the sort required for an increase of charity, then the substantial reward is also increased, because this reward is owed to the greater charity that follows upon the act, not to the charity that is the root of the act. But not all acts of charity are of this sort, as was said above; and therefore an increase of the substantial reward does not follow of necessity upon a multitude of acts of charity.

ARTICLE 4[a]   Whether charity's increase has a limit[b]

Objections:

Proceeding to the fourth, it seems that there is some limit to the increase of charity.

1. For a perfection does not exceed the capacity of the perfectible. But the soul's capacity is finite. Therefore it can only receive a finite perfection. But every motion that is toward something finite is finite. Therefore the increase of charity, which is a motion toward the soul's perfection, is itself finite.

2. Further, nothing is ordinately moved to what it cannot obtain,

a. Parallels: *In I Sent.* (*Lectura romana*) d. 17, q. 2, a. 2 (see below); *In I Sent.* d. 27, q. 2, a. 4; *In III Sent.* d. 29, a. 8, qa. 1, ad 2 (see below); *ST* II-II, q. 24, a. 7; *De caritate,* a. 10, ad 12.

b. The article asks *utrum augmentum charitatis habeat aliquem terminum.* The last word has been variously translated "limit," "definite limit," "term." Sometimes *in infinitum* has been translated as "indefinitely."

according to the Philosopher in *Physics* III and VI, just as he who cannot be in Egypt is not ordinately moved to going there.[a, 104] But no one
can *reach* something at an infinite distance, since no motion can *be* according to infinite distance. Therefore no motion is infinite. But the
increase of charity is a certain motion; therefore it comes to a definite
term.

3. Further, as the Master says below,[b] even God cannot make something greater than the grace of Christ. But if the increase of charity
and grace could go on indefinitely, there *could* be a greater charity and
grace than any given one [including Christ's]. Therefore such increase
is not indefinite. And one can say something similar of the Blessed Virgin, about whom Anselm says in chapter 18 of *On the Virgin Conception*[c]
that by her purity she shone so brightly that a greater purity beneath
God could not be conceived; and of the blessed, too, whose charity
cannot be increased—through all of which arguments it seems that the
increase of charity comes to a definite term, beyond which it cannot
be increased.

On the contrary:

1. Increase of charity takes place according to a greater likening to
God. But howsoever much one approaches to the likeness of God, one
always stands infinitely apart from him. Therefore one can always approach more. And so it seems that the increase of charity is not finite.[d]

2. Further, when an act of charity proceeds from a greater charity,
it is of greater power in meriting. But even an act of imperfect charity
merits an increase of charity. Therefore so much the more will it merit
when charity shall have been brought to a greater perfection; and so,
the increase of charity will never come to a stand-still.[105]

Response:

It should be said that we can speak of a limit to charity's increase in
two ways: either in regard to that which *is*, or in regard to that which
can be, even as we also say that there is not a highest evil than which
there *cannot be* anything worse, but nevertheless there is some highest evil than which nothing *is* worse. In like manner, I say that char-

a. Aristotle, implicitly at *Physics* III, ch. 5 (204b7–10); explicitly at *Physics* VI,
ch. 10 (241b3–11). For want of a better word, *ordinate* is rendered "ordinately."

b. Peter Lombard, *Sentences*, Book III, Distinction 13.

c. Anselm, *On the Virgin Conception*, ch. 18 (PL 158:451).

d. The Mandonnet edition (p. 422, line 14) mistakenly reads here *non infinitum*, where the argument clearly demands *non finitum*.

ity's increase comes to some limit in each man beyond which it is not (in fact) increased, but nevertheless it does not come to some term beyond which it cannot (in principle) be increased. The reason for this is from both that which is moved according to this increase and that *to* which it is moved. Now that *to* which the soul is moved in an increase of charity is the likeness of divine charity, to which the soul is likened; and this, being infinite, can be approached infinitely more and more, and will never be perfectly equalled. On the other hand, the reason for the possibility of infinite increase on the part of that which is moved is that the soul itself, to the extent that it receives more of the divine goodness and the very light of grace, is made all the more apt for receiving these; and therefore the more it receives, the more it is able to receive. The reason for this is that, while material powers are limited and finite owing to the needs and demands of matter[a] (and thus can receive [determination] only according to the proportion of the matter),[106] immaterial powers are not limited by matter, but rather are limited according to the amount of divine goodness received into them. Hence, as much more as is added of goodness, so much more is there of power for receiving,[b] as is evident in the Philosopher's example about sense and intellect (*On the Soul* III): for he says that the senses are corrupted by strong sensibles and their capacity is not increased, because they are material powers, whereas the intellect, to the extent that it understands difficult things more, is rendered that much more able to understand. So, too, the more charity the spiritual nature receives, the more it is able to receive.

Now certain ones, comparing the capacity of a spiritual substance to the capacity of a material substance, said that in charity's increase there is a limit according to the capacity of nature—namely, when it receives just so much charity as fills up the first capacity that was in its nature, it cannot receive any more. And they give the example of air, which has a limit to its subtleness, a limit it does not surpass; hence light can be intensified in it, insofar as it is more and more purified from mixed vapors, but when the purity of its own nature is attained, it cannot be still more purified, nor more illuminated by the same source of illumination.[107] But [this position is false, because] there is no parallel between the capacity of a material substance and that of a spirit, as was said.[c]

---

a. *secundum exigentiam materiae*
b. *potentia ad capacitatem*
c. See q. 1, a. 3 of the present Distinction.

Replies to objections:

1. To the first, therefore, it should be said that although the soul's capacity is actually finite, it can nonetheless be stretched more and more in its limit, according as it receives more and more.[a] Nevertheless, it will never *be* infinite, nor will it receive an infinite perfection, as is also clear in adding numbers to numbers, which can go on indefinitely[b] without there ever being some actually infinite number. For as the Commentator says in *Physics* III, the power of the addition of numbers[c, 108] is not a single power; instead, a power numerically other is brought about insofar as a new species of number is always made from each new addition. Hence, while *each* power of addition can go out into actuality, it is impossible that *all* should go out into actuality, because in each actuality a power is also added; and it is thus, too, with the soul's capacity.[109]

2. To the second, it should be said that any increase of charity whatsoever has a definite limit and is toward a limit man is able to attain; yet all the same this limit, since it is not pure act, is mixed with potency. Hence, there can still be a further increase that is numerically other than an increase that has already occurred,[d] and thus increase succeeds increase indefinitely. In this way may be understood the "limitless increase of charity."

3. To the third, it should be said that the grace of Christ, although it was finite according to its essence, was nevertheless infinite in a certain respect—namely, insofar as it was a disposition of congruity to the union of natures, and insofar as it concurred in the operation of Christ, which was of infinite power owing to his identity as a divine Person, and in other ways, too, as will be said in Book III;[e] and from this comes the position [of the Master] that his grace could not be increased. In response to what was objected concerning the Blessed Virgin, it should be said that increase of charity differs from increase of purity. For increase of purity is according to withdrawal from the contrary; and because in the Blessed Virgin there was purification from all sin, therefore she came to the highest purity; still, it was beneath God's purity,[f]

a. *potest plus et plus in finitum elongari, secundum quod plus et plus recipit.* The meaning could also be: although the soul's capacity at any moment is finite, it can nonetheless be elongated finitely such that the capacity is thereby increased.

b. *qui in infinitum est possibilis.* The Parma ed. mistakenly reads here *impossibilis.*

c. *potentia additionis numerorum*

d. An expansion of the phrase *adhuc potest esse aliud augmentum numero.*

e. See *In III Sent.* d. 17, q. 1, a. 2.

f. *sub Deo tamen*

for in him there is not that potential of falling away which is in any and every creature as such.[a] Increase of charity, on the other hand, comes about by means of approaching to the divine goodness; and therefore the Blessed Virgin did not have the highest charity than which a greater could not be conceived, since she too advanced in charity and grace. In response to what was objected concerning the blessed, it should be said that charity is not increased in them due to the condition of their state, because they are no longer on the way but have arrived at the end of the way. Hence a reward is given to them according to the charity that grew in them in the wayfaring state.

ARTICLE 5[b]   Whether charity admits of decrease

Objections:

Proceeding to the fifth, it seems that charity admits of decrease.

1. For contraries are apt to come to be in regard to the same thing.[c] But increase and decrease are contraries. Since therefore charity may be increased, it seems that it may also be diminished.

2. Again, Augustine says in the *Enchiridion*: "Where there is great cupidity, there is small charity";[d] and elsewhere, in the book of *Confessions*: "He loves you less, who loves something else along with you."[e] But it happens that cupidity increases; therefore it also happens that charity decreases.

3. Further, venial sin is an evil of guilt.[110] But every evil takes away some good opposed to it. Since therefore the good of grace or charity is opposed to the evil of guilt, venial sin will take away the good of charity. But it does not take away the *whole* of it, because it would then exclude one from the kingdom (for it is by charity alone that sons of the kingdom are distinguished from sons of damnation, according to Augustine in *On the Trinity*),[f] and were that the case, it would be mortal sin, not venial. Therefore it takes away *something* of charity, and thus it diminishes it.

4. Again, to the extent to which someone disposes himself to receiving charity and grace, to that extent does God infuse it into him:

a. *quantum in se est*

b. Parallels: *In I Sent.* (*Lectura romana*) d. 17, q. 2, a. 4 (see below); *ST* II-II, q. 24, a. 10; *De malo*, q. 7, a. 2.

c. *Contraria enim nata sunt fieri circa idem*

d. Augustine, *Enchiridion*, ch. 121 (CCSL 46:114).

e. Augustine, *Confessions* X, ch. 29 (CCSL 27:176).

f. Augustine, *On the Trinity* XV, ch. 18 (CCSL 50A:507).

for, according to Augustine,[a] the light of divine grace is present to all, but the fact that some do not receive it is because they avert themselves from it, like one who closes his eyes to the light of the sun. But it happens that someone disposes himself less to charity later on than he did before. Therefore he will participate less of the light of grace and of charity. [And so his charity will decrease.]

On the contrary:

Any created charity is finite. But every finite thing, according to the Philosopher in *Physics* I, is used up by the taking away of parts, if something be taken away again and again.[b] If therefore a venial sin did diminish something of charity, a subsequent one would diminish it too, and in this manner the whole of charity will be taken away by the multiplication of venial sins. But charity is taken away only by mortal sin. Therefore according to this argument many venial sins will constitute one mortal sin—which no one teaches.

If you say in response that this taking away of charity by venial sin happens like the division of the continuous, which can go on indefinitely as long as the division is made according to the same proportion and not according to the same quantity, against this I say: whenever there is division according to the same proportion, what is taken away afterwards is always less than what was taken away before—for example, if at first a third part of a line is taken away, and afterwards, a third of what remains of that, and so on, what is taken afterwards will always be less in quantity than what was taken before. It can happen, however, that a subsequent venial sin does not have less power than the first. Therefore, it takes away as much charity as the first sin did; and in this fashion, charity will be eventually consumed by this taking away.

Response:

It should be said that charity cannot essentially decrease, except perhaps by succession (namely, in such a way that the charity that was in someone is destroyed through mortal sin, and afterwards a lesser charity is infused owing to a lesser preparation for receiving it).[111] And the reason why this is impossible is that the cause of the decrease of char-

---

a. Mandonnet (p. 425) includes here a note: "Olim ad marginem: «*De spiritu et anima,* c. XVII,» ubi non habetur nisi aequivalenter." Augustine says something quite like this in *Expositions of the Psalms,* Ps. 99, n. 5 (CCSL 39:1396).

b. *consumitur per ablationem, ablato quodam semper et semper.*—Aristotle, *Physics* I, ch. 4 (187b25–26).

ity cannot be taken on God's part, since no defect can be traced back, as to a cause, to him who is complete actuality. If, then, charity were to decrease, it would be necessary that the cause of the decrease be taken on our part. Now defect happens on our part either (1) by cessation from acting or (2) by inordinateness in our acting. (1) According to what it is in itself,[a] charity cannot be weakened by cessation from acting, as can occur with the habits of acquired virtues. For the firmness of charity does not come from our act but from the source that infuses the habit,[b] as was said before.[c] Hence, even with the cessation of our acts, there remains nonetheless the same strength of charity. (Still, it is true that by frequent acts of charity all the powers of the soul are disposed [to contribute readily to such acts], and the members of the body are brought into the service of charity; and since fervor consists in such things, as was said, laziness therefore has the result of making charity's fervor grow cold.) The habit of acquired virtue, in contrast, has strength and firmness from our own works; hence, with the cessation of our works, the virtue's strength is weakened, even in itself.[112] (2) Now an act's inordinateness is either about the end or about things directed toward the end. If it is about the end—namely, such that the end is taken away[113]—then charity, insofar as it adheres (of itself) to the end, is also taken away, and this comes about through mortal sin. If, on the other hand, the inordinateness is about things directed toward the end—namely, such that while the end remains, a man gives inordinate attention or affection to things ordered to the end[d]—then this kind of inordinateness, which is a venial sin, does not touch charity, which has its being according to adherence to the end; and therefore it diminishes nothing of it.[114] Still, it is true that just as things directed toward the end are dispositive to the end, so correspondingly, inordinateness in them is dispositive to inordinateness about the end itself, and for this reason we say that venial sin is dispositive to mortal sin. Hence, by venial sins of this kind, a man is disposed to the loss of charity. And thence it is that charity is said to be diminished not with respect to essence, but with respect to rootedness and fervor—with respect to rootedness, insofar as a disposition to the contrary comes to be, so that charity's firm adherence [to God] is diminished; with respect to fervor, inasmuch as the obedience of lower powers to higher ones is impeded, from which obedience the aforementioned fervor was being caused.

a. *secundum quod in se est*   b. *principio influente*
c. In a. 2 of this question.
d. *inordinate aliquis immoretur circa ea quae sunt ad finem*

Replies to objections:

1. To the first, therefore, it should be said that contraries are apt to come to be in regard to the same thing, unless one of them is naturally in it.[115] And it is said to be "naturally in something" when it follows upon that thing's causes. Hence I say that increasability is naturally in charity, and not diminishability, because both on the part of the one receiving it and on the part of the one infusing it, there can be some cause of increase but not of diminishment, as was said in the response.

2. To the second, it should be said that the relationship of inverse proportion obtaining between cupidity and charity[a] can be understood in two ways: either with respect to the coming-to-be of charity, or with respect to its being. If understood with respect to its coming-to-be, then it is true that a man is less disposed to receiving charity or an increase thereof when, by inordinate acts, cupidity gains the upper hand in him, and this is so because our acts dispose us to having charity or advancing in it.[116] But if understood with respect to its being, then, seeing that our acts are not the cause of the very being of charity, inordinateness of acts caused by cupidity takes away nothing from charity with respect to its being, but only with respect to its fervor, insofar as the lower parts are dishabituated from obedience to charity.

3. To the third, it should be said that venial sin cannot deprive charity of anything, since it does not reach to that part of the soul where charity is. For just as the superior part of intellect consists in the consideration of principles of things known *per se*, through which all other things are known (so that regardless of how much doubt might arise about conclusions, nothing of the certitude of principles is diminished); so too, the superior part of affection consists in adherence to the end on account of which all things are loved. Hence, whatsoever inordinateness happens in regard to things directed toward the end, the very adherence to the end that comes about through charity is not diminished, unless a contrary end should be posited. Thus, precisely because it does not posit an undue end, venial sin does not reach to that highest affection where charity is. But just as venial sin is not sin simply speaking but only insofar as it is dispositive to mortal sin, so too it deprives one of the good that stands as a disposition to charity, i.e., fervor, which has its place in the facility of an act,[b] owing to the diligent obedience or subjection of lower powers to the higher part of affection where charity is.[117]

a. *commensuratio cupiditatis et charitatis per oppositum*
b. *qui contingit in habilitate actus*

4. To the fourth, it should be said that the disposition to receiving charity is a disposition according to the acts of the lower powers inasmuch as they operate about things directed toward the end, even as one arrives at the end through things that stand in relation to the end. But once the end is had, there is no longer a need for things that stand in relation to the end. Hence, whatever inordinateness comes to be in their regard does not redound to a loss of order to the end,[a] except in the manner of a disposition to such a loss, just as the knowledge of first principles is determined in us through the senses, and yet the certainty of principles would not be diminished even if the senses were destroyed, because this certainty is not acquired but is naturally implanted in us; and it is similar with infused charity.[118]

Notes on the text of Lombard

"Just as God is said to become great and rise up[b] in us . . ."

—insofar, namely, as he makes *us* great and lofty in him, which can happen only according to a fuller reception of his goodness; and therefore it is necessary to return to this point, that something *created* by God is put within us.

"Nevertheless, there are many who do not have him."

For they alone are said to have him, of whom he is as their inheritance; and these are they who enjoy him either in hope or in vision.[c]

"It is certainly the case that without the Holy Spirit we do not love Christ and cannot fulfill his commandments."

This can be understood in two ways: (1) that we cannot fulfill the commandments of God or love Christ through the gift of charity "without the Holy Spirit" had by us through charity, and this is true as regards doing things in a meritorious manner;[119] or (2) that [we cannot fulfill the commandments or love Christ] "without the Holy Spirit" operating in any of the ways in which he operates in things, and so taken, it is true that neither man nor any creature can have any operation at all without the Holy Spirit. But this latter interpretation is not Augustine's meaning in the text.

a. *deordinationem finis*
b. *magnificari et exaltari*
c. *vel in spe vel in re.* The Mandonnet ed. has mistakenly: *vel in spe in vel re* (p. 428, line 2).

"May the Holy Spirit who is in you be twofold in me."

This quotation seems irrelevant to the proposed topic, because, as a note explains, this is interpreted to mean that Elisha begged the two-fold *gift* (namely, of prophecy and of miracles) that was in Elijah, and that he did not beg to have the Holy Spirit more [than Elijah had him]. But it should be said that, even if we let that interpretation stand, Augustine's intention is supported: for if everyone were to receive the Holy Spirit equally, then if Elisha already *had* the Holy Spirit, he would not have *begged* for the Holy Spirit to come to be in himself, and if he did *not* have or did not know himself to have the Holy Spirit, he would simply have begged for the Holy Spirit. Hence the very fact that Elisha begged to have the Holy Spirit *in the way that* the Holy Spirit was in Elijah shows that Elijah had the Holy Spirit more excellently than Elisha had him.

"[The Holy Spirit is given until] the proper measure is completed."

There is said to be a proper measure of each thing both on the part of God—namely, so much as God has predestined to each one—and on the part of him who receives, taking both his natural capacity and his effort into consideration.

"It was said above that the Holy Spirit is the charity of the Father and of the Son."

Take note that the authorities that are brought against the Master say three things. For the ones who are brought forward first say that the charity by which God loves is other than that by which we love—which the Master interprets to mean other in *ratio*, or in the manner of understanding, and not in the thing itself.

Other authorities who are brought forward second say that love is from[a] the Holy Spirit; and thus, since the Holy Spirit is not from himself, the charity given to us will not be the Holy Spirit. But the Master responds that although the Holy Spirit is not from himself, nevertheless he is given by himself; and in this way charity is said to be from the Holy Spirit. But this response is insufficient, because it is said not only that charity is given *by* the Holy Spirit, but also that it is *from* him, which cannot be conceded about the Holy Spirit.[120]

---

a. The remaining sentences present a challenge to the translator, since the Latin *a/ab* can mean either "from" or "by" depending on context. We have used both. "From/by himself" is *a se*.

Other authorities who are brought forward third say that charity is a motion or affection of the mind, which is not true of the Holy Spirit.[a] But to this, the Master responds that that predication is made in reference to the cause, because charity is the *cause* of that motion or affection of the mind, "to love." And this explanation is true, although not according to the Master's meaning. For charity is the cause of affection as a habit eliciting an act, and not only as moving the soul to the act of love, which is what he means by what he said. Hence, he consequently raises the question: since the Holy Spirit (whom he calls "charity") moves the soul to *all* the acts of virtue, why is he especially said to move the soul to the act of *love*? And his response is right there in the text; but he never assigns the cause of what he takes for granted in the solution, namely, that the Holy Spirit causes this act, "to love," with no habit as the means [by which he causes it]; hence, the means remains undetermined.[b]

"For they [the saints] do not each have all [the gifts], but these have some, while others have others."

It should be known that not only is the uncreated gift common to the saints, but common also are gifts pertaining to the grace that makes one pleasing to God,[c] which are infused simultaneously, and without which the Holy Spirit is not had; whereas freely given charisms[d] are given more for the manifestation of the Spirit received than for conjoining the saint to the Spirit (and this is done on account of usefulness to others: 1 Cor. 12), and are distributed to different persons insofar as it agrees with usefulness for the Church.[e]

a. *Spiritui sancto non convenit*

b. *nullo habitu medio* [Parma ed.: *mediante*]: *unde medium adhuc remanet insolutum.* The last phrase could also mean "the middle term [in the argument] remains as yet unsolved," that is, the Master's solution is incomplete.

c. *gratia gratum faciens,* which is more familiarly called "sanctifying grace."

d. *dona gratis data* (or, in other texts, *gratia gratis data*), more familiarly called "gratuitous graces" or "charisms."

e. *dividuntur [scil., dona gratis data] diversis prout competit utilitati ecclesiae.* Most literally, "they are portioned out to different ones insofar as it [the manifestation of the Spirit] coincides with/lends itself to the usefulness of the Church."

DISTINCTION 17 (*LECTURA ROMANA*)[a]

QUESTION 1   On charity as something created in the soul

"Now let us approach [to the indicated mission of the Holy Spirit, by which he is invisibly sent into the hearts of the faithful]."[b] Here four things are sought. First, whether a supernatural light[c, 121] is required in order to love God. Second, given that it is, whether it is created or uncreated. Third, supposing that it is something created, whether it is an accident. Fourth, if it is an accident, whether someone can know for certain that he has it.

ARTICLE 1[d]   Whether a supernatural light is required in order to love God

Objections:

Proceeding to the first, it seems that something supernatural is not necessary in order to love God.

1. For as knowledge is of the true, so love is of the good. But because God is the highest truth, he is naturally known. Therefore because he is the highest good, he will be naturally loved. Therefore something supernatural is not necessary in order to love God.

2. Further, to the degree that something is stronger, it moves more and makes a greater impression. But God is infinite good. Therefore he most of all moves the will to love. Therefore [due to the strength of his impression], the will, of itself, most of all loves him, and not through something else [he has added on].[e, 122]

---

a. Latin text: *Lectura romana in primum Sententiarum Petri Lombardi,* ed. Leonard E. Boyle and John F. Boyle (Toronto: Pontifical Institute of Mediaeval Studies, 2006), 190–201. On the Roman version or *Lectura romana* of Book I of the *Sentences* commentary, see the Full Introduction (available at the website of the Catholic University of America Press) and the literature cited there.

b. The opening line of Lombard's Distinction 17.

c. *aliquod lumen supernaturale*

d. Parallels: *In III Sent.* d. 23, q. 1, a. 4, qa. 3 (see below); d. 27, q. 2, a. 2 (see below), esp. ad 1 and ad 4, and a. 3, ad 5.

e. *Quanto aliquid est fortius, tanto magis movet et imprimit. Sed Deus est infinitum*

3. Further, the will is moved by the good as understood or apprehended.[a] But we apprehend God through faith. Therefore faith alone is enough in order to love God. Therefore something other is not necessary in order to love God.

4. Further, to love is an act of the will. But the will is free. Therefore the will loves God by itself and not through something else [added to it].

On the contrary:

"The charity of God is poured out into our hearts by the Holy Spirit who has been given to us" (Rom. 5:5).

Response:

It should be said that love follows knowledge, since nothing is loved unless it is known. Whence as we know God, so do we love him. Now there is a threefold knowledge of God. One knowledge is that by which he is known only in his effects, as if, insofar as someone knows *being* or something *created*, he has some sort of knowledge of God the creator and his creation of it,[b] [namely an implicit knowledge]; and this knowledge is in all men naturally and from the beginning. Another knowledge is that by which God is considered in himself yet nevertheless is known through his effects, insofar as someone proceeds from the knowledge of his effects to the knowledge of God himself. And this can be had through the inquiry of natural reason, although not immediately. And it was thus that the philosophers and other wise men arrived at knowledge of God, to the extent that it is possible to attain it. The third knowledge is that by which he is known in himself and in those things that exceed all proportion to his effects. And this knowledge is neither naturally in men, nor had through the inquiry of natural reason, but had through an infused supernatural light. According to this threefold knowledge, a threefold love is found. One is that by which God is loved in his effects, insofar as when I love a creature I am said to love God. Another love is that by which God himself is loved on the basis of his effects, and this love is had through inquiry, as

---

bonum. Ergo maxime movet voluntatem ad diligendum. Ergo voluntas per se maxime diligit, et non per aliquid aliud. The phrases in brackets have to be supplied, otherwise the argument does not make sense.

a. *Voluntatem movet bonum intellectum seu apprehensum*

b. Or: "of God the creator, as creator of it," if one reads *ut* instead of *et.* The text reads: *Vna est qua cognoscitur in suis effectibus tantum, prout si in quantum cognoscit quis ens vel aliquid creatum, habet aliqualem cognitionem Dei creantis et creantis ipsum.*

when someone knowing God from his effects loves him. Another love is that by which man transcends all effects and every creature and directs his affection to God himself and loves the very goodness of God as our beatitude, so that we may have a certain fellowship with him; and this is altogether above nature and natural reason. Hence in order to love God in this way, a supernatural light is required, which elevates our affection to God himself, according as he is to be loved in and of himself.[a]

Replies to objections:

1. To the first, therefore, it should be said that God is loved as the highest good in one way naturally, but in another way supernaturally, as was said [in the response].

2. To the second, it should be said that God, as he is in himself, is infinitely lovable, but he is not infinitely loved by us due to a deficiency in our affection. For our affection follows apprehension, and one does not love more than one knows. Hence since our mind[b] does not perfectly know God, it does not perfectly love him. Hence, as something supernatural is required in order for him to be perfectly apprehended, so something supernatural is also required in order to love him perfectly.

3. To the third, it should be said that our affection is sometimes held back owing to many impediments. And therefore it is necessary for the will to be elevated by something supernatural to that which faith apprehends.[c] [123]

4. To the fourth, it should be said that, although the will is elevated and helped by something supernatural, it does not follow that it is not free, for since God works all things in all, even the very inclination and elevation of the will is from God, and so the freedom of the will is not taken away, because he alone has [the power] to be operative within the will.

a. *in ipsum Deum secundum seipsum diligendum*

b. *intellectus,* which must in this sentence function as the subject of both knowing and loving.

c. *affectus noster aliquando retardatur propter multa impedimenta, et ideo oportet quod voluntas elevetur per aliquid supernaturale ad id quod fides apprehendit*

ARTICLE 2ᵃ   Whether that [supernatural gift] is something created or uncreated

Objections:

Proceeding to the second, it seems that that supernatural [gift] is not something created.

1. For no creature has infinite power, since power flows from essence. But charity is of infinite power, since it moves over an infinite distance, uniting the creature to God. Therefore charity is not something created.

2. Further, what is infinitely distant cannot be united except by an infinite power. But no infinite power is a creature. Therefore that power which unites us to God is not a creature. But charity is this power. Therefore it is not created.

3. Further, it is certain that God creates things immediately. But creation corresponds to re-creation. Therefore, if God did not use any means in creating when he established nature, it seems that he also did not use any means in re-creating when he infused grace.

On the contrary:

Charity falls into the same category of virtue as faith and hope.ᵇ, 124 But these are created things, therefore charity also is.

Response:

It should be said that here the Master was deceived and believed that charity is not something created in the soul but that it is something uncreated. For it is to be known that when I say "faith" or "charity," I mean one of two things, since I mean either the act itself or the principle of the act; for "faith" sometimes refers to the very act, namely to believe, and again, the principle of the same act is also called "faith." And it is similar with charity, because charity sometimes means the very act of love, which is to love, and the Master asserts this to be something created; but with respect to the principle of the act of charity, he was deceived. For he said that the difference between charity and the other virtues is that the Holy Spirit moves us to the acts of the other virtues by means of the habits of those virtues, whereas the Holy Spirit moves us to the act of charity not by means of any habits, but

---

a. Parallels: *In I Sent.* (Paris version) d. 17, q. 1, a. 1 (see above); *ST* II-II, q. 23, a. 2; *De caritate*, a. 1.

b. *Caritas dividitur contra spem et fidem*

immediately. Hence he would have it that with respect to this activity, the Holy Spirit himself in the soul took the place of a habit that would move the will; and on this account, he was deceived, saying that charity is not something created in the soul. But this opinion is mistaken and impossible, for two reasons. First, since the Holy Spirit dwells in man through some effect of the Spirit's. Therefore if the Holy Spirit is not in man except according to the act of love, the Holy Spirit will not be in someone except when he is actually loving. And so, since man is not always actually loving—even a man in a state of grace[a] —but at times he is and at times he is not, it would follow [on this position] that he does not always have the Holy Spirit and grace, but at times does and at times does not. It would also follow that sleepers while asleep do not have the effect of the Holy Spirit, namely grace, since they are not actually loving. It is in every way unfitting to say this. Second, since the act of love is the noblest act, and one ought to be disposed in the noblest way to the noblest act. But one cannot be more nobly disposed than through the Holy Spirit himself; and therefore man must be disposed through him. And therefore he must have the Holy Spirit not only when he is actually loving, but also before, so that the Holy Spirit may dispose him to perform that act well and easily. And therefore we say that, as in the other infused virtues, the Holy Spirit brings about two effects: he moves a man to the act and, beyond this, he gives to the agent the capacity to act well and easily. And for this reason it is better to say something else [than the Master does]— that from one vantage charity is the Holy Spirit himself by whom we love God *effectively,* and in this regard it is something uncreated because it is the Holy Spirit himself; yet from a different vantage it is something created, insofar as we *formally* love God with the very charity given to the soul.[b]

Replies to objections:

1. To the first, therefore, it should be said that charity does not have infinite power of itself, but insofar as it is the effect and power of the Holy Spirit. In this regard, it is something uncreated, as was said [in the response].

2. To the second, it should be said that charity joins us to God not

---

a. *existens in gratia*

b. *Et propter hoc aliter dicendum est et melius, quod caritas est ipse Spiritus Sanctus quo diligimus Deum effective, et secundum hoc est quid increatum quia est ipse Spiritus Sanctus; est autem quid creatum in quantum secundum ipsam caritatem Deum formaliter diligimus*

by nature but by act, which is not unfitting;[125] and infinite power is not required for this.

3. To the third, it should be said that God does not re-create man without a *formal* means—for God, in justifying the soul, gives the *form* of holiness, which is charity—but he gives this form without a means of agency; for in the work of creation, too, even though there was no means of agency, nothing prevents there having been a formal means.[a, 126]

ARTICLE 3[b]   Whether that
[supernatural gift] is an accident

Objections:

Proceeding to the third, it seems that this created thing, which is charity, is not an accident.

1. For no accident is [nobler than] a substance. But charity is nobler than the soul [which is itself a substance]. Therefore charity is not an accident [but a substance].[c]

2. Further, something is nobler to the extent that it is simpler. But to the extent that something has more accidents, it is less simple, and consequently, less noble. Therefore if charity is an accident, the soul that does not have charity will be nobler, as being simpler.[d] But this is unfitting. Therefore charity is not an accident.

3. Further, an accident is caused by the subject's principles. But charity is not caused by the soul's principles. Therefore it is not an accident.

On the contrary:

Charity is a virtue. A virtue is an accident. Therefore charity is an accident.

---

a. *Ad tertium dicendum quod Deus non recreat homines sine medio formali – nam Deus iustificando animam dat formam sanctitatis quae est caritas – sed sine medio agente; nam et in opere creationis, etsi non fuerit medium agens, nihil tamen prohibet fuisse medium formale*

b. Parallels: *In I Sent.* (Paris version) d. 17, q. 1, a. 2 (see above); *ST* II-II, q. 23, a. 3, ad 3; *De caritate*, a. 1, ad 22.

c. The text reads: *Nullum enim accidens est substantia. Sed caritas est nobilior anima. Ergo caritas non est accidens.* However, to get both a middle term and a conclusion for the argument, one has to supply the bracketed phrases.

d. The MS reads *ut puta*, but the editors suggest *utpote* as the correct word for the context.

Response:

It should be said that no creature, by the very fact that it exists, has the perfection of its goodness, but only God, who alone is good and blessed of himself.[a] And therefore it is impossible that any perfection of any creature whatsoever be a substance. I say, then, that since the last perfection of man's goodness is charity, through which we are joined to God and are made, in a certain way, partakers[b] of the highest good and of our beatitude, it is impossible for it to be a substance, and therefore it must be an accident. It is also evident that it is an accident because we see that charity can be lost, which could not occur if it were not an accident.

Replies to objections:

1. To the first, therefore, it should be said that, although charity is nobler than the soul with respect to being *such* [namely, being united to God], it is not nobler with respect to being, simply speaking.[c]

2. To the second, it should be said that [the principle invoked in the objection] is true in immaterial things and in things in which there is nothing in potency. But things that are in potency must be perfected by something; and so, such a thing is more perfect to the extent that it has more perfections. Now, the soul is perfected by various perfections and virtues; hence a soul is nobler to the extent that it acquires more perfections and virtues.

3. To the third, it should be said that while a natural accident is caused by a subject's principles, an accident that is from an external source is not caused by a subject's principles. Charity, however, comes to the soul from an external source [and so it *is* an accident, but not an accident caused by a subject's own principles].

ARTICLE 4[d]   Whether a man can know
for certain that he has charity

Objections:

Proceeding to the fourth, it seems that a man *can* know for certain that he has this accident, charity.

1. For the Apostle says: "No one knows the things of man except

---

a. *nulla creatura eo ipso quod est habet perfectionem suae bonitatis, sed solus Deus qui est solus per se bonus et beatus*

b. *consortii*

c. *esse tale . . . esse simpliciter*

d. Parallels: *In I Sent.* (Paris version) d. 17, q. 1, a. 4 (see above); *In III Sent.*

the spirit of man, which is in him" (1 Cor. 2:11). Therefore it seems that a man can know the things that are in him. But charity is in a man. Therefore a man knows that he has charity.

2. Further, delight is a sign that a habit has been gained.[a] But a man knows when he is delighted in the love of God. Therefore a man knows that he has charity.

3. Further, according to the Philosopher in *Posterior Analytics* II,[b] it is unfitting that when we have the noblest habits they should remain hidden from us. Therefore since charity is the noblest habit, it seems that it is known with certainty by the one who has it.

On the contrary:
"No one knows whether he is worthy of love or of hatred" (Eccles. 9:1).

Response:
It should be said that only the intellectual part of the soul[c] turns back upon itself: for the intellect understands the understandable and understands itself to be understanding; the affection or will, too, loves something and loves its loving and also loves its understanding. And therefore concerning the acts of the soul's intellectual part, there can come to be a turning-back simply and *per se*. And in this way someone can know that he has acts of this kind. But further, and as a consequence, through [reflection on] the very acts a man can arrive at knowledge of the principles of those acts, and through them he can also know the soul's powers, habits, and essence. But it is to be considered that if the act is such as to be able to manifest the habits and essence with certainty, through it one arrives at knowledge of its principles with certainty; whereas if it is not such an act, we cannot have knowledge of its principles by means of it. Now, although we can know the act of charity insofar as each one knows that he loves, we cannot know its principle with certainty, both because it is in us through a certain configuration to the Holy Spirit, a configuration to which we

---

d. 23, q. 1, a. 2, ad 1 (translated in webnote 48); *De ueritate*, q. 10, aa. 9–10; *Super II Cor.*, ch. 12, lec. 1 and ch. 13, lec. 2; *Quodl.* VIII, q. 2, a. 2 [4]; *ST* I, q. 87, a. 2 and I-II, q. 112, a. 5.

    a. *Signum aggenerati habitus est delectatio*

    b. Aristotle, *Posterior Analytics* II, ch. 20 (99b25).

    c. The MS reads: *solum pars animae intellectivae,* but in the edition the last word is emended to *intellectiva* as being the phrasing obviously demanded by the argument.

do not attain through our own acts, and because it has a great likeness to the act of natural love. And therefore I say that no one can know for certain that he has charity.

Replies to objections:
[No replies are given in the manuscript.]ᵃ

QUESTION 2   On charity's increase and decrease

"Here the following is sought: [if charity *is* the Holy Spirit, then, since charity may increase and decrease in man, should it be conceded that the Holy Spirit can increase or decrease in man?"]ᵇ Here four things are sought. First, whether charity admits of increase.ᶜ Second, how much it can increase.ᵈ Third, how it increases. Fourth, whether it admits of decrease.

a. One of the editors of the critical edition of the *Lectura romana*, John Boyle, informed me in private correspondence that replies for this article's objections, as well as for the last article of the second question, are lacking in the MS, and no other indication (such as *sic patet*) is offered. The text could be missing. Notably, the MS contains a paragraph sign in d. 17, q. 2, a. 4, right where the *solutiones* ought to be, suggesting that the scribe was preparing to copy them. However, he might simply be following form, and then looking to the exemplar sees that there is nothing to copy. Boyle is inclined to think that there was nothing to copy, but that would not settle the question of whether, in that case, the exemplar is defective, and St. Thomas did in fact reply to the objections (with at least a *sic patet* . . .).

In any event, the first objection here plays on the notion that what is present to the soul should be most knowable, which is reminiscent of two objections in the Paris version (the third and the fourth, though neither of these invokes the authority from St. Paul), so some response can be compiled; moreover, the third objection here is identical with the second in the Paris version, so the response can be gathered from there (see above). However, it is interesting that the second objection here, which argues from delight as a sign of habit, matches no objection in the Paris version, where the connection between delight and habit is instead made in the response. Also, the rather weak fifth objection of the Paris version has been dropped from the *Lectura romana* altogether.

b. The beginning of ch. 5 in Distinction 17 of the Lombard's text.

c. The phrase *utrum caritas augeatur* suggests something a little stronger than "is increased." Attention is focused on the *nature* of charity, such that one asks: "Does it allow for, or admit of, increase—is it the sort of thing that can change in quantity, and if so, how?" The same is true of the opposite question *utrum minuatur.*

d. *quantum augeatur,* meaning here whether it has a limit or not.

ARTICLE 1[a]   Whether charity admits of increase

Objections:

Proceeding to the first, it seems that charity does not admit of increase.

1. For everything that increases is in motion. And everything that is in motion is a body. But charity is not a body. Therefore it does not admit of increase.[127]

2. Further, increase is a motion in terms of quantity. Yet charity is not a quantity, but rather a quality. Therefore increase does not belong to charity.

3. Further, charity is the life of the soul, as the soul is the life of the body. But the life of the body does not increase, for it does not admit of more and less. Therefore neither does charity, which is the life of the soul.

4. Further, accidents increase due to an increase in their causes. But the cause of charity is God, who cannot increase. Therefore neither can charity increase.

On the contrary:

Augustine says of charity: "Once it has been born, it then receives nourishment; when it has been strengthened, it reaches perfection."[b] Therefore charity increases according to certain specific degrees.

Response:

It should be said that certain ones asserted that charity does not *essentially* increase; and there were four opinions along these lines.

The first opinion is that of the Master, who asserted that charity is the Holy Spirit, who does not increase. Hence he said that charity does not increase in itself, but only in man, insofar as he progresses more or less in the act of loving God. But this position is untenable. For it was shown that there is in us not only uncreated charity, which is the Holy Spirit, but also a created habit of charity, which is what we are now inquiring about.[c]

Hence, another opinion is that one and the same charity does not

---

a. Parallels: *In I Sent.* (Paris version) d. 17, q. 2, a. 1 (see above); *ST* I-II, q. 52, a. 1; q. 66, a. 1; II-II, q. 24, a. 4; *Quodl.* IX, q. 6; *De uirt. in comm.*, a. 11; *De uirt. card.*, a. 3; *De malo*, q. 7, a. 2; *Sent. Eth.* X, lec. 3.

b. Augustine, *Tractates on the First Epistle of John*, Tractate 5, n. 4 (PL 35:2014).

c. "It was shown": in the present Distinction, q. 1, a. 2 (*Lectura romana*); cf. d. 17, q. 1, a. 1 (Paris version).

increase, but a lesser charity is taken away and a greater follows it. But again this cannot be, for since charity is not taken away except by mortal sin, it would follow that charity would not grow in anyone unless a mortal sin intervened, which is absurd.

A third opinion is that charity does not increase essentially, but increases insofar as it is more rooted in its subject. But those who held this did not realize what they were saying, since for an accident such as whiteness to increase is nothing other than for it to be applied more as a name to its subject, which means that it inheres more firmly in it.[a]

The fourth opinion is that charity does not increase essentially, but increases in regard to fervor. And if fervor is taken metaphorically (namely, as pertaining to the intensity of the act of love), it is evident that this view is impossible; for habits render their acts to be such as the habits themselves are; hence if an act of love is more intense, [this is a sign that] the habit of charity must itself also grow. If, however, fervor is understood as a certain disposition left behind in the soul's lower part due to the love of God, insofar as the lower powers follow the higher, in this way it happens that fervor does increase without charity being increased; for it is in this way that some people have greater fervor who do not have greater charity, in whom the lower appetitive power is more stirred up by the apprehension of divine things, either due to its newness, as in novices, or due to some other cause. But such an addition to fervor does not redound to merit;[b] for those who are more fervent in this way do not thereby merit more. For this reason,[c] therefore, if an increase of charity were only according to this fervor, man would not ever advance in meriting, which is false.

And therefore it should be said that charity itself [essentially] increases. But it should be known that increase is properly and *per se* found in quantity, as for example the great and the small, which are the terms of growth and lessening; and [the notion] is transferred from this scenario to other things, not in such a way that the forms of other genera have in themselves greatness or smallness or that increasing or diminishing [properly speaking] belongs to them, but only insofar as they are in a subject, namely insofar as the subject participates more or less in such a form, that is, the subject is brought[d] more or less into act

a. *Sed hi propriam vocem ignoraverunt; nihil enim est aliud accidens augeri, ut albedinem, quam magis denominari in suum subiectum, quod est ei firmius inhaerere*

b. *auget ad meritum*

c. *Secundum hoc,* taken to refer to the preceding statement.

d. *quod est reduci,* etc., which could also (though less plausibly) be translated as "which [subject] is brought . . ."

through such a form. Hence if a separate magnitude is understood, it can be understood as greater or less, but not if separated whiteness be understood, because in such things, what is abstract does not receive more or less, but only what is concrete, as whiteness is not said to be more or less, but what is white is said to be more or less. But that some form, even infosar as it is in a subject, does not receive more or less, occurs as a result of two things: in one way, on the part of the form itself, whose proper *ratio* consists in something determinate, as is evident in numbers and in those things that include numbers in their *ratio,* as a triangle, a square, and other such things. In another way, on the part of the formal effect or the manner in which they are united to the subject. For certain forms, namely substantial forms, give to the subject in which they are its being-what-it-is.[a] Now the being of each thing is one only; hence it is impossible that a substantial form receive more or less. And if even white were that which it is by the mere fact that it is white, then it could not be more or less white, since, if the substantial being of a thing were to vary, it would not be the same thing. Therefore since created charity is a certain form in man, the *ratio* of which form does not consist in something determinate, nor does it give substantial being to man, nothing prevents it from admitting of increase, just as other qualities that receive more and less [admit of increase].

Replies to objections:

1. To the first, therefore, it should be said that charity is said to increase not as though it were the *subject* of increase, for this manner of increase belongs only to bodies, but because increase may be attributed to it insofar as its subject participates in it more and less.[b]

2. To the second, it should be said that in charity and in other things that are great but not by greatness of mass, to be greater is the same as to be better, and to be better is the same as to be more perfect, as Augustine says.[c] And in this respect increase belongs to charity insofar as it is a certain perfection, although it is not in the genus of quantity; and this is what some people mean when they say that it has quantity of power, but not of mass.

3. To the third, it should be said that the life of the body consists in

---

a. *Quaedam enim formae scilicet substantiales dant subiecto in quo sunt esse hoc ipsum quod est*

b. *caritas non dicitur augeri quasi ipsa sit subiectum augmenti, hoc enim corporum tantum; sed quia secundum ipsam attenditur augmentum in quantum subiectum eius magis et minus participat ipsam*

c. Augustine, *On the Trinity* VI, ch. 8 (CCSL 50:238).

its substantial being (since for living things, to live is to *be*),ª but it is not the same with the life of charity, and therefore the two cases are not parallel.

4. To the fourth, it should be said that although God who is the cause of charity does not admit of increase, he is the cause of charity's increase, since [in general] he, being himself immovable, is the cause of motion in all things. For he does not cause charity according to a necessity of nature, but gives more or less of it according to the judgment of his will.

ARTICLE 2ᵇ   How much charity can increaseᶜ

Objections:

Proceeding to the second, it seems that charity cannot increase indefinitely.

1. For in John 3 it is set down as proper to Christ that the Spirit is not given to him according to a measure;[128] therefore, the Spirit is given to all others according to a measure. But the Holy Spirit is given according to his gifts, especially that of charity. Therefore charity cannot increase indefinitely.

2. Further, the charity of a comprehensorᵈ is finite. Therefore if the charity of a wayfarer increases indefinitely, it could happen that a wayfarer would have charity equal to that of a comprehensor, which is impossible.

3. Further, the grace of anyone merely a wayfarer is finite. Therefore if charity increases indefinitely, any wayfarer will be able to attain the charity of any comprehensor, and so a man will be able to progress by merit to the level of the Blessed Virgin or of the apostles [which is impossible].

4. Further, increase is a certain motion. But nothing moves boundlessly. Therefore charity does not increase boundlessly.

---

a. See Aristotle, *On the Soul* II, ch. 4 (415b13).

b. Parallels: *In I Sent.* (Paris version) d. 17, q. 2, a. 4 (see above); *In I Sent.* d. 27, q. 2, a. 4; *In III Sent.* d. 29, a. 8, qa. 1, ad 2 (see below); *ST* II-II, q. 24, a. 7; *De caritate,* a. 10, ad 12.

c. Throughout this article, although Thomas writes *caritas augetur* or *non augetur,* often the meaning is "charity *can* (or *cannot*) increase," as is evident from the first argument and the *sed contra.*

d. *caritas hominis comprehensoris,* i.e., a saint beholding God in the beatific vision.

On the contrary:

Gregory says that he who abandons the desire of making progress risks the danger of falling back.[a] Therefore however much progress a man makes, he can still make further progress, and thus his charity can increase indefinitely.[b]

Response:

It should be said that the increase of charity may be considered in two ways. In one way, insofar as it is in act; and in this way, since charity is the gift of God, who dispenses his gifts in a certain measure, in each one charity grows up to some determinate level, according to the saying of the Apostle in Ephesians 4:7: "To each is given grace according to the measure of the giving of Christ." In another way, increase of charity may be considered according to what is possible[c] [to the one who has it]; and in this way charity can increase indefinitely. And this is evident (1) from the *ratio* of charity itself, (2) from the *ratio* of its cause, and (3) from the *ratio* of its subject. (1) From the *ratio* of charity, for since charity makes us love God, we can never arrive at the point of loving God as much as he is deserving of our love,[d] because he is infinitely lovable; hence however much charity increases it still has room for growth. (2) From the *ratio* of its cause, since God, who causes charity, has infinite power and can always move man forward to a greater perfection. (3) From the *ratio* of the subject, for when charity is received, the recipient's capacity grows so that he may receive still more,[e] as happens also with regard to knowledge; for he who understands the greatest things does not understand lesser things less, but even more, as the Philosopher says in *On the Soul* III.[f]

a. According to the editors of the critical text, this statement is not from Gregory but from Leo the Great: see the latter's *Tractatus septem et nonaginta* 40.1 (CCSL 138A:224). Nevertheless, a formulation like it is to be found in Gregory's *Pastoral Rule*, Part III, Admonition 35 (PL 77:118), as well as in numerous works of Bernard of Clairvaux, listed here in an order of greater to lesser word-for-word correspondence: *Second Sermon for the Feast of the Purification* (PL 183:369); *Epistle* 385, n. 1 (PL 182:588); *Epistle* 254, nn. 4–6 (PL 182:460–61); *Epistle* 91, n. 3 (PL 182:223).

b. *caritatis augmentum est in infinitum,* literally, "the increase of charity is unto infinity."

c. This seems to be the meaning of Thomas's phrase: *secundum id quod potest esse,* which he contrasts with the earlier *secundum quod est in actu.*

d. *diligendus est a nobis*

e. *Ex ratione autem subiecti, quia capacitas hominis caritate recepta crescit ad ulterius recipiendum*

f. Aristotle, *On the Soul* III, ch. 4 (429b3).

Replies to objections:

1. To the first, therefore, it should be said that the measuring out of the Spirit is referred to charity's actual increase, as was said [in the response].

2. To the second, it should be said that although a comprehensor's charity is finite, as is that of a wayfarer, it is not of the same *ratio,* as can be seen by considering its root: for the charity of the fatherland follows upon manifest vision, whereas the charity of the wayfaring state follows upon the enigmatic vision had by faith. Therefore, just as no matter how much progress a man makes in the knowledge belonging to the wayfaring state, his knowledge will never be equal to that which is proper to the fatherland, so too no matter how much a man grows in the love belonging to the wayfaring state, his love will never be equal to that which is proper to the fatherland.

3. To the third, it should be said that for the sake of the beauty in the Church that arises from ordered diversity, God in his wisdom ordained to give more grace to some than to others, most of all and without measure to our head, Christ himself, while to others, namely the members, more and less, and most of all to those who were joined to Christ [in his earthly mission], as his mother and the apostles. Hence it is foolish to believe that anyone could, by his merit, attain the level of the Blessed Virgin or of the apostles.

4. To the fourth, it should be said that no motion is said to be boundless, in such a way that the very having of no bounds be the intended term of a motion; neither does the increase of charity occur as though it were intended for charity to arrive at boundless charity, but in such a way that however much it increases, a further increase is possible.

ARTICLE 3[a]   Whether charity grows by way of addition

Objections:

Proceeding to the third, it seems that charity grows by way of addition.

1. For increase is an addition to a magnitude that already exists. But charity increases. Therefore this happens by means of addition.

2. Further, in the increase of charity the Holy Spirit is invisibly sent. But the Holy Spirit is not invisibly sent unless some new gift is given.[b]

a. Parallels: *In I Sent.* (Paris version) d. 17, q. 2, a. 2 (see above); *ST* I-II, q. 52, a. 2; II-II, q. 24, a. 5; *De uirt. in comm.,* a. 11.

b. The phrase could also be rendered "unless by the giving of some new gift."

Therefore charity's increase happens by means of the infusion of new charity.

3. Further, it is by the same cause that something grows and is generated. But charity is not generated by our acts, as acquired habits are, but by infusion from God. Therefore it increases, too, by a new infusion.

4. Further, if it does not increase by way of infusion, it seems there would not be any other way it could increase except by means of our acts, even as our acquired habits increase. If, then, it increases by means of our acts, it follows that it increases in any and every act. But this seems to be false. Therefore the other explanation has to stand, namely that charity increases by the addition of newly infused charity.

On the contrary:

One simple thing added to another simple thing brings about nothing greater.[a] But charity is a simple form, since it is a spiritual gift. Therefore a greater charity cannot be brought about by the addition of charity to charity.

Response:

It should be said that, on the supposition that charity increases essentially, there are two opinions regarding the manner of its increase. For certain ones said that charity increases in man by the addition of new charity. But that position is not intelligible, for two reasons. First, charity increases in the respect in which it has magnitude. Now, it does not belong to it to have magnitude in itself, but only according as it is participated by a subject, as was said above.[b] Hence increase belongs to it only insofar as a subject participates in it more and more, which is to increase in intensity. Whereas to increase by addition is to increase in itself; hence such increase belongs only to things that are quantitative in themselves. Therefore those who held this position seem to have been deceived by a false imagination, interpreting the increase of charity as an increase in something quantitative. The second reason is as follows: addition is always of one thing to another. Therefore it requires multiplicity, and this, in turn, requires distinction; and in forms of a single species there is distinction only on account of a distinction of subject, as *this* whiteness is other than *that* whiteness because their subjects are different. Hence whiteness is not added to whiteness, ex-

a. *Simplex simplici additum nihil maius efficit*
b. In the present Distinction, q. 2, a. 1 *(Lectura romana)*; cf. *In I Sent.* (Paris version) d. 17, q. 2, a. 1.

cept insofar as one white subject is added on to another white subject, which does not make the resulting thing more *white*, but makes *what is white greater*.[129]

Now one would not say such a thing about charity, as is immediately obvious.[a] For it is manifest that charity increases not by addition but by intensity, that is, insofar as the subject is brought more into the actuality of the form in question, which is to participate more in it. But this occurs by the agent acting more forcefully[b] to bring the subject into the actuality of the form in question, even as something is made hotter by a more forceful heating. In like manner, charity grows due to the forcefulness of the action of God, who acts in things not to the extent that he is able, but to the extent that he wishes. Hence without change in himself he more and more impresses the effect, charity, in the soul.

Replies to objections:

1. To the first, therefore, it should be said that that proposition[c] is [correctly] understood about the increase of things which are in themselves quantitative.

2. To the second it should be said that charity's increase involves a new divine effect not because another charity is added, but because the charity that was previously present is intensified by the divine action.

3. To the third it should be said that while the increase of charity is indeed from God infusing it, this does not occur as if he adds charity to charity, but in the manner already explained [in the response].

4. To the fourth it should be said that although charity does not increase by way of addition, it does not thereby follow that it increases by our acts as the effective cause of this increase; our acts are only the meritorious cause. For he who uses well a gift given him merits that that gift should increase in him. Nevertheless it need not be the case that any act of charity should merit an increase of charity; this occurs only when someone uses charity not negligently but to the extent of the ability he has received. For a habit of the mind does not automatically bring about action but only does so when one wills to use it, and therefore by one and the same habit someone can act more intensely or more remissly.[d]

a. *Hoc autem non contingit dicere in caritate, ut per se patet*
b. *vehementius*   c. *verbum illud*
d. *Habitus enim mentis non est necessitate movens sed voluntate, et ideo uno et eodem habitu potest quis intensiv<i>us et remissius agere.* This succinct reply to an objection performs the function to which an entire article was devoted in the Paris version: see *In I Sent.* d. 17, q. 2, a. 3 (above).

ARTICLE 4[a]   Whether charity admits of decrease

Objections:

Proceeding to the fourth, it seems that charity admits of decrease.

1. For contraries are apt to come to be in regard to the same thing. Since therefore increase and decrease are contraries, it seems that if charity can increase, it can also decrease.

2. Further, in Revelation 2:4 it is said [to the angel of the church at Ephesus]: "I have a few things against you, that you have abandoned your first charity." But the text does not mean to say by this that she [the Ephesian church] had entirely lost charity; therefore the meaning seems to be that charity was diminished in her.[b, 130]

3. Further, the Holy Spirit is given to man according to participation in charity. But in Numbers 11:17 the Lord says to Moses: "I will take some of the spirit which is upon you and put it upon them."[131] Therefore it seems that charity can be diminished.[132]

4. Further, charity is the measure of merit. But sometimes someone has less merit than before; therefore he has less charity.

5. Further, "not to advance in the way of God is to fall back," as Gregory says.[c] But it is manifest that charity does not always advance in a man; therefore sometimes it would decrease.

On the contrary:

Charity is not diminished by mortal sin, but is entirely taken away. Similarly, it is not diminished by venial sin, for since man's charity is finite, many venial sins would eventually consume all his charity; since a second venial sin takes as much from charity as the first, *if* the second is equal to the first, therefore many venial sins will consume charity entirely, which is impossible, because heaven is promised only to those who have charity, and someone is not excluded therefrom owing to venial sins.[d]

---

a. Parallels: *In I Sent.* (Paris version) d. 17, q. 2, a. 5 (see above); *ST* II-II, q. 24, a. 10; *De malo*, q. 7, a. 2.

b. *Non autem persignificatur quod caritatem omnino amiserit; ergo videtur significari quod caritas sic diminuta in eo fuerit.* The *in eo* is a bit strange if the subject is the Church of Ephesus, which one would expect to be spoken of as a "she."

c. At times Thomas attributes this statement to Gregory (here; *ST* II-II, q. 24, a. 6, obj. 3), at times to Bernard (*In III Sent.* d. 29, q. 8, qa. 2, obj. 1; *De malo*, q. 7, a. 2, obj. 11). See the textual note to the *sed contra* of a. 2 above.

d. *Caritas non minuitur per peccatum mortale sed totaliter tollitur. Similiter nec per peccatum veniale, quia cum caritas hominis sit finita, multa peccata venialia totam consumerent caritatem; cum secundum peccatum veniale non <minus> de caritate auferat quantum primum, si sit secundum aequale primo, ergo multa peccata venialia totaliter*

Response:

It should be said that charity cannot be diminished, although some think differently. For no accident increases or decreases except due to some cause. Now the active cause of charity is God, while the receptive cause is the rational creature. Indeed, from God it comes about that a man has charity and that he advances in charity, whereas a failure in charity can only come about from our side, according to Hosea 13:9: "Your destruction is your own, O Israel, your help is from me."[a] Now on our side there is a reason why charity is withdrawn entirely from us by God, namely when we love something in contempt of God;[b] for this is contrary to charity, which loves God above all things. And in truth, this takes charity away, both by reason of contrariety in the subject and by reason of merit, or rather, demerit. For he who turns from God deserves that charity be taken away from him by God.

But charity's decrease cannot have a cause on our side either by way of disposition or by way of merit. For it could not be said that charity would decrease except by sin. But mortal sin takes it away entirely, as was said just now,[c] whereas venial sin cannot diminish it either (1) by way of merit or (2) by way of opposition or of disposition to the opposite. I say that this cannot happen (1) by way of merit, because the demerit of venial sin is not of infinite consequence.[d] Charity's decrease, on the other hand, has something infinite annexed to it, since when charity decreases, the eternal reward must also decrease. The comparison of venial sins to charity is as if points are taken away from a line: for as a line neither comes to be nor grows by the addition of any number of points, so it is not diminished by the subtraction of any number of points; and similarly no venial sins whatsoever diminish charity [as such]. I say, moreover, that neither does it happen (2) in terms of a contrary disposition, because venial sins are not opposed to the habit of charity, since they do not turn one away from the [ultimate] end to which charity tends,[e] although they make one dwell, more than is due, on things that lead to the end, inasmuch as that end

---

caritatem consument, quod est impossibile, quia propter peccata venialia aliquis excluderetur, quia non promittitur nisi habenti caritatem.

    a. Thomas quotes the verse as: *perditio tua Israel, ex me auxilium tuum.* Modern translations read the verse rather differently. Thus the RSV: "I will destroy you, O Israel, who can help you?"

    b. *dum scilicet aliquid contempto Deo diligimus.* "Contempt" should be taken in its older sense that survives in a phrase like "acting in contempt of the law."

    c. In the *sed contra* argument.   d. *ad aliquid infinitum*

    e. *innititur*

is constituted in them.[a, 133] However, venial sins *impede* the act of charity (although impediments to acts diminish neither a habit nor a natural power in itself—hence, too, it is said in *On the Soul* I[b] that if an old man were to receive the eye of a youth, he would see as a youth sees); but impediments of this kind can dispose one to the complete loss of a habit or of a virtue. And similarly venial sins do not diminish charity, but dispose one to the complete loss of charity, insofar as venial sin is a disposition to mortal sin.

Replies to objections:
[No replies are given in the manuscript.][c]

---

a. *licet faciant magis debito immorari circa ea quae sunt ad finem, secundum hoc quod in eis finis constituatur*

b. Aristotle, *On the Soul* I, ch. 10 (408b21).

c. Concerning the missing replies, see the textual note after the last article of the preceding question (q. 1, a. 4). Here, apart from the first objection, which is identical in both versions, the remaining objections (2–5) presented in this article vary considerably from those (viz., 2–4) given in the Paris version. There is some correspondence: Parisian objs. 2 & 3 run along similar lines to Roman obj. 2, inasmuch as they appeal to evidence of charity weakened or grown cold; Parisian obj. 4 loosely matches Roman obj. 5, each noting the possibility that by disposing oneself less to charity, one would, over time, end up with less charity than one had before. In a similar vein, Roman obj. 4 points to an effect, merit, and argues that if merit is sometimes less than it was before, so too must be its cause.

IN II SENTENTIARUM

�֍cↄ֍

DISTINCTION 3

QUESTION 4[a]   Whether angels, granted that
they had not been created in grace, would in
that state of innocence have loved[b] God above
themselves and more than themselves[c]

Regarding the third principal issue,[d] we now inquire about love—namely, whether angels, if they had not been created in grace,[134] would in that state of innocence have loved God above themselves and more than everything.

Objections:

1. And it seems that they would not have done so. For to love God in this way is an act of charity, which cannot exist in one who does not have charity. But angels in that state would not have had charity, since charity does not exist without grace, for it is never unformed by

a. Latin text: provisional critical ed. of the Leonine Commission; cf. Mandonnet, 125–28. Parallels: *ST* I, q. 60, a. 5; *In III Sent.* d. 29 (see below); *ST* II-II, q. 25, a. 2 and q. 27, a. 3.

b. *dilexerit.* The "state of innocence" here is a counterfactual hypothesis, so that it would be more accurate to say: Whether angels, if they had not been created with grace, would have loved God, etc.; and Thomas's answer should accordingly be understood: Even in this hypothetical state of innocence or pure nature, they would have loved God more than themselves and all others. (To avoid the misunderstandings that can result from failing to grasp that this discussion is, in key respects, hypothetical and counterfactual, Aquinas's indicative past tenses are translated into the past subjunctive.)

c. The Mandonnet ed. entitles this article: *Utrum angeli in illo statu innocentiae Deum supra se et plus quam se dilexerit, dato quod in gratia creati non sunt.* This is the title we have translated. The Parma ed. entitles the article differently: *Utrum angelus in statu suo naturali dilexerit Deum plus quam se et omnia alia.*

d. The division of this entire Distinction is confusing, at least in the Mandonnet ed., for at the start of Question 2, St. Thomas writes that he will inquire into three things: (1) whether an angel became evil at the very beginning of its creation; (2) of the angels' natural knowledge; (3) of the angels' love [*dilectio*]. But the first is then identified as *articulus primus* though it stands alone; it is followed by a Question 3 on the cognition of the angels, which is subdivided into four articles; and lastly comes a Question 4, a single inquiry, on the angels' love (translated here). Hence one must refer to the present selection as *In II Sent.* d. 3, q. 4.

grace. Therefore it seems that they would not have loved God more than themselves.

2. Further, according to Bernard, nature is always curved back upon itself.[a, 135] But [on our hypothesis] the love of the angels in their first state was from nothing else except a natural principle. Therefore the whole of that love was reflected back into the one loving, so that whatever the angels were loving, they were loving on account of themselves; and thus they did not love God above themselves.

3. Further, Avicenna says in his *Metaphysics,* tract IX, chapter 4, that no action of any nature is liberal[b] except God's alone, because of the fact that every other action than his pursues some benefit for the agent himself.[136] But the love by which someone loves God above himself is the most liberal of all. Therefore it seems that this kind of love could not belong to anyone except by grace.

4. Further, anything naturally seeks[c] to acquire its end. But everything that is desired by someone in order that he may acquire it for himself is loved on account of himself and less than himself. Since therefore angels in a state of natural endowments[d] would have loved God as their end, it seems that they would not have loved him above themselves.

5. Further, according to Dionysius,[e] natural goods remain in the angels even after sin. But it is obvious that a sinful man or sinful angel does not love God above all things. Therefore it seems that neither would they have so loved him in a state of natural endowments.

On the contrary:

1. Every love is either a love that uses or a love that enjoys.[f] If therefore the angels were loving God in a state of innocence, then they must have done so either as using him or as enjoying him. If they loved him in the sense of *using* him, then they used a thing that is only to be enjoyed, which is an act of great perversity, according to Augustine;[g] and so their love would have been sinful and not natural. If, on the other hand, they loved him in the sense of *enjoying* him, then they were

---

a. *natura semper in se curva est.* Mandonnet (p. 125, n. 2) suggests that the idea is gathered from *On Loving God,* ch. 8 (PL 182:988), though the phrase does not occur there word-for-word.

b. *liberalis,* free, generous, not self-seeking.

c. *appetit*; in the next line, the verb is *desideratur.*

d. *in statu naturalium*

e. Pseudo-Dionysius, *On the Divine Names,* ch. 4, n. 23 (PG 3:726).

f. *Omnis dilectio aut est usus aut fruitionis*

g. Augustine, *On the City of God* XI, ch. 25 (CCSL 48:345).

loving God for his own sake, since to enjoy is to cling to something by love, for its own sake.[a]

2. Further, that God should be loved above all things, because it is the natural law, was written in the angel's mind even more expressly than in man's mind. But acting against what is impressed upon the heart by the natural law cannot occur without sin. Therefore if the angels were not loving God above everything, they were sinning. Therefore as long as they were without sin, they would have loved God above all things.

Response:

It should be said that there is a twofold opinion about this matter. For certain ones distinguish the love of concupiscence from the love of friendship[b]—two loves that, if we diligently consider them, differ according to two acts of the will, namely to seek[c] (which is of a thing not had) and to love (which is of a thing had), according to Augustine.[d] And therefore the love of concupiscence is that by which someone desires something in order to make it his own,[e] which is good for him in some way; and by such a love, [say the proponents of one view,] the angels in a state of natural endowments would have loved God more than themselves by more vehemently seeking to behold[f] the divine good than their own, since this divine good would have been more pleasant to them; hence, they would have referred the whole of this

a. See *In I Sent.* d. 1, q. 1, a. 1 (above).

b. *dilectionem concupiscentiae et amicitiae.* In later works Thomas will prefer the language *amor concupiscentiae* and *amor amicitiae.* Most commentators on Thomas have translated these phrases as "love of concupiscence" and "love of friendship," and I see no reason to repudiate the custom, even if "concupiscence" here has to be taken to mean desire in general rather than sensuous desire alone. One can see from the passage at hand that originally *amor concupiscentiae* indicated a self-directed love and *amor amicitiae* a love directed to other persons. Eventually Thomas will make a decisive move to redefine them more formally as *kinds* of love—the former being the kind of love one has for a *good* for any person (for oneself *or* for another), the latter being the kind of love one has for a *person* (again, for another *or* for oneself). See webnotes 322, 339, and 349.

c. *appetere*; below, "by seeking" translates *appetendo.*

d. Augustine, *Expositions of the Psalms,* Ps. 118, Serm. 8, n. 4 (CCSL 40:1688).

e. *qua aliquis aliquid desiderat ad concupiscendum.* Grammatically, *ad concupiscendum* could modify *aliquid* or *desiderat.* But if it modified *aliquid,* the phrase would not be very different from saying "which is good for him in some way." In either case, one must take the phrase in connection with the previous statement: concupiscence relates to *seeking* something—it *may* be for oneself, though it need not be.

f. Mandonnet: *appetendo*; Leonine: *appetendo inspicere*

love back to themselves.[137] But the love of friendship is that by which
someone loves the likeness of something he has in himself *in the other,*
wishing good for him to whom he has this likeness.[a] And on account
of this the Philosopher says that like is friendly to like,[b] just as one virtuous man loves another, in whom alone is there true friendship;[c, 138]
and by such a love, [the argument continues,] the angels in a certain
way would have loved God above themselves, since they would have
wished[d] for him a greater good than for themselves, namely, that he
be *God,* which they would not have wished for themselves; whereas
for themselves they would have wished something less good. Nevertheless, this created good they would have more intensely wished for
themselves than the divine good for God.

But that explanation cannot stand. For one must lay down that the
angels would have had [in that natural condition] the love of friendship toward God, since, according to their natural goods, the divine
likeness would have shone forth in them. But it belongs to the *ratio* of friendship that, although friendship has pleasures and benefits
annexed to it, still the lover's eye does not look to these, but to the
good loved. In the lover's heart, therefore, the good loved outweighs
all benefits or pleasures that follow from the one loved. But there
would have been no good in the angel [in this state] that was not from
the beloved himself, namely, God. Therefore they would have loved
the divine good[e] more than the good that they themselves were or the
good that was in them; and this is the other opinion.

Replies to objections:

1. To the first, therefore, it should be said that "act of charity" can
be said in two ways: either one means an act that is *from* charity, and
this is only in one who has charity; or one means an act that is *toward*
charity, not as meritorious or generative, but as preparatory to having it; and in *this* sense, there can be an act of charity prior to the hav-

---

a. Mandonnet: *dilectio autem amicitiae est qua aliquis aliquid, vel similitudinem ejus
quod in se habet, amat in altero volens bonum ejus ad quem similitudinem habet*; Leonine: *Dilectio autem amicitie est qua aliquis similitudinem eius quod in se habet amat in
altero, uolens bonum ei ad quem similitudinem habet*

b. Leonine: *est simile simili amicum*; Mandonnet: *simile simili est amicus* ("like is a
friend to like"); Parma: *est similis a simili amari* ("it belongs to the like to be loved
by the like")—Aristotle, *Ethics* VIII, ch. 1 (1155a32ff.).

c. Mandonnet: *in quibus tamen est vera amicitia*; Leonine: *in quibus tantum est
uera amicitia*

d. *optabant;* in the next phrase, "wished" translates *uolebant.*

e. Mandonnet: *bonum amatum divinum*; Leonine: *bonum diuinum*

ing of charity as a habit, even as doing just things is prior to the habit
of justice. Or it can be said that in the friendship of charity, the spirit[a]
is moved to loving God from the likeness of grace,[139] whereas in natural love[b] the spirit is moved to loving God from the proper good of
nature,[c] which is also a likeness of the highest goodness. And for this
reason it is said that when we say that the one who has charity loves
God "on account of God himself," the "on account of" denotes the relation of an end *and* of an efficient cause, since God himself adds over
and above nature that [capacity] owing to which one tends into his
love,[d] whereas when we say of the one who lacks charity that he loves
God "on account of [God] himself," the "on account of" denotes the
relation of an end only, and not of a proximate efficient cause, except
in the sense in which God is at work in every nature at work.[e]

2. To the second, it should be said that nature is said to be "curved
back upon itself" because it always loves its own good. Yet it need not
be the case that the lover's intention rests in the fact that the good is
his own, but rather it can be the case that the intention rests in this,
that it is *good;* for unless it were good for him in some way, either in
truth or in appearance, he would never love it at all. Still, he loves the
good not because it is *his own,* but because it is *good;* for good is the *per
se* object of the will.

3. To the third, it should be said that, even though from its action
some benefit[f] accrues to any created nature whatsoever, it need not be
the case that that benefit be the object of intention, as is evident in the
friendship of noble-minded people.[g, 140]

4. To the fourth, it should be said that "end" is twofold. There is a
certain end proportionate to a thing, received in it as a perfection inhering in it, like the health that is sought by means of medical treatments; and since that end can have its existence only in him who acquires it,[h] therefore absolutely speaking, no one loves *it* more than
himself, but one loves existing *with* such a perfection more than merely existing.[i, 141] But there is a certain end, *per se* subsistent, not depending for its existence on the thing for which it is the end; and while one

a. *animus*   b. *dilectione naturali*

c. *ipso bono nature*

d. *Deus superaddit nature unde in eius dilectionem tendat* [Mandonnet: *tendit*]

e. *nisi sicut Deus in omni natura operante operatur*

f. *aliquod commodum*

g. *amicitia honestorum*

h. *iste finis non est secundum esse nisi in eo cui acquiritur*

i. *ideo absolute non amatur ab aliquo supra se; sed se esse sub tali perfectione, amatur
supra se esse simpliciter*

desires to acquire that end [for oneself], one loves it above what one acquires from it; and such an end is God, as was said above.[142]

5. To the fifth, it should be said that insofar as one considers natural goods absolutely, in their natural being, they remain intact after sin. Nevertheless, they are perverted with respect to the right order they had toward grace or virtue; and to love God above all things followed only upon this kind of rectitude.[a, 143]

a. *bona naturalia prout in esse nature absolute considerantur remanent integra post peccatum, tamen peruertuntur quantum ad rectum ordinem quem habebant in gratiam uel uirtutem* [Mandonnet: *gratia vel virtute*]. *Et hanc rectitudinem consequebatur super omnia Deum diligere.*

DISTINCTION 38[a]

ARTICLE 1[b] Whether there is only a single
end of right wills[c]

Objections:

Proceeding to the first, it seems that there is not only a single end of right wills.

1. For the charity by which we love God is not God, as was shown in Book I.[d] But the end of right wills is God, and charity too, as is shown in the text of Lombard. [This means right will is directed to both of these as ends.] Therefore, right wills do not tend to a single end.

2. Further, where there is found gradation[e] in referring a thing to an end, there is not a single end.[f] But in the three Persons there is found gradation when one considers the relation of things to an end; hence Hilary says:[g] "The head of all is the Son, but the head of the Son is the Father, and to the one God all things are referred by this gradation." Since therefore each of the three Persons is the end of right wills, as is said in the text, it seems that right wills tend to several ends.

3. Further, as natural things have species from their form, so moral things have species from their end; hence, they are right or perverse according to the end, as is said in the text. But there is not a single form for natural things. Therefore neither will there be a single end for moral acts, to which they ought to be directed.

---

a. This Distinction consists of five articles, of which the first two are translated here (Latin text: provisional critical ed. of the Leonine Commission; cf. Mandonnet ed., 967–73). The last three articles concern whether intention is an act of the will, whether the will by one and the same act wills both the end and things directed to that end, and whether the will should be judged right on the basis of the end willed.

b. Parallel: *ST* I-II, q. 1, a. 5.

c. *unus finis* has been rendered "single end" when this brings out the meaning more clearly.

d. See *In I Sent.* (Paris version) d. 17, q. 1, a. 1 (above); *In I Sent.* (*Lectura romana*) d. 17, q. 1, a. 2 (above).

e. *gradus.* Here, "grade, degree, step" do not work very well idiomatically; "gradation" is probably the best one can do without excessive paraphrase.

f. *ubi invenitur gradus in referendo res ad finem, ibi non est unus finis*

g. Hilary, *On Synods, or the Faith of the Orientals,* n. 60 (PL 10:521).

4. Further, the end of action is that on account of which action takes place. But each [rational] agent, while acting, thinks about that on account of which he is acting.[a] Since therefore many who are doing right acts are not actually thinking about God, it seems that God is not the end of all right actions; and thus different agents will have various ends, insofar as they have various considerations of the end.[b]

5. Further, that without which something would not come to be is that for the sake of which it comes to be.[c] But there are many who would not do spiritual works if they did not thereby acquire certain temporal things. Therefore those temporal things they seek to acquire are the end of their works and of their wills, and nevertheless they are not said to be sinning in doing this: for, as the Apostle says in 1 Corinthians 9:10, "the plowman should plow in hope and the thresher thresh in hope of a share in the crop," speaking to the literal sense of that passage.[d, 144] Therefore besides God and charity, there can be another end for right wills; and thus not all right wills tend to a single end.

On the contrary:

1. Every will that tends to different things is divided among many.[e] But a right heart is not divided, but unified; hence the saying of Hosea 10:2, "Their heart is divided; now they shall perish." Therefore there is a single ultimate end for a right heart.

2. Further, the *ratio* of the good is from the end. Therefore where the highest good is, there is the ultimate end. But the highest good is one alone, as was proved in Distinction 3.[145] Therefore there is a single ultimate end of right wills.

Response:

It should be said that things are referred to an end in the same order by which they proceed from a principle, because any agent orders its effect to a certain end; and therefore the order of ends is according to the order of agents. Now in the procession of things from a principle there is found one *first* principle of things common to them all, under which are found the other proper principles, which differ in dif-

a. *unusquisque agens cogitat in agendo de eo propter quod agit*
b. *videtur quod non omnium rectarum actionum finis sit Deus; et ita diversarum erunt diversi fines secundum quod agentium sunt diversae cogitationes de fine*
c. Leonine: *illud sine quo non fieret aliquid est hoc propter quod fit illud*; Mandonnet: *illud sine quod non fieret aliquid est propter quod fit illud*
d. *loquens ad litteram in casu isto*
e. *omnis voluntas quae in diversa tendit, divisa est in plura*

ferent things. So, too, in referring things to an end there is found one end[a] common to them all, which is the ultimate end [simply speaking]; but different proper ends are found according to the diversity of beings. For good is found in things according to a double order, as is said in *Metaphysics* XII:[b] (1) the order of one thing to another thing, which order is similar to the order that parts of an army have to each other; (2) the other, an order of things to an ultimate end, which is similar to the order of the army to the good of the leader; and since things are referred to an ultimate common end by means of the end proper to each, therefore a diversity in the proper end brings about diverse relations of things to the ultimate end.

Accordingly, therefore, it should be said that as there is a single ultimate end of all things, namely God, so there is a single ultimate end of all wills, namely God; nevertheless, there are other proximate ends, and if the due relation of the will to the ultimate end is preserved[c] in regard to those ends, the will will be right; but if not, it will be perverse. Now the due relation of the will to the ultimate end is preserved in regard to that end through which the will, in accordance with its nature,[d] is able to participate in the ultimate end, in which it is distinguished from other things that participate in the ultimate end in another way;[146] and this [subsidiary end] is charity or beatitude. And therefore it is not only God, but also charity, that is the end of all right wills.

Replies to objections:

1. To the first, therefore, it should be said that charity is not the ultimate end, since it is not the common end that all things desire; but charity is an end proper to the will, through which the will attains to the ultimate end; and so it does not follow that there are many ultimate ends.

2. To the second, it should be said that the Father and the Son and the Holy Spirit are a single ultimate end, as is said in the text, because to each one of them belongs the *ratio* of end, insofar as any [of the Persons] is the highest good; and these three are not three but one high-

a. Leonine: *unus finis*; Mandonnet: *ultimus finis*

b. Aristotle, *Metaphysics* XII, ch. 10 (1075a11–14).

c. "preserved": here, *seruatur* [Mandonnet, *servetur*]; in the next sentence, *saluatur.*

d. The phrase "in accordance with its nature" is meant to convey the force of the Latin *nata est* in the phrase *secundum illum finem quo uoluntas nata est ultimum finem participare.*

est good. Hence Hilary's statement—"To the one God all things are referred by this gradation"—should be understood of the gradation of
being in the leading-back of creatures to the Son, but not between the
Son and the Father, between whom, as Jerome says, there is no gradation. Yet if the term "gradation" be taken broadly for "order," in that
way there *is* gradation between the Father and the Son, i.e., the order
of a principle to that of which it is the principle, but not the order of an
end to that for which it is an end.

3. To the third, it should be said that moral acts are specified not by
the ultimate end, but by their proximate ends, and there are many of
these proximate ends for different moral acts, just as there are many
natural forms[a] [for different creatures].

4. To the fourth, it should be said that in order for the end of an action to be God or charity, it is not necessary for someone, in carrying
out that action, to be thinking of God or charity; nor, again, is it enough
for someone to have [as his end] God or charity by way of habit alone,
because according to that view, someone would be ordering even an
act of venial sin to God, which is false; but it is necessary for him to
have thought first about the end, which is charity or God, and for his
reason to have ordered the consequent actions toward this end in such
a way that the rightness of that ordering is [in fact] preserved in consequent actions—as is clear in the example Avicenna gives of the artisan,
who, if he were constantly thinking about the rules of his art while he
is working on an artifact, would be much hampered in his work; but
even as he thought it out beforehand [by those rules], so afterwards
was it executed [without hindrance].[b, 147]

5. To the fifth, it should be said that it is not necessary for that without which something could not come to be, to be that for the sake of
which it comes to be;[c] for everything that is required for action is that
without which an action cannot come to be, e.g., instruments; yet an
action [so performed] does not come to be for the sake of the instruments. So, too, they who, in the undertaking of spiritual works, seek
for temporal things do not seek them as the proximate or remote end of

a. Leonine: *forme naturales*; Mandonnet: *fines naturales*
b. Leonine: *Vt patet in exemplo quod ponit Auicenna de artifice, qui si dum opus
suum exercet* [Mandonnet: *exerceret*] *semper de regulis artis cogitaret, multum in opere
impediretur; set sicut prius excogitauit, ita postmodum operatur* [the Parma ed. adds: *et
sic in opere rectitudo salvatur*]. The *sicut . . . ita* refers to the verbs, i.e., precisely to
the artist's mode of action. A simpler way to state the meaning, but one that is
less literal, is "just what he thought out beforehand by the rules of his art, does
he afterwards accomplish by his work."
c. *illud sine quod non fieret aliquid est propter quod fit illud*

their actions, since a lesser good cannot be the end of a greater good; but they seek them for the support of nature and the upkeep of their status, so as to be able to undertake the spiritual works more becomingly.[a, 148]

ARTICLE 2   Whether beatitude or charity is the common and single end of right wills

Objections:

It seems that the common and single end of right wills cannot be charity or beatitude.[b]

1. For nothing that is less than the ultimate end[c] is a single end common to all. But charity is less than the ultimate end, namely, God; and in like manner, too, beatitude and good delight and things of this sort. Therefore things of this sort cannot be the common end of right wills.

2. Further, nothing undesired can be an end, nor can anything hidden be desired. Since therefore beatitude is hidden (according to what Isaiah 64:4 says: "Eye has not seen, O God, apart from you, what you have prepared for those who wait for you"), it seems that beatitude cannot be the end of right wills.

3. Further, bodily good is not the end of spiritual good, since the end is always better than what leads to the end.[d] But eternal life seems to name a certain bodily thing: the eternal conjunction of our soul to the body. Therefore eternal life is not the end of spiritual works.

4. Further, no end is possessed prior to the possession of what

---

a. *set querunt ea ad sustentamentum nature et conditionis sue, ut sic debite opera spiritualia exercere possint*

b. For this article as for the rest of the volume in general, "beatitude" was preferred to "happiness" as a translation of *beatitudo.* It is the kind of choice that leaves one feeling frustrated with the frequently non-overlapping territories of languages. "Beatitude" has in its favor a certain loftiness, somewhat like "blessedness," and so avoids the emotional fuzziness and vulgarity that so easily infect the term "happiness." The man who is *felix* may be pleased, but the man who is *beatus* is utterly fulfilled; a cat could be named Felix, but only a god or a godlike man (or angel) can be called Beatus. Yet for this very reason, "beatitude" is too rarefied a term for some of the arguments, which sound much more convincing when pitched in terms of "happiness," such as the second objection here and especially its reply, where the point is that everyone knows, in a rough and ready way, what "happiness" *means* ("a most perfect state"), but not everyone *sees* in this life what that state actually consists in, and so they can disagree radically about how to seek and find it.

c. *Nichil enim quod est citra* [Mandonnet: *circa*] *finem ultimum*; the editions differ thus in the next sentence also.

d. *eo quod est ad finem*

brings attainment of the end, since one arrives at the former by way of the latter. But charity is possessed prior to meritorious acts. Therefore charity is not the end of right works.

5. Further, a work is called "right" according as it is informed by some virtue. But just as an act is informed by charity, so too is it formed by other virtues. Therefore, just as charity is posited as an end, so too ought other virtues to be called ends.

6. Further, what is simply good is not ordered, as to an end, to what is good for this particular man, because what is simply good is better [than this particular man's good]. But to be engaged in activity is good *per se,* whereas delight is good for this particular man, namely, the one so engaged; hence right activity is better than delight. Therefore right operation is not ordered to delight as to an end.[a]

On the contrary:

An end without which there cannot be conjunction to the ultimate end must itself be intended as a common end. But without charity and beatitude and things of this sort, there cannot be the conjunction of man's will to the ultimate end, which is God. Therefore all those things have the *ratio* of a common end.

Response:

It should be said that, as was said above,[b] although there is one ultimate end of all things even as there is one first principle, nevertheless a proper end is due[c] to each thing even as there is a proper principle for each. And so,[d] just as things that belong to one genus share in the proper principle of that genus, so too they share in one end, which, indeed, is common to all in that genus, but not to all things; nor is it possible for anything to have its due relation[e] to the ultimate end except through the mediation of the end that is due to its genus.

Now the end proper to each and every thing, through which end it is ordered to the ultimate end, is its own proper activity. Hence, the end of the rational nature, through which it is ordered to its proper end, is the perfect activity proper to that nature. But perfection of ac-

a. *Sed operatio est bonum per se, delectatio autem est huic bonum, scilicet operanti; et sic recta operatio est melior delectatione. Ergo recta operatio non ordinatur ad delectationem sicut ad finem.*

b. In the preceding article.

c. *debetur;* the same word is used at the end of the paragraph.

d. Leonine: *principium proprium. Et ita, sicut;* Mandonnet: *principium proprium; ita ut sicut*

e. *debita relatio*

tivity consists in three things, namely, object, habit, and delight. For the higher is the object, the more beautiful and more perfect is the activity tending to that object; hence activity has its perfection from the object, and the highest perfection from the noblest object. In like manner, too, for man there is no perfect activity unless it comes from a habit. Hence, the more perfect is the habit, the more perfect will be the activity, and the most perfect activity will come from the noblest habit. Similarly, as the Philosopher says in *Ethics* X,[a] delight perfects activity as beauty perfects youth, for delight itself is a kind of gracing[b] of activity. Accordingly, it must be that something of each of the things [mentioned] is a common end of wills reckoned as right.[c] Now this perfect activity is beatitude; the highest object is God; the most perfect habit is charity; and the purest delight is spiritual delight, as is proved in *Ethics* X.[d] And therefore it is said in the text of Lombard that God is the end of right wills, and that charity, good delight, and beatitude are also the end of right wills—in such a way that God is nonetheless the ultimate end, and beatitude, embracing charity and pleasure, is like "an end under the end,"[e] conjoining one to the ultimate end, since activity tends to the object itself; nor is there a right relation of the will to God except by the mediation of these three things.

Replies to objections:

1. To the first, therefore, it should be said that an end that stands in relation to the ultimate end is not an end common to all things, but it can be common to all within some genus. And so it is with beatitude: for since irrational creatures cannot arrive at beatitude, beatitude is not their end; but it is the end of the rational creature that can arrive at it.

2. To the second, it should be said that, although beatitude is hidden with respect to its substance, yet the *ratio* of beatitude is openly known, for all understand by "beatitude" a certain most perfect state; but what that perfect state consists in, whether in this life or after this life, or in bodily goods or spiritual goods, and in which of these spiritual goods—this is hidden.[f]

a. Aristotle, *Ethics* X, ch. 4 (1174b31–33).
b. *sicut quidam decor*
c. This is a good guess at the meaning of an unusual phrase (as given by both Mandonnet and the Leonine editors): *Et ideo oportet quod aliquod istorum sit finis communis rectarum uoluntatum assignatarum.* Were the final word *assignatorum* it would agree with *istorum* and the translation would be: "of the things mentioned."
d. Aristotle, *Ethics* X, ch. 5 (1176a1–2).
e. *finis sub fine*
f. See the fuller discussion at *In IV Sent.* d. 49, q. 1, aa. 1–2 (below).

3. To the third, it should be said that "life" is said in two ways. In one way, life is the same as the *being* of the living, as when it is said in *On the Soul* II that "for living things, to live is to be";[a] and in this way, the life of man comes[b] from the conjoining of soul to body, and eternal life from their eternal conjunction; and so understood, eternal life is not the end of right wills. In another way, the *activity* of a living thing is called "life," and in this way, that perfect activity by which blessed men will see God in eternity is called eternal life, as is said in John 17:3: "This is eternal life, that they may know you, the only true God, and the one whom you have sent, Jesus Christ." And in this way, eternal life *is* the end of right wills, and is the very same as beatitude.

4. To the fourth, it should be said that charity may be considered in two ways: either simply as a habit, or according to the way that its good results in an act, just as the goodness of any habit results in an act proceeding from the habit. If therefore charity is taken in the first way, then good actions[c] done before the infusion of charity are ordered to charity as to an end, insofar as they dispose the soul to the reception of infused charity. But here, charity is not being understood in this way; rather it is being understood insofar as the good of charity results in an act, as when the Philosopher says in *Ethics* III[d] that "the brave man acts on account of the good of bravery," insofar as he refers his actions to the end of bravery, which is to act bravely. In like manner, too, the one who has charity refers his actions to the good of charity, which is the very activity proceeding from charity, namely, the love of God and neighbor.

5. To the fifth, it should be said that only an act proper to a virtue, or an act of another virtue commanded by it, is ordered to the good of any virtue; thus an act proper to bravery is ordered to the good of bravery, and an act of magnanimity, which is a tending toward the doing of great and difficult things, is ordered to an act of bravery insofar as bravery commands it. But no virtue universally commands all virtues except for charity, which is the mother of all virtues; and it has this [universal command] on the one hand from its proper object, the highest good, into which it is immediately borne, and on the other

a. Aristotle, *On the Soul* II, ch. 4 (415b13).

b. *relinquitur*

c. *operationes rectae*

d. At several points in the discussion of courage (*Ethics*, Book III, chs. 6–9), Aristotle underlines that the brave man acts not solely out of expertise in fighting or passion against foes but with choice and for the sake of the noble (see, e.g., 1115b13–23, 1116a10–15, 1116b30–1117a9). None of these texts says exactly what Thomas is saying, but they offer support to his argument.

hand from its subject, the will, which commands the other powers; and therefore charity alone among the virtues is called a common end of all right wills.[149]

6. To the sixth, it should be said that activity, simply speaking, is better than delight; and therefore, as medical doctors[a] say, nature placed delight in the act of generation, lest animals, content with their own preservation, should neglect the preservation of the species[b] that comes about through generation; hence, delight is for the sake of activity. But delight does not follow upon any activity whatsoever, but rather upon perfect activity;[150] and therefore just as imperfect activities are ordered to a perfect activity, so too they are ordered to delight, which adorns[c] perfect activity. Or it may be said that "end" can be attributed to something in two ways: either according as a thing is considered in itself, and in this way activity is not for the sake of pleasure but rather the converse; or on the part of what is tending toward an end, and in this way activity is completed[d] by delight and is for its sake, that is, for the sake of the activity's completeness—for proper delights, as is said in *Ethics* X,[e] bring about an increase in proper activities, because one who is doing such activities, insofar as he is refreshed by the delight they bring, goes about them more diligently.

a. *medici*

b. *ne animalia sua salute contenta salutem speciei negligerent.* In general, *salus* can mean health, well-being, preservation, or conservation (and of course, salvation, in a theological context). So, one could also say "lest animals, content with their own well-being, should neglect the well-being of the species."

c. *exornat*

d. "Completed" and "completeness" for *perficitur* and *perfectionem,* to emphasize that the pleasure "rounds off," gives a certain fullness, to the activity, and indeed promotes its continuance.

e. Aristotle, *Ethics* X, ch. 7 (1177b21).

IN III SENTENTIARUM

DISTINCTION 23[a]

QUESTION 1   On virtues in general

ARTICLE 4   On the division of virtues into intellectual, moral, and theological

SUBQUESTION 3[b]   Whether theological virtues ought to be distinguished from both kinds of virtue[c]

Objections:

Further, it seems that the theological virtues ought not to be distinguished from both kinds of virtue.

1. For a power does not need a habit added over and above its nature for those things to which it is naturally determined. But the knowledge of God is naturally implanted in all, as Damascene says,[d] and similarly the desire of the highest good, as Boethius says in *On the Consolation of Philosophy* III.[e] Therefore we do not need any *virtues* with God as their object, which is said to be a characteristic of theological virtues.

a. The commentary on Distinction 23 is structured as follows. *Question 1,* on the virtues in general, comprises five articles: a. 1, concerning the human need for habits; a. 2, in what way we have knowledge of the habits that are in us; a. 3, whether virtues are habits; a. 4, concerning the division of virtues into intellectual, moral, and theological (of which we have translated qa. 3); a. 5, concerning the number of theological virtues (also translated here). *Question 2,* on faith, again comprises five articles: a. 1, what is faith; a. 2, the act of faith; a. 3, the subject of faith; a. 4, whether faith is a virtue; a. 5, its relationship to other virtues (none of this question is translated). *Question 3* is about the formation of faith: a. 1, whether faith is formed by charity; a. 2, whether unformed faith is a gift of God; a. 3, whether unformed faith is found in the demons; a. 4, whether faith remains at the advent of charity (of these, a. 1 and a. 4 are given in translation).

b. Latin text: provisional critical ed. of the Leonine Commission; cf. Moos ed., 710–11, 714–16. Parallels: *ST* I-II, q. 62, aa. 1–2; *De ueritate,* q. 14, a. 3, ad 9; *De uirt. in comm.,* aa. 10 & 12.

c. The question is introduced as follows: *Vlterius uidetur quod uirtutes theologice non debeant distingui ab utrisque.* The *utrisque* refers to both types of virtue already discussed in the subquestions prior to this one, namely intellectual (qa. 1) and moral (qa. 2).

d. John Damascene, *On the Orthodox Faith* I, ch. 1 (PG 94:790).

e. In the Moos ed. the citation is given as Boethius, *On the Consolation of Philos-*

2. Further, as we [believers] posit the enjoyment of God to be the last end of all human acts, so the philosophers [for their part] posited happiness.[a] But they did not posit any virtues that would have happiness as their object. Therefore neither do we need any virtues with God as their object.

3. Further, to know principles and the things known from principles pertains to the same habit. But the end is the principle of things to be done, as the Philosopher says in *Ethics* VII and *Physics* II.[b] Therefore, the theological virtues that have the last end as their object should not be distinguished from the cardinal virtues, which direct us in regard to things that are toward the end.

4. Further, perfections are proportionate to things perfected by them. But in us there is no power capable of being perfected by a human virtue except the power essentially rational,[c] which is perfected by intellectual virtue, and the part rational by participation, which is perfected by moral virtue. Therefore there cannot be another kind of virtue besides the two already mentioned.

On the contrary:

1. The Apostle (1 Cor. 13) sets down these virtues—faith, hope, and charity—which are neither intellectual nor moral, as is evident by going one by one through the virtues enumerated by saints and philosophers. Therefore one must posit a third kind of virtue, which is called theological.

2. Further, God is more distant from creatures than any two creatures are from each other. But there are differences in some *creatures* that necessitate a difference in our habits. Therefore the virtues that have *God* as their object are [*a fortiori*] different from the other virtues.[151]

Response:

To the third question it should be said that, in all things that act for the sake of an end, there must be an inclination toward the end, and,

---

ophy, Book IV, prose 2 (CCSL 94:67), but the more probable reference is Book III, prose 2 (CCSL 94:38). Neither text is word-for-word identical, but the latter is nearer.

a. Thomas contrasts *fruitionem diuinam* with *felicitatem,* the happiness to which philosophers, untutored by revelation, had aspired.

b. Aristotle, *Ethics* VII, ch. 8 (1151a16); *Physics* II, ch. 2 (200a22).

c. The terms used here are *potentia* for the faculty and *uirtus* for the faculty's perfection.

as it were, a certain pre-presence of the end;ᵃ otherwise they would never act for the sake of that end. But the end to which the divine bounty ordered or predestined man, namely the enjoyment of God himself, is elevated altogether beyond the power of created nature, for "eye has not seen, nor ear heard, nor has it arisen in the heart of man, what God has prepared for those who love him," as is said in 1 Corinthians 2. Hence by natural endowments alone man does not have a sufficient inclination to that end.

And therefore something must be superadded to man through which he may have an inclination to that end, just as by his natural endowments he has an inclination to the end connatural to him. And those things superadded are called theological virtues on three accounts. First, as regards the object, for since the end to which we are ordered is God himself, the inclination that is prerequisite consists in an activity that has God himself as object.ᵇ Second, as regards the cause, for just as that end is ordained to be ours by God and not by our nature, so God alone effects an inclination to that end in us. And in this way they are called "theological" virtues, as being caused in us by God alone. Third, as regards knowledge, for since the [divine] end is above natural knowledge, the inclination to the end cannot be known by natural reason, but can be known only by divine revelation. And therefore they are called "theological" because they are made known to us by the divine words.ᶜ Hence the philosophers knew nothing about them.

Replies to objections:

1. To the first, therefore, it should be said that, although man is naturally ordered to God both by knowledge and by affection, insofar as he *naturally* participates in him, nevertheless, because there is a certain participation in him *above* nature, a certain knowledge and affection above nature is required; and theological virtues are needed for this.

2. To the second, it should be said that the happiness the philosophers posited is that to which man can attain by his natural powers, and therefore he has, of himself, a natural inclination to that end. Hence no virtues inclining to that end are prerequisite; what he needs are only the virtues that direct activities in relation to the end.ᵈ ¹⁵² It is not so in the case at hand [since we are speaking of an end above the natural end].

a. *inchoationem finis*   b. *que est circa ipsum Deum*
c. *quia diuino sermone sunt nobis manifestate*
d. *Vnde non preexiguntur alique uirtutes inclinantes in finem, set solum dirigentes in operibus que sunt ad finem*

3. To the third, it should be said that speculative principles are known by a natural habit, namely by simple understanding, whereas the habits by which conclusions are known are known by science.[a] In the affective part, by contrast, a natural habit does not come first, but from the power's very nature there is an inclination to the last end proportionate to the nature, as was said.[b] But in regard to the end elevated above nature, to which the natural inclination does not attain, freely given habits[c] must precede the other habits—both in the intellect (as faith) and in the affective part (as charity and hope).

4. To the fourth, it should be said that habits are distinguished not only by their subjects but also by their objects. Moral and intellectual virtues are therefore distinguished from one another on the part of their subject, as was said before,[d] but theological virtues are distinguished from both moral and intellectual virtues on the part of the object, which is above the natural ability of either part.[e] Hence a theological virtue such as faith regards knowledge and has a certain affinity[f] with intellectual virtues, while a theological virtue such as charity regards affection and has affinity with moral virtues.[153]

ARTICLE 5[g]   Whether there are more than three theological virtues

Objections:

Proceeding to the fifth, it seems that there are *more than three* theological virtues.

1. For a theological virtue has God as its object, as was said.[h] But fear of God has God as its object. Therefore it is a theological virtue.

---

a. *principia speculatiua cognoscuntur per alium habitum naturalem quam conclusiones, scilicet per intellectum, conclusiones uero per scientiam*

b. At the start of the article's response. The phrase "proportionate to the nature" belongs, of course, to "last end," not to "inclination."

c. Thomas begins in the singular (*habitum gratuitum*) but ends by mentioning three habits (*ut fidem . . . ut caritatem et spem*).

d. In the response to the preceding subquestion, viz., q. 1, a. 4, qa. 2: Whether moral virtues are distinguished from intellectual virtues.

e. That is, the rational by essence and the rational by participation.

f. *communionem quandam*

g. Latin text: provisional critical ed. of the Leonine Commission; cf. Moos, 716–18. Parallels: *In III Sent.* d. 26, q. 2, a. 3, qa. 1 (translated in webnote 158; cf. webnote 154); *ST* I-II, q. 62, a. 3; II-II, q. 17, a. 6; *De uirt. in comm.*, aa. 10 & 12; *Super I Cor.* 13, lec. 2 and lec. 4.

h. In the preceding subquestion (q. 1, a. 4, qa. 3).

2. Further, wisdom is about divine things, whereas science is about creatures. Therefore wisdom, too, is a theological virtue.

3. Further, adoration gives honor to God.[a] But the giving of honor to God has God as its object. Therefore adoration is a theological virtue.

4. Further, faith has God as its object insofar as he is the first truth, hope insofar as he is the highest bountifulness or majesty, and charity insofar as he is the highest goodness. Therefore since many other [perfections] are attributed to God, it seems that there are also more theological virtues than the three mentioned.

On the contrary:

5. It seems that there are *only two*, since working toward an end presupposes only knowledge of the end, which faith supplies, and desire for the end, which charity supplies. Therefore it seems that there are only two theological virtues.

6. Again, it seems that there is *only one*, since charity alone attains to God. But every virtue attains to its object. Therefore charity alone has God as its object, and so it alone ought to be called a theological virtue.

7. Again, it seems that there are *three*, because of what it says in 1 Corinthians 13: "Now faith, hope, and charity remain, these three."

8. Further, by theological virtues we are conformed to the Trinity. Therefore there ought to be three.

Response:

It should be said that theological virtues bring about in us an inclination to the last end, namely God, as was said.[b] Now, in everything that acts voluntarily for the sake of an end, prerequisite are two things that it must have in regard to the end before it can act for the end—namely, knowledge of the end and the intention of arriving at the end. But in order to intend the end, two things are required: the possibility of reaching the end (since nothing moves toward what is impossible to reach)[c] and the end's goodness (since intention is only of what is good).

And therefore faith is required, as making known the end; and hope, which gives someone confidence of attaining the last end as an end that is possible for him to attain;[d] and charity, through which the end is reckoned a good belonging to the very one intending it, insofar

---

a. *Latria colit Deum.* In religious contexts *colere* means "pay worship to" or "give honor to"; the nominative form is *cultus.*

b. In the preceding subquestion (q. 1, a. 4, qa. 3).

c. *possibilitas finis, quia nichil mouetur ad impossibile*

d. *spes, secundum quam inest fiducia de consequtione finis ultimi, quasi de re possibili*

as it makes man have affection for the end,[a] for otherwise he would never tend to it.[154]

Replies to objections:

1. To the first, therefore, it should be said that fear does not name a motion toward God, but rather a flight from him, insofar as man, in considering God's majesty, through reverence shrinks back to his own smallness.[b] And therefore it does not name something needed for motion toward the end.

2. To the second, it should be said that in the wayfaring state, wisdom is "about divine things" in the sense in which we come to know the Creator by reasoning about his creatures.[155] Hence it is not about God as he is in himself, i.e., as an end elevated above the ability of nature, as is the virtue of faith.

3. To the third, it should be said that adoration has as its object not God but that which we offer to God as due to him; but it has God as its proximate end.[156] Hence it is not a theological virtue but [part of] a cardinal virtue.

4. To the fourth, it should be said that theological virtues are distinguished not according to divine attributes, but according to the things that are needed in the one who acts for the sake of an end so that he may act for that end.[c, 157]

5. To the fifth, it should be said that knowledge of and affection for the end are not enough for man to begin to act for the sake of the end, if he does not have confidence of obtaining the end, since otherwise he would never begin to act at all, especially when the end is elevated above the nature of the one acting.[158]

6. To the sixth, it should be said that charity joins us *really* (in a sense) to God, and so really attains him, which faith and hope do not do. Activity in regard to God does not require this real union, but only that the one who acts be united to him as to the object of activity, as sight is united to what is seen, even at a distance.[d, 159]

---

sibi—literally, "hope, according to which confidence of attaining the last end, as of something possible to him, is present in him."

a. *in quantum facit quod homo afficiatur ad finem*

b. *in quantum homo ex ipsius maiestatis consideratione per reuerentiam resilit in propriam paruitatem*

c. *uirtutes theologice non distinguntur penes attributa diuina, set penes ea que exiguntur in eo qui operatur propter finem, antequam propter finem operetur.* The *antequam* is not to be taken in a temporal sense.

d. *caritas coniungit quodammodo realiter Deo et sic attingit ipsum realiter; quod non facit fides et spes. Nec hoc requiritur ad operationem que est circa Deum, set quod operans uniatur ei quasi obiecto operationis, sicut uisus uisibili etiam distanti.*

QUESTION 3[a]   On the formation of faith

ARTICLE 1[b]   The formation of faith through charity

SUBQUESTION 1[c]   Whether faith is formed through charity

Objections:

It seems that faith is not formed through charity.

1. For it belongs to form to precede,[d] since it is a thing's principle. But charity is posterior to faith, as was said.[e] Therefore faith is not formed through charity.

2. Further, everything has species from its proper form. But faith, according to its species, differs from charity. Therefore charity is not the form of faith.

3. Further, there are not different forms of one thing. But faith is formed through grace; therefore it is not formed through charity.

On the contrary:

1. Faith without charity cannot elicit a meritorious act, which it does elicit with the coming of charity. Therefore charity gives some force to faith, and thus it seems to form it in some way.

2. Further, the form of a thing is its beauty.[f] But faith comes to be beautiful, in such a way that it becomes acceptable to God, through charity. Therefore charity forms faith.

Response:

It should be said that in ordered agents the ends of the secondary agents are ordered to the end of the primary agent, as the whole universe is ordered to the good that is God, in the way that an army is ordered to the leader's good, as the Philosopher says in *Metaphysics* XI;[g] and therefore the action of the primary agent is both prior and poste-

a. For the division of articles in this and the preceding questions of the commentary on Distinction 23, see textual note a on p. 99.

b. Latin text: provisional critical ed. of the Leonine Commission; cf. Moos, 741–46.

c. Parallels: *ST* II-II, q. 4, a. 3 and q. 23, a. 8; *De ueritate*, q. 14, a. 5; *De caritate*, a. 3.

d. *forme est precedere*—that is, to precede other aspects of a thing in the order of being.

e. In a. 5 of the preceding question, on the priority of faith to all other infused virtues.

f. beauty . . . beautiful: *decor . . . decora*

g. Aristotle, *Metaphysics* XI, ch. 10 (1075a12ff.).

rior: prior in moving, because the actions of all the secondary agents
are founded upon the action of the first agent, the effect of whom—
since he is one, establishing all things commonly—is made specific in
this or that thing according to the requirements of each,[a] just as by one
command of the leader in charge of waging war, one soldier takes up
a sword, another equips a horse, and so forth; posterior, however, in
making use of the others' acts with a view to the end proper to him;
and thus, all the actions of the other agents are given their due mode[b]
through the primary agent's action.

Since therefore the will has the place of primary mover among the
powers of the soul, its action[c] is prior in a certain way to the acts of
the other powers, insofar as it *commands* them according to an intention of the last end and *uses* them for the attainment of this end. And
therefore the powers moved by the will receive two things from it.
First, they receive something of its form, according as every mover and
agent impresses its likeness upon the things moved by it and suffering
from it. Now this form is either according to the form of the will itself
(according to which all the powers moved by the will participate in
its freedom) or according to a habit perfecting the will, which is charity; and thus, all habits that are in powers moved by a will that is itself
perfected with charity[d] participate in charity's form. Nevertheless, this
form, in which the powers moved by the will participate, is common
to all of them. Hence, beyond this common form, the habits that are
the perfections of those powers have their own specific forms, which
perfect a power according to that which suits it by comparison to its
own acts and objects.[e] Second, they receive from the will consummation in the last end;[f] [160] and in this way charity is called the end of the
other virtues, insofar as they are joined to the last end through it.

Since, then, faith is in the intellect insofar as the intellect is moved
by the will, as was said above,[g] it follows that it is formed by the form
common to it and the other virtues—that is, through charity, which is
the will's perfection—yet beyond that common form it has also a spe-

---

a. *secundum exigentiam illius*

b. *modificantur*

c. Leonine: *actio*; Moos: *actus*

d. Moos/Leonine: *in uiribus motis a uoluntate caritate perfecta*; the Parma ed.
omits *caritate*.

e. *Vnde preter eam habitus, qui sunt perfectiones earum, habent speciales formas, secundum quod congruit potentie quam perficiunt, per comparationem ad actus et obiecta*

f. *recipiunt a uoluntate consumationem in fine*

g. In the present Distinction, q. 2, a. 2, qa. 1, response (Moos, p. 725, §140),
and ibid., a. 4, qa. 1, response (Moos, p. 736, §196–§199).

cific form derived from the *ratio* of its proper object and the power in which it is.[a] And in like manner, it receives consummation through charity.[161]

Replies to objections:

1. To the first, therefore, it should be said that faith, as such, precedes charity, since the act of will that is required for faith [namely, to be willing to believe] is able to exist without charity.[b] Formed faith, on the contrary, follows after charity.

2. To the second, it should be said that all virtues converge upon the last end; hence, their acts differ not according to the mode they receive from their order to this end, which mode charity gives to them, but rather according to the mode they have from the nature of the power in which they are, and its proper object. And according to *this* form, faith is distinguished from charity, and again, according to *this* form, is not formed by charity.[162]

3. To the third, it should be said that faith is formed by grace through the mediation of charity, since it is insofar as an act of faith comes from charity that it is accepted by God.

SUBQUESTION 2[c]   Whether unformed faith is a virtue

Objections:

Furthermore, it seems that unformed faith is a virtue.

1. For Augustine says in the book *Of True Innocence*[d] that virtues other than charity can be in the good and in the evil. Therefore faith, insofar as it is a virtue, can be in the evil. But the faith that is in the evil is unformed faith. Therefore unformed faith is a virtue.

2. Further, virtue is about difficult things, and gets praise owing to this, as the Philosopher says.[e] But it is most difficult to believe the articles of faith. Accordingly, Augustine says (and the quotation is given in

---

a. *Quia ergo fides, ut dictum est, est in intellectu secundum quod mouetur a uoluntate, ideo per caritatem, que est perfectio uoluntatis, formatur forma communi sibi et aliis uirtutibus. Tamen preter eam habet formam specialem ex ratione proprii obiecti et potentie in qua est.*

b. *Fides precedit simpliciter caritatem, quia uelle quod ad fidem exigitur sine caritate esse potest*

c. Parallels: *ST* I-II, q. 62, a. 3, ad 2 and q. 65, a. 4; II-II, q. 4, a. 5; *De ueritate,* q. 14, aa. 3 & 6; *De spe,* a. 3, ad 8; *Quodl.* VI, a. 4.

d. Moos (p. 742, n. 1) traces the reference to Prosper of Aquitaine's *Sentences,* no. 7 (CCSL 68A:258).

e. Aristotle, *Ethics* II, chs. 2–4 (1105a12–1106a1).

the following Distinction)ᵃ that "the praise of faith is to believe what it does not see."ᵇ Therefore it seems that unformed faith, which believes all the articles of faith, is a virtue.

3. Further, nothing is opposed to a vice unless it is either the contrary virtue or [another, incompatible] vice.¹⁶³ But the vice of infidelity is opposed to unformed faith. Since therefore unformed faith is not a vice, it seems that it is a virtue.

On the contrary:

1. Unformed faith is dead, as is said in James 2.ᶜ But nothing dead has the *ratio* of virtue.ᵈ Therefore unformed faith is not a virtue.

2. Further, no one makes a bad use of virtue, as Augustine says.ᵉ But some make a bad use of unformed faith.¹⁶⁴ Therefore unformed faith is not a virtue.

Response:

It should be said that it belongs to virtue to make an act perfect. But an act of a power that is moved by another power cannot be perfect unless both the superior and the inferior powers are perfected through habits—the superior, in order that it not fall short in directing or moving the act, and the inferior, in order that it not fall short in executing the act. This is evident in the act of the concupiscible power, the perfection of which requires that the concupiscible power be perfected through the habit of temperance, and, at the same time, that reason be perfected through the habit of prudence—because if prudence is lacking in the reason, then no matter how much of a disposition to the act of temperance there should be in the concupiscible power, that disposition will not have the *ratio* of virtue, as the Philosopher says in *Ethics* VI.ᶠ

Since, then, to believe is an act of the intellect insofar as it is moved by the will, it is necessary for the perfection of this act that both the intellect and the will be perfected—the intellect through the light of faith and the will through the habit of charity. And therefore unformed faith does not have a perfect act, and as a result it cannot be a virtue.

a. That is, in the opening lines of Lombard's Distinction 24, where the first *auctoritas* is this passage of Augustine.

b. Augustine, *On the Gospel of John* 14:29–31, tract. 79, n. 1 (CCSL 36:525).

c. "For as the body apart from the spirit is dead, so faith apart from works is dead" (Jas. 2:26, RSV).

d. The phrase here, *ratio uirtutis,* is to be taken in its most basic sense: a dead thing has no power to *do* anything, much less do something good.

e. Augustine, *On Free Choice of the Will* II, ch. 19 (CCSL 29:271).

f. Aristotle, *Ethics* VI, ch. 13 (1143b15ff.).

Replies to objections:

1. To the first, therefore, it should be said that Augustine uses the name "virtue" broadly for whatever disposition inclines to an act by which good is done.

2. To the second, it should be said that to have a virtue, it is not only necessary that a man *do* the things belonging to a virtue (e.g., that he do just or brave things), but also necessary that he do them in the *manner* in which the virtuous man does them[a]—even though in some way, from the very fact that he does the things belonging to a virtue, he can be praised. But as is clear from what has been said, this manner is wanting[b] in the act of unformed faith; and therefore it is not a virtue.

3. To the third, it should be said that even a disposition to virtue is opposed to vice; hence it is not necessary that unformed faith, which is opposed to infidelity, be a virtue.

SUBQUESTION 3[c]   Whether formed and unformed
faith differ in species

Objections:

Furthermore, it seems that formed and unformed faith differ in species.

1. For, as the Philosopher says in *Metaphysics* V,[d] things that differ in genus differ also in species. But formed and unformed faith differ in genus, since formed faith is a virtue, but unformed faith is not. Therefore formed and unformed faith differ in species.

2. Further, the species of a thing comes from its form. But charity is the form of faith. Therefore unformed faith does not belong to the same species as formed faith.

3. Further, an act that is the same in species belongs to what has the same form according to species. But the act of formed faith is to believe unto God,[e, 165] whereas this is not the act of unformed faith. Therefore formed and unformed faith differ in species.

a. In this sentence and the next, "manner" translates *modus.*

b. *Hic autem modus . . . deficit*

c. Parallels: *ST* II-II, q. 4, a. 4; *De ueritate,* q. 14, a. 7; *Super Rom.* 1, lec. 6.

d. The probable *locus* is *Metaphysics* V, chs. 9 & 10 (cf. *In Metaphys.* V, lec. 12), though a passage in ch. 6 is also relevant (1016b31–1017a3). Moos also sends us to *Metaphysics* X, ch. 8 (1058a17–28).

e. *credere in Deum,* to believe in such a way that one draws near to God through love.

On the contrary:

1. Habits are diversified by acts and objects. But formed and un-formed faith do not differ with respect to the proper object of faith, which is the first Truth.[a] Therefore formed and unformed faith do not differ in species.

2. Further, that which is outside the essence of a thing does not change its species, just as the light that comes to the air from a shining body [does not change the air's essence].[b] But charity is a habit sepa-rate from faith in essence. Therefore faith formed by charity does not differ in species from unformed faith.

Response:

It should be said that one comes to know a difference in habits from evaluating their acts.[c] Now it happens that some acts may be consid-ered in two ways: either according to natural species or according to moral species.[d, 166] And sometimes they converge in species with re-spect to one description but differ according to another,[e] just as killing the harmful and killing the innocent do not differ according to natural species, yet they do differ according to moral species, since one is an act of vice (viz., of murder), while the other is an act of virtue (viz., of justice); whereas the acts of killing a thief and giving him lashes[f] differ according to natural species, yet converge in moral species, since they are both acts of justice.

If therefore the acts of formed and unformed faith are considered according to natural species, in this way they are the same in species, since an act gets its natural species from its proper object; whereas if they are considered according to moral being,[g] then they differ as com-plete and incomplete in the same species, even as an act by which one does just things, but not precisely *as* just, differs from an act by which one does just things precisely as just. And similarly, formed and un-

a. Leonine: *ueritas prima;* Parma and Moos: *veritas una*

b. *Illud quod est extra essentiam rei non uariat speciem, sicut lumen adueniens aeri ex corpore lucenti.* The Parma and Moos eds. read, for the last phrase, *in corpore lucenti,* which makes no philosophical sense.

c. *differentia habituum pensanda est ex actibus*

d. *uel secundum speciem nature, uel secundum speciem moris*

e. *Et quandoque conueniunt secundum speciem quantum ad unum dictorum et differ-unt secundum aliud*

f. The example offered is notably different in the critical and non-critical edi-tions. The Leonine has *occidere latronem et uerberare;* the Moos has *occidere latronem et liberare innocentem.*

g. *esse moris*

formed faith are wholly the same in natural species, yet they differ in moral species—not as if existing in simply different species, but rather as perfect and imperfect in the same species, in the way that a *disposition* to virtue and the *habit* of virtue differ.[a]

Replies to objections:

1. To the first, therefore, it should be said that virtue is the genus of faith according to moral being. However, unformed faith is not wholly outside of this genus, but exists in it as something imperfect.

2. To the second, it should be said that a virtue gets its natural species from the form it has owing to the *ratio* of the power in which it is, as well as its proper object; but it gets its moral species from the form it has from the moving and directing power. And therefore it does not follow that formed and unformed faith differ in species, except as was explained.

3. To the third, it should be said (as was said above) that by those three descriptions, an act numerically one is designated with respect to different things.[b, 167] Hence, there is something in the act of formed faith that is not in the act of unformed faith, but nevertheless it is not wholly other.

ARTICLE 4[c]   The change from unformed
faith to formed faith

SUBQUESTION 1   Whether unformed faith is
emptied out at the coming of charity

Objections:

It seems that unformed faith is emptied out at the coming of charity.

1. "When what is perfect arrives, what is partial will be emptied out" (1 Cor. 13:10), as faith will be emptied out with the coming of vision. But unformed faith is imperfect with respect to formed faith.

---

a. *non quasi in diuersis speciebus existentes set sicut perfectum et imperfectum in eadem specie, sicut dispositio et habitus uirtutis*

b. *per illa tria unus numero actus designatur quantum ad diuersa*

c. The second and third articles are not translated here. (For a *divisio textus* of the commentary on d. 23, see textual note a on p. 99.) Latin text for a. 4: provisional critical ed. of the Leonine Commission; cf. Moos, 752–55. Parallels: *ST* II-II, q. 4, a. 4; *De ueritate*, q. 14, a. 7; *Super Rom.* 1, lec. 6.

Therefore unformed faith is taken away at the coming of formed faith.

2. Further, unformed faith is the principle of servile fear. But servile fear is taken away at the coming of charity; therefore unformed faith as well.

3. Further, grace, when it comes, does not have less efficacy in the faithful than in the infidel. But in the infidel it causes the habit of faith;[a] therefore it doe the same in the faithful who has formed faith. But formed and unformed faith are of the same species, as is evident from what has been said.[b] Therefore, since two forms of one species cannot be simultaneously in the same subject, it is necessary that unformed faith be taken away at the coming of charity and grace.

On the contrary:

1. Infused gifts are more permanent than acquired [habits]. But the coming of grace does not take away acquired habits; therefore much less does it take away the infused habit of faith.[168]

2. Further, nothing is corrupted except by its contrary. But unformed faith is not contrary to grace, because habits of good are not contrary to each other, but only habits of evil, or a habit of good to a habit of evil. Therefore unformed faith, strictly as a habit, is not taken away at the coming of charity.

Response:

It should be said that when that which does not pertain to a thing's species is removed, it need not be the case that a thing's substance is also taken away, just as if darkness is taken away from the air, the air still remains. Now the unformedness of faith does not pertain to the species of faith, because faith owes its species to the mode it has from the nature of the power in which it exists as in a subject, by relation to its proper object.[169] Now faith is called "formed" and "unformed" relative to something extrinsic, namely the will, as was said,[c] just as air is formed by light in relation to a luminous body;[d] and therefore it is evident that unformedness does not pertain to the species of faith [as such]. Since therefore charity, when it comes, takes away nothing from faith except its unformedness, it stands that the substance of the *habit* of faith still remains.

a. Leonine: *fidei habitum*; Moos: *totum fidei habitum*

b. In the last item translated prior to this article—a. 1, qa. 3 of the present question.

c. In the present Distinction (d. 23) and question (q. 3), a. 1, qa. 1, translated above.

d. *sicut aer formatur lumine per oppositionem luminosi corporis*

Replies to objections:

1. To the first, therefore, it should be said that the imperfection that faith has with respect to vision is according to the genus of knowledge, and therefore it pertains to the species of faith [as such]; and on account of this, faith is emptied out with the coming of vision. But it is not so in the case at hand, as was said.

2. To the second, it should be said that even servile fear is not taken away with respect to the habit of fear, but only with respect to its characteristic of servility.[170]

3. To the third, it should be said that, in the one who has faith, grace does not cause *another* habit of faith—and this is not because the grace lacks efficacy, but because the subject of grace cannot receive something that it already has.[a]

SUBQUESTION 2   Whether the act of unformed faith
is emptied out at the coming of charity

Objections:

Furthermore, it seems that even if unformed faith remains as a *habit,* it does not remain in regard to its *act.*

1. For even if something good is done by an act of unformed faith, nevertheless it is not something done well. But something *is* done well by an act of formed faith. Therefore at the coming of charity, unformed faith does not remain with respect to its act.

2. Further, a lesser light does not continue to give illumination once a greater light is present. But unformed faith is a lesser light than charity. Therefore, once charity is present, the act of unformed faith does not remain.

3. Further, each virtuous man works to the best of his ability,[b] just as nature does. But the act of formed faith, which the virtuous man who has charity exercises, is better than the act of unformed faith. Therefore in this man the act of unformed faith is left idle, just as one who can know something through a demonstrative syllogism does not care to consider the same thing through a dialectical syllogism.

---

a. *Et hoc non est per inefficaciam gratie, set accidit ex parte subiecti, quod non potest recipere id quod iam habet*

b. *Vnusquisque uirtuosus operatur quanto melius potest*

On the contrary:

1. Much less can something be in vain in moral things than in natural things, and especially with respect to infused habits. But a habit without an act is vain, because an act is its end, just as an act is also the end of a power. Therefore there is no *habit* of faith without a corresponding *act*.

2. Further, the act of unformed faith is to believe God or to believe in God.[a] But with the coming of charity, this act remains. Therefore the act of unformed faith is not emptied out.

Response:

It should be said that even as the habit of unformed faith remains but without its unformedness, so the act of the habit also remains but without *its* unformedness, since "a habit is that by which someone acts when the time for acting has come," as Augustine says.[b]

Replies to objections:

1. To the first, therefore, it should be said that the fact that someone does good through unformed faith pertains to the *substance* of the habit, and therefore this remains [with the coming of charity]; whereas the fact that he does something good but not well pertains to its unformedness, and therefore this does not remain.

2. To the second, it should be said that the light that is unformed faith and the light that is charity do not compete for the same intelligible territory; consequently, charity at its coming does not have the effect of darkening faith, but rather brings it to completion, since faith is as matter with respect to charity.[c]

3. To the third, it should be said that it is by reason of its unformedness that the act of unformed faith falls short of the act of formed faith, and according to this feature it does not remain.

---

a. *Actus fidei informis est credere Deo uel Deum*

b. Augustine, *On the Good of Marriage,* ch. 21, n. 25 (PL 40:390; the semi-critical edition of the *Corpus Scriptorum Ecclesiasticorum Latinorum* is reproduced, with modifications, in *Augustine: De Bono Coniugali, De Sancta Virginitate,* ed. and trans. P. G. Walsh [Oxford: Clarendon Press, 2001]).

c. Some liberties have been taken to make the reply more readable. Thomas writes: *lumen fidei informis et caritatis non sunt unius rationis, et ideo unum non obfuscat aliud, set perficit illud, cum unum sit materiale respectu alterius.*

SUBQUESTION 3   Whether unformed faith becomes
formed at the coming of charity

Objections:

Furthermore, it seems that unformed faith cannot become formed
faith.

1. For unformed faith is dead, as is said in James 2.[a] But a dead work
is not something that can be made alive. Therefore neither is unformed
faith made alive through the form of charity.

2. Further, faith is an accident. But as Boethius says, "accidents cannot be changed."[b] Therefore it seems that the very same faith that was
unformed cannot become formed.

3. Further, something one does not come to be out of two accidents.
But the arriving grace is one accident. Therefore it does not form the
prior unformed faith, but causes a new habit of formed faith.

On the contrary:

1. Nature always works in the shortest way; therefore, it is similar
in the workings of grace. But to form a habit hitherto unformed is a
shorter way than to infuse a new habit. Therefore what gets informed
is the same faith that was hitherto unformed.[c]

2. Further, infused habits have more in common with grace than
with a natural power. But an imperfect and unformed natural power
is formed at the coming of grace; therefore much more is the habit of
unformed faith so formed.

Response:

It should be said (as the Philosopher says in *Ethics* VI)[d] that prior
to the complete being[e] of moral virtue in a man, there exists a certain
natural inclination to that virtue, which is called "natural virtue"; and
this inclination takes on the *ratio* of virtue insofar as it receives perfection from a superior power, namely reason.

And in like manner, unformed faith preexists in the intellect prior

a. "For as the body apart from the spirit is dead, so faith apart from works is
dead" (Jas. 2:26, RSV).

b. Precisely as individual accidents: *this* white cannot be changed into *this*
black. The reference is to Boethius, *On Aristotle's Categories* I (PL 64:199).

c. *Natura semper operatur uia breuissima. Ergo similiter et gratia. Set hec uia est magis breuis, ut habitus prius informis formetur quam quod nouus habitus infundatur. Ergo
illa fides que prius erat informis formatur.*

d. Aristotle, *Ethics* VI, ch. 13 (1144b16).

e. *ante completum esse*

to the complete being of virtue, but it receives the *ratio* of virtue from the perfection of a superior power, namely the will. Hence, one and the same faith that beforehand was unformed afterwards becomes formed; nor is the faith that arrives something other [than the faith that was already there], since formed and unformed faith do not differ in species, as is evident from what has been said. But it is not possible for two forms of one species to exist at the same time [in the same subject], because forms are diversified in number by reason of a diversity of matter or subject.

Replies to objections:

1. To the first, therefore, it should be said that a dead work passes away, and cannot be taken up again the same in number, and therefore it cannot be made alive. But an unformed habit endures, and therefore it can be formed.

2. To the second, it should be said that an accident changes not as though *it* were the subject of change, but because its subject stands in various ways with respect to it, [and thus] its subject is the subject of change, as is evident in the intensification and remission of heat.[171]

3. To the third, it should be said not that one accident comes to be out of grace and faith, but rather, the mode of charity comes to be participated in in such a way that it gives rise to the perfection of faith, just as the mode of prudence is participated in in such a way that it gives rise to the perfection of moral virtue. And therefore charity, when it comes, is said to form the preexistent faith.

DISTINCTION 27[a] [LOVE AND CHARITY IN THEMSELVES]

Division of the text

"Since, however, Christ did not have the virtues of faith and hope but did have the virtue of charity. . ." After the Master has determined about faith and hope, here, in the third place, he determines about charity.

This consideration is divided into two parts. In the first, he considers the charity by which we love God; in the second, the charity by which God loves us (Distinction 32), where he says: "To the aforesaid should be added that which concerns the love of God by which he loves us."[b]

The former is divided into two parts. In the first, he determines about charity itself; in the second, about the duration of charity (Distinction 31), where he says: "Nor should it be overlooked that some assert that charity, once possessed, cannot be lost."[c]

The former is divided into two parts. In the first, he determines about the love of charity itself; in the second, about those things that are loved by charity (Distinction 28), where he says: "Here it may be asked whether in the commandment to love our neighbor, we are commanded to love the whole neighbor, i.e., soul and body, and the whole self."[d]

The former is divided into three parts. In the first, he makes a connection with preceding topics; in the second, he pursues his intention, where he says: "Charity is the love by which God is loved"; in the third, he makes a connection to subsequent topics, where he says: "But we ask: which things ought to be loved by this love?"

The second of these parts is divided into two parts. In the first, he determines about the love of charity as it is commanded by the two commandments [love of God and love of neighbor]; in the second, he shows that these two commandments mutually include one another,

---

a. Latin text: provisional critical ed. of the Leonine Commission; cf. Moos ed., 852–900.

b. For Aquinas's commentary on Distinction 32, see below at p. 307.

c. For Aquinas's commentary on Distinction 31, see below at p. 262.

d. For Aquinas's commentary on Distinction 28, see below at p. 183.

where he says: "Although there are two commandments of charity, one is often set down for both."

The first of these is divided into two parts. In the first, he considers the love of charity according to which we are commanded by two commandments to love two, namely God and neighbor; in the second he looks into the mode of love with respect to each object of love, where he says: "Next, we turn to the mode of each love."

Concerning the first, he does two things. First, he shows that God and neighbor are loved by charity; second, he shows that they are loved by the same charity, where he says: "Here we pose the question: is God loved by the same love by which the neighbor is loved?"

"Next, we turn to the mode of each love." Here he shows the mode of the aforesaid love, first with respect to love of neighbor, second with respect to love of God, where he says: "The mode of the love of God is implied when it is said 'from the whole heart.'"

And concerning this topic, he does three things. First, he shows the mode of our love with respect to God; second, he shows where that mode can be observed, where he says: "That commandment is not wholly fulfilled by man in this mortal life"; third, he raises a certain question, where he says: "But why is man commanded to pursue that perfection?"

Here we will treat three questions: first, about love in general [Question 1]; second, about charity [Question 2]; third, about the act and mode of charity [Question 3].

QUESTION 1   On love in general

Regarding the first, we will inquire into four things: (1) what love is; (2) that in which it is; (3) how it compares to other affections of the soul; (4) how it compares to things that are in knowledge.[a]

ARTICLE 1[b, 172]   What is love?

We proceed to the first article. In chapter 4 of *On the Divine Names*, Dionysius defines love thus: "Love is a unitive and concretive power [*uirtus*], moving superiors to exercise providence for those having less," i.e., their inferiors; "further, moving coordinated things," i.e.,

---

a. *de comparatione eius ad ea que in cognitione sunt*

b. General parallels: *ST* I, q. 20, a. 1; I-II, q. 28; *In De div. nom.* 4, lec. 12. More specific parallels will be noted where apposite.

equals, "to a communicative relationship with each other; and finally, moving subjects," i.e., inferiors, "to turn themselves toward better
things," i.e., their superiors.[a, 173]

Objections to the definition:

But it seems that here love is unfittingly defined.

1. For no passion is a virtue [*uirtus*], as is said in *Ethics* II.[b] But love is
a passion. Therefore it is not a virtue.

2. Further, Augustine says that love is of something now had.[c] But
whatever is now had, is in a certain way united to oneself. Therefore
love is not a *unitive* power, but one following upon union.

3. Further, that which is more preserved in unlikeness than in likeness does not have the force of uniting. But love is more preserved in
unlikeness, for we see that artisans of the same art, for example, pot-
ters, quarrel with each other, but with other artisans they live peace-
fully. Similarly, an empty stomach loves the food that a full stomach
abhors. Therefore love does not have the force of uniting.

4. Further, in *The Celestial Hierarchy* Dionysius sets down "piercing"[d]
and "burning"[e] among the properties of love,[f] and "melting," too, is set
down as love's effect, as in the Song of Songs: "My soul melted when
my beloved spoke" (5:6). In chapter 4 of *On the Divine Names* Dionysius
also sets down "ecstasy,"[g] i.e., being placed outside oneself, as love's
effect. But all these things seem to pertain to division. The piercing is
what divides by penetrating; the burning, what dissolves by exhalations. Melting, too, is a kind of division opposed to freezing. And that
which is placed outside itself is divided from itself. Therefore love is
more a divisive force than a unitive one.

5. Further, as every concretion is a certain union, it was therefore
superfluous to set down both "unitive" and "concretive" in the definition of love.

6. Further, love is a passion. But it does not belong to passion to
move, but rather to be an effect of motion and action. Therefore love is
not something *moving* superiors, as he says.

7. Further, it is from their proper forms that superiors are inclined

---

a. Pseudo-Dionysius, *On the Divine Names,* ch. 4, n. 15 (PG 3:714).

b. Aristotle, *Ethics* II, ch. 4 (1105b28).

c. Augustine, *Expositions of the Psalms,* Ps. 118, Serm. 8, n. 4 (CCSL 40:1688).

d. *acutum:* piercing, sharp, acute

e. *feruidum:* burning, fiery, seething

f. Pseudo-Dionysius, *The Celestial Hierarchy,* ch. 7, n. 1 (PG 3:206).

g. "Ecstasy" always and only translates the word *extasis,* and "melting," *lique-
factio.*

to act upon inferiors. But by acting upon them they provide for them. Hence, to move superiors to provide for their inferiors belongs not to *love* but to *nature*.

8. Further, everything that communicates something to something else is given preference to the recipient.[a] Therefore it does not belong to equals to share *mutually* with each other through love.

9. Further, everything which is done from love proceeds from an intrinsic principle, since what is done from love is voluntary. But the turning of inferiors toward superiors is from an extrinsic principle, namely, from the very action of the superiors by which they assimilate the inferiors to themselves. Therefore love does not turn inferiors toward superiors.

Response:

It should be said that love pertains to appetite. Appetite, however, is a passive power [*uirtus*]. Whence in *On the Soul* III the Philosopher says that the appetible good moves as an unmoved mover, whereas appetite moves as a moved mover.[b] Now, every passive principle is brought to perfection insofar as it is formed by the form of its corresponding active principle,[c] and in this [active principle, through being so informed,] its motion reaches its term, and it comes to rest. We see this in the case of intellect: before it is formed by an intelligible form, it inquires and doubts, but as soon as it is so informed, its inquiry ceases and the intellect fastens upon that form, and then the intellect is said to adhere firmly to that thing. Similarly, when the affection or appetite is wholly imbued by the form of a good that is an object for it, it finds the good suitable[d] and adheres to it as though fixed upon it; and then it is said to love it. Whence love is nothing other than a certain transformation[174] of affection into the thing loved.[e] And since anything that is made the

a. *Omne quod communicat aliquid alicui prefertur illi*

b. Aristotle, *On the Soul* III, ch. 10 (433b).

c. *Omne autem passiuum perficitur secundum quod formatur per formam sui actiui*

d. The phrase here is impossible to translate literally: *complacet sibi in illo.* Thomas is not saying that the affection or appetite "is pleased by" or "takes delight in" the good, for that would be *delectatio* or *gaudium*; one must think rather of *complacentia* in the philosophical sense Thomas develops for it, namely, a taking of the object to be well suited to oneself, experiencing the object as proportionate or fitted to oneself (cf. webnotes 54 and 173). *After* this initial stage, *out of* the basic adaptation of appetite to appetible, follow other acts of appetite such as desire for an absent good and delight in a present good.

e. *rem amatum.* Notice that Thomas is approaching the subject from a general and objective standpoint; he speaks here of a "thing loved," which could be, in principle, *any* object of love, personal or impersonal. Quite soon in the response, however,

form of something is made one with it, through love the lover becomes one with what is loved, which becomes the lover's form. And therefore the Philosopher says in *Ethics* IX that "a friend is another self";[a] and we read in 1 Corinthians 6:17: "Whoever adheres to God is one spirit."[175]

Now, each thing acts according to the demands and needs[b] of its form, which is the principle of acting and the rule of work. But the good loved is the end, and the end is the starting-point in matters of action, as first principles are the starting-point in matters of knowledge. Whence, just as the intellect, once it is informed by the essences of things, is directed thereby to the knowledge of the principles, which principles become known once the terms are known, and is directed further to the knowledge of conclusions that come to be known from the principles, so too, the lover whose affection is informed by the good itself—which has the *ratio* of an end, though not always of the last end—is inclined through love to act according to the demands and needs of the beloved, and such activity is most of all delightful to him, as being suitable to his form.[c] For this reason, whatsoever the lover does or suffers for the beloved, the whole of it is delightful to him, and he is ever more stirred up,[d] insofar as he experiences greater delight in the beloved in all he does or suffers for his sake.[176] And just as fire cannot be restrained, except by violence, from the motion that suits it according to the requirements of its form,[e] so neither can the lover be restrained from acting according to love; and on account of this, Gregory says that love "cannot be lazy, but rather, if it exists at all, it accom-

---

his ideas indicate that he has shifted to the domain of personal love, where the explanation given applies most clearly and fully (even as the *ratio* of appetite is verified most of all in rational appetite, less so in sensitive appetite, and least of all in the natural appetite of unconscious things). For this reason, it would be misleading not to acknowledge the implicit shift to the personal. This we have done by translating *amatum* later in the response as "beloved," though (as indicated in the Introduction, pp. xxiv–xxviii) the word's romantic connotations in modern English need not, and at times must not, be imported. It is not irrelevant to note, moreover, that the noun *amatum,* which is unambiguously neuter in the nominative case, more often appears in this passage in oblique cases, where neuter and masculine genders are identical (*amati, amatum, amato*).

a. Aristotle, *Ethics* IX, ch. 4 (1166a32).

b. The many connotations of *exigentia* should be borne in mind: exigency, necessity, neediness, demands, requirements. The paraphrase "demands and needs" I owe to Christopher Malloy.

c. *quasi forme sue conueniens*

d. *semper magis accenditur* could also be rendered: "he is ever more set on fire, aroused."

e. *Et sicut ignis non potest retineri a motu qui competit sibi secundum exigentiam sue forme nisi per uiolentiam*

plishes great things."[a] And since "every violent thing is saddening, as if repugnant to the will," as is said in *Metaphysics* V,[b] it is therefore painful to work against love's inclination, or even to disregard it,[c] whereas to work according to it is to accomplish those things that are suitable for the beloved.[d] For since the lover takes up the beloved as though he were the same as himself, he must, as it were, act as though he were the beloved in all that regards the beloved.[e] And so, in a way, the lover serves[f] the beloved insofar as he is guided by the beloved's ends.[g]

Accordingly, Dionysius, in the passage cited above, furnishes a most complete definition of love.[h] For where he says that "love is a unitive and concretive power," he sets down the very union between lover and beloved, which comes about through the transformation of the lover's affection into the beloved; and where he says "moving superior things," etc., he sets down love's inclination to accomplish those things that regard the beloved,[i] whether the beloved be a superior, an inferior, or an equal.

Replies to objections:

1. To the first, therefore, it should be said that the word *uirtus* is not used here to refer to a habit, as in *Ethics* II, but more broadly, for anything that can be the principle of some activity or motion. And since love brings about an inclination to activity, as was said, therefore Dionysius calls love a *uirtus*.

2. To the second, it should be said that love is said to be "of something already had" as that which is formed already has its form. But this formation is preceded by the desire that tends toward being formed, as reason precedes understanding or knowledge, and so [from the van-

---

a. Gregory, *Homilies on the Gospels,* Homily 30, n. 2 (CCSL 141:257).

b. Aristotle, *Metaphysics* V, ch. 5 (1015a28).

c. *etiam preter eam*: literally, to work beyond or beside love's inclination.

d. *operari ea que amato competunt*

e. *oportet ut quasi personam amati amans gerat in omnibus que ad amatum spectant.* The idiom *gerit . . . personam* can mean both "wear a mask" and "perform the role of *x*." Taking it in the latter sense, Thomas could be saying that the lover, by identifying himself with the beloved, performs the beloved's role, i.e., he loves the beloved as the beloved loves himself.

f. *inseruit,* which can also have the sense of "takes care of," "looks after," "is devoted to."

g. An attempt to get at the expression *amati terminis regulatur,* which could also mean "the beloved's goals are his rule" or "he is governed on the beloved's terms."

h. *amoris rationem*

i. *ad operandum ea que ad amatum spectant*

tage of desire] love is said to be of something *not* had. Whence love is called a unitive power *formally,* since it *is* the very union or connection or transformation by which the lover is transformed into the beloved and in a way is turned into him. Or it may be said that the quieting of affection suggested by the word "love" can exist only when two are found to be suited for each other, a fittingness that follows the extent of the participation of the one in that which belongs to the other, and in this way, the lover in a sense *has* the beloved.[a] Whence the conjunction implied in "to have" is the conjunction of thing to thing, and this is preceded by the union of thing to affection, which is love.[177]

3. To the third, it should be said that the root of love, absolutely speaking, is the likeness of the beloved to the lover, since it is owing to such a likeness that the beloved is good and suitable for him.[b] But it happens *per accidens* that unlikeness can be a cause of love and likeness a cause of hate, and this, in three ways. In one way, when the affection of the lover is not at rest within itself,[c] nor at rest in his condition or one of his qualities, as when someone hates something in himself. And then it behooves him to love someone else who, in that respect, is unlike himself, since from the very fact that the other is unlike him in condition, he is made like to his affection,[178] and, conversely, he hates whatever is like him and is not made like to his affection.

In a second way, this happens when someone who loves something is prevented from enjoying what he loves owing to that likeness [between himself and another possessor], and this occurs in regard to everything which cannot be possessed simultaneously by many, such as temporal things. Whence the one who loves to get profit or pleasure from a thing is impeded from the enjoyment of what he loves by another who similarly wishes to appropriate that thing to himself. And here is the source of jealousy, which does not allow any sharing of what is loved, and envy, inasmuch as the good of another is judged an impediment to one's own good.[d]

---

a. *quietatio affectus in aliquo quam amor importat non potest esse nisi secundum conuenientiam unius ad alterum, que quidem conuenientia est secundum quod ab uno participatur id quod est alterius, et sic amans quodammodo habet amatum*

b. Parallel treatments of likeness as a cause of love: *ST* I-II, q. 27, a. 3; *Expositio De ebdomadibus,* lec. 2; *Sent. Eth.* VIII, lec. 1; *Super Ioan.* 15, lec. 4.

c. *non sibi complacet:* there is something that strikes a person as repugnant, discordant, in his own being, and so he is not found "pleasing" to himself; his appetite is not at peace.

d. *boni proprii,* one's proper or private good. "Sharing" renders *consortium.* On *zelus* (jealousy, zeal) as an effect of love, see *ST* I-II, q. 28, a. 4; *Super I Cor.* 14, lec. 1; *Super II Cor.* 11, lec. 1; *In De div. nom.* 4, lec. 10; *Super Ioan.* 2, lec. 2.

In a third way, this happens when an unlikeness that comes before causes one to perceive more keenly a love that comes afterwards. For since we sense precisely when the sense-power is moved (which motion ceases when the sensible is now made the form of the power sensing), we do not perceive those things to which we have grown accustomed, as is evident with a builder whose ears are full of the sound of hammers. And it is for this reason that love is felt more keenly when the affection has been newly transformed into the beloved by the force of love. Hence, when someone does not have the beloved really present, he or she burns for the beloved and is in dire straits,[a] for the love is then more keenly perceived, although in the beloved's presence, love is not less, but only less perceived.[b]

4. To the fourth, it should be said that in love there is a union of lover and beloved, but there is also a threefold division. For by the fact that love transforms the lover into the beloved, it makes the lover enter into the interior of the beloved and *vice versa,* so that nothing of the beloved remains not united to the lover,[c] just as a form reaches to the innermost recesses of that which it informs and *vice versa.*[179] Thus, the lover in a way penetrates into the beloved, and so love is called "piercing"; for to come into the innermost recesses of a thing by dividing it is characteristic of something piercing. In the same way does the beloved penetrate the lover, reaching to his innermost recesses, and that is why it is said that love "wounds," and that it "transfixes the innards."[d, 180] But because nothing can be transformed into another

a. *magis feruet et artatur. Artatur* means wedged in, tightened, compressed, cramped. "In dire straits" seemed an idiomatic choice, but "hard pressed" might also work. Note, however, that some manuscripts read *anxiatur,* which makes good sense too: in the beloved's absence one tends to feel a greater anxiety.

b. Some manuscripts add at this point: "Whence Augustine says: 'Love is not felt so much when it does not show itself needy, because what is loved stands ever before it.'"

c. Here, as elsewhere, Thomas beautifully constructs his sentence to reflect the doctrine he expounds: *ut nichil amati amanti remaneat non unitum.* Grammatically, lover and beloved come as close together as possible; nothing stands between them. Other examples include, from the response, a threefold pattern which again echoes its content: "Cum enim *amans amatum* assumpserit quasi idem sibi, oportet ut quasi personam *amati amans* gerat in omnibus que ad amatum spectant. Et sic quodammodo *amans amato* inseruit in quantum amati terminis regulatur."

d. *transfigit iecur.* In medieval physiology the liver (*iecur*) was regarded as the origin of blood, and sometimes as the seat of the passions. The term itself, anatomical in its first imposition, signifies an organ or part of the body with many properties—the hidden innards, the seat of vital fire, the "domicile of life," the source of nourishment, the origin of veins and of blood, and so forth. Even if Thomas knew of only some of these properties, this would add subtle shades of meaning to the statement he makes here.

without withdrawing, in a way, from its own form, since of a single thing there is a single form, therefore preceding this division of penetration is another division by which the lover, in tending toward the beloved, is separated from himself. And according to this, love is said to bring about ecstasy and to burn,ª since that which burns rises beyond itself and vanishes into smoke.ᵇ, ¹⁸¹ Further still, because nothing withdraws from itself unless it is unbound from what was containing it within itself, as a natural thing does not lose its form unless the dispositions retaining this form in the matter are unbound,ᶜ it is therefore necessary that that boundedness by which the lover was contained within his own boundsᵈ be taken away from him. And that is why love is said to "melt the heart," for a liquid is not contained by its own limits, while the contrary disposition is called "hardness of heart."ᵉ, ¹⁸²

5. To the fifth, it should be said that union is twofold. For a certain kind of union unifies [only] in a qualified sense, like the union of things brought together by their surfaces touching; and such is not the union of love, since, as was said, the lover is transformed into the inner identity of the beloved.ᶠ There is another union that unifies simply speaking, like the union of continuous things and of form and matter; and such is the union of love, since love makes the beloved the lover's form. Thus, in addition to "union" Dionysius adds "concretion," in order to differentiate it from the first union, since those things are called "thoroughly mingled"ᵍ which are made to be simply one. Accordingly, another version gives "continuative."ʰ, ¹⁸³

a. The word *extasis* is being employed here in its strictly etymological sense: *ek-stasis,* a standing outside oneself. The phrase *dicitur amor extasim facere et feruere* means that love does this to, or in, the lover, as if to say: "love causes one to be in ecstasy and makes one burn."

b. *quod feruet extra se ebullit et exalat,* which could also be rendered "that which seethes, boils out of itself and evaporates" or "that which burns, rises outside itself into exhalations."

c. "unbound": *soluto . . . solutis*

d. "boundedness . . . bounds": *terminatio . . . terminos*

e. This reply parallels several articles of *ST* I-II, q. 28 on the effects of love, namely: a. 2 on mutual inherence (*mutua inhaesio*), a. 3 on *extasis,* and a. 5 on whether love is a passion that wounds the lover, which includes a discussion of four proximate effects of love—melting, enjoyment, languor, and burning. The notion of *mutua inhaesio* is briefly treated under the different wording *mutua penetratio per amorem* at *In I Sent.* d. 1, a. 1, while that of *extasis* is given rather full treatments at *ST* II-II, q. 175, a. 2, *In De div. nom.* 4, lec. 10, and *Super II Cor.* 12, lec. 1.

f. *amans in interiora amati transformetur*

g. *concreta,* which here has to be taken in its most literal sense: mingled or mixed together, and thus made solid, condensed, coherent.

h. That is, making the two continuous with one another. The *alia littera* is identified by Moos (p. 858, n. 4) as the version of Scotus Erigena (cf. PL 122:1137).

6. To the sixth, it should be said that appetite, as was said, moves while being moved. Thus passion, since it is moved by what is loved, moves in keeping with the demands and needs of what is loved.

7. To the seventh, it should be said that the very inclination of superiors to provide for inferiors, which is in them owing to their proper forms, is called their love, as will be evident below.[a]

8. To the eighth, it should be said that among things which are equal simply speaking, it is not unfitting that one be greater than another, in precisely that respect in which one is needed by the other.[184]

9. To the ninth, it should be said that the being-turned by which inferiors are turned toward superiors is their being-ordered to an end intended by the superiors.[b] And although the principle of this kind of being-ordered is from without insofar as the inferiors are ordered by those superiors to the ends of the superiors, nevertheless it is from an *intrinsic* principle insofar as there is a certain inclination to this in the inferiors themselves, whether from nature (as in natural love), or from the will (as in animal love). And it is on account of this that God is said to "dispose all things sweetly,"[c] insofar as singular things *of themselves* do that to which they are ordered.

ARTICLE 2[d]   Whether love is only in
the concupiscible power[e]

Objections:

Proceeding to the second, it seems that love is not only in the concupiscible power.

1. For Dionysius, in chapter 4 of *On the Divine Names*, sets down four

a. In article 2.

b. "being-turned": *conuersio*; "being-ordered": *ordinatio*

c. See Wis. 8:1.

d. Parallels: *In III Sent.* d. 26, q. 1, a. 2 (the Moos ed., p. 859, mistakenly lists q. 2, a. 1); *ST* I-II, q. 26, a. 1; cf. I, q. 80, a. 1 and ad 3; I-II, q. 29, a. 1.

e. Thomas simply writes *in concupiscibili*, but the context shows that he is speaking of a *power* or *part* of the soul as the subject of some act of love (hence the article's phrasing: whether love is *in* the concupiscible). There is a disadvantage to the customary translation of *concupiscibilis* as "concupiscible," since this technical-sounding term obscures in English the obvious connection in Latin between the adjective and the verb (e.g., *obiectum concupiscibilis est bonum concupiscenti*, "the object of the desiring power is the good of the one desiring"). On the other hand, the phrase "desiring power" has the fatal weakness of suggesting more than Thomas intends, since for him the concupiscible power, as is made clear further on, is *only* a power of sensitive appetition, its objects being sensi-

kinds of love: "divine, angelic, intellectual, and natural."[a] But whatever is in us pertains to intellect, to animality, or to nature. Hence love may be found in *all* the things that are in us.

2. Further, the commentator there sets down two definitions of love. The first is this: "Love is the connection or chain by which the totality of all things[b] is joined together in ineffable friendship and indissoluble unity." The second is: "Love is the end and quiet resting place[c] of the natural motion of all things that are in motion, beyond which no motion of the creature extends."[d] From these things it may be gathered that love is found in all things. Love, therefore, is in all the things that are in us, be they parts of the soul or parts of the body.

3. Further, every power takes pleasure in being joined with what is fitting to it. But pleasure is only taken in something loved. Thus, in any power whatsoever exists a love for what is fitting to it.

4. Further, as was said in the preceding article, and as can be gathered from the definition just mentioned,[e] love is the end and quieting[f] of appetitive motion. But within any power of ours is a desire for its proper good, and it tends toward this. Thus, love may be found in any power.

5. Further, at very least, the irascible power, too, pertains to the appetitive part. But the universal object of the appetitive part is the good. Since, therefore, love is always of some good, it seems that love is not only in the concupiscible power but also in the irascible power.

---

ble goods, whereas we (and he) are accustomed to speaking also of "desires of the will." Moreover, Latin has another word for "desire," *desiderium,* which is not, in Thomas at any rate, synonymous with *concupiscentia.* Also, the pair "concupiscible and irascible" has a familiar ring comparable to that of any famous pairing (substance and accident, intellect and will, faith and reason, etc.). Finally, "desiring" has the weakness of not catching the note of potentiality in *–ibilis.*

    a. Pseudo-Dionysius, *On the Divine Names,* ch. 4 (PG 3:714).

    b. *omnium rerum uniuersitas*

    c. *finis quietaque statio*

    d. "The commentator" is John Scotus Eriugena; the definitions are from his *Periphyseon (De Diuisione Naturae),* Book I, 519b26–30. In the provisional critical ed. of the *Scriptum* the wording of the two definitions matches exactly the text of Eriugena as given in the critical ed. of I. P. Sheldon-Williams, Scriptores Latini Hiberniae, vol. 7 (Dublin: The Dublin Institute for Advanced Studies, 1968), 210, but for a single word: where Eriugena writes *Amor est connexio ac uinculum,* Thomas writes *Amor est connexio uel uinculum.* Our translation is adapted from that of Sheldon-Williams, ibid., 211. I am grateful to John D. Jones for having identified for me the *commentator* and the *locus.*

    e. In the second objection.

    f. *quietatio*

On the contrary:

1. The Philosopher says in *Topics* II[a] that love is in the concupiscible power.

2. Further, the order found among parts of the soul corresponds to the order found among parts of the body. But among parts of the body, a single member can exercise a function that has regard to all the other members, as the foot carries not only itself but all the other members. [So too, among parts of the soul,] the concupiscible power desires and loves not only for itself but for all the others; and thus, the love of things pertaining to all powers seems to be in the concupiscible power.

3. Further, there is love only for something known. If, therefore, love of the proper good were in all powers, by the same reasoning knowledge of the proper good would also be in all of them—which is false.

4. Further, the object of the concupiscible power is a good befitting the one desiring, absolutely speaking.[185] But whatever is good according to any power is fitting to the one desiring. Therefore to desire the good of any power pertains to the concupiscible power, and for the same reason, pertains to love; and thus, love will exist only in the concupiscible power.

Proof of the major premise: If the object of the concupiscible power were not a good befitting the one desiring, simply speaking, its object would be the good fitting only to the concupiscible power. But a good is fitting to any power by comparison with its specific act, as the good fitting to sight is that which is good for seeing.[b] On this view, therefore, the object of the concupiscible power would be good under the aspect of "good for desiring." But this is impossible. To desire "what is good for desiring" happens in the wake of the concupiscible power's turning back upon its own act, insofar as it desires itself to desire or to desire well.[c] *That for which* something is good is desired first, since it is the end. But the turning back of a power upon its own act is preceded naturally by the simple act of the same power directly tending toward its object, as I first see color before I see myself seeing.[186] The object of the concupiscible power cannot, therefore, be something tended toward under the aspect of "good for desiring," since to desire this would be naturally both prior and posterior to the turning back of the concupiscible power

a. Aristotle, *Topics* II, ch. 7 (113b2).

b. *ad uidendum:* for the purposes of seeing, for the activity of seeing.

c. *concupiscere id quod est bonum ad concupiscendum sequitur reflexionem concupiscibilis supra suum actum, secundum quod concupiscit se concupiscere uel bene concupiscere*

upon its own act, which is impossible. Therefore it is necessary to give another account—namely, that the object of the concupiscible power is a good befitting the one desiring, absolutely speaking.[187]

Response:

It should be said that everything in pursuit of an end has to be determined to that end in some way, for otherwise it would not arrive at one end more than at any other. But such a determination has to emerge from an *intention* of the end—not merely out of nature tending to an end,[a] since if that were true, all things would be by chance, as certain philosophers have claimed. But to intend an end is impossible unless (1) the end is known precisely *as* end,[b] and (2) the relationship between things that are toward the end[c] [i.e., the means] and the end itself is also known. Now, the one who knows an end and things that are toward the end directs not only himself but also other things to that end, as the archer shoots an arrow at a target.[188]

So, therefore, something tends to an end in two ways. In one way, as directed of itself to an end, which happens only in one who knows the end and the *ratio* of the end. In another way, as directed by another; and in this way all things, in accord with their natures, tend to their proper and natural ends, as directed by the wisdom which established nature. We find two corresponding appetites: the *natural appetite,* which is nothing other than a thing's inclination to its natural end—an inclination given by the direction of the one who established nature; and a *voluntary appetite,* which is the inclination of one who knows an end and the ordering of things toward that end. Between these two there is a middle appetite, which proceeds from knowledge of an end, yet lacks knowledge of the *ratio* of end and the relationship between the end and things that are toward the end; and this is the *sensitive appetite.* These two kinds of appetite, sensitive and voluntary, are found only in natures to which living and knowing belong.[d]

---

a. *non solum ex natura tendente in finem.* Since Thomas consistently holds that God fashions the natures of things in such a way that even inanimate things tend, by their very natures, toward ends appropriate for them, this phrase must mean something like: "not merely as a result of the particular tendencies of elementary natural bodies, producing, by chance, favorable results in the composites and the larger order of the world, as certain philosophers (such as Empedocles) claimed."

b. *sub ratione finis*

c. *proportio eorum que sunt ad finem in finem ipsum.* On the translation of the phrase *ea quae sunt ad finem,* see the Introduction, p. xxix.

d. *tantum in natura uiuente et cognoscente*

Now, all that is proper to the nature of a living thing has to be led back to some power of the soul in the one that has a soul. Hence, there must be one power of the soul to which seeking after[a] belongs, contradistinguished from that power to which knowing belongs, even as separated substances, too, are divided into intellect and will, as philosophers say. It is therefore clear that natural appetite differs from voluntary appetite in this respect: the natural appetite's inclination is derived from an extrinsic principle and so it has no freedom, since "the free" may be defined as "that which is its own cause"; whereas the voluntary appetite's inclination is from the very one willing, and thus the will has freedom.[b] But the sensitive appetite's inclination is partly from the one desiring, inasmuch as it follows upon apprehension of an appetible[c] (hence, Augustine says that animals are moved by what they see), and partly from another, inasmuch as they lack knowledge of the ordering to an end; and owing to this, it is necessary that things useful for the end be provided to them by another who knows [what is useful for the end].[d] Hence, they are moved toward such things by a natural inclination.[189] On account of this, they do not have freedom in the full sense, but they do partake of some aspects of freedom.[e] Now, everything which is from God receives from him a nature by which it is ordered to its ultimate end. Hence, natural appetite will be found, of necessity, in all created things directed to ends[f]—even in the will itself, with respect to its ultimate end. Hence, by natural appetite, man wills happiness as well as those things that concern the very nature of the will.[g, 190]

Thus, it should be said that *natural* appetite exists in every power of the soul and in the parts of the body with respect to the proper

a. *appetere*

b. One cannot in English capture the linguistic connection: "the inclination of the *voluntary* appetite [*uoluntarii appetitus*] is from the very one *willing* [*ex ipso uolente*], and thus the will [*uoluntas*] has freedom." As we shall see, however, "the voluntary" can be understood more broadly than "the freely willed"; any animal that moves itself by its own desire for something known is said to act with some degree of voluntariness, but only man acts with perfect voluntariness, that is to say, *liberum arbitrium,* free will.

c. *ab appetente . . . appreensionem appetibilis*

d. *oportet quod ab alio cognoscente in finem expedientia eis prouideantur*

e. *non omnino habent libertatem, set participant aliquid libertatis*

f. *oportet in omnibus creatis habentibus aliquem finem inueniri appetitum naturalem.* This phrase does not imply that there are, or may be, creatures lacking ends; "in all creatures having some end" is equivalent to "all creatures as directed to their various ends."

g. *ea que ad naturam uoluntatis spectant*

good [of each power or part], but *animal* appetite, which is of a determinate good for which nature's inclination does not suffice,[191] belongs to some determinate power—either the will, the concupiscible power, or the irascible power. And thence it is that all the other powers of the soul[a] except for the will are compelled by their objects, since all the others have only a natural appetite with respect to their objects, whereas the will has, beyond its natural inclination, another of which the willer himself is the cause. And one should speak in a similar way about love, which is the termination of appetitive motion,[b, 192] since natural love is in all powers and in all things, while animal love, if I may so put it,[c] is in some determinate power—either in the will, insofar as this refers to the termination of the appetite of the intellective part, or in the concupiscible power, insofar as this refers to the termination of the sensitive appetite.[193]

Replies to objections:

1. To the first, therefore, it should be said that Dionysius takes "love" as a common term, applicable to natural love, sensitive love (which he calls "animal"), and intellective love (which he calls "intellectual" as far as men are concerned, "angelic and divine" as far as separate substances are concerned). And he sets down these five, because there cannot be more levels[194] of appetite: in God there is voluntary appetite only, for he determines all things and is not determined by anything; in angels, there is the voluntary with the natural, inasmuch as they are determined by God to the willing of something by nature; in man, the voluntary with the sensitive and the natural; in animals, the sensitive with the natural; and in other things, the natural only.[195]

2. Similarly, it should be said to the second that the commentator, in the passages cited, defines love insofar as it may be applied to all things in common.

3. To the third, it should be said that pleasure is caused by the conjunction of a suitable [good], for a suitable good, when it comes, perfects the one to which it comes, and gives rest to that one's inclination; and this being-at-rest,[d] insofar as it is perceived, is pleasure. For this

---

a. *uires anime*

b. *terminatio appetitiui motus*

c. By the phrase "animal love" is to be understood both sensitive love, as is found in mere (or "brute") animals, and rational love, as is found in rational animals. Hence Thomas can refer to both of these loves as "animal," qualifying his phrase with *ut ita dicam* so that we are not misled.

d. *quietat inclinationem . . . hec quietatio*

reason Plato said that pleasure is "a sensible generation into one's na-ture," i.e., a perceived emergence into what is connatural.[a, 196] Whence pleasure in no way exists in things that do not have knowledge. For beings with knowledge, however, there are two inclinations to what-ever is fitting: natural appetite and animal appetite. Each of these in-clinations is given rest when its object is present, and in each case the being-at-rest is perceived, too, so that pleasure is caused on both ac-counts.[197] The pleasure that is the being-at-rest of *natural* appetite is therefore found [to occur] in every power when its appropriate object is joined with it, whereas the pleasure that is the being-at-rest of *ani-mal* appetite arises only in the concupiscible power or in the will. If one is speaking with precision,[b] the former pleasure is only called *pleasure* and the opposite passion, *pain.* But the latter pleasure has in addition the name of *joy,* and the opposite passion is called *sadness.*[c] Whence, while pleasure and pain are in some way in all powers of the soul, joy and sadness are only in the concupiscible power or in the will.[198]

4. To the fourth one should reply as to the first, since the argument is based on natural appetite.

5. To the fifth, it should be said that animal love does not pertain to the irascible power, since the object of love is a good as such—not a good under the aspect of being, in addition, arduous or difficult, which sort of good is the proper object of the irascible power.[d, 199]

ARTICLE 3[e]   Whether love is the first and foremost[f] affection of the soul

Objections:

Proceeding to the third, it seems that love is not first and foremost among all the affections of the soul.

1. For motion toward a terminus precedes the terminus itself.[g, 200]

a. The phrase has been expanded to convey the sense; Thomas writes: *genera-tio sensibilis, id est cognita, in naturam, id est connaturalis.*

b. *proprie loquendo*

c. The four terms here are *delectatio, dolor, gaudium, tristitia.*

d. *quia obiectum amoris est bonum sine adiectione ardui uel difficilis, quod est propri-um obiectum irascibilis*

e. Parallels: *ST* I, q. 20, a. 1; I-II, q. 25, a. 2; q. 27, a. 4; q. 28, a. 6; *SCG* 3, ch. 19; *De ueritate,* q. 26, a. 4; *De spe,* a. 3; *In De div. nom.* 4, lec. 9.

f. *prima et principalior.* As "more principal" is unidiomatic, we will say "fore-most," since that is what is ultimately proved. Throughout the article, "pleasure" usually translates *delectatio.* In the quotation from Augustine in obj. 3, "pleasure" translates *uoluptas.*

g. *Motus enim precedit terminum*

But it is love that gives a terminus to appetitive motion, as is clear from what has been said.ᵃ Therefore desire, which brings about appetitive motion, precedes love, which has reference to the terminus.

2. Further, "that due to which anything is such as it is, is even more so itself."ᵇ But pleasure is a cause of love, which explains why a kind of friendship is founded upon the pleasurable. Therefore the affection of pleasure has precedence over that of love.

3. Further, Augustine says in *The Book of Eighty-Three Questions:* "There is no one who does not flee pain more than he desires pleasure."ᶜ But flight from pain causes hatred, just as desire for pleasure causes love. Therefore hatred is a more vehement passion than love.

4. Further, that which is conquered by another is less powerful. But love is conquered by anger, since anger gives birth to hatred, as Augustine says. Therefore anger is a more vehement passion than love.

5. Further, that for the sake of which things do whatsoever they do is most efficacious of all. But as Dionysius says in *On the Divine Names,* it is for the sake of peace that things do whatsoever they do.ᵈ Among all affections, therefore, peace is the most efficacious, even with respect to love.

On the contrary:

1. Augustine says that every affection is from love.ᵉ

2. Further, good is the object of affection. But that which first concerns the good is love. Therefore love is the principle of the whole of affection, and the foremost passion.

3. Further, love is compared to fire and even to death, as is clear from the Song of Songs 8:6.ᶠ But nothing is more vehement than these. No passion, therefore, is more vehement than love.

4. Further, Chrysostom says: "Great is love, nor is there anything which can resist its impetus."ᵍ

---

a. *amor est determinatio appetiui motus;* "From what has been said": in Article 1.

b. *Propter quod unumquodque, illud magis.*—Aristotle, *Posterior Analytics* I, ch. 2 (72b29).

c. Augustine, *The Book of Eighty-Three Questions,* Q. 36, n. 1 (CCSL 44A:55).

d. See Pseudo-Dionysius, *On the Divine Names,* ch. 11 (PG 3:947ff.).

e. Augustine, *On the City of God* XIV, ch. 9 (CCSL 48:425–30).

f. The verse reads: "Put me as a seal upon thy heart, as a seal upon thy arm, for love is strong as death, jealousy as hard as hell, the lamps thereof are fire and flames" (8:6, Douay-Rheims). The same verse is cited below at *In III Sent.* d. 31, q. 1, a. 1, obj. 3.

g. No reference is given in Moos (p. 864). A conceptually close text is found in Chrysostom's *Homily 49 on the Gospel of Matthew,* n. 1: "Talis est dilectio, talis amor, qui omnia gravia superet et expulset" (PG 58:496). The meaning is also

Response:

It should be said that love stands first among the soul's affections.[a] For love bespeaks the giving of a definite term to the power of affection,[b] by way of affection's being informed by its object.[c] Now, the following is found to be true in all matters: motion proceeds from a first immobile thing at rest. This is evident in natural things, since the first mover in any genus is not moved in regard to that genus of motion, as the first cause of alteration is not itself altered. The same likewise holds for intellectual things, since the motion of discursive reason proceeds from the [unchanging] principles and quiddities of things, by which the intellect, having been informed thereby, is provided with definite terms.[d] Since therefore affection is informed by love and given a definite term by love, as the intellect by principles and quiddities (as was just said), every affective motion must proceed from the being at rest, the giving of a definite term, proper to love.[e] And since everything that is first in any genus is more perfect—as is the understanding of principles in the realm of demonstrable things, and the motion of the heavens in the realm of natural things—it is therefore necessary that love be more vehement than the other affections, as will be evident by going through them one by one.

Replies to objections:

1. To the first, therefore, it should be said that, as in the operation of intellect a sort of circle is brought to completion, so also in the operation of affection. Starting from the certitude of the principles to which it immovably assents, intellect proceeds, by reasoning, to conclusions, in the knowledge of which it rests with greater certitude to the extent that those conclusions are resolved back into the first principles whose power is manifested in them.[f] Likewise, too, from love of an end (which is, as it were, the principle), affection proceeds, by way of desiring, to those things that are *toward* the end [the "means"], in which things affection can rest through love to the extent that it takes

---

found more diffusely in the same author's *Homily 9 on the Epistle to the Ephesians,* n. 4 (PG 62:74).

 a. *inter alias affectiones anime amor est prior*
 b. *amor dicit terminationem affectus*
 c. *per hoc quod informatur suo obiecto*
 d. *quibus intellectus informatus terminatur*
 e. *oportet quod omnis motus affectiue procedat ex quietatione et terminatione amoris*
 f. *in prima principia que in eis sunt uirtute.* That is, the power of the first principles is what enables the conclusions to be known.

them as containing the end in some manner.[201] And so, desire *follows upon* love of an end, although it *precedes* love of things that are toward the end. Love, too, is a more vehement affection than desire insofar as it bespeaks the bounding and forming of affection by the appetible object,[a] to which desire is [then] moved.[202]

2. To the second, it should be said that love naturally precedes pleasure, for pleasure comes about from a thing's being joined to something really suited for it,[b, 203] whereas love *makes* what is loved to be suitable and as if connatural to the lover, insofar as it unites the lover's affection to the loved, as was said. And so, pleasure arises from the real presence of the loved. But since pleasure, too, can be loved as a certain good, it thus happens *per accidens* that a love may be caused by pleasure,[204] as an act may be caused by an object or an end; for the one who loves something on account of pleasure chiefly loves pleasure itself. Accordingly, although a certain pleasure may be prior to a certain love, love, simply speaking, is prior to pleasure. Similarly, love is more vehement, since it comes about through the informing of the appetite by something appetible, whereas pleasure comes about when a thing is joined to something suitable and present to it.[c, 205] But the joining of thing to thing is not the same as the joining of appetite to appetible. The thing that causes pleasure upon its arrival is not joined [to the one pleased by it] according to nature, for *this* does not become *that*. Hence, in this case there is a joining in the manner of contact.[d] Appetite, by contrast, is of and toward the appetible itself,[e] according to its nature and substance. Hence, when an appetite is informed by something appetible, there is a joining in the manner of continuity and concretion.[f, 206] For this reason love unites more than pleasure does, since it makes the lover to *be*, in his affection, the very one loved, whereas pleasure comes about when the lover shares in something that belongs to the loved, insofar as the one loved is really present. Yet it should be understood that when the one loved is really present, in the manner in which this is possible, pleasure then occurs, as from the joining of what is most of all fitting [to the lover]. When, on the other hand, the one loved is altogether absent in reality,[g] then the lover

a. *terminationem et formationem affectus per appetibile*
b. *Delectatio enim contingit ex coniunctione rei conuenientis realiter*
c. *amor est per informationem appetitus ad appetibili, delectatio autem per coniunctionem rei ex re presente sibi conueniente*
d. *quasi coniunctio contactus*
e. *appetitus est ipsius appetibilis*
f. *quasi coniunctio continuitatis et concretionis*
g. *omnino absens secundum rem*

is most of all afflicted by the one loved,[a] even as pain may accompany the cutting apart of something continuous, for love is a force that makes for continuity, as was said; and this is why it is said that "love makes one grow faint and waste away."[b] But when the one loved is in one respect present and in another respect absent, the lover experiences pleasure mingled with affliction.[207]

3. To the third, it should be said that what is good is more vehement in acting than what is evil, since good does not necessarily have evil mixed up with it, whereas evil necessarily has good mixed up with it.[c] Again, what is good acts by its own power, but what is evil acts by the power of the good [mixed up with it], as Dionysius says in chapter 4 of *On the Divine Names*.[d] Hence, what is good is more loved than the evil opposed to it is hated.[208] Nevertheless, bodily pains are more evil than certain pleasures are good, since the pleasure of which Augustine is speaking in that passage comes about when a secondary perfection is added to the animal, as occurs in eating food or engaging in sexual intercourse, whereas the sadness or pain owing to which such a pleasure is abandoned[e] comes about from the removal of a primary perfection pertaining to a thing's very being, as when something continuous is cut into pieces.[f] Accordingly, if [instead of the sadness resulting from threats to life,] the sadness contrary to that sensual pleasure were considered, the pleasure would be more desired than the corresponding sadness would be fled, even as someone seeks pleasure in food, even if afterward he may suffer sadness from the food's being taken away, or something of this sort.[209]

4. To the fourth, it should be said that love is prior to anger and more vehement, for anger is caused by sadness, as was said earlier,[g] even as all the irascible passions are caused by concupiscible passions. And since love is prior to and more vehement than the other concupiscible passions, it will be prior to and more vehement than the

---

a. Thomas writes: *tunc maxime affligit,* he [the one loved] most of all afflicts the lover.

b. A poetic rendering of *amor languere facit:* love causes languor, illness, weakness.

c. *bonum not habet de necessitate ammixtionem mali, sicut malum habet de necessitate ammixtionem boni.* The liberty is taken of saying "what is good" and "what is evil" for *bonum* and *malum.*

d. *bonum agit in uirtute propria, set malum agit in uirtute boni.*—Pseudo-Dionysius, *On the Divine Names*, ch. 4, nn. 31–32 (PG 3:731).

e. *dimittitur:* also, scattered, dismissed, given up

f. *sicut ex diuisione continui*   g. *In III Sent.* d. 26, q. 1, a. 3.

irascible passions. Yet even though anger gives birth to hatred, still it does not destroy love; rather, anger comes *after* the destruction of love, since appetite cannot be moved to the point of harming something unless beforehand one's feelings toward the object have been distanced from love.[a, 210]

5. To the fifth, it should be said that peace is not distinct from love, but is something *of* love, for it bespeaks the resting, as it were, of the appetite [in what is loved]. Love, in addition to this, bespeaks the lover's transformation into, and his turning toward, the one loved. Thus peace is a mean between desire and love.[211]

ARTICLE 4[b, 212]   Whether knowledge[c] is higher than love

Arguments on behalf of the superiority of knowledge:

Proceeding to the fourth, it seems that knowledge is higher than love.

1. The highest act is that of the highest power. But the intellect is the highest power in us, as the Philosopher says in *Ethics* X.[d] Therefore knowledge is the highest operation of the powers within us, and so it is worthier than love.

2. Further, as Boethius says in *On the Consolation of Philosophy,* nature takes its origin from perfect things.[e] But knowledge precedes love; therefore knowledge is higher than love.[213]

3. Further, what is proper to man is nobler than what he has in common with brute animals. But understanding is proper to man, where-

a. *Quamuis autem ira odium pariat, non tamen amorem destruit, set amoris destructionem sequitur, quia non posset appetitus moueri in nocumentum alicuius nisi antea affectus ab amore separatus esset*

b. Parallels: *ST* I-II, q. 3, a. 4, ad 4; cf. *ST* I, q. 26, a. 2, ad 2; I, q. 82, a. 3; II-II, q. 23, a. 6, ad 1; *De ueritate,* q. 22, a. 11; *In IV Sent.* d. 49, q. 1, a. 1, qa. 2 (see below); *SCG* 3, ch. 26; *Quodl.* VIII, q. 9, a. 1; *Comp. theol.* I, ch. 107.

c. Since the English word "cognition" is, with its technical coldness, very distant from its medieval Latin forebear, and since the traditional meaning of the word "science" (*episteme, scientia*) has fared even worse because of the substitution of mechanistic materialism for the discipline of natural philosophy, we will translate *cognitio* and *scientia* as "knowledge." In the passages included in this translation, the two terms are being treated, for all intents and purposes, as synonyms. In the few cases where one or the other term is required for the sense of the argument, I have either translated literally or added a note.

d. Aristotle, *Ethics* X, ch. 7 (1177a20).

e. Boethius, *On the Consolation of Philosophy,* Book III, prose 10 (CCSL 94:53).

as love man has in common with brute animals. Therefore knowledge and understanding[a] are worthier than love.

4. Further, the contemplative life is nobler and higher than the active life. But knowledge pertains to the contemplative life, whereas love seems to pertain to practice, since its object is the good. Therefore knowledge is higher than love.

5. Further, the object of love is the good as such, but the true is better than the good as such, since the true is highest in the genus of goods, even as the best man is better than a man as such. Therefore knowledge is higher than love.[b]

6. Further, something is higher to the extent that it is more spiritual. But knowledge is more spiritual than love, since knowledge concerns a sort of movement from things toward the soul, whereas love concerns a sort of movement from the soul to things.[c] Therefore knowledge is more noble than love.

7. Further, a reward has pre-eminence to that which merits it.[d] But knowledge is the reward of love, according to John 14:21: "He who loves me will be loved by my Father, and I will manifest myself to him."[214] And Augustine says that "vision is the whole reward."[e] Therefore knowledge is more eminent than love.

Arguments on behalf of the superiority of love:

8. Ephesians 3:19 says: "The charity of Christ, surpassing knowledge."

9. Further, 1 Corinthians 13:13 states that charity is greater than faith. Thus, for the same reason, any love is greater and worthier than the knowledge corresponding to it.

10. Further, Hugh of St. Victor—commenting on Dionysius's words "mobile and piercing," etc., from chapter 7 of *The Celestial Hierarchy*—says: "Love surpasses knowledge and is greater than understanding, for more is loved than is understood, and love enters in where knowledge remains without."[f] Therefore love exceeds knowledge.

---

a. *scientia et intellectus*

b. Thomas actually writes: *Ergo et scientia uel cognitio est altior quam amor.*

c. The liberty has been taken of adding "a sort of" because neither the informing of the intellect with the intelligible nor the informing of the appetite and its inclination toward the good is a "motion" or "movement" in the ordinary sense of the word.

d. *premium est prestantius merito*

e. Augustine, *Expositions of the Psalms*, Ps. 90, n. 13 (CCSL 39:1277).

f. Hugh of St. Victor, *Commentary on* The Celestial Hierarchy *of Saint Dionysius the Areopagite*, Book VI, exp. of ch. 7 (PL 175:1038). "Understanding": *intelligentia*.

11. Further, in all things the end is most powerful. But the object of love is the good, which has the *ratio* of an end. Therefore, since activities are distinguished entirely by their objects, love is the most powerful among all the soul's activities.

12. Further, as power is to power, so is activity to activity. But the will is higher than all the other powers of the soul, since it moves all the others and is not subject to compulsion.[a] Therefore love, which is an activity of the will, surpasses all the other activities of the soul.

13. Further, as Dionysius says in chapter 5 of *On the Divine Names,*[b] that which is found in more is simpler and nobler, as *being* is nobler than *living,* although living things are nobler than things that merely exist, insofar as living things participate more nobly in being. But love is participated in by more things than knowledge, since, as was said in the preceding article, in all things there is love in some way, but not knowledge. Therefore love stands before knowledge. For instance, it would be ridiculous to say that in stones there is a natural knowledge, even as there is love or a natural appetite.

Response:

It should be said that a twofold perfection is found in all things: one, by which a thing subsists in itself; another, by which it is ordered to other things. Each of these perfections in material things is finite and determined, because a material thing has one determinate form through which it belongs to one species only, and also has an inclination and order, through a determinate power,[c] to certain things proportioned to it, e.g., heavy things vis-à-vis the center. In regard to both perfections, however, immaterial things possess infinity, in a way, because they are, in a way, all things[d]—either so far as the essence of an immaterial thing is an exemplar and likeness of all things, as happens in God, or so far as it has actually or potentially the likenesses of all things, as happens in angels and souls; and it is from this vantage that knowledge belongs to them.[e] In like manner, too, they have an inclination and order to all things, and it is from this vantage that will belongs to them, through which they are actually or potentially pleased or displeased by all things.[215] And to the extent that they participate in

a. *non cogitur*
b. Pseudo-Dionysius, *On the Divine Names,* ch. 5 (PG 3:815ff.).
c. *per determinatam uirtutem*
d. *res immateriales infinitatem habent quodammodo, quia sunt quodammodo omnia*
e. "happens in God": *in Deo accidit;* "it is from this vantage that knowledge belongs to them": *ex hac parte accidit eis cognitio*

immateriality, they are made participants of knowledge and will. This is the reason why even animals may be said *to know,* for the species of sensibles are *immaterially* received in their organs of sense, and—in accord with intentions spiritually gleaned from things—the animals are then *inclined,* by their sensitive appetite, toward various things.[a, 216] It is evident, therefore, that knowledge pertains to the perfection of the knower [and is that] by which he is made perfect in himself, whereas the will pertains to a thing's perfection as regards its order to other things. And so, the object of the knowing power is the true, which exists in the soul, as the Philosopher says in *Metaphysics* VI, while the object of the appetitive power is the good, which exists in things, as is said in the same place.[b, 217]

The knowing power can thus be compared to the appetitive power in three ways. First, according to their order: and in this way the knowing power is naturally prior, because the perfection of a thing in itself is prior to the perfection it has by being ordered to another.[218] Second, with respect to their capacity: and in this way they are equal, because just as the knowing power has some relation to all things, so too has the appetitive. For this reason they mutually include each other: intellect knows the will, and the will has appetite for or loves what pertains to intellect. Third, they can be compared according to eminence or dignity: and in this way they are related as exceeding and exceeded.[c] For, if intellect and will and the things that pertain to them be considered as *properties and accidents* of that being in which they exist, intellect is pre-eminent, along with what pertains to it. If, on the other hand, they be considered as *powers*—that is, according to the order they have to acts and objects—the will takes precedence, along with what pertains to it.

But if it be asked which of these is worthier simply speaking, it should be said, to begin the answer, that there are things superior to the soul and things inferior to it. Accordingly, since through willing and loving man is, in a way, drawn into the very things willed and loved, whereas through knowledge, on the contrary, things known are made to be in the knower by way of their likenesses, it follows that with respect to things above the soul, love is nobler and higher than

---

a. *in quantum species sensibilium immaterialiter in organis sensuum recipiuntur, et secundum intentiones spiritualiter ex rebus perceptas per appetitum sensibilem ad diuersa inclinantur*

b. Aristotle, *Metaphysics* VI, ch. 4 (1027b18ff.).

c. *ut excedentia et excessa:* each exceeds and is exceeded by the other in a certain respect. Two sentences further, *excedit* has been rendered "takes precedence."

knowledge, but with respect to things below the soul, knowledge is preferable.[a] And this holds of evil things, too, for loving them is bad, but knowing them is good.[219]

Replies to arguments on behalf of the superiority of knowledge:

1. To the first, it should be said that the Philosopher speaks there of powers insofar as they are properties of that in which they are. An alternative explanation would be that for the Philosopher the term "intellect" embraces both intellect and the will corresponding to it, as also the term "reason" at times embraces both reason and will. Therefore, one should not see in this passage a comparison of intellect to will, but rather of intellectual powers to inferior powers.[b]

2. To the second, it should be said that, while the first principle in any genus is most perfect, still it need not be the case that everything which is prior be more perfect, given that something can be prior in the way of generation which is less perfect than what will result in time, as a boy is less perfect than a man, and the one learning a science than the one who knows it.[c] And thus, too, does knowledge take precedence, in a way, over love.[220]

3. To the third, it should be said that that argument holds concerning intellect and will only with respect to the being in which they exist.[221] An alternative explanation would be that the other animals participate in intellect in some way, through a kind of obscure resonance, inasmuch as they have powers of sensing,[d] just as they participate in will inasmuch as they have sensual appetite—for which reason the "voluntary" is found in brute animals, as the Philosopher says in *Ethics* III, though they do not have will properly speaking.[e]

4. To the fourth, it should be said that will and love are not excluded from the contemplative life, as neither is intellect excluded from the active life; and therefore the ranking of these things (will, love, intellect, etc.) cannot be established according to the ranking of the two lives.[f]

5. To the fifth, it should be said that a particular has the *ratio* and

a. *potior,* which could also be rendered "better, more useful, more important."

b. Thomas simply says *intellectus ad inferiores uires,* but his argument requires taking *intellectus* to mean intellectual powers generally.

c. *cum aliquid sit prius in uia generationis quod imperfectius est, sicut puer uiro et addiscens sciente*

d. *in quantum sentiunt*

e. The relationship between the Latin words *uoluntarium* (voluntary) and *uoluntatem* (will) should be noted: *in brutis uoluntarium inuenitur . . . non quod simpliciter uoluntatem habeant.*—Aristotle, *Ethics* III, ch. 2 (1111b8).

f. *non potest horum gradus distingui secundum gradus duarum uitarum*

nature of the universal [under which it is subsumed] only to the extent that the universal nature is found in it. Hence, it is impossible that a universal *ratio* be more present in a particular than in the universal itself, although the *ratio* of something else might be found more in a particular than in the universal. For example, a man cannot be more of an animal than animal in common,[a] but he can be more *good*, or something of this sort. And so, neither the true nor any good, taken as a particular, can be said to be more eminent than the good itself.[b]

6. To the sixth, it should be said that that argument holds concerning things below the soul, and therefore less spiritual than it.

7. To the seventh, it should be said that, although the beatific vision will not be lacking love in the content of the reward, as neither in the gaining of merit was the wayfarer's love altogether lacking in knowledge of God, nevertheless, the reward is assigned more to knowledge and the meriting more to love, because reward has to do with a receiving by which someone is perfected in himself, while merit has to do with the activity by which someone stretches out toward the one who will reward him, and joins himself to him.[c, 222]

Replies to arguments on behalf of the superiority of love:

8 and 9. And since it is necessary also to respond to the other points that have been raised, it should be said to the eighth and the ninth that those arguments follow concerning the soul's knowledge of God, who is above the soul; hence, loving him is better than knowing him.[223]

10. To the tenth, it should be said that love enters more *into* a thing than knowledge, since knowledge is of the known insofar as it is received in the knower's capacity, whereas love is of the loved in a different way, the lover himself being transformed into the very thing loved, as was said before.[d] Thus, it was stated [in the main response] that will exceeds knowledge as regards the way in which the soul is perfected in its order to other things, to which way it pertains to be more or less intimate with a thing.

a. *animal commune:* animal as such, the universal notion, the nature.

b. *neque uerum neque aliquod bonum, particulare acceptum, potest dici prestantius quam ipsum bonum* (the "good" in common, parallel to *animal commune*).

c. *uisio illa non erit sine amore in premio, sicut nec amor fuit sine cognitione in merito: Ideo tamen premium magis attribuitur cognitioni, meritum uero amori, quia premium est secundum receptionem qua aliquis in se ipso perficitur, meritum uero secundum operationem qua aliquis in remuneratorem se extendit et ei se coniungit.*

d. The sentence has been amplified for clarity. The original: *cognitio est de re secundum id quod recipitur in cognoscente, amor autem est secundum <quod> ipse amans in rem ipsam transformatur.* "As was said before": see especially the first article of this question.

11. To the eleventh, it should be said that the *ratio* of end properly concerns motion and activity and the order something has to an end,[a] and not the very *being* of a thing, absolutely speaking. Hence, in mathematics, where there is neither activity nor motion, no end [i.e., final cause] is to be found, as is said in *Metaphysics* III.[b] Thus, the argument given in the objection is valid when taken according to the way in which will is said to be preeminent to intellect.

12. To the twelfth, it should be said that it pertains to the will to be the mover of other powers and not to be subject to compulsion by an object,[c] insofar as the will is the first power that determines for other human powers their ordering to the various things in regard to which they act, and insofar as the will itself is not determined by another. Hence, to the extent that it is determined by a natural inclination implanted by God, in a way it does *not* have freedom, but is, as it were, compelled by this natural inclination—as with respect to happiness, which no one is able not to will. From this vantage (namely, of man's being ordered by another), it was admitted that love exceeds knowledge.[224]

13. To the thirteenth, it should be said that love, properly speaking, exists only in things that are knowers;[d] but the term "love" is carried over to things to which the term "knowledge" cannot be extended. The reason for this is that love is spoken of whenever the one loving is ordered to another thing. Now, one thing can be ordered to another even when the ordering comes from an outside mover.[e, 225] Accordingly, the terms "love" and "appetite" can be given to things lacking knowledge, when they are ordered to something else by genuine knowers—and it is of these latter that love is properly said, insofar as they are ordered, in and of themselves, to what is loved. "Knowledge," on the other hand, is spoken of whenever a thing known comes to be in the knower according to the knower's mode—namely, according to spiritual and immaterial being. Yet such a disposition can exist in anything only owing to a property of its own nature. Hence, the term "knowledge" cannot be extended to things that do not have such a nature (as if one were to say that non-sensing things[226] naturally "know," as they naturally "love" or "desire").[227]

a. *ordinem rei ad rem*

b. Aristotle, *Metaphysics* III, ch. 2 (996a21–a34); cf. *Eudemian Ethics* II, ch. 6 (1222b15–b36); *Rhetoric* III, ch. 16 (1417a16–a36).

c. *non cogi ab obiecto*

d. *amor . . . non est nisi in illis in quibus est cognitio*

e. *Aliquid autem ad alterum ordinari potest etiam ab exteriori ordinante*

QUESTION 2   On charity

Charity is the next subject of inquiry; and concerning it, we will inquire into four things: (1) what charity is; (2) whether it is a virtue; (3) what its subject in the soul is; (4) how it stands in comparison with other virtues.

ARTICLE 1 ᵃ   What is charity?

Objections proposing various possibilities:

1. It seems that charity is the same as concupiscence. For Augustine says that charity is the virtue by which we desire to see and to enjoy God.ᵇ But to desire and enjoy are acts of concupiscence.ᶜ Therefore charity is concupiscence.

2. Again, it seems that it is the same as love, because, as Dionysius says in chapter 4 of *On the Divine Names,* "rational love is the same as love";ᵈ but in the text of the Master it says: "Charity is the rational love by which God is loved for his own sake, and one's neighbor for God's sake." Therefore charity is the same as love.

3. Again, it seems that it is the same as benevolence.ᵉ For it is owing to benevolence that we desire good things for someone,ᶠ but charity does just this, since it desires eternal life both for oneself and for others, and this is the reason why the one having charity is said to "love his neighbor as himself." Therefore charity is the same as benevolence.

4. Further, it seems that it is the same as concord. For charity causes the Church's unity, which consists in all of us speaking the same thing

a. Parallels: *ST* II-II, q. 23, a. 1; I-II, q. 65, a. 5; cf. *In III Sent.* d. 28, q. 1, esp. aa. 1 & 2, and d. 29, a. 4 (see below).

b. Augustine, *On Christian Doctrine* III, ch. 10, n. 16 (CCSL 32:87).

c. Thomas simply writes: *Hoc autem concupiscentie est.* Here, as before, one must bear in mind that *concupiscentia* need not, and here must not, be taken as sensual desire. It rather refers to a sort of hunger or thirst for goods (whether sensual or spiritual) needed by the one desiring, as well as pleasure taken in the satisfaction of such desires. What *concupiscentia* seems to exclude, therefore, is not the spiritual, as such, but the going-out toward another, the other-directedness, specific to friendship.

d. *dilectio est idem quod amor:* Pseudo-Dionysius, *On the Divine Names,* ch. 4, n. 12 (PG 3:710). In this article, "love" translates *amor* and "rational love" *dilectio* whenever the distinction between the two terms is relevant. See comments in the Introduction, pp. xxi–xxiv.

e. *beneuolentia:* literally, "wishing well" to another.

f. *qua alicui aliquod bonum optamus*

and there being "no schisms among us," as we read in 1 Corinthians 1:10. But this pertains to concord. Therefore charity is the same as concord.

5. Further, it seems that it is the same as beneficence.[a] For the measure of genuine charity is that we love not only in words,[b] "but in works and in truth" (1 Jn. 3:18). But to demonstrate love by deeds[c] pertains to beneficence. Therefore charity seems to be the same as beneficence.[228]

6. Further, it seems that it is the same as peace. For charity is the bond that makes for unity of spirits. But this is attributed to peace: "Be solicitous to serve the unity of the spirit in the bond of peace" (Eph. 4:3). Therefore charity is the same as peace.

7. Further, it seems that it is the same as friendship, since, as the Philosopher says in *Ethics* IX, "friendship is likened to a superabundance of love."[d, 229] But charity has the most superabundant love, a fact that gives it its very name "charity," for it esteems the beloved as the most cherished thing, placed beyond all price.[e, 230] Therefore charity is the same as friendship.

Objections to identifying charity as friendship:

8. But against that idea: as the Philosopher says, friendship exists between those who reciprocate their love.[f] But charity exists even toward enemies. Therefore it is not the same as friendship.

9. Further, the existence of a friendship is not hidden, whereas the existence of charity is most of all hidden to view.[g] It is therefore not friendship.

10. Further, friendship exists between people who live together and share in the same activities, whereas charity is directed toward God and the angels, whose manner of living and acting is not common to them and to us men.[h, 231] Therefore charity is not friendship.

a. *beneficentia:* literally, "doing well" by another, that is, doing good for another.

b. *non lingua tantum*

c. *diligere per effectum*

d. Cf. Aristotle, *Ethics* IX, ch. 4 (1166b1).

e. An attempt in English to catch the play of words in Latin: *unde et caritas dicitur, eo quod sub inestimabili pretio quasi carissimam rem ponat amatum.*

f. Aristotle, *Ethics* VIII, ch. 3 (1156a8). *Amicitia est redamantium,* which one could also render: "Friendship belongs to those who return love to each other" or "Reciprocation belongs to the reality of friendship."

g. *Amicitia est non latens. Set caritas maxime latet.*

h. Again, the original is terse: *Amicitia est eorum qui conuiuunt ad inuicem et com-*

11. Further, friendship seeks, above all, to talk with and to see a friend in person,[a] as the Philosopher says. But charity does not seek this, as Jerome says in his preface to the Bible.[b] It is therefore not the same as friendship.

12. Further, genuine friendship exists only among the few and the virtuous, whereas charity is toward all, even those who are evil. Therefore charity is not the same as friendship.

Response:

It should be said that love is a certain resting of appetite, as was said above.[c] Hence, just as appetite is found in the sensitive and intellectual parts of the soul, so too is love. Now, while things that pertain to the sensitive appetite get transferred to the intellectual appetite (such as the names of the passions), what is proper to the intellectual appetite is not applicable to[d] the sensitive appetite (such as the term "will"). And thus, love is found in each appetite. As found in the sensitive appetite, it is called "love" properly, for this implies a passion.[e] As found in the intellectual part, it is called "rational love," for this includes the element of choice,[f] which pertains to the intellectual appetite. Nevertheless, though the term "love" gets transferred from the lower part to the higher, the term "rational love" never gets transferred from the higher part to the lower.

All the other terms that seem to pertain to love either (1) are included within these terms already,[232] or (2) include them, and add some distinctive note beyond what is signified by "rational love" or "love."[g]

(1) For since love in a certain way unites lover to beloved, the lover therefore stands to the beloved as if to himself or to that which concerns his perfection.[233] But to himself and to that which belongs to him, he stands in the following ways. First, he wishes whatever concerns his perfection to be present to him; and therefore love includes

---

municant in eisdem operibus. Set caritas est ad Deum et ad angelos, quorum conuersatio non est cum hominibus.

a. *colloqui et uidere amicum.*—Aristotle, *Ethics* IX, ch. 11 (1171a27ff.).

b. Jerome, *Letter to Paulinus,* Letter 53, n. 1 (PL 22:540).

c. In the preceding question, article 1.

d. *conuenit*

e. Or: an undergoing. The "this" is ambiguous: either love, or the name "love," or both, imply passion. Similarly, *dilectio,* as well as the name *dilectio,* includes the element of *electio* or choice.

f. *dilectio . . . electio*

g. *uel includunt ea, quasi addentia aliquid supra dilectionem et amorem*

longing^a for the beloved, by which the beloved's presence is desired. Second, in his affections a man turns other things back to himself and seeks for himself whatever goods are expedient for him;^b and so far as this is done for the beloved, love includes the *benevolence* by which someone desires good things for the beloved. Third, the things a man desires for himself he actually acquires for himself by acting; and insofar as this activity is exercised toward another, love includes *beneficence*. Fourth, to the accomplishment of whatever seems good in his sight, he gives his full consent;^c and insofar as this attitude comes to be toward a friend, love includes the *concord* by which someone consents to things as they seem [good] to his friend—not, indeed, in speculative matters, since "concord in such matters," according to the Philosopher in *Ethics* IX, "does not pertain to friendship."^d And disagreement about matters like this can exist without injuring the friendship, because agreement or disagreement about speculative truths is not something subject to the will; valid argumentation compels the intellect's assent.^{234, 235} Nevertheless, over and above what belongs to the four things that have just been described, love adds a special note,^e namely, the appetite's resting in the beloved; lacking this, none of those four is able to exist.

(2) There are also terms that add some distinctive note beyond what is signified by "rational love" and "love."^f For *infatuation* adds, beyond love, the note of a peculiar intensity of love, as if a sort of blazing heat.^g *Friendship,* however, adds two notes: first, the fellowship of lov-

---

a. *concupiscentia*; "concupiscence" would be deceptive in this context.

b. *homo alia in se ipsum retorquet per affectum et sibi appetit quecumque sibi expediunt*

c. *homo ea que sibi bona uidentur implere consentit*

d. Aristotle, *Ethics* IX, ch. 6 (1167a25).

e. *Amor tamen super quatuor predicta aliquid addit*

f. *Sunt etiam quedam que super amorem uel dilectionem aliquid addunt*

g. *Amatio enim addit super amorem intensionem quandam amoris, quasi feruorem quendam.* One might despair of finding the right words for this sentence. *Amatio* has no exact English equivalent, though perhaps "infatuation" succeeds best. Its basic meaning is affectionate or passionate love, with an accent on the strength of feeling (consider the emphasis on *motion* when Thomas brings it up in *Comp. theol.* I, ch. 46, or on a "vehement impetus" at *Sent. Eth.* IX, lec. 5, ed. Leon. 47:518.34–42). It approaches, in a way, what might be called a "romantic" love. In English of a bygone age one could have said "fondness" (see *Crabb's English Synonymes* of 1816, rev. ed., ed. John H. Finley [New York: Harper & Brothers, 1917], s.v. affection; *The Concise Dictionary of English Etymology* of 1884 [repr. Ware, Hertfordshire: Wordsworth Editions, 1993], s.v. fond), or, in a euphemistic sense, "kindness" (see C. S. Lewis, *Studies in Words*, 2nd ed. [Cambridge: Cambridge University Press, 1967], 33). In a number of passages (e.g., *In IV Sent.* d. 29, a. 3, qa. 2, ad 1; *ST* II-II, q. 23, a. 1) Thomas speaks of *mutua amatio* or *redamatio*, reciprocated or requited love, as a condition for genuine friendship. See

er and beloved in a mutual love,ᵃ such that they love each other and *know* that they love each other; second, that they act out of free choice, not merely from passion. Hence the Philosopher says that friendship is like a habit, but infatuation like a passion.ᵇ Accordingly, it is clear that friendship, which includes in itself all that has been mentioned, is the most perfect among things pertaining to love. And for this reason charity—which is a friendship between man and God, by which man loves God and God loves man, bringing about an association of man with God, as is said in 1 John 1:7: "If we walk in the light, just as he himself is in the light, we have fellowship with each other"—ought to be placed in a genus of this kind.

Replies to objections:

1. To the first, therefore, it should be said that any friendship includes concupiscence or desire, and adds something beyond it, as was said.²³⁶

2. To the second, it should be said that charity adds something beyond rational love and love.

3–5. And a similar response should be made to the third, about benevolence, to the fourth, about concord, and to the fifth, about beneficence.

6. To the sixth, it should be said that peace may be traced back to concord—except that, to be precise, peace is spoken of more in regard to removal of disagreement between parties, while concord is spoken of more in regard to the union itself between them.²³⁷

7. To the seventh, it should be said that charity is a friendship, but adds something beyond friendship commonly so-called, namely, a specification of who the friend is, since it is friendship toward God, who is more precious and dearer than all things.ᶜ

8. To the eighth, it should be said that a friend loves not only the friend with whom he is joined in friendship, but also everything that

---

In I Sent. d. 10, a. 5, ad 1 (Mandonnet, 271): "[T]he will tends toward another, and there can be reciprocation, so that from two [persons] proceeds one conformity of will which is the union of both." At *Sent. Eth.* VIII, lec. 5 (ed. Leon. 47:458.105–13), the same notion is contrasted with the *amatio simplex* that can be had even toward inanimate things such as wine or gold. *Fervor* conveys the sense of intense heat, boiling, burning, being aroused, being feverish, though it would be a mistake to assume that Thomas always has in mind the more violent aspects.

a. *societas quedam amantis et amati in amore*

b. Aristotle, *Ethics* VIII, ch. 5 (1157b28).

c. *caritas est amicitia, set aliquid addit supra ipsam, scilicet determinationem amici, quia est amicitia ad Deum, omnibus pretiosorem et cariorem*

pertains to the friend (for example, his sons, his brothers, and such-like), even if he is not loved by them in return. In like manner, charity causes one chiefly to love God, who loves those loving him and who anticipates them in his loving,[a, 238] but it also causes one to love men insofar as they belong to him. Hence when it was said that friendship concerns a returning of love, this has to be understood with respect to those between whom the friendship chiefly exists.

9. To the ninth, it should be said that, when friendship is spoken of as "not hidden," it is not because a friend's love is known with certain-ty, but because the mutual love of friends can be gathered from prob-able signs. Charity, too, can be manifest in the same way, for someone seeing the signs of charity in himself can make a probable judgment that he has charity.[b]

10. To the tenth, it should be said that insofar as men are made God-like by charity, they are indeed above mere men,[c] and their "con-versation is in heaven"; and it is in this way that they live together with God and the angels, insofar as men stretch themselves toward similar things, in accord with what the Lord teaches: "Be perfect, even as your heavenly Father is perfect" (Mt. 5:48).[239]

11. To the eleventh, it should be said that, while true friendship does desire to see the friend in person, and makes one rejoice in speak-ing together with the one who is the primary object of friendship, still the pleasure that comes from mutual beholding and enjoyment is not set as the *end* of true friendship, as is done in the friendship of pleasure.[d, 240] And this is what Jerome intends to remove, by teach-ing that the friendship of charity is not directed chiefly toward being with and speaking with other men but rather "is joined by the glue of Christ," and that the pleasure of companionship with friends should not be sought as the main thing.[e, 241]

12. To the twelfth, it should be said that that objection has truth in regard to that toward which the friendship mainly looks,[242] not about those who are loved insofar as they pertain to the main friend; for in this way, the friendship of charity extends to many.

a. *qui amantes se amat et in amando preuenit*

b. See earlier discussions of this point, above: *In I Sent.* (Paris version) d. 17, q. 1, a. 4; *In I Sent.* (*Lectura romana*) d. 17, q. 1, a. 4.

c. *in quantum homines per caritatem deiformes efficiuntur, sic supra homines sunt*

d. *amicitia uera desiderat uidere amicum et colloquiis mutuis gaudere facit ad quem principaliter est amicitia, non autem ita quod delectatio, que est ex mutua uisione et perfru-itione, finis amicitie ponatur, sicut est in amicitia delectabilis*

e. *scilicet quod non est amicitia caritatis principaliter ad homines, set "est Christi glut-tino copulata", et quod delectatio principaliter de amicis non est querendum*

ARTICLE 2ᵃ   Whether charity is a virtue

Objections:

Proceeding to the second, it seems that charity is not a virtue.

1. For charity, as was said, is a certain friendship between man and God. But friendship is not set down as a virtue by the philosophers, although it has virtue for its foundation, since it exists on account of the noble goodᵇ that virtue is. Therefore charity is not a virtue.

2. Further, the commandments of the law are about acts of the virtues. But "the end of the commandments is charity" (1 Tim. 1:5).ᶜ Therefore charity is the end of the virtues. But the end of the virtues is not virtue, but happiness. Therefore charity is not a virtue.

3. Further, "virtue" bespeaks the ultimate a power can do, as is said in *On the Heavens* I.ᵈ ²⁴³ But pleasure is something more ultimate than love, since it comes about in the very joining of lover and the object of his love, which is the union love seeks.ᵉ Therefore pleasure ought to be called a virtue more than love. But since pleasure is not set down as a virtue, neither should charity be called a virtue.

4. Further, if nature suffices in the doing of some work, there is no need for nature to be elevated by a virtue. But insofar as man is able to know by natural reason that God is the highest good, man is able, owing to something naturally in him, to love God above all things—and this is the act proper to charity. Therefore it would be needless to add, over and above this, any *virtue* of charity.

5. Further, in order to strive for an end, it is enough to know it and desire it. But charity causes more than that, since it makes one love God and have friendship with him. Therefore it was not necessary for charity to be a theological virtue, but desire would have been enough.²⁴⁴

6. Further, "Virtue is about difficult things," as is said in *Ethics* II.ᶠ But loving is not difficult; on the contrary, love lightens all difficult things. Therefore charity is not a virtue.

---

a. Parallels: *ST* II-II, q. 23, a. 3; *De caritate*, a. 2.

b. *bonum honestum*

c. This is what the phrase says when translated directly from the Latin text (as it is in the Douay-Rheims). The RSV translates it "the aim of our charge is love," as if it were referring to Paul's pastoral mission.

d. *Virtus est ultimum potentie.*—Aristotle, *On the Heavens* I, ch. 11 (281a11).

e. *Set delectatio est magis ultimum quam amor, quia est ex ipsa coniunctione rei amate, quam amor querit*

f. Aristotle, *Ethics* II, ch. 2 (1105a9).

On the contrary:

1. The commandments of the law are about acts of the virtues. But charity fulfills all the commandments of the law, since "love is the fullness of the law" (Rom. 13:10). Therefore charity is a virtue.

2. Further, spiritual existence is caused by virtue.[a, 245] But there is no spiritual existence without charity. Hence the Apostle says: "If I should have all faith, yet lack charity, I am nothing" (1 Cor. 13:2). Therefore charity is most of all a virtue.

3. Further, nothing expels sin except virtue. But charity, "which covers a multitude of sins" (Prov. 10:12), does this most of all. Therefore charity is a virtue.

Response:

It should be said that the end of human life is happiness.[b] Hence, according to the diverse lives men lead are distinguished diverse kinds of happinesses corresponding to them.[c] Those who are outside civic life cannot arrive at civic happiness, which belongs to[d] the height of that life. In like manner, if someone is going to arrive at contemplative happiness, he has to become a partaker of that life. Consequently, the happiness that man can arrive at by the exercise of his natural powers is a happiness at the level of human life;[e] and this is what the philosophers spoke of, for which reason it is said in *Ethics* I: "Happy, however, as men."[f, 246] But since to us is promised a happiness in which we shall be equal to the angels, as is evident from Matthew 22:30[247]—a happiness exceeding not only the powers of man but also the powers of angels, who, like us, must be led to this end by grace, for to God alone is such happiness natural—it follows that if man is to attain that divine happiness, he must be made a partaker of the divine life.[248] Now, that which most of all causes one to live together with another is friendship,[g] as the Philosopher says in *Ethics* IX: "Each one keeps company with his friend in the activities he especially loves and takes as the center of

a. *Esse spirituale est a uirtute*

b. Here and throughout the response, unless otherwise noted the term Thomas uses is *felicitas.*

c. *secundum diuersas uitas etiam diuerse felicitates distinguntur*

d. *attingit*

e. *felicitas, ad quam homo per sua naturalia potest deuenire, est secundum uitam humanam*

f. *Beatos autem ut homines:* Aristotle, *Ethics* I, ch. 10 (1101a20).

g. *Illud autem quod ad alterum conuiuere facit maxime amicitia est*

his life, as if [above all] wishing to live with his friend."ᵃ Thus we find that some go hunting together, others drink together, others talk philosophy together, and so on in regard to other things that people value. Accordingly, [if a man is going to keep company with God as with a friend], there needs to be a certain friendship with God by which we would live together with him; and this is charity, as was said. But this sharing of divine life exceeds the faculties of nature, as also does the happiness to which the sharing is ordered. And for this reason, nature has to be brought to this perfection by some superadded gift, which is the very *ratio* of [an infused] virtue.²⁴⁹ Hence charity must be called a theological virtue, which is poured out "into our hearts by the Holy Spirit, who is given to us" (Rom. 5:5).

Replies to objections:

1. To the first, therefore, it should be said that the kind of friendship discussed by the Philosopherᵇ is caused either by an inclination of nature (as in friendships based on pleasure or utility) or by the inclination of a virtuous habit, with that natural inclination presupposed (as in friendship based on what is noble)ᶜ, insofar as everything that makes people alike tends to cause love between them.ᵈ ²⁵⁰ And so, friendship is set down not as a virtue of theirs,ᵉ but rather as something following upon the virtues. Yet the friendship we have with God cannot have any such foundation, since it exceeds the boundaries of nature.ᶠ We must therefore be lifted up to this friendship by a special gift; and this gift we call a virtue.

---

a. A defensible translation of a difficult sentence: *unusquisque conuersatur cum amico suo in illis que maxime diligit, et que suam uitam reputat, quasi amico conuiuere uolens,* which could also be expanded: "Each one is on intimate terms with his friend in regard to the things he most of all loves and reckons to be the point of his life, as if indicating that he wants most of all to live together with his friend so as to share these things with him." The reference is to Aristotle, *Ethics* IX, ch. 12 (1172a5).

b. In the objection it was not Aristotle in particular but philosophers in general who were mentioned (*amicitia a philosophis non ponitur uirtus*). In the reply, the Leonine editors capitalize the word *Philosophus,* but it is possible to read the reply in the same way as the objection—as referring to the limits of the analysis of "a philosopher," someone analyzing natural friendships from the vantage of natural reason.

c. *quantum ad amicitiam delectabilis et utilis . . . quantum ad amicitiam honesti*

d. *in quantum omne quod facit similitudinem cum aliquo inclinat ad amorem illius*

e. *Et ideo non ponitur ab eis uirtus.* This could also be rendered (more literally, but not necessarily more accurately) as "And so, friendship is not set down *by them* as a virtue," as if to say: virtuous men do not themselves consider noble friendship to be a virtue, but rather a consequence of and context for virtue.

f. *nature metas,* literally, "the pillars or columns of nature."

2. To the second, it should be said that charity is not said to be the end of the commandments as if it were the ultimate end of the virtues, but rather as being that by which all the other virtues are given their proper ordering to the ultimate end. And in the passage cited,[a] the Apostle excludes from charity three things repugnant to true friendship: first, insincerity,[b] as found in those who simulate friendship, when they are not really friends,[c] which he excludes by saying "a faith not insincere" (taking faith here to mean fidelity); second, an evil foundation, as found in people who come together to share a certain sin and become friends on that account, which he excludes by saying "with a good conscience"; third, an ulterior motive,[d] as found when someone loves a friend for the sake of lucre, which he excludes by saying "of a pure heart."

3. To the third, it should be said that, since the acts of the virtues are praiseworthy, they must have a point of origin within us.[e, 251] By contrast, pleasure, since it comes from being joined with something fitting, is spoken of as a certain reception, and so as a passion, which originates from an agent.[f] For this reason, pleasure belongs rather to the aspect of reward. But love signifies the stretching out of the appetite into the thing loved and implies this activity. Accordingly, charity is set down as a virtue, but enjoyment, which pleasure implies, is set down as a dowry.[252]

4. To the fourth, it should be said that charity, as is evident from what was said before,[g] includes friendship, love, and desire. But a natural desire can only be for a thing that is capable of being possessed naturally; hence a natural desire for the highest good is in us by nature—in the sense that, and so far as, this highest good can be participated in by us through its natural effects.[h, 253] Similarly, love is caused by likeness; hence the highest good is naturally loved above all things, insofar as we have a likeness to him[i] through natural goods. But since

a. In the Douay-Rheims (translating from the Vulgate), 1 Tim. 1:5 reads: "Now the end of the commandment is charity, from a pure heart, and a good conscience, and an unfeigned faith." Thomas takes these up in reverse order.

b. *fictio*, which could also be rendered pretense, dissimulation.

c. *sicut est in simulantibus amicitiam, cum non sint amici*

d. *obliquata intentio*

e. *oportet quod habeant principium in nobis*

f. *cuius principium est ab agente*

g. In the preceding article.

h. *Vnde desiderium naturale summi boni inest nobis secundum naturam, in quantum summum bonum participabile est a nobis per effectus naturales*

i. *ipsum,* which can be translated either "it" or "him"—though the context

nature cannot arrive at the highest good's activities, which are his very life and happiness—cannot arrive, that is, at the vision of the divine essence—for the same reason, it does not attain the intimacy with him of a friendship that makes friends live together and share in the same works.[a] And so there is a need for charity, by which we would have friendship with God, to be added above [what is possible to nature]—both that we might love him as he is in himself, having been made like unto him through sharing in spiritual gifts, and that we might desire him as sharable by his friends in the state of glory.[b, 254]

5. To the fifth, it should be said that desire does not suffice; there also has be a sharing of life, as was said.[c]

6. To the sixth, it should be said that the difficulty found in works of virtue is not always a difficulty of labor or of something saddening. Rather, the things with which virtue is concerned are correctly said to involve difficulty inasmuch as they are above and beyond the powers of those who lack that virtue.[d, 255]

ARTICLE 3[e]   Whether reason is the subject of charity

Objections:

Proceeding to the third, it seems that the subject of charity is reason.[f]

---

strongly favors the latter, as Thomas is not speaking about a *notion* of some highest good, but about the actually existing highest good which is God.

a. Thomas writes *ideo etiam ad amicitiam non pertingit, que facit amicos conuiuere et in operibus communicare,* which has been expanded to "the intimacy with him of a friendship that makes friends" etc., in order to bring out the point that in the philosophical life one does have some relationship to God, namely through an admiring contemplation and assimilation of divine effects, but it is not that special relationship called friendship. Moreover, since there can be a sort of friendship which is called such metaphorically, as when a person joins an organization called "Friends of Whales" or when a philosopher is called a "friend of truth" (for this would also be metaphorical unless he is joined to a person who *is* Truth), we have construed the second phrase as a description of the *sort* of friendship the natural contemplative life fails to attain.

b. *et ipsum amemus, assimilati ei per participationem spiritualium donorum, et desideremus ut participabilem per gloriam ab amicis suis*

c. In the response. The phrase is *communicationem in uita.*

d. *set proprie ea quorum est uirtus dicuntur habere difficultatem, in quantum supra uires eleuantur eorum qui uirtutem non habent*

e. Parallels: *ST* I-II, q. 56, a. 6; II-II, q. 24, a. 1; *De uirt. in comm.,* a. 5; cf. *In III Sent.* d. 27, q. 1, a. 2 (see above).

f. Throughout the article, "reason" translates *ratio.* The phrases *est in ratione* and *est in uoluntate* have often been translated "has reason/will for its subject."

1. For as is said in *Ethics* I, the subject of every virtue is either the rational by participation or the rational by essence.[a] But charity is a virtue, as was said. Since its subject is not the rational by participation—for if it were, it would be a moral virtue—it seems, therefore, that its subject has to be the rational by essence. [But this is nothing other than intellect or reason. Therefore charity has reason for its subject.]

2. Further, whenever there are two things one of which always casts out the other, they must have their existence in the same subject.[b] But charity and mortal sin mutually cast each other out. Since every mortal sin is either in the superior reason or in the inferior reason (as was said in Book II, Distinction 24), it therefore seems that charity, too, has reason for its subject.

3. Further, as charity is chief among virtues freely given,[c] so prudence is chief among moral virtues. But reason is the subject of prudence; therefore, it is also that of charity.

4. Further, since charity is a theological virtue, it cannot be in the soul's sensitive part, which cannot have God for its object. It must therefore be in the soul's intellectual part. But it is not in free will,[d] since free will has for its object a contingent thing that can be brought about and chosen by us, whereas charity is of the ultimate end, which in no way belongs to the class of contingent, workable, choosable things.[e] Nor, likewise, can charity be in the will, since the will does not have a determinate act of its own but commands all the other acts of the soul—so that, if charity were in the will, for the same reason every other virtue would also be in the will [, which is false]. Therefore the only option remaining is that charity has reason for its subject.

5. Further, in their treatments of virtue, philosophers did not posit any virtue in the will, positing instead intellectual virtues in the part of the soul that is rational by essence and moral virtues in the part that is rational by participation, to which part belong the irascible and concupiscible powers, as is clear from *Ethics* I.[f] Since charity is a virtue, it therefore seems that it is not in the will.

a. That is, the part of the soul that is rational by participation (appetite) and the part of the soul that is rational by essence (intellect). The reference is to Aristotle, *Ethics* I, ch. 13 (1103a3).

b. *Ea que mutuo se expellunt oportet esse in eodem*

c. *caritas principatur in gratuitis uirtutibus*

d. "free will": *liberum arbitrium*; "will" (below): *uoluntas*

e. *supra quod non cadit contingentia nec operatio nostra nec electio:* literally, "upon which befalls neither contingency, nor activity or choice of ours"

f. Aristotle, *Ethics* I, ch. 13 (1102b13–1103a3).

On the contrary:

1. Reason's object is the true, whereas charity's object is not the true but rather the good. Therefore charity has the will for its subject, not reason.

2. Further, love pertains to appetite, whereas reason pertains to knowledge. Therefore charity does not have reason for its subject.

Response:

It should be said that, in order to know what power some virtue is in, one must consider the power to which the virtue's *act* is related. Now the chief act of charity is to love God, which indeed belongs to reason as directing, but to appetite as executing; hence it must be traced back to appetite.[256] But this act cannot be executed by sensitive appetite, since this appetite cannot have God for its object. Therefore this act must pertain to the intellectual part's appetite—not insofar as it chooses things that may lead to the end, but insofar as it is related to the ultimate end itself, and this, too, belongs to the will. Hence charity has the will for its proper subject. Certain ones, however, say that charity is in the concupiscible power. But this cannot be the case, since the concupiscible power is part of the sensitive appetite, and even if the concupiscible power be styled "human" [to distinguish it from the power as found in brute animals], still it does not have this humanness except by participating in reason—unless perhaps someone might wish, speaking equivocally, to call the will itself irascible and concupiscible.

Replies to objections:

1. To the first, therefore, it should be said that "the part of the soul that is rational by essence" does not mean reason alone, but also includes the appetite annexed to reason, namely, the will. Hence the Philosopher says in *On the Soul* III that "the will is in reason."[a] And so, charity is neither a moral virtue (since it is not about the passions belonging to the sensitive appetite, which is rational by participation) nor an intellectual virtue (for it is not with respect to powers of apprehension that it exists in the part rational by essence), but it is a theological virtue.[257]

2. To the second, it should be said that mortal sin is not always said to be "in the reason" as in a subject, since it has for its subject at times

---

a. Aristotle, *On the Soul* III, ch. 9 (432b5).

the irascible power, at times the conscupiscible;[258] but mortal sin is always "in the reason" as in the power directing the act of sin, and "in the will" or free will as in the power commanding and eliciting the act of sin. In this way, charity, too, has reason—or rather, understanding—as director of its acts.[259]

3. To the third, it should be said that prudence is chief among moral virtues insofar as it directs all of them, and on this account it pertains to reason;[260] whereas charity is chief by way of commanding various acts and conjoining the lover to an end and forming the appetite, all of which pertains to the will.[a]

4. To the fourth, it should be said that charity's subject, properly speaking, is neither sensitive appetite nor free will but simply the will, which, although related in a certain way to all human acts as their cause, nevertheless does not stand in the same relation toward all. For certain acts it elicits of itself, inasmuch as it is a specific power (for example, the very act of willing), while other acts it commands, inasmuch as it is universal mover of the soul's powers. Accordingly, virtues that bring to perfection acts merely commanded by the will do not have the will itself for their subject, but instead, whatever specific powers elicit those acts, whereas the virtues that bring to perfection acts that the will elicits *do* have the will for their subject; and so, the same account cannot be given for all of them. To love,[b] however, is an act elicited by the will, for it implies a resting of the will and a certain transformation into the thing loved. Thus, charity, which brings *this* act to perfection, has the will for its subject.

5. To the fifth, it should be said, as was said above,[c] that virtues are necessary for us in order that the soul's natural powers should be determined to good.[261] Thus, for matters in regard to which natural powers are, of their nature, determined to good, virtues[d] are not required. Now the will has for its object the good, which is the end. Hence, as far as its own nature is concerned,[e] the will is naturally determined to good—the good proportionate to human nature.[262] And

a. Filling out what the original sentence implies: *Set caritas est principalis per modum imperantis et coniungentis fini et informantis, quod pertinet ad uoluntatem.*

b. Here, *diligere,* not *amare.*

c. See *In III Sent.* d. 23, q. 1, a. 1.

d. *Vnde in illis in quibus potentie naturales sunt ex sui natura ad bonum determinate, non requiruntur alie uirtutes.* Thomas can write "other (*alie*) virtues" because the *potentie naturales* are themselves *uirtutes* in his philosophical vocabulary. We, however, would not call functional eyesight a "virtue," so much has our usage been narrowed to the moral arena.

e. *quantum in se est*

for this reason the philosophers posited no virtue in the will with respect to the ultimate end.²⁶³ Nevertheless, some acquired virtue must be posited in the will insofar as the will is concerned with things that lead to the end—the virtue, namely, of justice, as will be explained below,ª which has to do with goods that come into the use of daily life.ᵇ Even so, justice is counted among moral virtues, since, although the will according to its essence is in the part of the soul that is rational by essence, nevertheless, owing to a likeness between its act and theirs it is grouped together with the irascible and concupiscible powers, which are called rational by participation. Moreover, the will itself in some way participates in reason, insofar as it is directed by reason in the latter's function of apprehending goods.ᶜ According to the doctrine of the faith, however, an ultimate end is given that exceeds natural inclination. It is therefore necessary, according to theologians, to posit some virtue in the will, for the purpose of lifting it up to this end; and this we call charity.

ARTICLE 4   Whether charity is one virtue or many

Proceeding to the fourth, [we divide the article into four subquestions: (1) whether charity is a single virtue; (2) whether charity is distinct from other virtues; (3) whether charity is the form of the other virtues; (4) whether there can be an unformed charity.]

SUBQUESTION 1ᵈ   Whether charity is a single virtue

Objections:

It seems that charity is not a single virtue.ᵉ

1. For habits are distinguished by their acts, and acts by their objects. But charity has two objects at the greatest distance from each other, namely, God and neighbor. Therefore it is not a single virtue.

a. See *In III Sent.* d. 33, q. 2, a. 4, qa. 2.
b. *circa bona que in usum uite ueniunt*
c. *in quantum a ratione appreensiua dirigitur*
d. Parallels: *ST* II-II, q. 23, a. 5; *De caritate,* a. 4.
e. *caritas non sit una uirtus:* we have mostly written "single virtue" rather than "one virtue," because the force of the question is not: Is charity *a* virtue or *one kind of* virtue, but precisely: Is charity a *single* virtue, rather than many virtues grouped under a single name?

2. Further, theological virtues are different from moral virtues because moral virtues direct a person in regard to things that lead to the end, whereas theological virtues are about the end itself. But charity is about both the end itself and things that lead to the end, inasmuch as both God and neighbor are loved by charity. Therefore charity contains two virtues, of which one is moral and the other theological.

3. Further, virtues are ordered to specific sorts of acts, since virtue is productive of the best, as is said in *Ethics* II;[a] and they place an appropriate manner of acting in their acts,[b] since virtue consists not only in doing good things, but in doing them well; and again, acts of the virtues are commanded by the commandments of the law. But charity has two acts, two manners of acting, and two commandments. Therefore it is not a single virtue.

On the contrary:

1. There is only one [first] mover in any given genus. But charity moves all the other virtues to their ends by means of their proper acts. Therefore charity is a single virtue.

2. Further, since it is a theological virtue, charity's object is God. But God is supremely one. Therefore charity, too, is only one virtue.

Response:

It should be said that a virtue derives its species from its object according to the *ratio* under which the virtue chiefly tends to the object.[c] Hence, since charity chiefly loves God, and does not love anything else except insofar as it is *of* God, it is apparent that charity receives unity and is a single virtue from the unity of divine goodness to which it first has reference.[264]

a. Aristotle, *Ethics* II, ch. 5 (1106b22). Thomas writes: *Virtutes ad actus aliquos ordinantur, quia uirtus est optimorum operatiua.* That is, a given virtue is not about just any species of act done in any way, but it produces just the right species of act in just the right way; it is "operative of the best things" in that area of life.

b. *modum aliquem in suis actibus ponunt. Modus* in this sentence is best rendered "an appropriate manner of acting." A *modus* of activity is the manner in which it is done, such as cooking breakfast well or poorly, quickly or slowly, cheerfully or irritably. A virtue makes it possible not only to do what is "materially" the right thing, such as to refrain from drinking too much wine, but also to do the right thing in the best *way*, such as to refrain from excess without regrets or complaint, and to find it pleasant to drink the right amount. *Modus* can also be translated as "measure," and in some sentences this seems a better choice.

c. *uirtus specificatur ex obiecto suo secundum illam rationem qua principaliter in ipsum tendit*

Replies to objections:

1. To the first, therefore, it should be said that the neighbor is not the chief object of charity, as was said.

2. To the second, it should be said that theological virtues direct one also as regards things that lead to the end—not, indeed, according to the proper *rationes* of the things that lead to the end, but according to the nature of the end.[265] For even as faith causes one to believe certain things about creatures on account of the first Truth from which one receives faith,[266] so, in like manner, does charity cause one to love men insofar as they are capable of participating in the divine goodness, which is the ultimate end.

3. To the third, it should be said that a material diversity of objects suffices for numerical diversity of acts, but only a diversity of formal objects brings about diversity of species among acts.[a] Now a formal diversity of object derives from that *ratio* of the object to which either a habit or a power chiefly refers. Accordingly, while loving God and loving neighbor are indeed diverse acts, they still pertain to the same habit, just as seeing white and seeing black, or seeing something close at hand and seeing something far away, are numerically different acts of sight taking place in different ways,[b] yet pertain to one seeing power.[267] And thus, too, diverse commandments are given about acts of charity, according to the diverse measures[c] they have.[268]

SUBQUESTION 2[d]   Whether charity is distinct
from other virtues

Objections:

Furthermore, it seems that charity is not distinct from other virtues.

1. Whatever falls within the definition of virtue as such cannot be that which distinguishes one virtue from another.[e] But charity is this kind of thing. Hence, Jerome says: "To sum up briefly the whole definition of virtue: virtue is the charity by which God and neighbor are loved."[f] And Augustine says that "virtue is the order of

a. *materialis diuersitas obiectorum sufficit ad diuersificandum actum secundum numerum, set secundum speciem actus non diuersificantur nisi ex formali diuersitate obiecti*
b. *diuerse uisiones secundum numerum et diuersos modos habent*
c. *modos*
d. Parallels: *ST* II-II, q. 23, a. 4; *De malo*, q. 8, a. 2 and q. 11, a. 2; *De caritate*, a. 5.
e. *Quicquid cadit in diffinitione uirtutis non distinguitur a uirtutibus*
f. *uirtus est caritas, qua diligitur Deus et proximus.*—In fact it is Augustine, *Letter to*

love."[a] Therefore charity is not a virtue distinct from other virtues.[b]

2. Further, virtues are distinguished from one another by their acts. But the acts of all other virtues are attributed to charity, as is clear from 1 Corinthians 13. Therefore charity is not a virtue distinct from other virtues.

3. Further, any special virtue has a special object.[269] Charity, by contrast, has, not a special object, but one common to all, namely, the good. Therefore charity is not a special virtue.

4. Further, the commandments of the law are about acts of the virtues. But the commandment that pertains to charity is not contradistinguished from the other commandments, but rather it contains all the other commandments in itself. Therefore charity is not a virtue distinct from other virtues.

On the contrary:

1. Whenever a genus is divided into species, the members so divided are distinct from one another.[c] But charity is distinguished from the other theological virtues, according to 1 Corinthians 13 and according to Gregory, who says that charity is symbolized by one of the daughters of Job.[d] Therefore it is a special virtue.

2. Further, in *Ethics* V the Philosopher proves that justice is a special virtue because it has a special vice contrary to it alone.[e] But charity has a special vice contrary to it alone, namely, hatred. Therefore charity is a special virtue.

Response:

It should be said that, as was said [in the preceding article], habits derive their species from their correlative objects, according to that *ratio* of an object to which a habit chiefly refers. Now, an object's *ratio* is taken according to the relationship between the thing toward which the habit or power exercises its activity, and the act of the soul in which the habits or powers exist.[f] Since, however, it happens that things which in reality[g] are joined together and are supremely one

---

Jerome, Letter 168, ch. 4, n. 15 (PL 33:739), and the exact wording is: "virtus est charitas qua id quod diligendum est diligitur."

a. Augustine, *On the City of God* XV, ch. 22 (CCSL 48:488).

b. *caritas non distinguitur ab aliis uirtutibus*

c. A paraphrase of *Omne quod condiuiditur contra alia est distinctum ab illis.*

d. Gregory, *Morals on the Book of Job* I, ch. 27 (CCSL 143:45).

e. Aristotle, *Ethics* V, ch. 4 (1130a14).

f. Literally, the proportion of the thing to the act of soul: *Ratio autem obiecti sumitur secundum proportionem rei circa quam est operatio habitus uel potentie ad actum anime in qua sunt habitus uel potentie.*

g. Here and elsewhere, "in reality" translates *secundum rem.*

are sometimes divided by the soul's activity, it therefore happens that where a *thing* is the same, there may yet be diverse *rationes* of the object, as, for example, the same thing [wealth] is the object of liberality as able to be given away freely to another, and of justice as having the nature of a debt owed to another.[a] And likewise, where a thing is really common, the object's *ratio* is particular and proper, as, for example, first philosophy, although it considers being as common to all, is a special science precisely because it considers being under a special *ratio*, namely, being insofar as it does not depend on matter and motion. The case is similar in the topic under discussion. The chief and proper object of charity is the divine goodness. Now, while there is some divine good aspired to in all the other virtues, yet this very good, common in reality,[270] has itself a special *ratio*.[b] And so, charity is a special virtue distinct from all the others.

Replies to objections:

1. To the first, therefore, it should be said that just as in the realm of sciences perfection is imparted to all the other sciences by a single special science distinct from them, namely, first philosophy, insofar as its object is common in reality to the objects of all the other sciences, so, too, is it in the realm of virtues: that which pertains to a single virtue can be placed in the common definition of virtue, as is evident with prudence, which perfects the *ratio* of virtue in all the moral virtues. And so, right reason, which pertains to prudence, is placed in the definition of virtue as such, as is evident from *Ethics* II: "Virtue is a choice-productive habit consisting in a mean determined by reason, as a wise man would determine it";[c] nor from this should it be concluded that prudence is not a special virtue, but rather, that it is a general rule of all virtues.

And so it is that charity, too, which perfects all the other virtues, is placed in the common definition of virtue; nor from this should it be concluded that charity is a general virtue, but rather, that it is a general perfection of the virtues. Nevertheless, Augustine's statement that "virtue is the order of love" can be understood in two ways: either interpreting "love" to mean the love of charity itself, and then the aforesaid

a. *sicut eadem est obiectum est liberalitatis ut est donabilis, et iustitie ut habet rationem debiti*

b. *In omnibus autem aliis uirtutibus est aliquod bonum diuinum, set tamen hoc quod est commune secundum rem habet specialem rationem*—namely, its very status as supreme and essential Good, of whose beatitude man can become partaker.

c. Aristotle, *Ethics* II, ch. 6 (1106b36).

response holds; or interpreting "love" to mean love in general,ᵃ and in this way "love" is taken for that natural love which exists in any power whatsoever with respect to its object, to which love virtue gives a suitable determination, since virtue is the ordering of the soul's affections.ᵇ Certain ones, however, not paying attention to the difference between *natural* love and appetite and *animal* love and appetite, erred to the extent of maintaining that the concupiscible was not a special power but [something] diffused in all the other powers;ᶜ and, in like manner, maintained that charity was indistinct from the other virtues.²⁷¹

2. To the second, it should be said that acts of other virtues are attributed to charity, not as though it elicits them itself, but rather because it commands them. It does, however, have a special act to elicit, namely loving God.

3. To the third, it should be said that charity's object is not any good whatsoever, but the *divine* good; and this good also, although it is in some way present in all goods, nevertheless has a special *ratio* [distinctly its own and not common to any other good], as was said.

4. To the fourth, it should be said that the commandment pertaining to charity does not embrace all the other commandments as though it were a sort of universal in comparison to those things, but instead in the manner of a sort of leading-back of the others to it,ᵈ ²⁷² since all commandments are ordered to that one, just as the acts of all the other virtues are ordered to the act of charity, insofar as it commands them all. Hence, from this fact is established, not that charity is a general virtue, but that it is a general *mover* of all the virtues.

SUBQUESTION 3ᵉ   Whether charity is the form of the other virtues

Objections:

Furthermore, it seems that charity is not the form of the other virtues.²⁷³

a. *amore caritatis . . . amore in communi*

b. *et sic amor sumitur pro amore naturali, qui inest cuilibet potentie respectu sui obiecti, quem uirtus determinat, quia est ordinatio affectionum anime*

c. *uim . . . uiribus*

d. *non compreendit omnia alia commandmenta sicut uniuersale ad illa, set per quandam reductionem*

e. Parallels: *In II Sent.* d. 26, a. 4, ad 5 (translated in webnote 285); *In III Sent.* d. 23, q. 3, a. 1, qa. 1 (see above); *ST* II-II, q. 23, a. 8; *De ueritate*, q. 14, a. 5; *De malo*, q. 8, a. 2; *De caritate*, a. 3.

1. For every form is either an exemplar form or an intrinsic form.[274] But charity is not the exemplar form of the virtues, since on that supposition all the other virtues would be drawn into the same species;[275] nor is it an intrinsic form, since then it would give being and species to the other virtues, and in that way all the virtues would be of the same species and would be in the same subject as charity is, nor would they be distinct from it.[276] Therefore in no way is charity the form of the virtues.

2. Further, charity differs from grace. But grace is said to be the form of all the virtues, since it makes an act meritorious. Therefore charity is not the form.

3. Further, as power stands to power, so habit stands to habit. But reason imposes an appropriate manner of acting on all the other forces[a] of the soul; therefore a habit existing in the reason imposes such a manner on all the other habits. And thus, faith—or even prudence, which is described by the philosophers as the form of all the other virtues—is more the form of the virtues than charity.

4. Further, form, agent, and end do not come together in something numerically one, as is said in *Physics* II.[b] But charity is the end of the commandments and thus of the virtues, and it is a mover, too, insofar as it commands the acts of the virtues. Therefore it is not a form.

5. Further, habits are revealed through acts proceeding from them. But any virtue whatsoever imposes its manner of acting or its form upon the act proceeding from it, so that, accordingly, a just man works justly, and a brave man acts bravely. Therefore the virtues are not formed through charity but are formed through themselves.[277]

On the contrary:

1. Ambrose says that charity informs all the other virtues and is their mother.[c]

2. Further, that which is foremost even in bodily things is formal with respect to others in the same order, as fire is in a certain way the form of air, and air of water, and water of earth, as is said in *Physics* IV.[d]

a. *uiribus*

b. *Forma et efficiens et finis non incidit in idem numero.*—Aristotle, *Physics* II, ch. 7 (198a25).

c. Moos sends us to Ambrosiaster, *Comments on First Corinthians* 8, 2 (PL 17:226), but no relevant text is there. Shortly thereafter (PL 17:239) we find a text saying that charity is "the mother of all good things." Another more likely source is Ambrose Autpert's *Lives of Saints Paldo, Tuto, and Vaso,* n. 17 (CCCM 27B:902), which speaks of charity as "mother of all virtues." Neither text, however, speaks of "forming" or "informing."

d. Aristotle, *Physics* IV, ch. 5 (213a1ff.).

But charity has first place among the virtues. Therefore it itself is the form of the virtues.

Response:

It should be said that charity may be compared to all other virtues as their mover, as their end, and as their form.

(1) That it is the *mover* of all the other virtues is evident from the fact that the good itself, which is charity's object under the *ratio* of final end, is the [common] end of the virtues. But in all powers or arts of a single order, it happens that the art or power that has to do with the ultimate end orders the acts of other arts or powers to their proper ends, as the military art, which exists for the sake of victory (to which every particular military task[a] is ordered), orders the equestrian and naval arts to their ends. And so, charity is called "mother" of the other virtues, insofar as she brings forth their acts from her conception of the end, which functions in the manner of a seed, since the end is the point of departure for matters of action, as the Philosopher says.[b] Now, [a virtue that has to do with the end] is said to command the acts of lower virtues insofar as it makes them do their work for the sake of its end, and in this way it moves other lower arts toward its end. Hence charity also moves all the other virtues toward its end, and in this way it is said to command their acts. For there is this difference between eliciting and commanding an act: a habit or power elicits that act which it produces in regard to its own object, without the mediation of anything else; but it *commands* an act when that act is produced by the mediation of a lower power or habit in regard to that power's object.[278] In this way, therefore, charity is the mover of the other virtues.[279]

(2) Charity is likewise their *end.* For it belongs to all the virtues in common that their acts are their proximate ends, since activity is second perfection and habit first perfection, and the less complete is ordered to the more complete as to an end. Now the end of a lower power or habit is ordered to the end of a higher-ranking one, just as a military end is ordered to a civic end.[280] Consequently, the acts of all the other virtues are ordered to the act of charity as to an end. And it is for this reason that charity is called "the end of the commandments" (1 Tim. 1:5).[c]

a. *officium bellicum*

b. *principium in operabilibus*: Aristotle, *Ethics* VII, ch. 8 (1151a16).

c. According to the Vulgate's rendering of the Greek: *Finis autem praecepti est caritas de corde puro et conscientia bona et fide non ficta.* The RSV has a different take on the verse: "The aim of our charge is love that issues from a pure heart and a good conscience and sincere faith."

(3) It is likewise evident that charity is the *form* that causes the *ratio* of virtue to be perfectly realized in each and every virtue.[a] For a lower power does not have the perfection of virtue except by participating in the perfection of a higher-ranking power, as for example a habit in the irascible power does not have the nature of virtue, as is said in *Ethics* VI,[b] except inasmuch as it receives understanding (i.e., discretion) from reason, which is perfected by prudence; and accordingly, prudence places a form and an appropriate manner of acting into all the other moral virtues. Now, all the virtues that can merit eternal life— and it is from this vantage that we are now speaking of virtues—exist in powers subject to the will, since a power's act can be meritorious only to the extent that it has something of the voluntary in it, and voluntariness has place whenever the will moves and commands the acts of other powers.[c, 281] Hence it is impossible that a habit existing in some power of the soul should have the nature of virtue—if one is speaking of meritorious virtues, as we are doing here—except to the extent that such a power participates in something of the perfection of a will that is perfected by charity.

And therefore charity is the form of *all* the other virtues, as prudence is the form of the *moral* virtues. And this is one way in which charity is the form of the other virtues. The other two ways [in which charity is the form of the virtues] can be taken from the fact that charity is mover and end, insofar as a mover communicates something of its manner of acting to the instrument,[d, 282] and insofar as things that lead to the end are directed in accord with the *ratio* of the end [as it preexists in the agent].[e, 283] And it is thus that charity's manner of acting is participated in by the other virtues, insofar as they are moved by charity and are ordered to it as their end.

Replies to objections:

1. To the first, therefore, it should be said that charity is the exemplar form of the virtues. But there are two kinds of exemplar form. One is the original in imitation of which something is made; and for this [sort of imitation to occur], nothing other than a mere likeness is required, as we say that real things in the world are exemplar forms of

---

a. *forma perficiens unamquamque uirtutem in ratione uirtutis*

b. Aristotle, *Ethics* VI, ch. 13 (1144b1ff.).

c. *in quantum habet aliquid de uoluntario, quod contingit ex hoc quod uoluntas mouet*, etc.

d. *in quantum mouens ponit modum suum in instrumento*

e. *et ea que sunt ad finem diriguntur ex ratione finis*

paintings.ᵃ Another kind of exemplar form is that according to the likeness of which something is made *and* through participation in which it has being, as the divine goodness is the exemplar form of every goodness, and the divine wisdom, of every wisdom; and such an exemplar form need not be of one and the same species with the effects caused by it, since participants do not always participate [in the perfections of their cause] in the mode of that cause in which they participate.ᵇ And this is the way in which prudence is the form of the other moral virtues, for, by impressing upon lower powers a sort of seal of prudence, prudence gives to the habits found in the lower powers the *ratio* of virtue.ᶜ And something similar holds for charity with respect to all the other virtues.

2. To the second, it should be said that lower powers are not perfected by the perfection of virtue except by participating in the perfection of higher-ranking ones. Now, since higher-ranking things are formal with respect to lower-ranking things, as being more perfect, what is participated in from the higher-ranking is formal in the lower-ranking. Hence, for the perfection of virtue in any power is required [a participation in] as many forms as are higher-ranking with respect to that power. For example, reason is higher-ranking than the concupiscible appetite, as placing order in it; and so prudence, which is reason's perfection, is the form of temperance, which is a virtue in the concupiscible appetite. Similarly, the will is higher-ranking than reason, insofar as reason's act is viewed as a voluntary and meritorious act; and so charity is the form of prudence and temperance alike. Similarly, the soul's essence is superior to the will, insofar as the will and all the other powers of the soul flow from the soul's essence; and so grace, which is the perfection of the soul's essence, establishing it in spiritual being, is the form of charity, prudence, and temperance alike. Nor would charity be a virtue if it were [*per impossibile*] without grace, as neither would prudence be a virtue if it were without charity, nor temperance, without charity and prudence—as long as we are speaking of infused virtues ordered to gaining merit.²⁸⁴ Certain ones, however, say that charity and grace are the same in essence; but this was discussed in Book II, Distinction 26.²⁸⁵

  ᴶ   a. *una ad cuius representationem aliquid fit, et ad hanc non exigitur nisi similitudo tantum, sicut dicimus res ueras picturarum esse formas exemplares*

     b. *talis forma exemplaris non oportet quod sit unius speciei cum causatis, quia participantia non semper participant per modum participati*

     c. *in quantum sigillatio quedam prudentie in inferioribus uiribus dat habitibus qui ibi sunt rationem uirtutis*

3. To the third, it should be said that reason imposes a manner of acting on all the powers under its governance, and the will, likewise, on all the powers lower than it.[a] But the philosophers did not maintain that virtue was given form by anything other than prudence, because neither in the will, so far as it pertains to the ultimate end, nor in the soul's essence, did they posit any perfection added over and above that of human nature.[286] Nevertheless, the natural perfection that all the virtues share in remains.[b, 287]

4. To the fourth, it should be said that exemplar form comes together with the agent and the end in something numerically one, as is evident with God, but intrinsic form does not.[288]

5. To the fifth, it should be said that lower things participate in the perfections of higher things after the former's own manner; and so the participants' participations are determined for them by their own capacity and nature. Accordingly, any virtue in a lower power has a certain form by which it is constituted *a* virtue owing to its participation in a higher power's perfection, while it has the form by which it is *this* virtue from the nature of the particular power in which it exists, through that power's determination to its proper object. And any virtue places into its own act *this* form and manner of acting *as well as* the form or manner it has from the higher power, as, for example, [infused] temperance places into its act a manner of acting proper to temperance, as well as that which it has from prudence, from charity, and from grace.

SUBQUESTION 4[c]   Whether there can be an unformed charity

Objections:

Furthermore, it seems that charity can exist while being unformed by grace.[d, 289]

1. For just as faith continues to exist in one who believes but does not act rightly, so too can the love by which God is loved exist in such a person, since even sinners and infidels love God.[e] But faith lacking

---

a. *ratio imponit modum omnibus uiribus que sunt sub ipsa, et uoluntas similiter omnibus uiribus inferioribus ea*

b. *Naturalis autem perfectio constat quod in omnibus uirtutibus participatur*

c. Parallels: *ST* I-II, q. 65, aa. 2 & 4; II-II, q. 23, a. 7; immediately above, qa. 3, ad 2.

d. The formulation is briefer: *quod caritas possit esse informis.*

e. *Sicut enim fides est in eo qui non operatur bene, ita etiam et dilectio qua Deus diligitur, quia etiam peccatores et infideles Deum diligunt*

good works is unformed by grace; in like manner, therefore, charity lacking good works is unformed by grace.

2. Further, no one knows whether or not he has grace. But someone can know that he has love. Therefore the love of God can exist without grace, and so it can exist in an unformed state.[a]

3. Further, from faith arise both fear and love. But fear can exist in an unformed state, as servile fear proves.[290] Therefore, so can love.

On the contrary:

1. The Holy Spirit cannot be present and active without grace being present and active.[b] But "the charity of God is poured out into our hearts by the Holy Spirit" (Rom. 5:5). Therefore charity [is accompanied by the presence and action of the Holy Spirit, and so] cannot exist while being unformed by grace.

2. Further, a form cannot be unformed, but charity is the form of all the other virtues. Therefore it cannot itself be unformed.

Response:

It should be said that charity can never exist while being unformed by grace; and on this point all authorities agree. According to some, however, this happens because of the fact that charity is nothing other than the Holy Spirit. But in Book I, this position was destroyed.[c] According to others, charity is the same as grace—which was rejected in Book II.[291] It is therefore necessary to assign other reasons. From what has been said up to this point, two such reasons can be gathered. The first is taken from charity's effect; for, since charity is a certain friendship that requires friends to live together,[d] there cannot be charity unless there be a sharing of divine life, which comes through grace; and therefore charity cannot exist without grace. The second reason can be gathered from the fact that charity is the mover and form of all the virtues. Hence, inasmuch as every sin is opposed to the act of some vir-

a. Both times "love" is *dilectio*. If *dilectio* is understood psychologically, as a formation of the will, we can be aware of its presence even as we are aware of our own thoughts; but the objector equivocates by assuming that, since *caritas* is a kind of *dilectio*, the same is true for it, too. The reason this does not follow has already been discussed above: see *In I Sent.* (Paris version) d. 17, q. 1, a. 4; *In I Sent.* (*Lectura romana*) d. 17, q. 1, a. 4.

b. An interpretative rendering of *Spiritus Sanctus non potest esse sine gratia.*

c. *In I Sent.* (Paris version) d. 17, q. 1, aa. 1–2 (see above); *In I Sent.* (*Lectura romana*) d. 17, q. 1, a. 2 (see above).

d. *conuictum inter amicos*, a common life among friends—those who share their meals together; compare the unfortunate English derivative "convicts."

tue, every [mortal] sin takes away charity.[292] And since grace cannot be taken away except by sin, it follows that charity is taken away as soon as grace is removed.[a, 293]

Replies to objections:

1. To the first, therefore, it should be said that to faith is specifically opposed not every sin, but rather, every infidelity; and so, just as the habit of faith is entirely taken away when a man errs about one article of faith, as was said above,[b] so the habit of charity is entirely taken away when any sin opposed to charity is committed. Hence, nothing ever remains unformed in charity, whereas this can happen in the other virtues.[c, 294]

2. To the second, it should be said that a man does not know whether or not the rational love he is aware of having is specifically the rational love that is *charity*.[d] Hence, just as a man does not know whether or not he has grace, so he does not know whether or not he has charity.

3. To the third, it should be said that fear does not require a sharing of divine life, as does the love of charity. And therefore love and fear are not similar in this respect.

QUESTION 3   On the act of charity for God

The next thing to be inquired about is the act of charity by which God is loved, since the place for inquiry about loving one's neighbor will come later. We will inquire into four things here: (1) whether it is possible for us to love God in his very essence, directly and immediately; (2) whether he can be totally loved; (3) whether the love by which we love God has any measure; (4) whether the measure of acting contained in the commandment of charity—namely, "with all your heart, with all your soul," etc.—can be fulfilled in the wayfaring state.

---

a. *caritas tollitur, ablata gratia*
b. *In III Sent.* d. 23, q. 3, a. 3, qa. 1.
c. *Vnde in caritate nichil manet informe, sicut in aliis uirtutibus*
d. *dilectio illa quam aliquis scit se habere, nescit de ea utrum sit dilectio caritatis*

ARTICLE 1^a   Whether God can be immediately loved by wayfarers

Objections:

Proceeding to the first, it seems that God cannot be loved by us directly and immediately, as long as we are in the wayfaring state.^b

1. For intellect is quicker than affection; hence Augustine says that "intellect flies ahead, but affection lags behind or comes not at all."^c But our intellect in the wayfaring state cannot see God directly and immediately; therefore neither can our affection love him in that way.

2. Further, love cannot be had for the unknown and the unseen; hence the Philosopher says in *Ethics* IX, "No one begins to love a beauty in which he did not already take delight."^d But in the wayfaring state we do not see the divine essence. Therefore neither can we love it in its essence, directly and immediately.

3. Further, knowledge had in the heavenly fatherland exceeds knowledge had in the wayfaring state, insofar as man in the fatherland sees God directly and immediately in his essence. If therefore in the wayfaring state man could love God directly and immediately, the charity of the fatherland would not surpass the charity of the wayfaring state. [And this is false. Therefore, man cannot so love God in the wayfaring state.]

4. Further, in the wayfaring state we are unable to see God directly and immediately because of the fact that we rise from visible things to the knowledge of invisible things. But in like manner, we go from love of visible things to love of invisible things. Hence Gregory says in one of his homilies: "The kingdom of heaven is spoken of under the likeness of earthly things, so that, by way of what the soul already knew to love, it might learn also to love what is unknown."^e And in the Pref-

---

a. Parallels: *ST* II-II, q. 27, a. 4; *De ueritate*, q. 10, a. 11, ad 6; *De caritate*, a. 2, ad 11.

b. Note the various phrasings of the question. "Is it possible for us in this life (that is, *in uia*, as wayfarers to heaven) to love God *per essentiam*, to love him as he is in himself?" which is equivalent to the question "Can we as wayfarers love him '*immediate*,' without any created intermediary, with nothing intervening between him and us?" *Immediate* emphasizes that the act in question has its term directly in God, and is not by way of a power or habit that has something else as its object, such as a creature of God.

c. Augustine, *Expositions of the Psalms*, Ps. 118, Serm. 8, n. 4 (CCSL 40:1689).

d. Aristotle, *Ethics* IX, ch. 5 (1167a3–5): "Goodwill seems, then, to be a beginning of friendship, as the pleasure of the eye is the beginning of love. For no one loves if he has not first been delighted by the form of the beloved . . ."

e. Gregory, *Homilies on the Gospels*, Homily 11, n. 1 (CCSL 141:74).

ace it says: "that by knowing God visibly, we may, through this, be borne off into love for what is invisible."[a] In like manner, therefore, in the wayfaring state we do not love God directly and immediately.

5. Further, the will, which is the first root of sin, ought to be corrupted more by sin than any other power of the soul is corrupted. But [in man's fallen condition] the intellect cannot exercise its act, which is *to see*, toward God as direct and immediate object.[b] Therefore neither can the will exercise an act of love having God as direct and immediate object.

On the contrary:

1. Augustine says in the *Confessions*: "Woe to those who love your traces in place of you."[c] The phrase "traces of God," however, refers to the participation of divine goodness found in creatures. Therefore holy men and women[d] in the wayfaring state love God directly and immediately, and not only insofar as his goodness is participated in by creatures.

2. Further, the knowledge proper to the wayfaring state is enigmatic and destined to be emptied out, owing to the fact that it knows God through the mediation of created things; but "charity will never fail" (1 Cor. 13:8). Therefore charity does not love God through the mediation of any created thing.[e, 295]

3. Further, that which is a middle term of knowing something is the reason for that knowledge;[f] and it ought to be similar with rational love. But creatures are not the reason for loving God; quite the contrary, God is the reason for loving creatures, most of all when we are speaking about the love that is charity. Therefore [even in this life], God is directly and immediately loved in his essence.

Response:

It should be said that for ordered powers, the following truth obtains: where a prior power's activity has its terminus, there a subse-

---

a. *Vt dum uisibiliter Deum cognoscimus, per hunc in inuisibilium amorem rapiamur.* From the Preface appointed for Masses of the Christmas season.

b. *intellectus non potest actum suum, qui est uidere, exercere circa Deum immediate*

c. Augustine, rightly *On Free Choice of the Will* II, ch. 16, n. 43 (CCSL 29:266). "Traces": *nutus*, which first means "nod," then comes to mean "command" or "will," and finally "things commanded or willed."

d. *sanctis*

e. *Cognitio uie, propter hoc quod Deum mediantibus creaturis cognoscit, euacuatur et est enigmatica. Set "caritas numquam excidet", I Cor. XIII. Ergo non diligit Deum mediante creatura.*

f. *medium cognoscendi . . . ratio cognitionis*

quent power's activity begins,ᵃ as it is evident that sensation ends in imagination, which is a motion produced from sense-in-act, and intellect begins where imagination ends, since the intellect takes phantasms for its object, as is said in *On the Soul* III.ᵇ Consequently, about things that have no phantasms,ᶜ the intellect can gather no knowledge, except on the basis of things whose phantasms are represented to it.ᵈ Hence in the wayfaring state, in which it gathers [intelligible forms] from phantasms, the intellect cannot see God directly and immediately, but has to arrive at a knowledge of him on the basis of visible things whose phantasms it grasps. Now, although it does not directly and immediately see his very essence, the intellect's knowledge nevertheless ends in [a knowledge of] God himself, since from his effects it apprehends that he exists.ᵉ Hence, the will's activity can be directly and immediately about God himself, with no intervening middle term on the will's part[296]—but nevertheless, with many preceding middle terms on the intellect's part, by which it comes to the knowledge of God.ᶠ ⁽²⁹⁷⁾

Replies to objections:

1. To the first, therefore, it should be said that intellect is quicker to this extent, that it precedes affection [by giving it its object]; but in the act of loving, affection reaches more into a thing's innermost being,ᵍ as was said above.ʰ

2. To the second, it should be said that love must be of that which is *somehow* known and seen, but not necessarily of that which is known and seen directly.ⁱ Hence that which is known in another can yet be loved directly.

a. *ubi terminatur operatio prioris potentie, ibi incipit operatio sequentis.* "Ends" has to be taken here in the sense of "has its terminus" or "terminates," not "ceases to act."

b. Aristotle, *On the Soul* III, ch. 7 (431a15ff.).

c. That is, things of which there cannot *be* phantasms from which to abstract.

d. *illarum rerum que non habent phantasmata cognitionem non potest accipere, nisi ex rebus quarum sibi representantur phantasmata*

e. And so, that he can be loved. *Quamuis autem ipsam essentiam non uideat immediate, tamen cognitio intellectus ad ipsum Deum terminatur, quia ipsum esse ex effectibus appreendit.* Right after this sentence, Moos includes two sentences that are found in some manuscripts, a translation of which may be helpful to the reader although their authenticity has been rejected by the Leonine editors: "Hence, since affection follows upon intellect, affection's (or the will's) activity begins where intellect's activity terminates. It was said, however, that the intellect's operation, viz., knowledge of him, has its term in God himself, whose being it apprehends from his effects."

f. *nullo medio interueniente . . . multis tamen mediis precedentibus*

g. *affectus in amando magis pertingit ad intima*

h. See *In III Sent.* d. 27, q. 1, a. 1 (above).

i. "directly": *in se*

3. To the third, it should be said that a good is more lovable to the extent that it is more fully known—especially that good which is the end, and in which is found nothing offensive to affection. And therefore since God is more fully known in the fatherland than now, so he will be more fully loved. But that difference on the part of knowledge[a] will be due to something proper to knowledge (namely, to know something *per se*, not in and through another); and accordingly there will not be the same *ratio* of knowledge [in the fatherland as in the wayfaring state]. There will be a difference in affection, however, not in regard to what pertains to it *per se*, but rather due to the difference in knowledge. So, the nature of this love will remain the same, but the love will differ in its intensity, as the greater from the lesser.[b]

4. To the fourth, it should be said that the fact that love tends from visible to invisible things does not derive from something on *its* part, but rather from something on the part of knowledge, namely, the kind of knowledge preceding it. Hence in each authority adduced mention was made of knowledge.

5. To the fifth, it should be said that neither the nature of the soul's powers nor that which follows upon them according to their nature is taken away through sin.

ARTICLE 2[c]   Whether God can be totally loved

Objections:

Proceeding to the second, it seems that God cannot be totally loved.

1. For love[d] presupposes knowledge, but God is not totally known, even by the saints in the fatherland. Therefore neither can he be totally loved by any creature.

2. Further, just as the divine light is infinite, so also is the divine goodness. But by reason of its infinity the divine light cannot be comprehended by the intellect in such a way that it would be totally seen.

a. That is, the difference between wayfaring and heavenly knowledge, mentioned in the objection.

b. *inde erit eadem ratio amoris, set differet amor per magis et minus,* i.e., the love will be of the same species here and there—in both states, it is the same charity; but it will differ in heaven by being more intense than it is here, for the reason given.

c. Parallels: *ST* II-II, q. 27, a. 5; *De caritate*, a. 10, ad 5. This inquiry overlaps to a large extent with the more specific inquiry into whether a Christian in the wayfaring state can love God perfectly: in addition to a. 4 below, see, for example, *ST* II-II, q. 24, a. 8; q. 44, a. 4; q. 184, a. 2; *De perfectione*, chs. 3–7 (ed. Leon. 41:B70–72).

d. Throughout this article, "love" renders *dilectio* and *diligere*.

Therefore neither can the divine goodness be totally comprehended by the affection in such a way that it would be totally loved.

3. Further, God does not love himself more than totally. If therefore some creature could love God totally, some creature's love would equal the divine love, which is false.

On the contrary:

"Love the Lord your God from your whole heart" (Deut. 6:5). This will be fulfilled, at least in the fatherland. Therefore God can be totally loved by man.

Response:

It should be said that three things concur in the activity of loving, namely lover, love, and beloved;[a] and to each of these corresponds its own mode.[b] For a thing loved has a mode by which it is lovable, and the lover has a mode by which he is dilective, that is, apt to love something.[c] But the mode of *love* is discerned[d] in the comparison of lover to beloved, since love is the medium between the two. And it is similar in the case of vision.[298]

If therefore "totally" be taken to refer to the mode of *the thing loved and seen,* in this way the saints in the fatherland love God totally and see him totally, since, just as there is nothing of his essence which they do not see and love (for which reason they are said to see the whole and love the whole),[299] so also nothing of the mode according to which God exists remains unseen or unloved by them.[e, 300] Hence they see

a. *diligens, dilectio, et dilectum*

b. In this discussion, *modus* is a difficult concept to grasp. Any thing or activity has a mode, measure, manner, of existing or of acting that is suitable to it, and on the basis of which the relationship of other things to it can be judged. Thus, a runner's *modus* might be described as how well or how far he can run, these being a certain "measure" of his ability. To say that a thing loved has a *modus* by which it is lovable means that to each good there corresponds a certain "measure" of lovability. A thing is as lovable as it is good: the goodness *measures* its lovability. The mode that goes along with a cake is relatively dim, for we love it only to a modest point. The mode that goes along with bodily life as opposed to death is quite intense as compared with other natural goods, but still finite because there are greater goods than it, for the sake of which one should be prepared to lay down one's life. However, the mode that goes along with God, the infinite good, is itself infinite; he is as lovable as he is good.

c. *natus diligere,* "born to love": compare the idiom "someone is a born runner." We are speaking of the activity most natural to something, the work it naturally performs.

d. *attenditur*

e. *ita etiam nichil de modo quo Deus est remanet ab eis non uisum aut non dilectum*

and love totally, that is, they see and love the whole mode according to which God exists.

It is similar, too, if "totally" be taken to refer to the mode of *the ones loving,* since according to the whole mode [of their power to love and to see], that is, according to their whole capacity,ᵃ they will love and see, nothing of their power being withdrawn from the divine vision and love. And in this way is understood "to love [God] from the whole heart."

If, however, "totally" be taken to refer to the mode of *the love,* in this way they will neither totally love nor totally see, since the mode of love and of vision, as was said, is discerned in the comparison of the lovable and the visible to the one seeing [and loving]. Now the mode in which God is lovable and visible exceeds the mode by which man can love or see, since his light and his goodness is infinite. And therefore he is not totally seen and loved by others, since he is not loved as intensely and fervently, nor seen as clearly, as he is lovable and visible, except by himself. And thus he alone comprehends himself by loving and by seeing.

Replies to objections:

1–4. And from this response, the solution to all the objections is clear.

ARTICLE 3ᵇ   Whether the love by which we
love God has any measureᶜ

Objections:

Proceeding to the third, it seems that the love by which we love God has a mode.

1. For every finite thing has a measure.ᵈ But mode is caused by

a. *totum suum posse*
b. Parallels: *ST* II-II, q. 27, a. 6; *De caritate,* a. 2, ad 13; *Super Rom.* 12, lec. 1.
c. The question can be understood only if one bears in mind the variety of meanings *modus* can have: mode, manner, way. So, to ask whether a certain activity has a *modus* is to ask whether a limit is imposed on it by some external measure. For instance, the activity of eating is measured, or given its functional limits, objectively by food that is appealing and good to eat, subjectively by the sensation of hunger giving way to satiety. Here, to ask if there is any *modus* to our loving of God is to ask if the activity itself should be "measured," moderate, limited in any way (see the *sed contra*). I have at times preferred "measure" to "mode," since the former more idiomatically conveys the truth Thomas wishes to convey: there simply is no limit, nor could there ever be, to how much God deserves to be loved or how much we should love him.
d. *mensuram*

measure, as was said in Book I, Distinction 3. Since therefore the love by which we love God is finite, it must have a mode.

2. Further, as Bernard says, "Charity progresses to wisdom."[a] But wisdom has a mode, according to Romans 12:3: "Do not be wiser than is necessary."[b] Therefore love has a mode.

3. Further, every act of virtue is moderate, since what is immoderate is reprehensible and vicious.[c] But the love by which we love God is especially an act of virtue. Therefore it has a mode.

4. Further, all the acts of the other virtues are done from charity. If therefore charity has no mode in its act, neither will the other virtues have a mode. [But they do; therefore charity, too, has a mode.]

On the contrary:

1. Bernard says in *On Loving God:* "The reason to love God is God; the measure, to love without measure."[d]

2. Further, love ought to take its measure from the lovable thing. But the divine goodness is measureless. Therefore love of him has no measure.[e]

Response:

It should be said that "mode" implies a certain measuring.[f] But an act is measured by that which is the *ratio* for acting, just as mercy, in giving aid to misery, takes its measure from the quantity of misery that moves mercy. Now, whereas the cause of loving God is the divine goodness, which is infinite, the act of a creature is finite, since it proceeds from a finite potency; and therefore it cannot be commensurate to the *ratio* for loving. And owing to this, the love of God has no limit[g] placed upon it beyond which it would be unnecessary to progress, but howsoever much this love should love him, it always stretches itself to

---

a. Rightly William of St. Thierry, *On the Nature and Dignity of Love,* ch. 2, n. 5 (PL 184:383).

b. *Non plus sapere quam oportet.* The whole verse: "For I say, by the grace that is given me, to all that are among you, not to be more wise than it behoveth to be wise, but to be wise unto sobriety and according as God hath divided to every one the measure of faith" (Douay-Rheims).

c. *moderatus . . . immoderatum,* i.e., "moded" and "unmoded."

d. *Causa diligendi Deum Deus est, modus sine modo diligere.*—Bernard of Clairvaux, *On Loving God,* ch. 1, n. 1 (PL 182:974; SC 393:60).

e. *Dilectio mensuranda est ad diligibile. Set diuina bonitas est immensa. Ergo et dilectio ipsius non habet modum.* A sign of the conceptual closeness of *modus* and *mensura* can be seen in the fact that the *sed contra* articles here employ both terms as if they were interchangeable.

f. *mensurationem*   g. *modus*

what [still] lies before it.ᵃ And for this reason, too, it is said that charity does not have a mode, namely, a pre-set mode, beyond which it must not progress.

Replies to objections:

1. To the first, therefore, it should be said that since the love by which we love God is finite, it has [as a matter of fact] a certain mode to which it attains [at any given moment]; but it does not have a mode according to which it stops or ought to stop, as have the other virtues.[301]

2. To the second, it should be said, as was said above,ᵇ that through knowledge things are in a certain way drawn into the one knowing; and therefore things pertaining to knowledge are measured by the knower's own capacity, although the *truth* of the knowledge is measured by the thing itself. But through love the lover is drawn toward the very one loved, and therefore love is to be measured by the very thing loved rather than by the one loving.

3. To the third, it should be said that no matter how much God is loved, the act will not be immoderate, since it does not exceed the proportion [fitting] to its object.

4. To the fourth, it should be said that when it is stated that "charity has no mode," we should understand the statement in regard to the act charity elicits, not in regard to the acts it commands, since those acts *ought* to receive modes in accordance with the various natures of their proper objects, concerning which those acts are done.[302]

ARTICLE 4ᶜ   Whether the mode of loving specified in the commandment can be fulfilled in the wayfaring stateᵈ

Objections:

Proceeding to the fourth, it seems that the mode contained in the commandment *can* be fulfilled in the wayfaring state.

1. For Jerome says: "The one who says that God has commanded

---

a. *propter hoc in dilectione Dei non ponitur aliquis modus ultra quem non oporteat progredi, set quantumcumque diligat semper ad anteriora se extendit.* An allusion to Phil. 3:13–14, where St. Paul writes: "Brethren, I do not count myself to have apprehended. But one thing I do: Forgetting the things that are behind and stretching forth myself to those that are before [Vulg.: *in priora*], I press towards the mark, to the prize of the supernal vocation of God in Christ Jesus" (Douay-Rheims).

b. In the present Distinction (d. 27), q. 1, a. 1.

c. Parallels: *ST* II-II, q. 24, a. 8, q. 44, a. 6, and q. 184, a. 2; *De caritate*, a. 10; *De perfectione*, chs. 3–6 (ed. Leon. 41:B70–71); *Super Philem.* 3, lec. 2.

d. The commandment is, of course, "You shall love the Lord your God with all your heart, and with all your soul, and with all your mind, and with all your

something impossible, let him be anathema."[a] But God commanded this ["Love the Lord your God with *all* your heart," etc.] to all wayfarers. Therefore it is heretical to say that it cannot be observed in the wayfaring state.

2. Further, charity is a virtue more necessary than other virtues. But the commandments given about the acts of the other virtues can be fulfilled in the wayfaring state; therefore, too, the commandment given about the act of charity can be fulfilled.

3. Further, every commandment of the law binds, since "law" is derived from "binding."[b] But no one may leave undone that to which he is bound, without incurring sin. If, therefore, the law were to command something that could not be done, it would kill—not only by furnishing an occasion for sinning, as the Apostle says, but also directly;[c] and so it would be evil, which is unfitting.

On the contrary:

1. As long as we remain in this life, we cannot be without sin, as is clear from the first Epistle of John, chapter 1. But whenever someone sins, he does not love God with his whole heart. Therefore that commandment cannot be totally fulfilled in the wayfaring state.

2. Further, the heart of man cannot be occupied at the same time with many things.[d] But while we are in this life we sometimes have to fix our hearts upon temporal things. Therefore man cannot love God in this life with his whole heart.

Response:

It should be said that the whole and the perfect are the same, as the Philosopher says.[e] The *ratio* of the perfect, however, consists in this: that nothing be lacking to it. But this happens in two ways: ei-

---

strength" (Mk. 12:29; cf. Lk. 10:27, Mt. 22:37, and Deut. 6:5). Taking it as already established that one *can* love God and neighbor in this life, here a further question is posed: Is it possible to do so in this life *according to the mode specified,* namely "with *all* your heart, *all* your soul," etc.?

a. In a note Moos simply writes "Jerome, *Exposition of the Catholic Faith,*" but in fact this statement appears to be from a confession of faith that Pelagius addressed to Pope Innocent I (PL 45:1718, n. 10).

b. *lex a ligando dicitur*

c. *non solum occasionaliter, ut dicit Apostolus, set etiam directe occidet*—i.e., not only by providing an occasion for convicting fallen man of his helplessness and need for grace, but also by its very content, which would be simply impossible to fulfill.

d. *homo non potest simul cor ad multa habere,* literally, man cannot have (or relate) his heart toward many things at once.

e. Aristotle, *Metaphysics* X, ch. 4 (1055a12).

ther (1) when something lacks nothing that it is capable of having,[a] or (2) when something lacks nothing that it *ought* to have, just as someone is of the perfect quantity [of body] when he has such quantity as human nature requires, even if he does not have the quantity of a giant, which is nevertheless possible in human nature. Accordingly, (1) the first perfection of human nature is in the state of glory, when man will have the whole of what can possibly exist in human nature; but (2) the second perfection is of nature built up[b]—namely, when a man has the whole of what he ought to have at a given time.

Following upon this distinction, a twofold totality in the love of God may be considered: (1) one, by which a man gives all to the love of God, in no way falling short of what is possible for him to give;[c] and indeed, that *this* perfection or totality should be enacted is not commanded of us [in this life], but rather *shown* to us, in order that we might know the final state we shall come to, as Augustine says. And this perfection or totality excludes everything that would be able to interrupt the act of love, even for a time.[d] (2) Another totality may be considered, by which a man withholds none of the things he ought to do for love of God, at some given time; and this perfection or totality is laid down in the commandment in such a way that even now it is meant to be fulfilled—namely, that a man should omit none of the things he ought to do for love of God. And this totality excludes everything that is contrary to it, as being repugnant to divine love—not, however, that which interrupts the act of love for a time, since always to act with the act of some virtue cannot happen except in those who are in the state of blessedness: for the perfection of the blessed[e] consists in operation, whereas the perfection of the virtuous consists in habit.

Replies to objections:

1. To the first, therefore, it should be said that what the law commands to be done can be fulfilled and is fulfilled by all in the state of salvation.[303]

2. To the second, it should be said that the acts of the other virtues are not "the end of the commandment," as is the act of charity. The act of charity therefore has a mode which belongs in one way to the end

a. *nichil desit eorum que natum est habere*
b. *nature condite*
c. *Vna qua nichil deerit de his que homo potest expendere in amorem Dei, quin in dilectione ponat*
d. *etiam ad tempus*
e. "of blessedness": *beatitudinis*; "blessed": *felici*

and, in a different way, to the wayfaring state. It is not the same, however, with other virtues.

3. To the third, it should be said that, insofar as charity is laid down as a commandment of the law, it binds us to whatever is to be fulfilled in the wayfaring state; whereas in regard to that which will be fulfilled of charity in the fatherland, it is laid down rather as an article of faith[a] than a commandment of the law.

4, 5. The solution to the contrary arguments is evident from what has been said.

Notes on the text of Lombard

"Therefore now he [the evil man] does not love himself."[304]

But against this: every sin, according to Augustine, comes from self-love.[b] Therefore it seems that the evil man loves himself immoderately. In response, it should be said that what he loves in himself is his exterior nature, which he reckons himself to be, but not the intellectual nature, according to which he truly is what he is. And so he loves what he reckons himself to be, but not what he truly is, since "each thing is properly that which is most powerful in it, just as the city is the king," as the Philosopher says in *Ethics* IX.[c]

"So built is the human mind [that it would never fail to remember its own possessions, never fail to understand itself, never fail to love itself]."[d]

On the things mentioned in this statement, see the discussion in Book I, Distinction 3.[305]

"'With your whole heart' [means with your whole intellect, 'with your whole soul' means your will, 'with your whole mind' means your memory]."

It should be known that something is required for charity in three ways: (1) in one way, as the subject of charity, which is the will itself; (2) in another way, as something preceding charity, like memory and intelligence; (3) in a third way, as following upon charity, like the irascible and concupiscible, and also the bodily members that execute the

a. *documentum fidei*

b. Augustine, *On the City of God* XIV, ch. 28 (CCSL 48:451).

c. Aristotle, *Ethics* IX, ch. 8 (1168b31).

d. In Distinction 27, ch. 5, n. 2, the Lombard quotes at length from Augustine's *On the Trinity* XIV, ch. 14, n. 18 (CCSL 50A:445; cf. Grottaferrata ed., 2:165), beginning with the statement cited here by Aquinas.

command of charity. Since therefore the act of charity (even as the act of any virtue whatsoever) must be perfect, the commandment concerning the act of charity includes the perfection of all the aforesaid powers, and this all commentators admit though they expound the text differently[a]—namely, that neither in the will, nor in all the powers preceding or following the act of the will, should there be anything that resists charity (speaking of the perfection fitting to the wayfaring state) or anything that can interrupt its act (speaking of the perfection of the fatherland).

And thus, according to one explanation, the commandment is saying: "with your whole mind," i.e., with the whole memory, that it be without forgetfulness; "with your whole heart," i.e., with the intellect, that it be without error; "with your whole soul," i.e., with the will, that every contrary affection might be removed.

The same is explained in another way: "with your whole heart," as regards the concupscible and "with your whole soul" as regards the irascible, so that no passion of the sensitive appetite should impede the love of God; "with your whole mind" as regards the rational, which includes both will and intellect.

Again, Gregory of Nyssa[b] offers this explanation: "with your whole heart," as regards the vegetative soul; "with your whole soul," as regards the sensitive soul; "with your whole mind," as regards the rational soul. But in Deuteronomy 6 is also laid down "with your whole strength," which is to be referred to the exterior members that carry out charity's command; or [it may be referred] also to the irascible, as some say; or [it may be that the phrase] lays down a characteristic of this love, viz., that it should be firm.

---

a. *ideo preceptum de actu caritatis includit perfectionem omnium predictorum secundum diuersas expositiones:* I have filled out this phrase a bit to make Thomas's point clear. All the Church Fathers understand Jesus to be commanding a perfection or totality of love embracing all of man's powers, but they differ among themselves regarding the exact meaning of each term (heart, soul, mind, strength).

b. Gregory of Nyssa, *Treatise on the Creation of Man,* ch. 8 (PG 44:143).

DISTINCTION 28[a]
[OBJECTS OF CHARITY]

Division of the text

"Here it may be sought whether by that commandment [of the love of neighbor we are commanded to love the *whole* neighbor, that is, soul and body," etc.]. Here, the Master determines the truth about charity in point of its comparison to the object of love.[b]

This consideration is divided into two parts. In the first, he asks what should be loved from charity; in the second, in what order [they should be loved], where he says (Distinction 29): "After the aforesaid, the order of charity [should be treated]."[c]

The first is divided into three parts. In the first, he shows to which things the commandment of charity extends with respect to men; in the second, with respect to angels, where he says: "Here, however, a question arises"; in the third, he draws a certain distinction from what was said, at the words: "Here it should be noted."

Concerning the first, he does two things. First, he determines the truth; second, he removes a doubt, where he says: "Augustine seems to hand down this [opinion, that by the commandment of charity we are not bound to love ourselves]."

Here, we will address seven questions: whether from charity one should love (1) virtues, (2) inanimate things; (3) angels; (4) demons; (5) evil people; (6) whether from charity a man can love himself or (7) his own body.

ARTICLE 1[d]   Whether virtues should be loved from charity

Objections:

Proceeding to the first, it seems that virtues should be loved from charity.

a. Latin text: provisional critical ed. of the Leonine Commission; cf. Moos ed., 902–17.
b. *de caritate per comparationem ad ipsum diligibile*
c. For Aquinas's commentary on Distinction 29, see p. 202.
d. Parallels: *In I Sent.* (Paris version) d. 17, q. 1, a. 5 (see above); *ST* II-II, q. 25, a. 2; *Super Rom.* 12, lec. 2.

1. For Augustine says: "He who loves his brother, loves more the love by which he loves."ᵃ But the love by which a neighbor is loved is the virtue of charity. Therefore virtues should be loved from charity, since the neighbor is loved from charity.

2. Further, "that due to which anything is such as it is, is even more so itself."ᵇ But true friendship loves the friend on account of what is noble.ᶜ Hence it loves what is noble even more than the friend. Therefore charity, which is a certain friendship, as was said,ᵈ is more loving of the virtues than even of neighbors.

3. Further, first acts pertain to the same power as the acts reflective upon them, since they are of the same *ratio,* e.g., understanding something understandable and understanding oneself to understand it. But acts of the same *ratio* are perfected by one and the same virtue. Therefore since the neighbor is loved through charity, through charity is likewise loved the love by which the neighbor is loved; and for the same reason, other virtues are so loved by charity.

4. Further, things having reference to our final beatitude should be loved from charity. But we are led to beatitude by the virtues, and they will remain with us in beatitude. Therefore the virtues should be loved from charity.

5. Further, charity is love of the ultimate end. But the ultimate end of our life is beatitude. Therefore we ought to love beatitude from charity. But when they reach consummation, virtues and grace will pass into beatitude. Therefore the virtues should be loved from charity.

On the contrary:

1. Augustine sufficiently enumerates the things that should be loved from charity, and he makes no mention of virtues, as is evident in the text.

---

a. *Qui diligit fratrem, dilectionem qua diligit magis diligat.*—A semi-quotation of Augustine, *On the Trinity* VIII, ch. 8 (CCSL 50:286), where we find a statement already cited by the Lombard (and by Aquinas) in Book I, Distinction 17: *magis novit dilectionem qua diligit quam fratrem quem diligit.* There is no textual variation in Augustine that would read "magis *diligit* dilectionem." There is, however, another text further on that differs in structure but has the same meaning: "Cum de dilectione diligimus fratrem, de Deo diligimus fratrem; nec fieri potest ut eandem dilectionem non praecipue diligamus qua fratrem diligimus" (ibid., ch. 12, p. 288). Perhaps St. Thomas had this assertion in mind, but confused the actual statement with the preceding statement about the *knowledge* of one's own love. Here and throughout the Distinction, "love" is usually the noun *dilectio* or the verb *diligere.*

b. Aristotle, *Posterior Analytics* I, ch. 2 (72b29).

c. *honestum.* On the concept of *honestum,* see webnote 140.

d. See *In III Sent.* d. 27, q. 2, a. 1 (above).

2. Further, what we love only on account of ourselves is not loved from charity, since "charity does not seek after its own" (1 Cor. 13:5). But we love virtues only on account of ourselves, since, being accidents, they do not subsist of themselves; hence neither do they have goodness except insofar as they exist in us. Therefore they should not be loved from charity.

3. Further, those alone should be loved from charity that share beatitude with us. But virtues, since they are accidents, are not capable of beatitude, or even of life. Therefore they should not be loved from charity.

Response:

It should be said that, since charity includes love but adds something more, it happens in two different ways that something can be loved from charity.[a]

In one way, something can be loved from charity as that in which the friendship of charity has its term; and in this way, nothing is loved from charity except that to which friendship is capable of being extended.[b] Now friendship cannot be extended to virtues or any accidents, for two reasons. First, because friendship makes a man want his friend to exist and to have what is good. But accidents do not exist on their own, nor have they goodness on their own; being and well-being are theirs only when they exist in substances. Hence, we do want virtues or accidents to exist, yet not for themselves, but for a *subject* to which we want being or well-being to come by way of those accidents. Second, because friendship consists in a certain association in which friends return love to one another and do the same things and live their lives together.[c] Hence, friendship can exist only toward something that is naturally capable of acting; and since acting belongs not to accidents but to subjects, there can be no friendship for virtues or for any other accidents. And therefore virtues cannot be loved from charity, as that in which charity has its term.

In another way, something can be said to be loved from charity as that in which the love or rational love that is incorporated into charity has its term,[d] even though it is not the object of friendship. And this

a. "love . . . loved from charity": *amorem . . . diligi ex caritate*

b. *illud ad quod nata est amicitia esse*

c. *amici se ipsos redamant, et eadem operantur, et simul conuersantur*

d. *amor, seu dilectio, qui in caritate includitur.* Here one has to find a way of distinguishing *amor* and *dilectio* in English; elsewhere the need is not so pressing, as explained in the Introduction. The *includitur* is translated "is incorporated into" be-

love, which is called "love of concupiscence,"ᵃ is ordered to the love of something else that is chiefly loved, as a friend is said to love the health of his friend. And in this way, the virtues *are* loved from charity.

Replies to objections:

1. To the first, therefore, it should be said that Augustine is speaking there of the love which *is* God, and by this love the neighbor is loved effectively and exemplarily.[306]

2. To the second, it should be said that virtue or what is noble is not the *final* cause on account of which a friend is loved; rather it is that which makes him lovable *formally*. Hence it does not follow that virtue is more lovable than a friend is, or lovable for the same reason a friend is, even as it does not follow that whiteness is more white than a white body.

3. To the third, it should be said that it does pertain to charity to love love,ᵇ but not as if it were that in which charity has its term.

4. To the fourth, it should be said that charity has its term in things that are referred to beatitude, precisely as things capable of participating in beatitude. In this way, virtue is not referred to beatitude, since virtue itself cannot become blessed.

5. To the fifth, it should be said that the end in which charity chiefly has its term is uncreated beatitude itself. But as for *created* beatitude, the same reasoning applies as was given above of the virtues.[307]

ARTICLE 2ᶜ   Whether irrational creatures[308] are to be loved from charity

Objections:

Proceeding to the second, it seems that irrational creatures are to be loved from charity.

1. For every meritorious love pertains to charity. But a person can love irrational things meritoriously, as when he loves them by referring them to God, or loves them because they are made by God or because they aid those who are on their way to God. Therefore irrational creatures are to be loved from charity.

---

cause the sense is that charity builds upon and makes use of loves that are already there, but for its own end, in its own manner. "Includes" might be too weak.

a. *concupiscentie dilectio*
b. *diligere dilectionem*
c. Parallels: *ST* II-II, q. 25, a. 3; *De caritate*, a. 7.

2. Further, charity conforms man's loving to God's. But God loves irrational creatures from charity, according to Wisdom 11:25: "You love all the things that exist." Therefore man, too, ought to love irrational creatures from charity.

3. Further, rational creatures are to be loved from charity, since in them a likeness to God is found. But some likeness to God is found in irrational creatures, although not so great a likeness as is found in rational ones. Therefore irrational creatures are to be loved from charity.

4. Further, faith, like charity, is a theological virtue. But faith extends in its scope even to irrational creatures, insofar as man believes them to be created by God and to be ruled by divine providence. Therefore charity also extends in its scope to them.

On the contrary:

1. Augustine says: "Those alone are to be loved from charity who, by belonging with us to a certain society, are referred to God [as their happiness]."[a] But irrational things are not of this sort. Therefore they are not to be loved from charity.

2. Further, charity includes benevolence, as was said above.[b] But benevolence cannot exist toward irrational things, as the Philosopher says in *Ethics* VIII;[c] therefore neither can charity.

Response:

It should be said that there can be no friendship with irrational things for the same reasons there can be no friendship with accidents. For though they have an existence in which they subsist and they have certain activities, they do not share a human life with us,[d] as regards either existence or the activities of life. Consequently, toward them we cannot have the benevolence according to which we wish a friend to exist and to have what is good, which we do not wish for irrational things except insofar as they are related to man. Nor can we have with them the unity of hearts according to which we *want* and *do* the same things for our friends[e]—neither of which can occur with irrational things, since they cannot share with us the same activities.[309] Therefore, they cannot be loved from charity as that in which charity has its term.

a. Augustine, *On Christian Doctrine* I, ch. 23, n. 22 (CCSL 32:18).
b. *In III Sent.* d. 27, a. 1 (see above).
c. Aristotle, *Ethics* VIII, ch. 2 (1155b27).
d. *non tamen nobiscum in uita communicant humana*
e. *neque concordia, secundum quam eadem uolumus et agimus amicis*

Nevertheless, there is a way they *can* be loved from charity: as that in which the love that charity incorporates into itself, namely love of concupiscence, has its term, the same way that a friend loves the possessions and animals belonging to his friend, but still does not have friendship with them. And such a love[a] is not merely commanded by charity, it is also elicited, because charity elicits an act of love not only for objects toward which charity is chiefly directed, but also for those that are ordered to that end. And in this way inanimate things are loved from charity, insofar as they are ordered to that which is chiefly and directly the object of charity.

Replies to objections:

1. To the first, therefore, it should be said that a love for inanimate things does pertain to charity [in the manner explained], yet such things are not charity's object.

2. To the second, it should be said that, while God loves all creatures *from* charity, nevertheless he has charity only *for* rational creatures that he created for beatitude, through which they are made sharers of his own life.

3. To the third, it should be said that the likeness of image that is found in rational creatures makes them capable of sharing one and the same life with God and with each other, namely, the life of glory. The likeness of trace that is found in other creatures does not suffice for this. Whence there is no parallel.

4. To the fourth, it should be said that faith does not imply some association [i.e., friendship] between the believer and the one believed in, as charity implies between the lover and the beloved. Hence the same reasoning does not apply to both.

ARTICLE 3[b]   Whether angels are to be loved from charity

Objections:

Proceeding to the third, it seems that angels are not to be loved from charity.

---

a. "the love that charity incorporates . . . love of concupiscence . . . such a love": *amor quem caritas includit . . . amor concupiscentie . . . ista dilectio.* This is a good example of Thomas not troubling himself much over the distinction between *amor* and *dilectio* as long as the former is being taken generally rather than restrictively.

b. Parallels: *ST* II-II, q. 25, a. 10; *De caritate,* a. 7, ad 9; *Super Rom.* 13, lec. 2.

1. For as was said before,[a] man's charity does not extend to things that do not share in human life. But angels do not live a human life. Therefore charity does not bring it about that men love angels.

2. Further, charity, since it is a friendship, exists between those who are naturally suited to converse with each other. But the conversation of the angels, who are called gods, "is not with men," as is said in Daniel 2:11. Therefore angels are not to be loved from charity.

3. Further, charity, since it is a friendship, is a certain equality. But angels are much superior to us. Therefore charity or friendship cannot be had toward them.

4. Further, since they are incorporeal and thus of another genus [i.e., pure spirits], angels stand further from us than irrational animals, which belong to the same genus we do [i.e., animals]. But we cannot love irrational animals from charity; therefore much less can we love angels.

On the contrary:

1. Neighbors are to be loved from charity. But angels are neighbors to us, as is said in the text of the *Sentences*. Therefore they are to be loved from charity.

2. Further, friendship causes friends to will the same thing and to be friends of the same ones. But God loves the angels from charity just as he loves us from charity. Therefore we, too, should love the angels from charity.

Response:

It should be said (as has been already said)[b] that charity or friendship can exist only between those who participate in the same life. Now, the life of men and of angels is twofold. One life belongs to them in accordance with their nature, and in this respect, men and angels do not share the same life, but men share a human life with one another, and angels an angelic life with one another, for it pertains to each [rank of being] to be occupied with the same kinds of activities. Yet both have another life through grace, in which they become participants of the divine life; and this life they *do* share with each other and with God. Therefore, according to *this* life, they can have friendship with each other, and this friendship is charity.

a. In articles 1 and 2.
b. In the preceding article.

Replies to objections:

1. To the first, therefore, it should be said that "human life" may be spoken of in two ways: either that kind of life which accords with [mere] human nature, and if spoken of in this way, angels do not share in human life; or that kind of life which belongs to man by his participation in the divine life, and if spoken of in this way, the angels *do* share in human life.

2. To the second, it should be said that men and angels are naturally suited to converse with each other in the fatherland, where we shall be equal to the angels, as is said in Matthew 22:30. And we converse in some way with the angels even in this life, insofar as we lead an angelic life on earth.

3. To the third, it should be said that friendship requires not a strict equality but a proportionate equality[a]—in other words, that one friend behaves toward the other in keeping with his own proportion, as is said in *Ethics* VIII.[b] Nevertheless, a great inequality dissolves friendship, namely, when they do not share the same life.

4. To the fourth, it should be said that when it comes to our souls, we share more in common with angels than with brute animals, but when it comes to our bodies and bodily powers,[c] we share more in common with brute animals than with angels. But, as the Philosopher says in *Ethics* IX, man is more that which falls on the side of the soul than that which falls on the side of the body, because each thing is [in a way] that which is most powerful in it.[d] Simply speaking, therefore, we stand further from brute animals than we do from angels.

---

a. *non equalitatem equiparantie set equalitatem proportionis*

b. Aristotle, *Ethics* VIII, chs. 7–8 (1157b26ff.) Aristotle writes in ch. 7: "In all friendships implying inequality the love also should be proportional, i.e., the better should be more loved than he loves, and so should the more useful, and similarly in each of the other cases; for when the love is in proportion to the merit of the parties, then in a sense arises equality, which is held to be characteristic of friendship."

c. *uirtutes corporeas*

d. Aristotle, *Ethics* IX, ch. 18 (1168b30ff.). Put differently, a thing is more its species than its genus; the specific difference points more to *what it is* than any of its generic "natures." Thus, since man is man precisely by being rational, his rationality defines more what he is than anything he has in common with lower animals. See *infra* a. 6, ad 5 and a. 7, ad 4; cf. *In III Sent.* d. 27, Notes on the Text, first note (above).

ARTICLE 4ª   Whether we ought to have
charity for evil peopleᵇ

Objections:

Proceeding to the fourth, it seems that we cannot have charity for evil people.

1. For charity requires sharing in the divine life, which comes about through grace, as was said.ᶜ But this divine life is not in sinners. Therefore they are not to be loved from charity.

2. Further, just as likeness is the cause of love, so unlikeness is the cause of the contrary. But evil people are unlike good people. Therefore they are not to be loved from charity.

3. Further, as the Philosopher says in *Ethics* IX, friendship cannot exist between those who do not rejoice in the same things.ᵈ But the good and the evil do not rejoice in the same things, but in contrary things. Therefore they cannot have friendship with each other.

4. Further, friendship involves a return of love, as the Philosopher says.ᵉ But those who are evil do not love us in return; instead, they hate those who are good. Therefore neither ought good people to love evil people from charity.

5. Further, it is characteristic of friends to extend their friendship to the same people.[310] If, therefore, those who are good loved from charity those who are evil, the latter, too, would love themselves.[311] This, however, is false, since the Philosopher proves in *Ethics* IX that no evil person is a friend to himself.ᶠ Therefore evil people are not to be loved from charity.

On the contrary:

1. "Love your enemies" (Mt. 5:44). But everyone who is responsible for enmity is evil.ᵍ Therefore evil people are to be loved from charity.

2. Further, whatever people are supposed to be the objects of our

a. Parallels: *In II Sent.* d. 7, q. 3, a. 2, ad 2 (translated in webnote 316); *ST* II-II, q. 25, a. 6; *Super Gal.* 6, lec. 2; *De caritate,* a. 8, ad 8 & 9; *De duobus praeceptis* (*Opuscula theologica,* Marietti ed., 2:252–53, nn. 1183–1192).

b. *ad malos homines*

c. *In III Sent.* d. 27, q. 2, a. 2 (see above).

d. Aristotle, *Ethics* IX, ch. 3 (1165b27).

e. Aristotle, *Ethics* VIII, ch. 2 (1155b28); ch. 3 (1156a8).

f. Aristotle, *Ethics* IX, ch. 4 (1166b17). See the first of Aquinas's Notes on the Text immediately following this question.

g. *omnis qui inimicatur malus est*

beneficence are to be loved from charity. But we ought to benefit evil people by converting them and by aiding them in their necessities. Therefore evil people are to be loved from charity.

Response:

It should be said that in evil people there are two things to be considered: the nature by which they are men, and the malice by which they are evil. Since by their very nature they bear in themselves the image of God and are capable of receiving divine life, they are therefore to be loved from charity according to that nature. Their malice, however, is contrary to divine life, and it is therefore to be hated in them. Hence Augustine says: "Men are to be loved in such a way that their errors are not also loved."[a, 312]

Replies to objections:

1. To the first, therefore, it should be said that charity does not require actual communication in divine life; it is enough that the communication exist in potency, since what is in potency already in a certain way *is*.

2. To the second, it should be said that we ought to hate in evil people that according to which they are unlike us and ought to do all in our power to destroy it.[313] And to do this is precisely to love their *nature*, because their malice is repugnant to the good of nature.

3. To the third, it should be said that, while evil people do not rejoice in the same things right now, still it is possible that they may come to rejoice in the same things the good rejoice in. For this reason, the Philosopher says in *Ethics* IX that friendship should not be immediately broken off with one who, having been good, becomes evil, but on the contrary we should help such ones recover the good of virtue even more than we would help them recover lost temporal goods.[b]

4. To the fourth, it should be said that while evil people do not actually return love right now, nevertheless they are naturally capable of returning love, especially in the future life; and it is the sharing of *that* life that charity especially takes into consideration. Hence return-

---

a. The statement is drawn from Prosper of Aquitaine's Augustinian anthology, the *Liber Sententiarum*, n. 2 (PL 45:1859).

b. I have taken liberties with this sentence to make it read smoothly: *Et ideo dicit Philosophus in IX Ethicorum quod non confestim dissoluenda est amicitia ad eum qui ex bono factus est malus, set multo plus adiuuandi sunt ad recuperandam bonitatem uirtutis quam ad recuperandam possessionem bonorum temporalium.*—The reference is to Aristotle, *Ethics* IX, ch. 3 (1165b13–22).

ing love for love can certainly take place, even among those who were never acquainted with each other in this life.

5. To the fifth, it should be said that an evil person is divided in himself, because owing to his affection for malice he fights against the goodness of his nature; and it is in view of this inner strife that he is said to "hate himself." We, however, ought to love evil people with respect to the nature they have, not with respect to their malice.[314]

ARTICLE 5[a]   Whether demons are to
be loved from charity

Objections:

Proceeding to the fifth, it seems that demons are to be loved from charity.

1. For Leviticus 19:18 states: "Love your neighbor," on which a gloss reads: "Neighbor should not be understood in terms of nearness of blood but in terms of the fellowship of reason." But demons and the damned have fellowship with us in reason; they should therefore be loved from charity.

2. Further, it was said in the preceding article that we ought to love evil people in view of their nature, which is good in them. But, as Dionysius says in chapter 4 of *On the Divine Names*, a good nature is to be found in demons, too, since they did not forfeit their natural goods through sin.[b] They should therefore be loved from charity.

3. Further, every rational creature that God loves, he loves from charity. But God loves demons, because he loves all that he has made. He therefore loves them from charity, since they are rational creatures. And for the same reason we, too, ought to love them from charity.

4. Further, we ought to love from charity whatever contributes to the increase[c] of our merit and to the glory of God. But insofar as they tempt us [and we resist], demons profit us, as was said in Book II, Distinction 6; and again, God's glory is manifested in them. Therefore, they should be loved from charity.

a. Parallels: *In III Sent.* d. 31, q. 2, a. 3, qa. 1, response (see below); *ST* II-II, q. 25, a. 11; *De caritate*, a. 7; *Super Rom.* 13, lec. 2.

b. Pseudo-Dionysius, *On the Divine Names*, ch. 4, n. 23 (PG 3:726).

c. *cumulum*

On the contrary:

1. There should be sharing among friends. But all manner of inter-action with demons is forbidden to us,[a] for in Isaiah 38 (verses 14 and following), those who are said to have formed a pact with death and hell are reprehended. Therefore demons are not to be loved from char-ity.

2. Further, Augustine says that a neighbor is loved from charity ei-ther because he is just, or in order that he might become just. But the demons are neither just nor able to be just; therefore they are not to be loved from charity.

Response:

It should be said, as was said before, that something is loved from charity in two ways: in one way, as its direct object; in another way, as something that the love included in charity somehow aims at, insofar as such an indirect object is ordered to something belonging to the di-rect objects of charity.[b, 315] In the first way, demons are not to be loved from charity, since neither in act nor in potency do they share with us in the divine life; and the same holds for the damned. Hence the Phi-losopher says in *Ethics* IX that "friendship is to be broken off with those who are incurable on account of abundant malice."[c] Now, there are some people in this life who seem incurably bad if mere human pow-ers are taken into account, and yet are not really incurable if one takes into account the order of divine mercy by which they can be rescued; yet they would remain incurable after this life, if they died without repentance.[d] Now charity looks to what is divine, whereas [natural] friendship looks to what is human. For this reason, political friend-ship is broken off with those who, according to human considerations, have become incurable, which does occur sometimes in this life; but charity is not broken off with *anyone* in this life, no matter how evil he

---

a. *Cum amicis communicandum est. Set omnis communicatio ad demones est nobis in-terdicta.*

b. "Direct object" and "indirect object" are introduced to make sense of the contrast that Thomas describes more elliptically: *Dicendum, quod, sicut predictum est, ex caritate diligitur aliquid dupliciter: uno modo sicut id ad quod habetur caritas; alio modo sicut id ad quod terminatur aliquo modo amor quem includit caritas, in quantum or-dinatur ad aliquid eorum ad que habetur caritas*

c. Aristotle, *Ethics* IX, ch. 3 (1165b18, 36).

d. *Hec autem insanabilitas, quamuis in hac uita contingat in quibusdam, considera-tis humanis uiribus, non tamen contingit nisi post hanc uitam, considerato ordine diuine misericordie*

may be, since at least according to the order of divine mercy there remains some possibility of the life of grace for him. But after this life, when such a possibility ceases, charity does not abide for the one who is evil; and therefore neither the damned nor the demons are to be loved from charity in the first way described.[a, 316] In the second way [having to do with charity's indirect object], however, the *nature* of the demons can be loved from charity, insofar as this nature is God's creature; but not the demons themselves, since this name "demon" chiefly designates their vice.[317]

Replies to objections:

1. To the first, therefore, it should be said that this gloss should be understood in regard to that fellowship of reason in which an order to the life of grace remains, since charity requires sharing of this kind.[318]

2. To the second, it should be said that as long as they are in this life, a potential for grace[b] remains in sinners, at least by reason of their nature; but no such potential remains in the damned and in the demons. Hence the same argument does not apply.

3. To the third, it should be said that God loves the nature of the demons, not as though he has charity for it, but insofar as it is his effect. And this is the way we, too, ought to love it.

4. To the fourth, it should be said that the fact that demons are useful to us in our meriting[c] and that their acts and life redound to the glory of God is *per accidens* and beyond their intention; and no judgment about anything should be based on what is *per accidens*.

ARTICLE 6[d, 319]   Whether a man ought to love himself from charity

Objections:

Proceeding to the sixth, it seems that a man ought not to love himself from charity.

1. For, as Gregory says, "charity cannot exist between fewer than two."[e] Therefore it cannot exist in someone with regard to himself.

---

a. *Set post hanc uitam non manet, et ideo per modum predictum neque dampnati neque demones sunt ex caritate diligendi*

b. *possibilitas ad gratiam*

c. *prosint nobis ad meritum*

d. Parallels: *ST* II-II, q. 25, a. 4; *De caritate*, a. 7.

e. *Caritas minus quam inter duos haberi non potest.*—Gregory, *Homilies on the Gospels*, Homily 17, n. 1 (CCSL 141:117).

2. Further, friendship requires reciprocal love, sharing of life, and other such things, which cannot exist in a man with regard to himself. But charity is a certain friendship. Therefore, there is no charity in a man with regard to himself.

3. Further, charity is a certain love, and "love is a unitive power," as Dionysius says.[a] Seeing that union pertains only to diverse things, it seems there cannot be charity toward oneself.

4. Further, friendship, like justice, consists in equality, as is said in *Ethics* VIII.[b] But justice does not exist with regard to oneself, properly speaking, as the Philosopher says in *Ethics* V.[c] Therefore neither is there friendship or charity toward oneself, properly speaking.

5. Further, nothing reprehensible comes from charity. But to love oneself is reprehensible, as is clear from 2 Timothy (3:2): "Men will be lovers of self."[320] Therefore a man does not love himself from charity.

On the contrary:

1. A man ought to love his neighbor as himself. But he ought to love his neighbor from charity; therefore himself, too.

2. Further, charity gives rise to mercy. But man ought to be merciful first toward himself [and only in second place, toward his neighbor].[d] Therefore he ought also to love himself first from charity.

Response:

It should be said that the progression of love bears a likeness to the progression of knowledge.[e] Now, in things known there is found something that the knower's intellect first fixes upon, such as first principles, and from these it is led on to other things. And insofar as it stands in the principles, knowledge receives the name of "understanding," while insofar as it is led to conclusions that are known from the principles, it receives the name of "science." But since the knowledge

a. Pseudo-Dionysius, *On the Divine Names,* ch. 4, n. 15 (PG 3:714); cf. *In III Sent.* d. 27, q. 1, a. 1 (above).

b. Aristotle, *Ethics* VIII, ch. 8 (1158b1) and ch. 11 (1159b26).

c. Aristotle, *Ethics* V, ch. 15 (1138a5ff.).

d. *Misericordia ex caritate causatur. Set homo sibi ipsi primo misericors esse debet.* Alternately, "charity gives rise to pity, but a man can take pity on himself." The scriptural background is Ecclesiasticus 30:24 (iuxta Vulg.): "Have pity on thy own soul, pleasing God, and contain thyself: gather up thy heart in his holiness: and drive away sadness far from thee" (Douay-Rheims). A non-Vulgate based translation is not nearly as relevant (cf. Sir. 30:23 in the RSV).

e. "Progression" seemed the least inadequate term for *processus,* the "going-forth" of love or knowledge. "Process" has too many other connotations; "going-forth" is too awkward. Perhaps "development" could also be used.

of principles is in the conclusions as a cause is in its effect, and conversely the knowledge of the conclusion is in the principles as an effect is in its cause, conclusions are therefore also said to be "understood," and principles are said to be "known."[a] In like manner, too, a lover's affection is first fixed upon the lover himself, and is extended from him to others, as the Philosopher says in *Ethics* IX: "From the affections a man has for himself come those that are for his friend, he relating to the friend as to himself."[b, 321] On account of this, it even stands in the commandment of the law that "one should love his neighbor *as himself*."[c] Nor is this to be wondered at, since things that are *united* bear a likeness to things that are *one*.[d] And although the name "friendship" is given, properly speaking, to a love that diffuses itself to others,[e] nevertheless even the love one has for oneself can be called friendship and charity,[f, 322] insofar as the love one has for another proceeds by way of likeness to the love one has for oneself.

Replies to objections:

1. To the first, therefore, it should be said that Gregory is speaking with respect to the first imposition of the name "charity."[323]

2. To the second, it should be said that that reasoning holds concerning friendship insofar as it implies a love diffused to others.

3. To the third, it should be said that those things which are already one by nature can still be *made one* at the level of affections.[g, 324] Consequently, there can be love, even properly speaking, toward oneself.

4. To the fourth, it should be said that friendship consists in an equalizing with regard to affection, whereas justice consists in an equalizing

a. The point Thomas is making depends to some extent on the underlying Latin. Knowledge (*cognitio*) of principles is called understanding (*intellectus*); knowledge of conclusions is called science (*scientia*). But because the former exists in the latter as its cause, and the latter preexists in the former as its effect, we can say that we "understand conclusions" (*intelligere conclusiones*) and "know principles" (*scire principia*). In other words, though these knowledge-words have proper meanings, their substitution for one another can be justified in view of the relationship of principle and conclusion.

b. The phrase in Aristotle is a marvel of compactness: *ex his que sunt hominis ad se ipsum uenerunt ea que sunt hominis ad amicum, dum scilicet se habet ad amicum sicut ad se ipsum.—Ethics* IX, ch. 4 (1166a1).

c. *Propter quod etiam in precepto legis est ut quis proximum sicut se ipsum diligat.* The reference is to Lev. 19:18 and 19:34; cf. Mt. 19:19, Rom. 13:9, Gal. 5:14, and Jas. 2:8.

d. *Nec est mirum, quia unita ad similitudinem se habent eorum que sunt unum*

e. *nomen amicitie imponatur proprie secundum quod amor ad alios se diffundit*

f. "love one has for oneself": *amor quem quis habet ad se ipsum*

g. *illa que sunt unum secundum naturam possunt adhuc uniri per affectum*

of things. But even as diverse things can be taken as one by means of the soul's activity, so the same thing can be taken as many, which occurs when the soul's act is turned back upon the agent himself.[325] Accordingly, in regard to oneself there can be friendship more than there can be justice—although it is possible to apply the term "justice" metaphorically to a man with regard to himself, in view of the fact that within a man things really diverse are found, namely diverse powers, whose equalization in that which belongs to each one brings about a (metaphorical) justice, as is said in *Ethics* V.[a]

5. To the fifth, it should be said that to love oneself with respect to the exterior man deserves great reproof, but to love oneself with respect to the interior man deserves much praise; and this [kind of love] belongs to charity.[326]

ARTICLE 7[b]   Whether our bodies are to be loved from charity

Objections:

Proceeding to the seventh, it seems that our bodies are not be loved from charity.

1. For charity does not flee from involvement[c] with that to which charity is extended. Yet charity makes one flee from involvement with the body, as is clear from Romans 7:24: "Who will free me from the body of this death?" Therefore the body is not to be loved from charity.

2. Further, the Philosopher says in *Ethics* IX that "it is reprehensible for a man to love himself with regard to what is exterior in himself."[d] But our body is the most exterior [part of us]. Therefore it is reprehensible to love our body; and so it is not loved from charity.

3. Further, our beatitude will consist in the enjoyment of God. But our body cannot participate in that enjoyment; hence it is no participant of our beatitude. Therefore it is not to be loved from charity.

4. Further, the part is not set down in numerical distinction against the whole. But our body is a part of us. Therefore our body ought not to be set down as something lovable distinct from ourselves.

a. Aristotle, *Ethics* V, ch. 15 (1138b6).
b. Parallels: specifically on the love of one's body, *ST* II-II, q. 25, a. 5; as to there being four objects fittingly loved from charity, including the body: *ST* II-II, q. 25, a. 12; *De caritate*, a. 7.
c. *conuersationem*
d. Aristotle, *Ethics* IX, ch. 8 (1168b15).

5. Further, we ought to love our neighbor as ourselves. But the neighbor's body is not set down as something lovable distinct from the neighbor. Therefore our bodies, too, ought not to be set down as something lovable distinct from ourselves.

On the contrary:

1. "Men ought to love their wives as their own bodies" (Eph. 5:28). But they ought to love their wives from charity; therefore also their own bodies.

2. Further, everything capable of being made blessed is to be loved from charity. But the body is capable of being made blessed. Therefore it is to be loved from charity.

Response:

It should be said that our body is one of four things which are to be loved from charity. For, as is clear from what has been said, the love of charity has for its foundation chiefly the sharing of the blessed life, and of the life of grace insofar as it is ordained to that goal. Now this [blessed] life has a threefold relation to the possessor of charity.[a] In one way, it exists in someone as in a source diffusing that life into others; this is how it is in God. In another way, it exists in the [human] lover as the one who participates in that life, which occurs in two ways—chiefly in regard to the soul, and secondarily in regard to the body, through a certain overflowing into the body of what is in the soul. Lastly, this blessed life exists in others, too, as co-participants with us; this is how it is in our neighbor. Accordingly, there are four things that are to be loved from charity: God, the neighbor, ourselves, and our body.

Replies to objections:

1. To the first, therefore, it should be said that charity flees from involvement with the body, not insofar as the body is capable of glory, but only insofar as it is subject to the misery that impedes this glory.

2. To the second, it should be said that for a man to love himself according to his exterior nature in things repugnant to reason is reprehensible; but it is worthy of praise for a man to love himself in things wherein his exterior nature harmonizes with his interior.[327]

3. To the third, it should be said that while the body does not enjoy God immediately, nevertheless there will be a certain overflowing of glory into the body from the soul enjoying him.

---

a. *ad habentem caritatem*

4. To the fourth, it should be said that each man is properly said to be what is most noble in him, as the Philosopher says in *Ethics* IX.[a] Hence, "love of oneself" is understood with respect to those things that pertain to the soul; and therefore "love of one's body" is distinguished from "love of oneself" not as a part is distinguished from a whole, but as a part from another part.[b]

5. To the fifth, it should be said that the neighbor's body and soul stand in the same relationship to the one having charity, as far as the blessed life is concerned—namely, both his body and his soul are destined to share in that beatitude. For this reason, the neighbor's soul and body are not distinguished as altogether diverse objects of love.

Notes on the text of Lombard

"Of the second and fourth [objects of love, i.e., ourselves and our body],[c] no commandments ought to have been given."

But against this statement: Law ought universally to direct a man concerning everything that pertains to the virtues. Moreover, the love of God was likewise naturally implanted in all things.[328] It should be said in reply that just as speculative knowledge stands to things to be known, so the law stands to things to be done. Hence, just as in a speculative science instruction is not given about principles *per se* known (since they are known to us by nature), but only about conclusions known through them, so neither does the law make an explicit determination about the love of self to which nature inclines, but rather does this about the love of neighbor arising out of that love as conclusions arise from principles. Now, while it is true that the love of God is naturally implanted in us, we do not love God by this natural love in the same way as we love him by charity,[d] as was said above. Furthermore, from the very fact that we are commanded to love God spiritually, we are taught to love ourselves spiritually as well.

---

a. Aristotle, *Ethics* IX, ch. 8 (1168b31–33).

b. See above, a. 3, ad 4.

c. Recall the text of Augustine from *On Christian Doctrine* I, ch. 23, n. 22, cited by Lombard: "Four things are to be loved: one that is above us, namely God; another that is we ourselves; a third that is alongside us, namely the neighbor; a fourth that is beneath us, namely the body" (cf. Grottaferrata ed., 2:168.10–13).

d. *Dilectio autem Dei, quamuis nobis naturaliter insit, non tamen hoc modo quo per caritatem diligitur*

"No one ever hated his own flesh."

But against that statement: Many commit suicide owing to their abundant malice, as the Philosopher says in *Ethics* IX.[a] It should be said in reply that each and every man naturally loves his bodily life; but the fact that some long for bodily death occurs *per accidens*, either insofar as bodily life is an impediment to some good they love more than bodily life, as happens in those who seek another life [after death], or insofar as evils in some way accompany their bodily life, which evils they reckon it better to lack than to continue having bodily life [under their burden].

But a further question arises here. [A difficulty about those who are greatly superior to us.]

It seems that love for the angels and for the Blessed Virgin and for Christ as man are not contained in love of one's neighbor, but rather should be reduced to the love of God, seeing that they are above us. It should be said in reply that God is above us as the one who pours eternal life into us. In this way, of course, neither angels nor the Blessed Virgin nor Christ as man are above us, since, even as the Trinity alone created us to the life of nature, so it alone sanctifies us by the life of grace and will beatify us by the life of glory. They, on the other hand, are to be loved as participating together with us in the eternal life that comes from God; and so far as this is concerned, they are alongside us, even though in their fuller participation they are above us.

a. Aristotle, *Ethics* IX, ch. 4 (1166b8–9).

DISTINCTION 29[a]
[THE ORDER OF CHARITY]

Division of the text

"After the aforesaid matters, the next topic of treatment is the order of charity, [for the Bride says: 'The King has brought me into his wine-cellar, and has made charity well-ordered within me' (Song 2:4).]" After the Master has determined what is to be loved from charity, here he determines about the order of charity.

This consideration is divided into two parts. In the first, he determines the order of charity with respect to its objects, so far as the amount of love is concerned (Distinction 29); in the second, he determines the same, so far as the amount of merit is concerned (Distinction 30), at the place where it says: "Here it is customary to inquire [which is better and more meritorious—to love one's friends or to love one's enemies]."[b]

The former is divided into two parts. In the first, he determines about the order of charity with respect to diverse grades among the very objects of love; in the second, he determines the same order, but with respect to the state of the lover, at the place where it says: "It should also be known [that the degrees of charity are diverse. For there is beginning charity, advancing charity, perfect charity, and most perfect charity]."

The former is divided into two parts. In the first, he determines about the order of charity with respect to the objects of love; in the second, he raises certain questions about the matters determined, at the place where it says: "It is also customarily asked [if, should our parents or children or siblings be evil, they are to be loved more or less than other good people who are not joined to us in the same way]."

Concerning the former, he does two things. First, he shows that charity does have an order; second, he shows according to what realities that order is to be looked to,[c] at the place where it says: "Hence,

---

a. Latin text: provisional critical ed. of the Leonine Commission; cf. Moos ed., 921–49.

b. For Aquinas's commentary on Distinction 30, see p. 242.

c. *secundo ostendit secundum quid attendendus sit ordo iste.* How does one ascertain

upon this matter, a question is often raised [which has been rendered perplexing due to various sayings put forward by the saints]."

And concerning this, he does two things. First, he sets down diverse points about these opinions; second, he determines what seems true to him, at the place where it says: "It is true that the previously quoted words [of Ambrose seem, for those who analyze them diligently, to unfold the order of love more in regard to affection than in regard to effect]."

Concerning the former, he does two things. First, he sets down diverse opinions and the arguments in support of them; second, he shows how the first opinion responds to the arguments given in favor of the other position, at the place where it says: "But certain ones say [that what was said above regarding the order of love is to be understood in reference to the outward display of the work of charity]."

Concerning the former, he does two things. First, he sets down the opinion of certain ones who say that an order of charity is to be looked to only according to charity's *effect*; second, he sets down the opinion of certain ones who say that this order is to be looked to not just according to charity's effect, but also according to one's *affection* [for the object of love], at the place where it says: "Some resist [the aforementioned opinion by citing the commandment of the law about loving one's parents]."

At the words "But certain ones say [that what was said above regarding the order of love is to be understood in reference to the outward display of the work of charity]," he shows how the first opinion responds to the arguments given in favor of the other position. And concerning this, he does two things. First, he shows how the first opinion responds to the arguments in favor of the second. Second, he shows how the first opinion says, in addition, an unequal love is to be given to the neighbor as far as affection is concerned, [an affection] like that which is given to oneself,[a] at the place where it says: "Several authorities teach that by the affection of charity we are to love our neighbors just as much as we love ourselves."

At the words "It is also customarily asked [if, should our parents or children or siblings be evil, they are to be loved more or less than other good people who are not joined to us in the same way]," he raises cer-

---

the proper order in which to love objects of love—what criteria does one consult, what aspect(s) of things does one look to?

a. *in secunda ostendit quomodo prima opinio addit inequalem dilectionem esse impendendam proximo quantum ad affectum, sicut et sibi ipsi, ibi: Quorum etiam nonnulli.* The Leonine ed. has *inequalem,* but Moos reads *aequalem.*

tain questions about the truth he has determined. And this is divided into two parts, according to the two questions he raises, the second beginning where it says: "It is also customarily asked [why the Lord commanded us to love enemies. . .]."

Here [in this Distinction], we will inquire into eight things: (1) whether it belongs to charity to have an order; (2) whether that order is to be looked to regarding both affection and effect, or merely regarding affection; (3) whether God is to be loved above all things; (4) whether loving him permits looking to a reward; (5) whether we ought to love our neighbor as much as we love ourselves; (6) whether among neighbors, those who are close to us are to be preferred to those who are strangers;[a] (7) the order of love in regard to those who are close to us; (8) the perfection of charity and the degrees enumerated in the text.

ARTICLE 1[b, 329]   Whether charity has an order

Objections:

Proceeding to the first, it seems that charity does not have an order.

1. For Bernard says that "love knows no grade, it considers no dignity."[c] But every order involves some grade. There is not, therefore, any order in charity.

2. Further, the Philosopher says that "friendship is a certain equality."[d] But equality belongs to what is uniform, allowing no diversity, even as unity does not allow division. Therefore charity does not have an order.

a. *Utrum inter proximos, propinqui extraneis preferendi sint.* In the genus of "neighbor" (*proximus*), the "one who is close by" (*propinquus*—see a. 7 below) occupies a special place; everyone else is an "outsider" (*extraneus*). *Propinqui* has been translated "those who are close to us" rather than "relatives" because, as will become evident in the relevant articles, for Thomas the term applies not only to family members (though they are the most obvious and important instance of *propinqui*) but also to friends, fellow citizens, fellow Christians, etc.—anyone who is "close" to us on account of something shared, whether blood, country, knowledge, interests, or charity. By contrast, a stranger or outsider, *extraneus*, is someone with whom one does not have such things in common.

b. Parallels: *ST* II-II, q. 26, a. 1 and q. 44, a. 8, ad 2; *De caritate*, a. 9.

c. Cf. Bernard, *Sermons on the Song of Songs*, Serm. 64, n. 10 (PL 183:1088); Serm. 79, n. 1 (PL 183:1163); Serm. 83, n. 3 (PL 183:1182). "Grade" seems the best translation in this context for *gradus*, since the point concerns whether objects of love are "graded" as more and less worthy of love, whether there is a gradation among them.

d. Aristotle, *Ethics* VIII, ch. 7 (1157b36).

3. Further, to put things in order belongs to reason, whose function it is to gather things together. But charity is not in the reason but in the will, which is not a collecting force. Therefore in charity there is no order.

4. Further, order requires distinction. But charity is the most unitive of the virtues.[a] Since therefore in the other virtues an order is not assigned,[330] neither should an order be assigned in charity.

5. Further, everything that pertains to the act of a virtue, e.g., certain necessary circumstances, falls under a commandment. But the order of love does not fall under a commandment, since, if I give someone what I owe him, the law does not forbid me to give more to someone else to whom I have no such obligation. Therefore, the order of love is not a due[b] circumstance in charity.[331]

On the contrary:

1. As Dionysius says in chapter 4 of *On the Divine Names*: "What is evil for man is to be against the good of reason."[c] But to be against virtue is [likewise] evil for man. Consequently, the good of reason must be present in any virtue. But it belongs to the good of reason that man should do whatever he does in an orderly way. Since, therefore, charity is a virtue, it must have an order.

2. Further, the acts of the virtues are diversified according to the requirements of the objects. But the good, which is the object of charity, has an order, since some goods are better than others. Therefore charity too ought to have an order.

3. Further, wherever one thing is on account of another, some order is to be found. But charity loves something on account of another, for it loves all things on account of God. Therefore charity has an order.

Response:

It should be said that there must be a mode[d] in any act of virtue whatsoever, for a man is truly just not when he merely does just things, but when he does just things *justly*. But the mode belonging to an act of virtue comes from its commensuration to its object, in such a way that the act receives its measure from the same thing from which it derives

a. *magis unitiua inter alias uirtutes*—that is, it takes away distinction.
b. "owe . . . due": *debeo . . . debita*
c. Pseudo-Dionysius, *On the Divine Names* ch. 4, n. 32 (PG 3:734).
d. That is, a proper manner or measure of acting. See textual note b on p. 159; textual note b on p. 175; textual note c on p. 176.

its species.³³² But the good is charity's object in such a way that "the good as such is lovable as such, whereas to each man his own proper good is lovable," as the Philosopher says in *Ethics* VIII.ᵃ Hence, since there happen to be a great diversity and many different grades as regards this [object], insofar as one object of love is better or closer than another, the act of love must also have an order, if it is to be virtuous.

Replies to objections:

1. To the first, therefore, it should be said that in love a twofold grade can be discerned: one is of an object of loveᵇ vis-à-vis another object of love, and it is of this grade we are speaking; the other is of the lover to the object of love, and it is of this grade Bernard is speaking. Nevertheless, there is a way in which love knows this grade, and a way in which it does not. For it knows it with respect to the exterior effect, since it does not give the same thing to superiors and to equals; but it does not know it with respect to affection, insofar as it unites the lover to the beloved. And meanwhile, something of the affection does shine out in the effect—namely, that we bear ourselves more trustingly to superiors and more sociably to inferiors.³³³

2. To the second, it should be said that friendship does not consist in a strict equality alone, since it can be had with superiors, inferiors, and equals alike; rather it consists in a proportionate equalityᶜ—an equality that does not exclude a diversity of quantity, since 3:2 and 6:4 are the same proportion, viz., sesquialter, even though the excess quantity is unequal in the two cases.

3. To the third, it should be said that the act of reason precedes love. Prior things, however, leave behind something of themselves in things that come after. Thus, the order that reason brings about is found in love, so that love itself is ordered—not that love is responsible for bringing about that order, but because love tends in an orderly way toward goods that have been placed in order by reason.

4. To the fourth, it should be said that some virtues, such as faith, temperance, and others of this sort, order a person within himself. Justice, on the other hand, orders a person to someone else, insofar as the person is made equal to that other in regard to the matters with which justice is concerned.ᵈ But charity orders a person to someone else by

a. Aristotle, *Ethics* VIII, ch. 7 (1157b26).

b. "love . . . object of love": *amor . . . diligibilis*

c. *equalitate equiparantie . . . equalitate proportionis.* Cf. *In III Sent.* d. 28, a. 3, ad 3 and a. 6, ad 4 (above).

d. *Iustitia uero ordinat ad alium, secundum quod equatur ei quantum ad res circa quas est iustitia*

uniting him to the other in affection. Thus charity's proper object is [not some *thing* that needs to be equalized between two persons, but] the very rational nature toward which charity is to be had; and there are many diverse grades of rational nature found in reality. And for this reason, one may attribute an order to charity more than to any other virtue.[334]

5. To the fifth, it should be said that in one genus there can be only one highest. So, if I love something other than God as ultimate end, I cannot love God as ultimate end. Thus, by the very fact that I place what is to be loved less on equal terms of love with what is to be loved more, I do not give the *whole* of the love that I ought to give to the one who is to be loved more; and something similar is true in other cases.[335] Hence the order of charity is present in the commandment of love, and "whoever acts in disregard of proper order commits a sin," as is said in the text.[a]

ARTICLE 2[b]   Whether the order of charity is to be looked to regarding affection or effect

Objections:

Proceeding to the second, it seems that the order of charity is not to be looked to[c] according to affection, but only according to effect.

1. For just as the first Truth on which faith depends is one in all, so the highest goodness on which charity depends is one. But faith is equally certain about all the things which are believed on faith. Therefore charity, too, has equal affection for everything loved from charity. And so there is no order of affection in charity, but only an order of effects.[d]

a. The phrase is *peccat qui prepostere agit,* which could also be rendered "whoever acts in a disorderly way commits a sin."

b. Parallels: *ST* II-II, q. 26, a. 6 and q. 44, a. 8, ad 2; *De caritate,* a. 9. The distinction employed here is also brought to bear elsewhere for the solution of particular problems: cf. *ST* II-II, q. 32, a. 6, obj. 1; q. 106, a. 5, obj. 1 and corp.

c. *attendendus.* The word here means "considered, looked to, determined." The discussion is about whether the order that has been proved (in a. 1) to belong to charity is an order according to a greater or lesser *affection* (disposition of will) toward the objects of love, or according to a greater or lesser *exhibition* of love in works done in regard to those objects. The question could be paraphrased: Should the order of charity be considered, and in practical terms followed, as an order of my interior dispositions or as an order of the things I do for people?

d. To complete the statement of the argument (as Thomas usually does but here omits to do), a concluding sentence has been supplied in objections 1–4.

2. Further, an act takes its measure from the *ratio* of the object. But although many things are loved from charity, in all there is a single *ratio* for loving,[a] namely the divine goodness, which is charity's object. Therefore there is an equal affection toward everything loved from charity. And so there is no order of affection in charity, but only an order of effects.

3. Further, when a person has greater affection for someone, he desires a greater good for him. But for all whom we love from charity, either we desire the same good if it is not yet fully possessed, or we are pleased with the same good when it *is* possessed—namely, eternal life. Therefore all are loved with equal affection. And so there is no order of affection in charity, but only an order of effects.

4. Further, the order of charity is present in the commandment of love. In the commandment, however, there is nothing to do with affection, since as long as I actually do for anyone what I am supposed to do for him, even if I do it without affection, I am not guilty of breaking the commandment. Therefore the order of charity is not looked to according to affection, but only according to effect.

5. Further, where there is greater affection there is also greater merit, since merit is measured in reference to the root of charity [viz., the will]. But a man does not merit more in loving those who are close to him than in loving other people, or even in loving himself than in loving others.[b] Therefore the order of love is not to be gauged according to affection.

On the contrary:

1. "Love is proved by outward deeds," Gregory says.[c] If, therefore, there is an order of love according to effect, there must also be an order according to affection.[336]

2. Further, the good is the object of charity, as far as affection is concerned. But the order of charity, as was said,[d] is looked to according to a diversity of goods. Therefore charity has an order not only according to effect, but also according to affection.

a. *una ratio dilectionis*

b. An implicit premise of the objector should be added: We have naturally a greater affection for self than for others, and for relatives than for non-relatives; hence it is easier to love them, requires less exertion of will, and so is less meritorious.

c. *probatio dilectionis est exhibitio operis*, literally, "the proof of love is the exhibiting of a work."—Gregory, *Homilies on the Gospels*, Homily 30, n. 1 (CCSL 141:256).

d. In the body of the preceding article.

3. Further, just as charity chiefly concerns affection, so beneficence chiefly concerns the effect. If, therefore, an order were to exist only regarding effects, this would be an ordering not of charity but rather of beneficence—which is against the authority of the Song of Songs invoked in the text.[a]

Response:

It should be said that an exterior effect only pertains to charity inasmuch as it proceeds from affection, in which the act of charity first has its being. Hence, if order were to be looked to only regarding the effect, that order would in no way pertain to charity, but rather [it would pertain] to other virtues, for instance liberality or mercy. Accordingly, since charity is held to be ordered, an order must be observed in one's affections, and one must proceed from affection to effect—not in the sense that more effects are bestowed upon the one who is loved with more affection, but in the sense that a man should be *prepared* to bestow more upon him if it becomes necessary, since sometimes the one who is more loved does not need our aid at a given time. And this is clear, too, through something similar found in nature, since the Creator endows each natural thing with as much natural love for something as the creature needs in order to carry out appropriate actions in regard to it. And in like manner, divine law commands an order of affections that corresponds to the gradation [of lovable things]—a gradation we must respect and abide by in our actions.[b]

Replies to objections:

1. To the first, therefore, it should be said that the object of faith is the first Truth, not insofar as it simply exists in reality, but insofar as it is divinely announced to us, since "faith comes by hearing" (Rom. 10:17). Since therefore all the things which are of faith are announced to us in the same way, an equal certitude is had about all of them. But the object of charity is the good insofar as it really exists in things. Consequently, since the divine goodness is found in different things differently, our affection must be extended to those things in different ways.

2. To the second, it should be said that, although in everything may

---

a. Song 2:4, quoted in the *divisio textus* of the present Distinction.

b. *Et hoc etiam patet per simile in natura, quia unicuique rei naturali tantum inditum est a creatore de amore naturali erga aliquid quantum necessarium est ut effectum circa id exhibeat. Et similiter secundum gradum qui necesse est ut obseruetur in effectu, ordo affectus lege diuina imperatur.*

be found the same *common* aspect according to which they are loved, nevertheless individual things do not participate equally in that aspect, and therefore neither is an equal affection owed to them.

3. To the third, it should be said that the intensity of an act, especially in acts of the soul (which does not necessarily act according to its whole capability, as natural things do), takes its measure not merely from an object's quantity but also from an agent's efficacy and effort in acting. Hence he who sees better is not the one who sees a bigger thing, but the one who sees a thing more clearly. And therefore, too, I need not have equal affection for those for whom I desire an equal good.[337]

4. To the fourth, it should be said that, even though a person who gives to another what he owes him yet has no affection in doing so is not guilty of breaking the commandment that concerns the act of justice, he *is* guilty of breaking the commandment that concerns the act of charity. Hence in Romans 1, to be without affection is deemed a vice.[a]

5. To the fifth, it should be said that the treatment of the amount of merit corresponding to various objects of love will come in the following Distinction, and is therefore reserved until then.[b]

ARTICLE 3[c, 338]   Whether God is to be loved above all things from charity

Objections:

Proceeding to the third, it seems that God is not to be loved above all things from charity.

1. For as Dionysius says in chapter 4 of *On the Divine Names*, "love is a unitive power."[d] But anyone is more united to himself than he is to God. Therefore he ought from charity to love himself more than he loves God.

2. Further, the Philosopher says in *Ethics* VIII that "anyone finds lovable that which is good for him."[e] But whatever a man loves owing to the fact that it is good for him, he loves on account of himself. Therefore whatsoever he loves, he loves on account of himself. There-

a. Rom. 1:30 attributes to the pagans, among other qualities, being "faithless, heartless, ruthless."

b. See *In III Sent.* d. 30, which begins below at p. 242.

c. Parallels: *In III Sent.* d. 30, a. 4 (see below); *ST* I, q. 60, a. 5; I-II, q. 109, a. 3; II-II, q. 26, aa. 2 & 3; *De caritate*, a. 4, ad 2 and a. 9.

d. Pseudo-Dionysius, *On the Divine Names*, ch. 4, n. 15 (PG 3:714).

e. Aristotle, *Ethics* VIII, ch. 7 (1157b27).

fore he loves himself more than everything he loves; and so, he does not love God above all things.

3. Further, the Philosopher says in *Ethics* IX that "friendly feelings for another come from friendly feelings toward oneself."[a] But the first in any genus is the most powerful. Accordingly, the love someone has for himself is more powerful than the love he has for another, and so, by nature, a man loves himself more than he loves God—and the same is true even by charity, since grace does not destroy nature.

4. Further, as Gregory says, "love's proof is a deed done."[b] But a person does as much to preserve grace or possess created beatitude as he does for the sake of God. Therefore a person loves grace or created beatitude as much as he loves God. But the love by which we are said to love virtue or some accident is referred to the subject of the accident, the one for whom that accident is desired. Therefore someone having charity loves himself as much as he loves God.

5. Further, a person loves her neighbor only to the extent that she loves *God* in the neighbor. But a person loves God in himself as much as she loves God in a neighbor or in herself, because God is no better in himself than he is wherever he is. Therefore a person loves herself or her neighbor as much as she loves God; and thus God is not loved above all things from charity.[c]

On the contrary:

1. The end is more to be loved than things ordered to the end. But God is the end of everything that is loved from charity. Therefore he is to be loved most of all.

2. Further, each and every man finds his proper good lovable, according to the Philosopher.[d] But God is a greater good than any other, and is more proper to someone than any other, since he is more intimately present to the soul than even the soul is to itself, as is said in *On the Spirit and the Soul.*[e] Therefore God is to be loved above all things.

3. Further, that which is a cause of others in any genus is supreme

a. Aristotle, *Ethics* IX, ch. 4 (1166a1): *amicabilia que sunt ad alterum uenerunt ex amicabilibus que sunt ad se ipsum*—"The 'friendly things' [affections, intentions, deeds] that are toward another come from the 'friendly things' that are toward oneself."

b. Gregory, *Homilies on the Gospels,* Homily 30, n. 1 (CCSL 141:256).

c. Feminine pronouns are employed in this objection so as to escape the confusion that would result from more conventional usage.

d. Aristotle, *Ethics* VIII, ch. 2 (1155b23–24).

e. Pseudo-Augustine [Alcher of Clairvaux], *On the Spirit and the Soul,* ch. 14 (PL 40:791). Cf. St. Augustine, *Confessions* III, ch. 6, n. 11: "Tu autem eras interior intimo meo et superior summo meo" (CCSL 27:33).

in that genus, as is said in *Metaphysics* II.ᵃ But God is the cause and the
reason why all things are loved from charity, since the divine goodness
is charity's *per se* object. Therefore God is more to be loved from charity than anything else.

Response:

It should be said that, since the good is the object of love, there are
two ways in which someone can tend to something's good. (1) In one
way, he can tend to it such that he refers that thing's good to another,
as when I desireᵇ one thing's good for the sake of another, should that
other lack it, or when it pleases me that the other has that good, just
as someone loves wine insofar as he greatly desires the wine's pleasant
taste, and rejoices not because the wine possesses that pleasant taste,
but because he is enjoying it.ᶜ ³³⁹ And this love is called by some the
"love of concupiscence." That love, however, does not have its ultimate term in the thing that is said to be loved, but is bent toward that
person for whom that thing's good is desired. (2) In another way, love
is borne to the good of something such that it has its term in that very
one, inasmuch as the lover is pleased that the object of his love has
whatever good he has, and desires for him the good he as yet lacks.ᵈ
And this is "love of benevolence," which is the beginning of friendship, as the Philosopher says in *Ethics* IX.ᵉ Hence, the degrees of charity
are to be gauged in accordance with this kind of love, since charity includes friendship, as was said above.ᶠ

a. Aristotle, *Metaphysics* II, ch. 1 (993b24).

b. "Desire," "greatly desires," "is desired" render *opto, preoptat, optatur,* etc.

c. "Pleasant taste" renders *dulcedinem,* which need not be limited to the notion
of sweetness but includes also, more generally, agreeableness. The argument thus
far is crafted at a very abstract level ("someone can tend to something's good";
"the good of one thing, *bonum unius rei,* for the sake of another, *alteri*") but clearly
Thomas is speaking of the basic structure of love as he understands it—someone
loving some *thing* for the sake of some *person*. In this text we see one of Thomas's
first efforts to articulate the distinction between *amor concupiscentiae* and *amor amicitiae* (called *amor beniuolentie* in this paragraph, *amor amicitie* later on in the response).

d. These two sentences read: *Amor autem iste non terminatur ad rem que dicitur amari, set reflectitur ad rem illam cui optatur bonum illius rei. Alio modo amor fertur
in bonum alicuius rei ita quod ad rem ipsam terminatur, in quantum bonum quod habet complacet quod habeat, et bonum quod non habet optatur ei.* The thrust of the argument demands that the *rem illam* or *rem ipsam* is no mere "thing," but always
a person; see the Introduction for a full explanation of why we do not translate
such a formally-intended Latin neuter with an impersonal equivalent in English.

e. Aristotle, *Ethics* IX, ch. 5 (1167a3).

f. *In III Sent.* d. 27, q. 2, a. 1 (see above).

Now, the good that each person most of all wishes to see preserved is that good that is more pleasing to him, because this good is more in conformity with the appetite informed through love. This good, however, is his own good.[a] Hence, it is to the extent that something's good is (or is reckoned to be) more the lover's own good that he wishes that good to be preserved in the one loved. The lover's own good, however, is found more where it is more perfect. And thus, since any part whatever is imperfect in itself but has perfection in its whole, it follows that even by natural love the part tends more to the preservation of the whole than to its own conservation. Accordingly, an animal naturally interposes its arm in defense of the head on which the health of the whole animal depends, and particular men, too, expose themselves to death for the preservation of the community of which they are a part.[340]

Since therefore our good is perfect in God, as in the first and perfect universal cause of good things, it follows that the good's being in him naturally pleases us more than the good's being in us.[b] And thus, too, with love of friendship, God is naturally loved by a man more than a man loves himself. And since charity perfects nature, it follows according to charity as well that man loves God above himself and above all other particular goods. However, charity adds to the natural love of God a certain fellowship in the life of grace, as was said earlier.[c]

Certain ones, on the other hand, say that a man naturally loves God more than himself with a love of concupiscence, insofar as the divine good is more delightful to him [than his own good is], whereas he naturally loves himself more than God with a love of friendship, because he wishes himself to exist and to live and to have some goods more than he wishes the same for God; but [they go on to say] that charity then has the function of so elevating nature that a man loves God more than himself even with love of friendship. But the first opinion is more defensible, since the inclination of human nature, as such, never contradicts the inclination of virtue, but is in conformity with it.[d]

a. "Each person": *unusquisque*; "his own good": *suum bonum*

b. *Quia ergo bonum nostrum in Deo perfectum est, sicut in causa uniuersali prima et perfecta bonorum, ideo bonum in ipso esse magis naturaliter complacet quam in nobis ipsis.* That is, we are by nature more pleased that the good is in God than that it is in us. This rendering seems necessary in order to connect the statement with the preceding paragraph.

c. *In III Sent.* d. 27, q. 2, a. 1, end of the response (see above).

d. *inclinatio nature hominis, in quantum est homo, numquam contratendit inclinationi uirtutis, set est ei conformis*

Replies to objections:

1. To the first, therefore, it should be said that love is not essentially a union of things themselves, but a union of affection. However, it is not unfitting that what is *less* conjoined in reality should be *more* conjoined in regard to affection, since it often happens that things really conjoined to us are displeasing to us and most of all conflict with our affection.[a] But love does bring about a real union with things,[b] so far as this is possible. And therefore divine love makes a man, so far as this is possible, live not his own life but the life of God, as the Apostle says: "I live, yet it is not I but Christ who lives in me" (Gal. 2:20).

2. To the second, it should be said that although each person finds lovable that which is good for him, it is nevertheless not necessary that the object of love be loved on account of that (viz., that it is good for him) as though this were the lover's *goal,* since friendship does not turn back to oneself the good desired for another. For we love our friends, even if nothing might come of it to us.[c, 341]

3. To the third, it should be said that friendly feelings[d] toward another come from friendly feelings toward oneself, not as if the latter were the final cause of the former, but in the manner of what is prior in the process of generation, because, just as each person is first known to himself before another person (even God) is known to him, so too, in the process of generation, the love anyone has for himself is prior to the love he has for another.[342]

4. To the fourth, it should be said that, properly speaking, our works are not proportioned to the affection by which we love God in himself, since nothing accrues or is able to accrue to him from our works. But if it *were* possible that something could accrue to him from our works, the person who has charity would do much more for the sake of preserving God's beatitude than for the sake of securing the person's own beatitude.

5. To the fifth, it should be said that, while God is everywhere equally loved,[343] nevertheless the divine good existing in some particular being is not as lovable as that very being is in God, since the divine good does not exist equally perfectly in everything.

a. *ab affectu maxime discedant*
b. *amor ad rerum unionem inducit*
c. *quamuis unicuique sit amabile quod sibi est bonum, non tamen oportet quod propter hoc sicut propter finem ametur, quia est sibi bonum, cum etiam amicitia non retorqueat ad se ipsum bonum quod ad alterum optat. Diligimus enim amicos, etiam si nichil nobis debeat inde fieri.*
d. *amicabilia*

ARTICLE 4[a]   Whether the love of God permits consideration of a wage[b]

Objections:

Proceeding to the fourth, it seems that love of God forbids looking to some wage.

1. For in John 10, the wage-seeker is reproved, but "wage-seeker" signifies one who seeks a wage.[c] Therefore the love of God from charity cannot admit consideration of a wage.

2. Further, Augustine says: "Although it is impossible to serve God and gain no reward, nevertheless he is to be served without looking to a reward."[d] But a reward is nothing other than a wage for labor done. Therefore God is to be served without consideration of a wage.

3. Further, although civic friendship brings with it many delights and benefits, still for all that it does not look to them, but has the noble good as its foundation.[e] But the friendship of charity is more noble than civic friendship; therefore neither does it look to any benefits.[f]

a. Parallels: *ST* II-II, q. 27, a. 3; cf. q. 27, a. 8. If one is considering the much broader question of the relationship between love of God (or love of the good as such, on its own account) and love of self (or love of the good as shared in or possessed by one's own activity), one will find a plethora of texts in Aquinas on this subject, which is discussed under several headings: the natural inclination of the will to the good of the willer; the nature of hope as a theological virtue aimed at *possessing* beatitude; the relationship between the end itself and the *obtaining* of the end. Just in this translation, one may consult the articles immediately before and after this one (a. 3 and a. 5) as well as *In II Sent.* d. 3, q. 4 and d. 38, aa. 1 & 2 (see above).

b. *Merces* will be rendered "wage" to parallel the singular verbs used with it, and also to bring out that Thomas is interested not in wages in general but in the wage of eternal life. Although the second objection tries to equate "wage" (*merces*) and "reward" (*premium*), there seems to be a subtle difference: a wage is a benefit worked for, earned by that very work, while a reward is some good conferred on a worthy candidate. It may be, of course, that the worthiness is constituted by working well; in this sense a wage can be, and usually is, the reward for good work or faithful service. Both a wage and a reward have the note of a *debitum*, something owed in justice.

c. *mercenarius . . . mercedem.* The *mercenarius* is the hired worker who works only for the sake of the pay. Hence the pejorative term "mercenary," applied either to soldiers who fight not for love of country but for love of money, or in general to anyone who makes personal gain the object of his efforts.

d. Implicit in Augustine, *Sermon* 385, ch. 4 (PL 38:1692); explicit in Bernard, *On Loving God*, ch. 7, n. 17 (PL 182:894).

e. *supra honestum fundatur*

f. The unspoken premise is that a wage is a benefit (*utilitas*) and not a noble good (*bonum honestum*) because, unlike moral virtue, it is not worth having for its own sake but is worth having only as a means to something else. Therefore if

4. Further, a wage is the end of things done for the sake of a wage. But an end is more loved than things that stand relative to the end. If, therefore, God were loved for the sake of a wage to be gained, something else would be loved more than God—which is contrary to the nature of charity.

5. Further, just as a person secures a reward through charity, so too does he escape punishment through charity. But charity, most of all when it is perfect, banishes the fear of punishment. Hence it also seems to exclude looking to a wage.

On the contrary:

1. As is said in a gloss on Matthew 1, "hope generates charity." But hope is the expectation of a wage.[a] Therefore charity can co-exist with looking to a wage.[344]

2. Further, in Hebrews 11:26 it is said of the holy fathers that "they looked for repayment." But there is no question that they loved God from charity. Therefore the love of God from charity is compatible with looking to a wage.

3. Further, friends seek to enjoy one another.[b] But our wage is nothing other than to enjoy God by seeing him. Therefore not only does charity not exclude having an eye to a wage, but it even makes one do so.

Response:

It should be said that a wage properly signifies the reward that someone earns[c] from labor or from some work. Now, a reward is what is rendered to someone for his benefit.[d, 345] Hence a wage, insofar as it fits this description, implies something referable, through love, to that one whose wage is rendered, for a person loves a wage on account of himself. Nonetheless, it does not belong to the *ratio* of a wage that it be the *end* of a person's intention, since it often happens that someone to whom a wage is given does not, in fact, seek a wage from his work.[346] Now, those things that someone loves on account of himself are either

---

even the friendship of fellow citizens is capable of going beyond utilitarian concerns, how much more should charity go beyond them?

a. *Set spes est expectatio mercedis*

b. Literally, it is of friends—it belongs to what it means to be friends—that they seek to enjoy one another: *Amicorum est quod querant inuicem perfrui.*

c. "wage . . . earns": *merces . . . meretur.* The accent is on earning a reward precisely by work done.

d. *Premium autem est quod alicui in bonum eius redditur* (here, *in bonum eius* means "for his good," i.e., for his benefit).

formal perfections in him, e.g., health, virtue, activity, love, and such-like, or they bring into being or preserve these things or impede their contraries. Hence, if someone loves something outside of himself on account of himself, that thing can be called a wage insofar as from it something else is obtained by him or is preserved in him.[a] But, as was said above, it belongs to the *ratio* of friendship that a friend be loved for his own sake.[b] Hence within friendship a friend does not have the *ratio* of a wage, properly speaking, even though the many good things that are brought about for us by a friend (for example, the delights and benefits that we, the lover, obtain from him) can have the *ratio* of a wage, by reason of which the friend himself is called a "wage" in the manner of a cause, just as God is called our "wage" by reason of those things that exist in us from him.

It is clear, therefore, that setting up some wage as the end of love, on the part of love's object, contradicts the definition of friendship.[347] Hence in this way charity cannot have an eye to a wage, for this would be to set up as the ultimate end not God, but the goods that derive from him.

On the other hand, to set up a wage as the end of love on the part of the lover (but still not as his ultimate end), taking into consideration that love itself is a certain activity of the lover, does not contradict the definition of friendship, because this very activity, since it is an accident, is not said to be loved except on account of its subject, as is clear from what was said before.[c] And, without prejudice to friendship,[d] there *can* be an order among things that a man loves on account of himself. Hence, friendship notwithstanding, I can love the very activity of love, on account of something else. Nevertheless it will contradict the *ratio* of virtue if the activity of a virtue is loved on account of some other inferior power,[e] of which sort are temporal goods.[348]

It is therefore clear that the person who has charity cannot have an eye toward a wage in such a way that he would be setting up anything else as the end in comparison with the one loved,[f] viz., God, for this would contradict the definition of charity *as friendship*; nor in such a way that he would be setting up some temporal good as the end of

---

a. *in quantum ex eo aliquid in ipso relinquitur uel conseruatur*

b. *amicus sui gratia diligatur*

c. *In III Sent.* d. 28, a. 1 (see above).

d. *salua amicitia*

e. "Virtue" and "power" are both *uirtus*.

f. *ut ponat aliquid quodcumque finem amati*, that is, to set up an end beyond the one loved—to make God the means to some further end.

his love, because this contradicts the definition of charity *as virtue*. But, since beatitude is the end of the virtues, the person who has charity can have an eye toward a wage in such a way that he sets up created beatitude as the end of his [exercise of the virtue of] love (not, however, as the end in comparison with the one loved), for this contradicts neither the definition of friendship nor the definition of virtue.[349]

Replies to objections:

1. To the first, therefore, it should be said that the wage-seeker we read about in that passage signifies one who undertakes a spiritual work for the sake of a temporal wage.

2. To the second, it should be said that "God is to be served without looking to a reward" in such a way that a reward is not set up as the end of the one loved and served [as if there were some end beyond God], but is set up as the end of that very service or love [insofar as they are the lover's activities].

3. To the third, it should be said that friendship does not look to the delights and benefits supplied by friends as if these were the end on account of which a friend loves.

4. To the fourth, the solution is clear from what was said in the response.

5. To the fifth, it should be said that the good with which hope is concerned has more consonance with love than the evil with which fear is concerned. As a result, although perfect charity altogether banishes the fear of punishment,[a] it is not necessary that it banish looking to a wage.

ARTICLE 5[b]   Whether from charity a man ought to love himself more than his neighbor

Objections:

Proceeding to the fifth, it seems that a man ought not to love himself more than he loves his neighbor from charity.

1. For that on account of which something else is given up is more loved. But charity makes a man in a way give up his very self and

---

a. *perfecta caritas foras mittat timorem pene*

b. Parallels: *ST* II-II, q. 26, aa. 4–5; q. 44, a. 8, ad 2; *De caritate,* a. 9 and a. 11, ad 9; *De perfectione,* ch. 14 (ed. Leon. 41:B84–85); *Super II Tim.* 3, lec. 1. These parallel texts discuss two queries that happen to be merged in this article of the *Scriptum,* namely: should a person love him*self* more than he loves his neighbor; should he love his *body* more than he loves a neighbor.

cleave to the beloved, since, as Dionysius says, love places a man out-side himself and places him in the beloved.ᵃ Therefore he loves his friend more than himself.

2. Further, we love God more than ourselves inasmuch as our good is found more perfectly in him than in us. But in like manner, it is found more perfectly in some of our neighbors than in us, since they have the goods that we have, yet more perfectly. Therefore we should love our neighbor more than ourselves.³⁵⁰

3. Further, what someone most of all loves in himself is to live and to exist. But charity makes one lay down one's bodily life on behalf of one's brethren; for even certain pagans,ᵇ owing to love of friends, ex-posed themselves to death, without any hope of eternal life. Therefore friendship, and charity too, makes one love one's neighbor more than oneself.

4. Further, we love people the more in proportion to how much we desire goods for them and prevent evils befalling them. But, as the Phi-losopher says in *Ethics* IX, when we are sorrowing we should be slow to call upon friends, yet go promptly to share in their sorrows, where-as in regard to joys the converse holds, since one should promptly call upon friends to share in one's joys, but thrust oneself cautiously into their joys.ᶜ ³⁵¹ Therefore charity makes one love one's neighbor more than oneself.

5. Further, beneficence is an effect of charity. But those who are benefactors to their friends receive greater praise than those who are benefactors to themselves. Therefore charity makes one love one's neighbor more than oneself.

6. Further, friendship makes a man rejoice in the company and con-versation of his friends.ᵈ But a man is more delighted by the company and conversation of his friends than by his own company and [inter-nal] conversation. Therefore he loves friends and neighbors more than himself.

On the contrary:

1. To the extent that someone loves anyone's salvation, to that ex-tent he shuns his sin. But a man ought more to shun his own sin than another's. Therefore he ought to love his own salvation more than the salvation of another.³⁵²

a. Pseudo-Dionysius, *On the Divine Names,* ch. 4, n. 13 (PG 3:711).

b. *gentiles*

c. Aristotle, *Ethics* IX, ch. 11 (1171b15ff.).

d. "company and conversation of his friends": *conuersatione cum amicis*

2. Further, mercy arises out of love. But according to what Augustine says, a person ought to begin by having mercy on himself [before he extends mercy to others].[a] Therefore love, too, ought to begin from himself [and then spread out to others].

3. Further, what is natural is more vehement than what is only voluntary. But love of self comes from an inclination of nature, whereas love of others comes only from rational will.[b,353] Therefore a man loves himself from charity more than he loves others.

Response:

It should be said that, just as something is found more perfectly in a perfect and universal cause than in a particular effect, so too something is found more perfectly in a thing itself than in its likeness. Hence, since the proper good of a man is found (1) in God as in a universal cause, (2) in himself as in a particular effect, and (3) in the neighbor as in a likeness, it follows that, just as he ought to love God more than himself by the love of benevolence, so he ought also to love himself more than his neighbor.

But it should be known that since in a human being there is a twofold nature—the interior (viz., the rational nature) which is called the "inner man," and the exterior (viz., sensual nature) which is called the "outer man"—a man ought to love himself more in regard to the interior nature than in regard to the exterior nature. And therefore he ought to desire more those things that are goods of the interior nature than those things that are goods for him according to the exterior nature.

Now, all the works of virtue—among which are included those works by which someone behaves appropriately toward a friend—are goods for a man according to his interior nature. And therefore more exterior goods are to be bestowed upon friends than upon ourselves, insofar as the good of virtue, which is our greatest good, consists in this [kind of activity]; but in regard to spiritual goods, we ought always to bestow them more upon ourselves and will them more for ourselves than for our friends; and the same holds about avoiding evils.[354]

---

a. *incipere misereri.* He ought to have pity on, and take steps to remedy, his own sinful condition first, before being concerned with the condition of others. Cf. Augustine, *Sermon* 106, ch. 4 (PL 38:626): "Quid est, facite misericordiam? Si intelligis, a te incipe."

b. *ex uoluntate rationis*

Replies to objections:

1. To the first, therefore, it should be said that in love the one loved *qua* beloved is more powerful than the one loving *qua* lover. But since the one loving is [not only lover of another but] also an object of love to himself, it follows that he can be more powerful in regard to love than is an extrinsic object of love, insofar as he is an object of love to himself and his affection is concentrated more upon himself than upon the extrinsic object of love.[a]

2. To the second, it should be said that, although it is possible that the good I have is found more perfectly in a neighbor than in myself, nevertheless it is always found more perfectly in me as something *proper,* since the good that is in him is not mine except by way of likeness. The good that is in God, however, is mine too, by virtue of God's causing of my good.[b, 355]

3. To the third, it should be said that to hand oneself over to death for the sake of a friend is the most perfect act of virtue; accordingly, a virtuous man desires this act more than he desires his own bodily life. Hence, that a man lays down his own bodily life for the sake of a friend happens not because he loves the friend more than himself, but because he loves the good of virtue in himself more than he loves his bodily good.[356]

4. To the fourth, it should be said that the very fact that a man wishes not to be burdensome to his friend by sharing his own sorrows with him, but instead wishes to be generous and delightful, shows that he is acting according to virtue; and so he renders more spiritual good to himself than to his friend.

5. To the fifth, it should be said that, as far as spiritual goods are concerned, we bestow more upon ourselves than upon our friends, but as far as bodily goods are concerned, we bestow more upon friends than upon ourselves, for the reason that was given in the response.[357]

6. To the sixth, it should be said that the company and conversation of friends is delightful to us insofar as we are acquainted with their

a. The original reads: *in amore amatum ut amatum potius est quam amans ut amans. Set quia amans etiam est amatum a se ipso, ideo potius potest esse in amore, in quantum est amatum, quam aliud amatum extrinsecum, et magis collocatur in ipso affectus amantis quam in exteriori amato.* Note the careful wording: Thomas explains how it is that *some* beloved is less loved than oneself, viz., another creature. The same logic does not apply to God, because the very good the lover loves in himself is more perfectly found in God than in himself, as Thomas has already explained earlier.

b. *Bonum autem quod est in Deo est meum etiam secundum causam*

good, which pleases us as if it were our own. And since we are better acquainted with things through sight than through any other sense, friends most of all desire to *see* each other. And since a man can get to know things that belong to another better than he can get to know those that belong to himself, he takes more delight in sharing conversation with a friend than in conversing with himself, although the virtuous man pleasantly converses with himself, insofar as within himself he turns over memories and plans and the hope of good things, all of which bring delight to him, as is said in *Ethics* IX.[a, 358]

ARTICLE 6[b]   Whether from charity a man ought to love strangers more than those who are close to him[c]

Objections:

Proceeding to the sixth, it seems that from charity a man ought to love strangers more than those who are close to him.

1. For charity, like friendship, has the noble good as its foundation. But a greater nobility or virtue is sometimes found in strangers more than in those who are close to us. Therefore strangers are sometimes more to be loved from charity than those who are close to us.

2. Further, charity brings about a conformity of man to God. But God loves those who are strangers to us, if they are better, more than he loves those who are close to us. Therefore we, too, ought to love them more.

3. Further, effect corresponds to affection. But in some affairs, as in the distribution of ecclesiastical benefices, we ought to show a greater effect of love to strangers than to those who are close to us, if the strangers are better. Therefore strangers are sometimes to be loved with greater affection, too, than those who are close to us.

4. Further, concord is both implied in and effected by charity. But concord sometimes exists more with strangers than with those who are close to us, as occurs in a time of war, when the commander of the army is to be obeyed more than one's own father. Therefore [in such circumstances] strangers are more to be loved than those who are close to us.

5. Further, what is owed should take precedence over what is not

a. Aristotle, *Ethics* IX, ch. 4 (1166a3ff.).

b. Parallels: *In III Sent.* d. 31, q. 2, a. 3, qa. 2 (see below); *ST* II-II, q. 26, a. 7, where the question is posed as: Whether we ought to love those who are better more than those who are joined to us.

c. On the meaning of *propinqui,* see textual note a on p. 204.

owed. But the returning of benefits is something owed to benefactors. Now, sometimes benefitting those who are close to us is not something owed. Therefore benefits are to be given more to strangers than to those who are close to us; and so, at least with respect to the effect of friendship, strangers should take precedence over those who are close to us.

On the contrary:

1. "Let us do good to all men, but most of all to those who are of the household of the faith" (Gal. 6:10). Therefore those who are close to us are to take precedence over strangers.

2. Further, "whoever does not take care of his own, and most of all of the members of his household, has denied the faith and is worse than an infidel" (1 Tim. 5:8). Therefore care is to be taken more of those who are close to us than of others.

3. Further, man ought to love himself more than others. Therefore when some are closer to him, he ought to love them more.

Response:

It should be said, as was said above,[a] that we love neighbors inasmuch as our good is found in them by way of likeness (speaking here of the love of benevolence). Now, this likeness is attended to according to the manner in which we share things in common with them,[b] for which reason the Philosopher distinguishes different friendships according to different manners of sharing things in common. For there is a *natural* sharing in common, according to which some people share a natural origin; and upon that sharing is based the friendship of father and son and of other blood relatives. Another sharing in common is *economic,* according to which men share domestic duties with each other.[c] Still another sharing in common is *political,* according to which men share things in common with their fellow citizens. A fourth sharing in common is *divine,* according to which all men share in the one body of the Church, either actually or potentially; and this is the friendship of charity, which is extended to all, even to enemies.

Therefore, since charity implies benevolence, which desires good things for friends and does good things to them, it follows that, in any

a. In the preceding article, response to the final objection.

b. *cum eis communicamus.* In the response, *communicatio* will be rendered "sharing in common."

c. The term *yconomica* is, of course, used with the ancient meaning "things having to do with the household or family management," not the modern meaning "things having to do with a society's production and consumption, labor and capital, etc.," which is perhaps better named "political economy."

of the aforesaid friendships, friends are to be loved at the level of the goods pertaining to that sharing in common upon which the friendship is based. Hence, to our fathers and blood relatives we ought to bear ourselves more amicably in that which pertains to the preservation of nature; to members of the household, in that which pertains to household government; to fellow citizens, in that which regards civil life, such as conversing together and assisting in civic works;[a] and to all men, in that which regards God, so that we desire eternal life for all and work for their salvation according to our station and means.[b]

Nevertheless, simply speaking, there ought to be a greater love by that friendship which more closely approaches what deserves to be more loved. Now, God is to be loved most of all, and after this, a man ought to love himself most of all, as was said above.[c] And since the last of the aforesaid friendships, namely that of charity, approaches more nearly to the love of God, if it were separated from those prior friendships and taken by itself, it would be more powerful without the others, simply speaking, than the others would be without it. These different friendships are not, however, really separate with respect to anyone who is still living this mortal life; but after death, the damned are separated from the friendship of charity.[359] Hence I ought to love a Christian man more than my dead infidel father, simply speaking, although when it comes to natural affection it is permitted that we be drawn more toward that which is more conjoined to us by nature. The first friendship [the natural] is closer to that [love] by which someone loves himself than the second [the domestic], and the second than the third [the political], and the third together with the fourth [that of charity] than the fourth by itself.[360]

Consequently, Ambrose sets down this order of love: first, that blood relatives are loved, with whom the first friendship exists; second, that "domestics" are loved—with whom the second friendship [the domestic, narrowly speaking] exists in regard to those who live together with us in the same household,[d] and with whom the third friendship [the political] exists in regard to those familiar acquaintances who undertake with us civic and noble deeds;[e] third, that enemies are loved, to-

---

a. *simul conuersari et iuuare in operibus ciuilibus. Conuersari* can also refer more generally to the various activities that people do when they dwell together.

b. *secundum modum nostrum*—could convey the sense of "according to individual circumstances" or "according to the possibilities afforded by one's state in life."

c. In the preceding articles, esp. 3 and 5.

d. *quantum ad illos qui in domo conuersantur nobiscum*

e. *quantum ad illos qui nobis in ciuilibus et honestis actibus familiares sunt*

ward whom we have only the fourth friendship. And this ordering is to be understood under the proviso: "simply speaking." Yet in a certain respect that order can be changed, so that, for instance, to a familiar acquaintance who undertakes noble works in common with me, I should bear myself more amicably in regard to our association in such things than I do to my father, if he does not share them in common with me.[361] And the same qualification should be understood in the other cases as well.

Replies to objections:

1. To the first, therefore, it should be said that political friendship has for its basis a sharing in noble works, which some men pursue in common, whereas natural friendship has for its basis a *natural* sharing, and this sharing is closer to that whereby a man has something in common with himself.[a, 362] Hence, just as a man, simply speaking, ought to love himself more as far as *nature* is concerned, even if he is evil, than he ought to love another man who is good, so too he ought to love more the *nature* of his [evil] father, simply speaking, than he ought to love another man who is good—not, of course, insofar as the father is evil, but to the end that he might become good.

2. To the second, it should be said that we are conformed to God in this: that we love those more who have more in common with us, even as he loves more those who have more in common with him—although they who have more in common with us and they who have more in common with him are not necessarily the same ones.

3. To the third, it should be said that in regard to things that do *not* pertain to what we naturally share in common with our father or other blood relatives, we need not confer benefits upon our blood relatives more than upon others, but should rather benefit those who are more conjoined with us in regard to the precise sharing in common to which the goods in question pertain. Ecclesiastical benefices, accordingly, are not to be granted more to blood relatives, but to those who are more suitable for ruling the Church, since they share more in common with us insofar as we are dispensers of divine things. Whereas when it comes to the disposing of one's own patrimony and of those things that a man privately and lawfully acquires,[b] one can and should benefit blood relatives in preference to others, unless from another

---

a. *amicitia politica fundamentum habet communicationem in operibus honestis in quibus simul aliqui conuersantur. Set amicitia naturalis habet fundamentum communicationem naturalem, et hec communicatio propinquior est illi qua homo sibi communicat.*

b. *de patrimonio proprio et de his que homo proprio et licito lucro acquirit*

point of view there is something that weighs more heavily, such as poverty to be met or advantage to be gained.[a, 363]

4. To the fourth, it should be said that the solution is clear in what has been said, since we ought to bear ourselves more amicably to anyone in precisely those things that pertain to the sharing in common proper to that friendship by which they are joined to us.

5. To the fifth, it should be said that in things pertaining to the preservation of [human] nature we are debtors more to our parents, from whom we have received that nature,[364] than to any others; and consequently, we are debtors also to blood relatives because of their connection to our parents.[b] We are therefore more obliged to deliver our father from death than to deliver a stranger from death, even if the same stranger in a similar case would have delivered us.[365] But in regard to other benefits, there are times when we may bear ourselves more amicably to strangers than to those who are close to us.

ARTICLE 7[c]   Concerning the order of charity to be observed among those who are close to us[366]

Objections:

Proceeding to the seventh, it seems that one's father is not to be loved most of all [among those who are close to us].

1. For effect corresponds to affection, and makes the latter manifest. But we ought to show love's effect more to children[d] than to fathers, for, according to 2 Corinthians 12:14, children ought not to lay up wealth for their parents, but conversely. Therefore children are more to be loved than parents.

2. Further, the order of charity is not repugnant to the order of nature, since charity does not destroy nature but perfects it. But a man naturally loves his child more than his father, just as a benefactor naturally loves the one benefitted more than the other way around, insofar as the former's own good shines out more in the latter, as is said in

a. *nisi ex alia parte sit aliquid quod preponderet, uel indigentia uel utilitas*

b. "and consequently . . . parents": *et consanguineis consequenter*

c. Parallels: *ST* II-II, q. 26, aa. 8–12; *De caritate*, a. 9 (esp. ad 15 & ad 18); *Super Eph.* 5, lec. 10; *Super Matth.* 10; *Sent. Eth.* VIII, lec. 12; ibid., IX, lec. 7.

d. In this article, *filii* has been rendered "children" and *fratres* "siblings" wherever the sex of the child or sibling makes no difference to the content of the argument. There is only one instance where the sex makes a difference in the argument, namely in objection 5, where Thomas speaks of daughters (*filie*) having more resemblance to their mother than to their father, and hence to their *sorores* than to their *fratres*.

Ethics IX.ᵃ Therefore according to charity, too, children are to be loved more than parents.

3. Further, after God, each one ought to love himself more than any other. But a man ought to love his wife as himself, since he is one body with her. Therefore he ought to love his wife more than any other.

4. Further, we ought to love more those who love us more. But mothers love their children more than fathers do. Therefore children ought to love their mothers more than their fathers.

5. Further, likeness is the cause of friendship. But daughters are more likened to their mothers than to their fathers. Therefore daughters, at least, ought to love their mothers more than their fathers, and [for the same reason] their sisters more than their brothers. And so the order set down in the text is not universal.ᵇ

6. Further, Peter's siblings are closer to his father than Peter's children are. If, therefore, the father were to be loved above all others, it would follow that one's siblings should be loved more than one's children, of which the contrary is said in the text.

On the contrary:

1. We ought to love God above all. But the love we bear toward a father has a greater likeness to the love we bear toward God, who is our Father, than has any other love. Therefore we ought to love a father above all others.³⁶⁷

2. Further, the one to whom a sufficient return can never be made is to be loved most of all. But as the Philosopher says in *Ethics* VIII,ᶜ we can never make a sufficient return to our fathers, from whom we have received being, nourishment, and education. Therefore among neighbors we ought to love fathers most of all.

---

a. Aristotle, *Ethics* IX, ch. 7 (1167b17ff.): "It is disputed why benefactors are more fond of the benefitted than the benefitted of their benefactors. The opposite seems to be just. One might suppose it happens from consideration of utility and what is profitable to oneself; for the benefactor has a debt due to him, while the benefitted has to repay a debt. This, however, is not all; the reason is partly the general natural principle: activity is more desirable. There is the same relation between the effect and the activity, the benefitted being as it were an effect or creation of the benefactor."

b. The reference must be to Lombard's citation of Jerome's *Commentary on Ezekiel* 44:25: "After God, the Father of all, is loved one's father and mother in the flesh, then one's son and daughter, [and one's] brother and sister" (Grottaferrata ed., 2:173.19–22). This is the only authority that seems to put father before mother, son before daughter, brother before sister; all the other authorities cited speak generally of *parentes* and *filii* and *fratres*.

c. Aristotle, *Ethics* VIII, ch. 14 (1162a2ff.).

3. Further, as a friendship is greater, so is it firmer. But the friendship a child has for a father is more firm than the converse, since sons cannot repudiate their parents, as fathers can repudiate their sons and, on account of some crime, accuse them and throw them out, as is said in *Ethics* VIII.ª Therefore fathers are to be loved more than children.

Response:

It should be said that the friendship of those who are close to us, as was said above,ᵇ is founded upon a natural sharing of something in common. Now every natural sharing is based upon the origin in regard to which father and child are constituted as such;ᶜ for siblings are called siblings because they are born of the same father, and so on in succession.³⁶⁸ Hence the entire friendship of those who are close to us is based upon the friendship of father and child; and therefore this friendship is greater than any other friendship with those who are close to us. Yet in this sphere of friendship, children in a certain way take precedence over parents, and parents in a certain way take precedence over children, in accordance with the two modes of love. For something is loved as a distinct thing, e.g., as I love a human being, and something is loved as existing in or for another, e.g., as I love my hand or another bodily member by the one love by which I love myself.

Speaking, therefore, of the love of something in itself, in this way parents are more loved than children. But speaking of the love by which something is loved as existing in another, in this way children are more loved than parents. The reason for this is that each thing is more loved the closer it is to us. But something that has an essential order to someone is closer to him than something that is ordered to him accidentally. Now, a cause is essential to an effect as genus is essential to species, whereas an effect is related accidentally to a cause. This is because the effect follows upon the being of the cause as species follows upon genus³⁶⁹—unless the effect is something *of* the cause, since in that case the effect will be compared to the cause in the manner of an integral part, which is actually and essentially in the whole, while insofar as the effect is something *of* the cause, it is not distinct from it but is one with it.

a. Aristotle, *Ethics* VIII, ch. 16 (1163b18ff.).

b. In the preceding article.

c. *super originem, secundum quam est pater et filius.* Thomas's argument will eventually show that the father as such has a special place. Hence "parent" cannot be substituted for *pater.* On the other hand, it makes no difference to the argument of the response whether one is speaking of a son or of a daughter; hence *filius* can be "child."

Accordingly, if we consider father and child as certain persons[a] distinct in themselves, the father is more loved than the child, because the father is a cause, whereas the child is an effect. But since the child is a certain "part of the father,"[b, 370] which does not hold conversely [the father is not a "part of the child"], the child is therefore loved by another love, insofar as the child is a "part of the loving father" as though one of his own members.[c] Hence the Philosopher says that what is generated from someone is closer to him, as though it were a bodily member, say a foot or a tooth.[d] And since in this way it is loved by a love that is as one with that love by which someone loves himself, it follows, from this vantage, that the child is more loved than the father.[371]

And according to this way of viewing the matter, the Philosopher assigns three reasons why children are loved more than parents. The first is that children are like members of their father; hence someone loves his child even as he loves himself. The second is that a father knows better who are his children than his children know who is their father.[e] The third is that the good of the father shines forth in the child as the good of the cause shines forth in the effect—for which reason any artisan naturally loves his works as though they were his children.[f] But since the love by which something is loved in itself [rather than in another] has more the character of benevolence, which is the source and root of friendship, therefore one has friendship (and likewise charity) more for one's father than for one's child, although in a way one's love is more for one's child.

Certain ones, however, say that children are more loved by natural affection, but fathers are more loved by the affection of charity. But this opinion displeases me, since in natural things nothing is inordinate, yet an inclination of nature that inclined someone to love *more* what in reality is to be loved *less* would be inordinate. Hence charity does not change the order of nature, but perfects it. Further, in certain respects a man is naturally more inclined to the love of his father than to the love of his child, even as a man more easily drives away a child from himself than a father, whom he does not drive away except

a. *quedam persone*

b. *res patris*

c. *Set quia filius est quedam res patris et non e conuerso, ideo filius diligitur alia dilectione, in quantum res patris diligentis est, ut membrum ipsius*

d. Aristotle, *Ethics* VIII, ch. 12 (1161b20–24).

e. *patres sciunt magis aliquos esse suos filios quam e conuerso*

f. These reasons are given in various places in the *Ethics*: V, ch. 6 (1134b8–12); VIII, ch. 12 (1161b17–33); IX, ch. 7 (1167b33–1168a9). Aristotle does not, however, limit the arguments to fathers, but in most cases mentions mothers too.

on account of superabundant malice, as the Philosopher says in *Ethics* VIII.[a] In like manner, too, certain animals have a greater natural inclination toward their parents in certain matters than toward their offspring, as Basil in *Hexaemeron,* Book VIII,[b] relates about storks, which, when their parents are worn out by old age, cover them with their feathers, feed them, and support them in flight.

Hence it is clear that, according to both natural inclination and charity, there is need of a distinction [between the love of something in itself, and the love of something as in or for another].

Replies to objections:

1. To the first, therefore, it should be said that the father is a cause of the child. Now, it belongs to a cause to flow into the caused, and not conversely. Hence, natural love for a child is gauged according to the father's natural inclination of affection to benefit his child, whereas the love of a child for his father is gauged according to the child's natural inclination to subject itself to its father; and this latter inclination is not less than the former, but greater. Hence, it requires greater malice in a man to arrive at the point of turning away from the latter inclination than to arrive at the point of turning away from the former. Now, although in some cases a father is inferior to his child insofar as he needs the child's help, nevertheless this inferiority does not attach to the father *qua* father, since *qua* father he is always superior and [has the dignity of] a cause. And therefore, since nature always inclines to what is always and *per se* the case, not to what may chance to occur in particular cases,[c] there is not so great a natural inclination on the part of the child to benefit its father as there is on the part of a father to benefit his child. Yet this inclination [of offspring to parent] is brought about by reason, which in men supplies that for which na-

---

a. Aristotle, *Ethics* VIII, ch. 14 (1163b19–27).

b. Basil, *Homilies on the Six Days of Creation,* Homily 8, n. 5 (PG 29:175). Albert the Great had also commented on this behavior of the storks in his *De animalibus,* Book XXIII, ch. 24: "When feeding its young, it regurgitates this macerated food and serves the nourishment to its delicate fledglings. . . . According to legend, the stork tends to the wants of its parents for the same length of time as the parents had nurtured its needs during infancy. Hence, the ancients revered the stork as a model of filial piety." See James J. Scanlan's translation of Books XXII to XXVI, *Man and the Beasts* (Binghamton, NY: Medieval & Renaissance Texts & Studies, 1987), 213–14. As a probable source for Albert, Scanlan cites Ambrose's *Hexae-meron,* Bk. V, ch. 16 (PL 14:243–44).

c. *quia natura semper inclinat ad illud quod per se est et semper, non ad illud quod ac-cidit in casu*

ture by itself does not suffice. In other animals, however, in which it frequently happens that sires owing to old age need the help of their offspring,[a] nature endows the offspring (since they lack reason) with the inclination to provide for their sires, even as conversely [the sires are endowed with a natural inclination to provide for offspring], as was said about storks.

2. To the second, it should be said that that reasoning applies to love for a child in the sense in which he is loved as a good of the father; for in this way, the one benefitted is naturally more loved than the benefactor, insofar as he is the benefactor's accomplishment.[b]

3. To the third, it should be said that a wife is a woman who is taken to oneself for the act of generation. Hence it seems that, in terms of the love of benevolence, she is to be placed in the same category as children who are generated in this union.[c, 372]

4. To the fourth, it should be said that mothers naturally love their children more than fathers do, for three reasons.[d] The first is that they labored more in their generation; they thus put more of themselves into them. The second is that mothers know better than fathers which children are their own. The third is that, right after birth, they take their infants to themselves and nurture them, which fathers do not do; and this makes a difference, even as we love among our relatives those with whom we have regular interaction more than we love the more distant ones, since by such interaction social friendship is joined to natural friendship. And all these reasons amount to this—that the mother puts more of herself into a child than the father does. But more of that which is *of* the son is contributed by the father than by the mother, since the father gives the form while the mother gives the matter.[373] Consequently, a man by nature loves his father and relatives on his father's side more than he loves relatives on his mother's side.

5. To the fifth, it should be said that in regard to things that pertain to perfection, which she loves more in themselves, a daughter is more likened to her father than to her mother; but in regard to things that pertain to defect, she is more likened to her mother than to her father,[374] and a likeness of this sort is not a rationale for loving. And consequently, too, a person by nature loves brothers more than sisters,

a. Thomas writes *patres . . . indigent filiorum* speaking of the brute animals, but it is not so idiomatic in English to speak of "animal fathers and children."

b. *factura*

c. *dicendum, quod uxor in actum generationis assumitur. Vnde uidetur in eodem gradu ponenda esse, quantum ad amorem beniuolentie, cum filiis.*

d. Cf. Aristotle, *Ethics* VIII, ch. 12 (1161b17–30); IX, ch. 7 (1168a21–27).

insofar as brothers more perfectly imitate their father than sisters do.

6. To the sixth, it should be said that, although brothers are closer to the father, nevertheless children are closer to us [than brothers are]. Now, we ought to love ourselves more than our fathers; therefore, we ought to love our children more than our brothers.

ARTICLE 8   Concerning charity's perfection and degrees

Proceeding to the eighth, [we divide the article into three subquestions: (1) Whether these degrees are fittingly distinguished; (2) whether all are bound to the practice of perfect charity; (3) whether one who has attained perfect charity is bound to everything that belongs to perfection.]

SUBQUESTION 1[a]   Whether the degrees of charity are fittingly distinguished

Objections:

It seems that those degrees of charity [given in the text of Lombard[b]] are unfittingly distinguished.

1. For the perfection of charity consists in this: that God is loved with one's whole heart. But this is not possible in the wayfaring state, as was said above.[c] Therefore charity in the wayfaring state cannot be perfect. [Hence, "perfect charity" should not be mentioned in a list that has to do with the present life.]

2. Further, that which is always on the increase can never be perfect. But as long as we are in this life, charity can always be increased, as was said in Book I, Distinction 17.[d] Therefore it cannot be perfect.

3. Further, in any motion whatsoever, an infinity of intermediate points can be taken between the first and the last points.[e] But beginning charity is like the starting-point of a motion, and the perfection of

a. Parallels: *ST* II-II, q. 24, a. 9; *Super Isaiam* 44.

b. The subject of Lombard's third chapter in this Distinction, the grades or degrees are: *incipiens, proficiens, perfecta,* and *perfectissima* (Grottaferrata ed., 2:177), which have been rendered here: beginning, advancing, perfect, and most perfect.

c. *In III Sent.* d. 27, q. 3, a. 2 (see above).

d. *In I Sent.* (Paris version) d. 17, q. 2, a. 4, and *In I Sent. (Lectura romana)* d. 17, q. 2, a. 2 (see above for both).

e. *inter primum et ultimum*—that is, between the *terminus a quo* and the *terminus ad quem.*

charity is like the term. Therefore infinite degrees can be assigned between these. [Hence, it is unfitting to set down only four.]

4. Further, as soon as someone begins, he is already advancing forward. Therefore "advancing charity" ought not to be distinguished from "beginning charity."

On the contrary:

The spiritual life bears a likeness to natural life. But determinate degrees of age are assigned in the advance of natural life. Therefore determinate degrees ought to be assigned in charity, too, since the spiritual life of the soul is according to it.[a]

Response:

It should be said that, just as diverse ages[b] are distinguished in bodily growth according to some notable effects to which nature advances when before, in an earlier stage, it was unable to exercise these effects, so, too, in spiritual growth diverse degrees of charity are assigned according to some notable effects that charity produces in the one who has charity.[375]

The first effect of charity is that a man draws back from sin; and therefore the mind of the one who has charity is at first occupied most of all with this—that he should be cleansed from past sins and avoid future ones. And with respect to this effect, charity is called "beginning." The second effect is that the one who is now confident of having liberation from sins should extend himself to gaining good things.[c] And with respect to this effect, charity is called "advancing"—not because it does not advance in other states as well, but because in this state its special care is to gain good things; during it, a man is always panting for progress. The third effect is that a man, now thoroughly nourished with those good things, possesses them as (in a certain way) natural to him, and rests in them and is delighted by them. And this pertains to "perfect" charity.

The intermediate state, however, can be viewed under two aspects: one, according to which it is compared to the first state, since

a. *Vita spiritualis similatur uite naturali. Set in profectu naturalis uite assignantur determinati gradus etatum. Ergo et in caritate, secundum quam est spiritualis uita anime, debent determinati gradus assignari.*

b. *etates,* which could also be rendered "stages": the age/stage of infancy, the age/stage of childhood, the age/stage of youth, etc.

c. *in bonum adipiscendum se extendat:* he not only seeks escape from evils, but exerts himself to do good works, to form virtues, to practice the Beatitudes, to follow the promptings of the Holy Spirit, etc.

it is strengthened against the evils that beginning charity is careful to avoid; the other, that it is nourished, according to which it tends toward the third state, as always incorporating good things more and more into itself.[376]

In like manner, perfect charity has two degrees: one, according to which it rests securely in the good things that are commonly required of all, and in respect to this it is called "perfect";[a] the other, according to which it sets its hand to any difficult task whatsoever, and in respect to this it is called "most perfect"—or [according to another explanation] "perfect" as regards the wayfaring state, "most perfect" as regards the state of the fatherland.

Replies to objections:

1. To the first, therefore, it should be said that that commandment is fulfilled, in a certain way, in both the wayfaring state and the fatherland, but not in the same way. In the wayfaring state the commandment is fulfilled as regards the perfection here attainable; in the fatherland, it is fulfilled as regards the perfection there attained.[b]

2. To the second, it should be said that, although charity may always be increased as regards the intensity with which the same effects are willed, nevertheless it is not increased in such a way that there would be added to it some notable effects which were absent before.

3. To the third, it should be said that, although infinite intermediate points can be taken in any motion, nonetheless they do not all have a notable diversity.[377]

4. To the fourth, it should be said that, although a beginner does advance, still his mind is more occupied with removing evils than with advancing in the good. Consequently, he is not called "advancing" with respect to his *state,* since moral things receive their names from the end aimed at.

---

a. *unus est secundum quod in bonis communibus, quasi iam secura, conquiescit, et secundum hoc dicitur perfecta*

b. *preceptum illud quodammodo seruatur in uia quantum ad perfectionem uie, quodammodo in patria quantum ad perfectionem patrie*

SUBQUESTION 2   Whether all are bound
to perfect charity[a]

Objections:

Furthermore, it seems that all are bound to aim for the practice of perfect charity.[b]

1. For, as Bernard says, "to stand still in the way of God is to fall backwards."[c] But everyone who advances in the way of God is tending to the goal of perfection. Therefore all are bound to tend to the perfection of charity.

2. Further, each man is bound to love his neighbor more than his own body. But to lay down one's bodily life for one's brethren is something that belongs to perfect charity. Therefore each man is bound to perfect charity.

3. Further, those who denied God owing to fear of death are not excused from sin. Yet they would not have sinned unless they were *bound* to do the opposite. Therefore each one is bound to dying for Christ, which belongs to perfect charity.

4. Further, the Philosopher says in *Ethics* VIII that, in the honors we give to parents and to God, we cannot make a return of something equivalent to what has been given to us, so that justice in this instance is to make whatever return to them we can.[d] Now, all are bound to the work of justice. Therefore each man ought to do for God the whole of what he can. But a man can extend himself to works of perfection. Therefore he is bound to those works.

On the contrary:

Anyone sins by omitting that to which he is bound. If, therefore, all were bound to perfect charity, all the imperfect would be damned, which is false.

---

a. Parallel: *De caritate,* a. 11.

b. *omnes teneantur ad caritatem perfectam:* the query concerns whether everyone is bound to pursue and practice perfect charity, as opposed to settling for something less. Thus the first objection phrases it this way: *omnes tenentur ad perfectionem caritatis tendere.* Throughout these subquestions the language of "being bound to *x*" has to be taken in a strong sense, as the correlative to what God has commanded; to omit the practice of a commandment is to suffer the loss of salvation.

c. Bernard, *Letter to the Abbot Garinus,* Letter 254, nn. 4–6 (PL 182:460–61); see textual note a on p. 71 on the various formulations of this idea in Leo, Gregory, and Bernard.

d. Aristotle, *Ethics* VIII, ch. 16 (1163b16).

Response:

It should be said that the quantity of charity can be viewed in two ways (and this distinction applies to the quantity of any virtue,[a] whether moral or natural): in one way, according to the intensity of charity; in another way, according to its object. And in keeping with this distinction, a twofold perfection of charity can be considered: one according to intensity, viz., that it should love perfectly; the other according to its object or effect, viz., that it should do perfect things. Now, in regard to charity, each of these perfections can be viewed in two ways. For (1) it has perfection with respect to its being, insofar as it is perfect in its species; and this is the perfection of sufficiency, to which all of us are bound even as we are bound to [have the virtue of] charity itself, since in both ways charity has a determinate quantity beneath which it does not extend.[b] And in this [having of sufficient quantity] stands its *essential* perfection. (2) It has a further perfection with respect to *well-being*, and in regard to this perfection, too, a distinction is to be made, since one is bound to *tend* to (though one is not bound to *have*) the perfection that has to do with *intensity*, whereas someone is not bound, simply speaking, either to tend to or to have the perfection that has to do with charity's *objects*, but he is bound not to despise it or harden himself against it.[378] And the reason is that the essential reward to which we are bound to tend is measured not by the greatness of one's deeds but by the intensity of one's charity, since God thinks more of how much charity a deed was done from, than how much was done. Nevertheless, one is bound in particular cases to do some works similar to works of perfection, as will be said.

Replies to objections:

1. To the first, therefore, it should be said that Bernard's statement is rightly understood of advancement in regard to intensity, for which a man always ought to strive.

a. *uirtus*, where the term means either a "virtue" as we commonly speak of it, or some natural power or potency such as motility, sight, or free-will.

b. *citra quam non porrigitur*, i.e., a minimum threshold beneath which charity cannot exist. This is a roundabout way of saying that to "have charity" is the same as having at least the minimum being of the virtue, less than which no virtue exists at all; being bound to charity *means* being bound to what is here called the *perfectio sufficientie*. Thomas describes this *perfectio* along the lines of the basic perfection of a natural being, namely that it have its form or *species*. A human being is human by having the human form, the rational soul; this is his first and most fundamental perfection. Likewise, charity is "perfect" in one sense when it simply exists as a virtue in the will.

2. To the second, it should be said that, when we know that a brother can be freed from the death of his soul through the death of our body without danger to our own soul, then handing over our life for the brethren does not belong to perfection but is a matter of necessity; in other circumstances, however, such an act belongs to perfection.

3. And similarly, it should be said to the third that for a man to hand himself over freely to persecutors when danger to the faith presses is a matter of perfection; but for him not to deny the faith if he is caught is a matter of necessity.

4. To the fourth, it should be said that, in things not determined to one, a power in its totality cannot be bound to something one, since, were this the case, its character of contingency, according to which something can fail in the lesser part, would perish. Since, therefore, men in this wayfaring state do not have their free will determined to one, it is not required of them that the totality of free will be expended in the service of God—for this will be so only in the fatherland, when it will be impossible for anything less than perfect to occur—but it suffices that we expend nothing of our power *against* God, and that we do those things that are determined for us [e.g., obey the commandments]; for if it were the other way [i.e., if we were bound to do all we could], the essence of our state [as wayfarers] would perish. Hence, just as God does not demand from us as much as he gave to us, since it is impossible for us to make an equal return to him, so he does not demand from us as much as we are *able* to do, since this, too, would run contrary to the essence of our state as wayfarers.[a]

---

a. *Ad quartum dicendum, quod in illis que non sunt determinata ad unum non potest tota potentia obligari ad aliquid unum, quia periret ratio contingentie, secundum quam aliquid deficere potest in minori parte. Cum ergo homines in statu isto non habeant liberum arbitrium determinatum, non exigitur quod totum posse expendatur in seruitium Dei—hoc enim erit in patria quando iam defectus incidere non poterit—set sufficit quod nichil de posse nostro contra Deum expendamus et illa que nobis determinata sunt faciamus; alias periret ratio nostri status. Vnde sicut Deus non exigit a nobis quantum ipse dedit nobis, quia non possumus, ita non exigit a nobis quantum possumus, quia hoc esset contra rationem nostri status.*

SUBQUESTION 3[a]   Whether one who has attained perfect
charity is bound to everything that belongs to perfection

Objections:

Furthermore, it seems that one who has attained perfect charity is
bound to everything that belongs to perfection.[b]

1. For, as Gregory says, "when gifts increase, the reckonings of the
gifts also increase";[c] and in Luke 12:48 it is said: "To whom more is
committed, from him more is required." But more is committed to
him who has perfect charity. Therefore he is bound to more, in keeping with the demands arising from the gifts he has received. And so it
seems that he is bound to [all] those things that belong to perfection.

2. Further, as an imperfect man stands to what is commonly required of Christians,[d] so a perfect man stands to those things that belong to perfection. But the imperfect one is bound to what is commonly required; therefore the perfect one is bound to those things that
belong to perfection.

3. Further, the Apostle was *bound* to evangelizing, which is a work
of perfection; for he says: "If I should not preach the gospel, woe unto
me, for a necessity presses upon me" (1 Cor. 9:16). This "necessity"
pressed upon him for no other reason than that he had perfect charity.[e]
Therefore those who have perfect charity are bound to those things
that belong to perfection.

On the contrary:

4. When someone has more charity, he has more freedom, since
"where the Spirit of the Lord is, there is freedom" (2 Cor. 3:17). But
the one who has perfect charity has charity most of all. Therefore he

a. Parallels: *ST* II-II, q. 186, a. 2; *De caritate*, a. 11, ad 12; *Quodl.* I, q. 7, a. 2; *Contra impugn.*, ch. 2.

b. The phrasing is: *uidetur quod habentes caritatem perfectam teneantur ad omnia
que sunt perfectionis.* The idea is: if a person should reach the grade of perfect charity, is he then bound always to do or to suffer everything at that level, both in
what he does and in *how* he does it, or would he be permitted at times to do
something less than perfect, or less than perfectly?

c. Gregory, *Homilies on the Gospels*, Homily 9, n. 1 (CCSL 141:58).

d. *Sicut se habet imperfectus ad communia*; here *communia* indicates everything
that believers are bound to do in common (e.g., go to Mass on Sundays and feast-
days, fast when the Church declares a fast, obey legitimate pastors in the Church,
etc.) as opposed to *ea que perfectionis sunt*, to which only certain ones are bound
(e.g., those who have taken vows of poverty, celibacy, religious obedience).

e. After the citation of 1 Cor. 9:16, the phrasing is: *quod est perfectionis, non nisi
quia habebat perfectam caritatem.*

is under less of an obligation and, consequently, is not obliged to do as great things as others are.

5. Further, it belongs to perfection not to give offense by one's speech and to avoid venial sins. But no one succeeds in doing this [perfectly], not even the Apostles. Therefore those who are perfect are not obliged to those things that belong to perfection.[379]

Response:

It should be said that "one who has perfect charity" can be understood in two ways. (1) In one way, according to the perfection of charity considered with respect to its objects, as those people are called "perfect" to whom it pertains to do works of perfection either from vow, e.g., religious, or from office, e.g., prelates. And so, in terms of what is owed, such "perfect" people are not bound to anything to which others are not bound except for those specific things they vowed to do or things connected with their office. Hence neither prelates nor religious are bound to all of the counsels.[380] (2) In another way, according to the perfection of charity considered with respect to its intensity, as might be found in a layman in the world who is fervent in charity. And such a man is not obliged to undertake works of perfection except in the way that others are, but he *is* obliged to love God more intensely for the goods he has received; he is also inclined to do this from his habit of perfect charity.

Replies to objections:

1. To the first, therefore, it should be said that the one who has perfect charity is bound to love God more, that is, to act more intensely and more perfectly [in regard to what is required of all], but is not bound to perform other, additional works on the basis of what God has given him, although perhaps another man is more bound to perform such works on the basis of what God has forgiven him.[a] Now, although what is given is much more [valuable] than what is forgiven, since good is more good than evil is evil, nevertheless, the one who is a debtor from being forgiven is bound to some things, such as making satisfaction for sins, to which the other one is not bound.

2. To the second, it should be said that this reasoning supposes something false, unless it be understood about perfect ones who vowed some works of perfection, to which works they are bound above other men.

a. *tenetur ad plus diligendum Deum, id est intensius et perfectius agendum, set non ad opera alia facienda ex commisso, quamuis alius forte plus teneatur ex dimisso*

3. To the third, it should be said that this work of evangelizing pertained to Paul on account of the office of prelate [in which he was installed].

4, 5. Nevertheless it should be known that the argument made in support of the opposite position goes too far,[a] since the perfect are not less *bound*, but are merely less moved from *debt*, since love moves them more than debt, even in those things in which they are debtors; and it is in this respect that greater liberty is said to be in them.

Notes on the text of Lombard

"The charity of many is inordinate."

In this passage the term "charity" is being used broadly for love or friendship.

"Who, if they [Christian neighbors] are good, are to be given preference to bad children . . ."

But not in those affairs that have reference to what parent and child naturally share in common, like the distribution of an inheritance, education, and things of this sort; unless perhaps the superabundant malice of those children makes them unworthy of fatherly favor.

"It is perfect charity that someone be ready to die for the brethren."

But against that statement an objection could be raised: One who is imperfect is not ready to die even for God; therefore one who is perfect loves his neighbor more than one who is imperfect loves God. In response, it should be said that this difference between them arises from the fact that the one who is perfect loves his bodily life less than does the one who is imperfect. Moreover, the one who is perfect lays down his life for the brethren from a *superabundance* of divine charity, for it is impossible that any instantiation of charity should cause a love of neighbor as great as another instantiation of charity causes a love of God.[b] But these two loves are not of the same kind; one kind of love, [the love of God,] is love of the end and cause of all loving, while the other kind of love, [the love of neighbor,] is love of that which is for the end and receives the *ratio* of being lovable from another, viz., from

a. *nimis concludit*

b. *Non enim potest esse ut aliqua caritas tantum diligat proximum quantum aliqua Deum*

God; hence the two are not comparable in the way that the objection compares them.

"In order that he [the Apostle] might arrive at perfection, he says: 'I desire to be dissolved and to be with the Lord' (Phil. 1:23)."

We seem to have a contrary example in the case of blessed Peter, to whom the Lord said: "You will extend your hand, and another will lead you where you do not wish to be led" (Jn. 21:18), [as if indicating that Peter had no such desire to be dissolved and hence was not perfect]; and in blessed Martin, too, who did not refuse to keep on living.[a] In regard to Peter's case, it should be said that the Lord's words are understood as referring to natural will, whereas the words of the Apostle [Paul] are understood as referring to rational will.[b, 381] In regard to Martin's case, it should be said that perfect charity, insofar as it has something of the love of concupiscence, wishes above all else to enjoy God in the way Paul describes; but inasmuch as it consists more chiefly in benevolence, it makes one desire above all what is pleasing to God. And it was according to this aspect of charity that blessed Martin spoke his words.[382] The increase of charity, however, was discussed in Book I, Distinction 17.[c]

a. Thomas is alluding to the story of how St. Martin of Tours as an elderly bishop felt "torn" between staying with his flock and quitting this life to be with the Lord. As narrated in the *Legenda aurea* written around 1260 by the Dominican friar Jacobus de Voragine: "When he had spent some time in the above-named diocese [of Candes], his strength began to fail, and he told his disciples that his days were numbered. They wept and asked him: 'Why are you deserting us, father? To whom are you leaving us, orphans? Fierce wolves will ravage your flock!' Moved by their entreaties and tears, Martin wept with them and prayed: 'Lord, if I am still needed by your people, I do not refuse the labor! Thy will be done!' He really was not sure which he preferred, because he wanted neither to leave these people nor to remain separated from Christ any longer" (*The Golden Legend,* trans. William G. Ryan, 2 vols. [Princeton: Princeton University Press, 1993], 2:298). As Thomas explains, there is no reason to find Martin's words objectionable, for St. Paul had said exactly the same thing in the text to which Lombard points us, Phil. 1:21–26.

b. *de uoluntate naturali . . . de uoluntate rationis*

c. *In I Sent.* (Paris version) d. 17, q. 2; *In I Sent. (Lectura romana)* d. 17, q. 2 (see above for both).

DISTINCTION 30[a]
[LOVE OF ENEMIES; MERIT]

Division of the text

"Here, it is customary to inquire which is preferable [and more meritorious, to love one's friends or to love one's enemies"]. After the Master has determined the order of charity with respect to diverse objects of love as regards the quantity of love, he here determines this order as regards the efficacy of meriting.

This consideration is divided into two parts. In the first, he pursues his intention; in the second, he raises a doubt on the basis of what was said, at the words: "The statement that follows moves us more."

The former is divided into two parts. In the first, he poses the question; in the second, he answers it, at the words: "But this comparison [is implicit]."

And concerning the answer, he does three things. First, he answers the question. Second, he gives an objection to the contrary, at the words "Augustine, nevertheless, seems to feel that it is a greater thing to love an enemy than a friend." Third, he solves the objection, at the words: "If someone simply [does not wish to concede] this point, [saying one loves a friend more intensely than an enemy, and therefore the one is preferred to the other . . .]."

At the passage beginning "The statement that follows moves us more," he does three things. First, he raises a doubt. Second, he sets down a faulty solution, at the words: "Certain ones, wishing to hold simply what was said here, [say that love of enemies is given as a commandment only to those who are perfect, whereas to lesser souls it is given as a counsel]." Third, he sets down his own opinion, at the words: "But it is better to understand [that by that commandment all are commanded to love everyone, even enemies]."

Here in this Distinction, we will inquire into five things: (1) whether all are bound to love enemies; (2) whether all are bound to show them signs of love;[b] (3) what is of greater merit, to love an enemy or

---

a. Latin text: provisional critical ed. of the Leonine Commission; cf. Moos ed., 951–65.

b. *signa dilectionis*

to love a friend; (4) what is of greater merit, to love God or to love one's neighbor; (5) whether the whole power of meriting is based on charity.[a]

ARTICLE 1[b]   Whether all are bound to love enemies

Objections:

Proceeding to the first, it seems that not all are bound to love enemies.

1. For on the verse "Love your enemies" (Lk. 6:27), a gloss says: "This belongs to the perfect."[c] But not all are bound to those things that belong to perfection, as was said above.[d] Therefore not all are bound to love enemies.

2. Further, men are not bound to more things under the New Law than under the Old, as is evident from Mark 8, where the gloss (interpreting the lines "And taking the loaves," etc.) says: "He does not preach anything other than what was written, but he shows that the Law and the Prophets are heavy."[e] But under the Old Law men were

a. *utrum tota uirtus merendi penes caritatem consistat.* The last phrase could also be rendered "is established according to charity," namely, the virtue of charity which is the principle of all good works.

b. Parallels: *ST* II-II, q. 11, a. 4, q. 25, a. 8, and q. 83, a. 8; *De perfectione,* chs. 14–15 (ed. Leon. 41:B84–87); *De caritate,* a. 8; *Super Rom.* 12, lec. 3; *De duobus praeceptis* (*Opuscula theologica,* Marietti ed., 2:252–53, nn. 1183–92). The status of love of enemies in the fatherland is treated at *In III Sent.* d. 31, q. 2, a. 3, qa. 1 (see below).

c. Leonine: *Luc. <VI>, "Diligite inimicos uestros," dicit Glosa, "Hoc perfectorum est."* Moos: *Mat. V, 44: "Diligite inimicos vestros," dicit Glossa Hieronymi,* etc. The two scriptural verses are identically worded. Moos refers to PL 26:41 (it should be 26:42) for the gloss on Mt. 5:44, but nothing exactly corresponding to the phrase is found there. A similar idea is however expressed: *Sciendum est ergo Christum non impossibilia praecipere, sed perfecta: quae fecit David in Saul et in Absalon* (the examples of St. Stephen and St. Paul are then mentioned).

d. In the preceding Distinction, a. 8, qa. 2 (see above).

e. The provisional Leonine ed. has *ut patet Marc. <VIII> super illud "Et accipiens panes"* etc., which would send us to Mk. 8:1–10 where the episode of the feeding of the four thousand with seven loaves is recounted (cf. the parallel at Mt. 15:29–39). The Moos ed. has *ut patent Mat. XIV,* which would send us to Mt. 14:13–22, where the feeding of five thousand with five loaves is recounted (cf. the parallel at Mk. 6:33–45). The Parma ed. in fact quotes Mt. 14:19 (or the identical Mk. 6:41), *accepte quinque panibus,* instead of the *Et accipiens [septem] panes* of Mk. 8:6 (or the identical Mt. 15:36). To add to the confusion, Moos sends us to PL 114:136 for Strabo's gloss on Mt. 14, but no such thing is to be found there; in reality, Thomas is (mis?)quoting the gloss on Mk. 6:41 (PL 114:203), which reads in full: *Non nova cibaria creat quia incarnatus, non alia quam quae scripta erant*

not bound to loving enemies, for in Matthew 5:43 we read: "It was said of old, Love your friend and hate your enemy." Therefore neither are we bound to love enemies.

3. Further, nature does not incline to something contrary to charity. But every nature is inclined to detest its contrary. Since therefore an enemy, precisely as enemy, is contrary to us, it seems that we are not bound, from charity, to love enemies.

4. Further, we do not love those for whom we desire evils and about whom we rejoice in evils [that befall them]. But it is permissible to desire evils for enemies and to rejoice over their evils. Hence in Sacred Scripture, imprecations against enemies are frequently included, and the destruction of hostile forces is retold[a] for the consolation of the faithful. Therefore we are not bound to love enemies.

5. Further, charity conforms man's will to the divine will. But there are some whom God hates, as is said in Malachi 1:3: "I have hated Esau."[b] Therefore it is permissible to hate enemies.

6. Further, this [hatred] seems to be clearly expressed in the Psalm that says: "I have hated them with a perfect hatred" (139:22). But every perfection comes from charity. Therefore not only does charity *not* make one love enemies, it makes one rather hate them.

On the contrary:

1. "You shall not seek revenge, nor shall you be mindful of the injury [sustained at the hands] of your fellow citizens" (Lev. 19:18).

2. Further, "If your enemy should fall, you shall not rejoice" (Prov. 24:17).

3. Further, charity looks to the image of God in man, according to which image it is possible for any man to share with us in the life of grace, as was said above. But this image is found in enemies. Therefore we are bound from charity to love enemies.

---

praedicat: sed legem et prophetas mysteriis gravida esse demonstrat. Compare Thomas's citation: *Non alia quam que scripta erant predicat, set legem et prophetas grauia esse demonstrat.*

a. *inducitur,* literally "brought in." The most vivid examples would be the stages in the conquest of Canaan recounted in the Book of Joshua, involving the destruction of Jericho (Josh. 6), of Ai (Josh. 8), and of numerous smaller towns (Josh. 10–12), with all their inhabitants, including women and children, and, in some cases, livestock.

b. The full verse: "'Is not Esau Jacob's brother?' says the Lord. 'Yet I have loved Jacob but I have hated Esau; I have laid waste his hill country and left his heritage to jackals of the desert" (Mal. 1:2–3).

Response:

It should be said that we are bound to love someone according as he shares something in common with us. Now our enemy has in common with us a sharing in human nature, on the basis of which it is possible for him to have in common with us a sharing in the divine life. Accordingly, we ought to love him in regard to things that pertain to his nature and to the possession of grace, whereas we ought not to love the enmity he has against us, since according to it he has something in common neither with us nor even with himself, but rather something that is contrary [both to us and to himself], as was said also concerning other sins.[a, 383]

Replies to objections:

1. To the first, therefore, it should be said that loving enemies to the extent of showing signs of benevolence to them belongs to perfection, and not all are bound to do this. But to desire for one's enemy that he receive God's grace and inherit eternal life, which is charity's special concern, is something everyone must do.[b]

2. To the second, it should be said that even under the Old Law men were bound to love their enemies, as is evident from the authority of Leviticus brought forward. Hence the saying "You shall hate your enemy" is not taken from the Law, since this is nowhere found in the text of Scripture, but was added on from the perverse interpretation of Jews who, on the basis of the fact that love of neighbor was commanded, concluded [falsely] that enemies were to be hated. What the New Law did add, however, is the counsel to show signs of benevolence to an enemy.[384]

3. To the third, it should be said that nature inclines to hating an enemy not insofar as he is similar to us by agreement in nature or receptivity to grace, but insofar as he is dissimilar. Now this dissimilarity comes about insofar as he is exercising enmity toward us, which ought to displease us exceedingly.

4. To the fourth, it should be said that charity looks to certain goods *per se,* viz., to the goods of grace, but looks to certain other goods *per accidens,* insofar as they are ordered to those *per se* goods.

Now temporal goods, which charity looks to *per accidens* and secondarily, can impede each other in various ways, since one man's prosper-

a. See *In III Sent.* d. 28, a. 4 (above).
b. *Set quod homo inimico suo optet gratiam Dei et uitam eternam, quod specialiter caritas respicit, hoc necessitatis est*

ity may lead to another's adversity. Hence, since charity has an order, and since anyone ought to love himself more than another, and neighbors more than strangers, and friends more than enemies, and the common good of many more than the private good of one, someone can, while preserving charity, desire temporal evil for someone and rejoice if it happens—but not precisely _as_ that person's evil, but rather, as an evil that prevents other evils from occurring to another, whether of the community or of the Church, whom he is bound to love more. Something similar can be said about [desiring or rejoicing in] the evil of someone who falls into temporal evil, insofar as the evil of punishment frequently impedes the evil of [further] guilt on his part.

The goods of grace, on the other hand, do not mutually impede each other, since spiritual goods can be integrally possessed by many. Consequently, with respect to these goods it is impossible for anyone, while preserving charity, to desire [corresponding spiritual] evils for another or to rejoice about such evils, except insofar as the goodness of divine justice, which one is bound to love more than any man, shines forth in the evil of guilt [that God has permitted] or of someone's punishment of damnation. But this is not to rejoice about evil _per se_, but rather about a good to which an evil is conjoined.

5. To the fifth, it should be said that God, too, does not will someone's evil, speaking of the evil of guilt, but only permits it; and this permission is good. Now, when it comes to the evil of punishment, of which he _is_ the author, again God wills it not insofar as it is evil—since he does not rejoice in punishments—but insofar as it is just.

6. To the sixth, it should be said that the Psalmist did not hate them with a perfect hatred except insofar as they were enemies of God; but that they are such is the result only of their sinning. Hence, in them whom he hated with a perfect hatred, the Psalmist hated nothing except their sin.[385]

ARTICLE 2[a]   Whether all are bound to show signs of friendship to enemies

Objections:

Proceeding to the second, it seems that all are bound to show signs of friendship to enemies.

---

a. Parallel: _ST_ II-II, q. 25, a. 9; otherwise the same as the parallels listed for the preceding article. See, in addition, _De perfectione_, chs. 16–17 (ed. Leon. 41:B87–89).

1. For acts of kindness and help[a] to friends are the signs of friendship *par excellence*; but a man is bound to do such things for his enemies, as it says in Proverbs 25:21: "If your enemy shall hunger, feed him." Therefore one is bound to show signs of friendship to enemies.

2. Further, the Church prays for enemies, as is evident from a gloss on Matthew 5 and from the Collect *Pietate tua*, where we find the phrase "to give abundantly true charity to our friends and enemies."[b] But prayer is the foremost act of kindness and help that someone can bestow. Hence, since an act of the Church belongs to any member of the Church, it seems that anyone who is a member of the Church is bound to be a benefactor to enemies.

3. Further, no one ought to have a pretended love. But a love that does not show itself in works is not true love, since "love is proved by outward deeds," as Gregory says,[c] and since in 1 John 3:18 it is said: "Let us not love by tongue and by words, but in works and in truth." Therefore since each man ought to love his enemy, it follows that each man is bound to extend works of love to him.

4. Further, in Matthew 5 it is commanded simultaneously that we love enemies and do what benefits them. For the same reason, therefore, men are obliged to do both [if they are obliged to do either]. But all are bound to the first; therefore also to the second.

5. Further, to refuse a man signs of familiarity and acts of kindness and help is to take a sort of vengeance upon him. But man is bound not to avenge himself, as is clear from Romans 12:19: "Beloved, never avenge yourselves." Therefore one is bound not to withdraw his acts of kindness and help from enemies.

a. This phrase renders the term *beneficia*. In this article *beneficere* has also been rendered "doing acts of kindness." The question is, are we supposed to help out our enemy, do him a good turn (and in this sense, "benefit" him)?

b. In the Dominican missal, among the *orationes votivas ad diversa*, specifically those *pro vivis et defunctis*. Strabo's gloss on Mt. 5:44 is typical and could have been the one Thomas has in mind: "The Church is fought against in three ways: by hatred, by [evil] words, by bodily torture. The Church, on the contrary, loves, blesses, prays. This is the new commandment, this is what makes children of wrath into children of God; hence it follows, 'That you may be sons.' For the adoption of sons is acquired only through charity. . . . [By] 'brethren' are to be understood not only those who now believe, but also those who are going to believe, for whom we should pray that they be joined to us in fraternal accord" (PL 114:97–98).

c. Gregory, *Homilies on the Gospels*, Homily 30, n. 1 (CCSL 141:256).

On the contrary:

6. A gloss on Matthew 5 says that to do acts of kindness to one's enemies and to pray for them is the peak of perfection. But not all are bound to those things that belong to perfection. Therefore neither are all bound to offer acts of kindness to enemies.

7. Further, in the Old Law the sons of Israel were frequently commanded to pursue their enemies to the death,[a] and not to enter into a covenant with them. Therefore they were not bound to do acts of kindness to enemies. Therefore neither are we bound to do so now.

8. Further, we see that even now the Church suggests that war should be waged against tyrants and infidels; hence it is permissible to do evil to enemies. Therefore much less is it necessary to do them acts of kindness.

Response:

It should be said that charity's effect ought to correspond to charity's affection. Hence, insofar as someone is bound to have the affection of charity toward an enemy, so also is he bound to extend to him its effect. Now charity, as was said,[b] considers the goods of grace, which all the living share in common, actually or potentially. Consequently, the friendship of charity is more common and more extensive than any other kind of friendship, since other kinds extend to fewer, inasmuch as they are founded upon some sharing in common which does not include everyone.[c] Now in all things, that which is common is more vehement, but that which is proper embraces more in act; and the perfection of the common consists in its extension to those things that the proper embraces, as the genus is perfected through the addition of the difference. For example, being inheres in a thing more vehemently than being-alive; and yet being-alive embraces something in act that being has only in potency, so that being has its perfection insofar as it is extended to life.[d] [386]

In keeping with this principle,[e] therefore, charity more vehemently desires[f] for someone the goods of grace, with which goods it is chiefly concerned, than any other friendship desires for someone the goods

a. *persequerentur hostes suos*

b. In the preceding article, ad 4; cf. *In III Sent.* d. 28, a. 4 (above).

c. *Et ideo est communior et latior quam aliqua alia amicitia que ad pauciores se extendit, in quantum fundatur super communicatione aliqua que non ad omnes est*

d. "being . . . being-alive": *esse . . . uiuere*

e. *Sic ergo*

f. Throughout this paragraph, "desire" translates the verb *optare*.

corresponding to that friendship. All the same, that charity should extend itself to those goods [to which the other friendships extend, e.g., doing acts of kindness and assistance] does not pertain to its necessity, but rather to its perfection. And therefore anyone is bound of necessity to desire *eternal* goods for one who hates him, but he is not bound to desire *temporal* goods for him; yet it belongs to charity's perfection that it should extend even to such things as these, too. But since in the order of generation the removal of evil precedes the attainment of good, it follows that no one's affection desires a good for someone for whom he desires an evil, insofar as it is evil. Hence, although it belongs to charity's perfection that we desire temporal goods for enemies, nevertheless it is a matter of necessity that we not desire evils for them precisely as evils, but rather *per accidens,* as was said before.[a]

And something similar holds concerning the effect, since a man is bound—in accordance with place, time, and his condition—to cooperate in doing, even for an enemy, things having to do with eternal life, at least by praying for all men in common, not excluding an enemy from his prayers (although perhaps he does not make special mention of him, even as he need not offer a special prayer for everyone toward whom he has charity, but prayer with a common intention suffices). In regard to other [viz., temporal] goods, a man is not bound to cooperate with an enemy, unless the enemy be under a pressing necessity; to extend even to such goods belongs rather to charity's perfection. Yet a man is bound not to do any evil to an enemy, except insofar as it would impede a greater evil or promote a greater good, as the good of justice or something of this sort.[387]

Replies to objections:

1. To the first, therefore, it should be said that friendly acts of kindness and help proceed from generosity, not from obligation.[b] Necessity, however, makes all things common; and therefore, in cases of necessity, even enemies are to be aided. But this is rather an effect of justice than of friendship.

2. To the second, it should be said that prayer is about goods that pertain to the sharing in common of spiritual life—the sharing that charity chiefly considers. Accordingly, one cannot make the same argument for this and for the other goods.[c]

3. To the third, it should be said that there is no dissimulation in

a. In the preceding article.
b. *ex debito*
c. *Et ideo non est simile de hoc et de aliis,* viz., spiritual goods and temporal goods.

love when as much is shown forth in deeds as is had in affection.[388]

4. To the fourth, it should be said that those two [loving and doing acts of kindness] run with an equal step, as was said.[389]

5. To the fifth, it should be said that it would be revenge to deny signs of familiarity to a man when necessity beckons,[a, 390] or if he should beg one's pardon, or when a man who was considered an enemy should bear himself familiarly toward one (if it may be presumed that he is not dissimulating or doing it in mockery), since under such circumstances he loves, and is to be counted among one's friends. But it belongs to perfection that someone should carry himself beyond this to the point of familiarity with an [actual] enemy.

6. To the sixth, it should be said that the gloss speaks about the sort of benefitting that follows upon perfect charity, according to which it moves ahead into the sorts of behavior that belong to other particular friendships.[b, 391]

7. To the seventh, it should be said that it was commanded of old that they should pursue enemies and should not form a covenant with them insofar as they were drawn into idolatry through their friendship, and insofar as they were executors of divine justice, acting from the command of him who had authority [over life and death], but not in such a way that they should do it from revenge.

8. And to the eighth, likewise, it should be said that it is in this way that the Church promotes war against enemies—either that such war might bring about justice or that it might thwart a greater evil or lead to a greater good.[392]

ARTICLE 3[c, 393]   Whether it is of greater merit to love a friend or an enemy

Objections in favor of the enemy:

Proceeding to the third, it seems to be of greater merit to love an enemy than a friend.

1. For in Matthew 5:46, the Lord says: "If you should love those who love you, what reward will you have?" But merit is spoken of in connection with reward. Therefore it is of greater merit to love an enemy than a friend.

---

a. *quando necessitas expeteret,* i.e., when he is lacking in bare necessities and so is (objectively) calling out for help from a fellow human being.

b. *procedit in illa que sunt aliarum specialium amicitiarum*

c. Parallels: the following article (a. 4), ad 3; *ST* II-II, q. 27, a. 7; *De caritate,* a. 8.

2. Further, that which belongs to perfection is of greater merit, since perfect charity merits more than imperfect charity. But to love an enemy belongs to perfect charity, whereas to love a friend does not. Therefore to love an enemy is of greater merit.

3. Further, where there is greater difficulty there is greater merit, since it pertains more to virtue, which is about difficult matters. But to love an enemy is more difficult than to love a friend; therefore it is of greater merit.

4. Further, according to Gregory, services are more pleasing to the extent that they are less owed.[a] But one owes love to an enemy less than one owes it to a friend.[b] Therefore it is more pleasing to God and more meritorious.

5. Further, the power of meriting is from grace. But grace alone moves us to love our enemies, whereas nature together with grace moves us to love our friends. Therefore it is more meritorious to love an enemy than to love a friend.

Objections in favor of the friend:

6. But against this: the better an act is, the more meritorious, too. But it is better to love a friend than an enemy, since it is an act falling more under love's proper matter.[c][394] Therefore it is better to love a friend than an enemy.

7. Further, when necessity presses, a lesser good is to be dismissed for the sake of a greater good. But love of enemies would be dismissed more readily than love of friends, which is evident from the effect that is proportioned to the affection, since whenever we cannot aid friends *and* enemies when both are under extreme necessity, we are bound more to aid friends than enemies. Therefore to love a friend is better than to love an enemy.

8. Further, that which is common and first according to nature is better than that which is superadded, just as "being" is better than "liv-

---

a. *seruitia tanto sunt magis accepta quanto minus debita. Accepta* could also be rendered "welcomed, credited." Elsewhere Thomas attributes to Gregory a similar idea: *servitia tanto magis sunt grata, quanto magis sunt libera* (*In IV Sent.* d. 49, q. 5, a. 3, qa. 2, obj. 2). Still other formulations are found at *ST* II-II, q. 104, a. 1, obj. 3 (*servitia, quanto sunt magis gratuita, tanto sunt magis accepta*) and II-II, q. 186, a. 5, obj. 5 (*illa servitia sunt Deo maxime accepta quae liberaliter et non ex necessitate fiunt*). In these *ST* texts, Thomas no longer mentions Gregory; in the last text he derives the idea from 2 Cor. 9:7.

b. *minus est debitum diligere inimicum quam diligere amicum.* We owe it to a friend, as friend, to love him and perform services for him, whereas we do not owe the same to an enemy.

c. Leonine: *propriam materiam;* Moos: *debitam materiam*

ing" (if the latter be considered apart from being),ᵃ as Dionysius says in chapter 5 of *On the Divine Names.*ᵇ But to love a friend is the common and first foundation of charity, to which the love of enemies is super-added. Therefore to love a friend is better than to love an enemy.ᶜ

Response:

It should be said that the aforesaid comparison of loves can be understood in two ways, viz., with respect to action and with respect to habit.

If it be understood with respect to action, it should be known that when we are seeking which is the better and more meritorious of two acts, the question has to be understood of those things when speaking of them *per se,* according to their genus. For it can happen that what is less good or less meritorious according to its genus is rendered more good or more meritorious by some additional factor attaching to it, as a small work done from great charity is more meritorious than a great work done from small charity.

Now the goodness of an act is measured by two things from which it receives goodness—namely, from the term or object, and from the principle, which is the will. An act has the species of goodness from the term, while it has the *ratio* of meriting from the will, since it is in the power of the one doing it precisely on account of its proceeding from the will. If therefore we compare the love of friend and of enemy with respect to the terms or objects, it is better to love a friend than an enemy, since a friend is an object more suited to the nature of loveᵈ than an enemy. On the other hand, if we compare the two aforesaid loves to the principle [of the act of love], which is the will, there must be greater merit where there is greater effort of will, since the greater the will's effort, the more fervent is the will concerning the end on account of which it attends to something that, taken in itself, is more repugnant to the will—although the will is more remiss, at times, about that to which it is more impelled [by nature].ᵉ ³⁹⁵ Merit, however, consists

---

a. *si sine esse consideretur*
b. Pseudo-Dionysius, *On the Divine Names,* ch. 5, n. 3 (PG 3:818).
c. The Parma ed. adds here: "and more meritorious"—a point implicit, at any rate, in the very conclusion that one love is better than another.
d. *magis competens dilectioni*
e. *Si uero comparemus duas predictas dilectiones ad principium quod est uoluntas, sic ubi est maior conatus uoluntatis, ibi oportet esse maius meritum, quia quanto est maior conatus uoluntatis, tanto est feruentior uoluntas de fine, propter quem attemptat illud quod secundum se sibi est magis repugnans, quamuis sit magis remissa quandoque circa id ad quod magis conatur*

in the fact that the will is affected [in a certain way] toward the *end*.

And if, therefore, we compare the *acts* of such loves, the love of enemies is more meritorious insofar as it is just this sort of thing (i.e., a love of *enemies*), since, insofar as it is, it requires a greater effort and a greater fervor about the [ultimate] end, even though the love of a friend is more intense about its object. But the love of a friend is better with respect to the essential goodness that accompanies the species of an act, since an act has its species from its object. If, however, the aforesaid loves are compared with respect to the *habit*, in this way the question posed must be understood either in regard to the love of enemies that is a matter of necessity (and from this vantage there is no question of comparison, since the same habit is equal with respect to both enemies and friends), or in regard to the love of enemies that pertains to perfection, in which case "love of enemies" includes love of friends, but not conversely; and from this vantage, the love of enemies is better.[396]

Replies to objections:

1. To the first, therefore, it should be said that while the love by which *only* friends are loved does not proceed from grace, and therefore cannot be meritorious or have a reward, nevertheless, if the act of love by which we love friends *is* informed by grace, it is meritorious and does have a reward.[397]

2. To the second, it should be said that not *every* way of loving one's enemies belongs to perfection;[398] but insofar as loving one's enemies does belong to perfection, it is made more meritorious according as it requires a greater effort.

3. To the third, it should be said that difficulty does not make for merit except to the extent that it causes the need for a greater inclination and effort of will toward something.[399]

4. To the fourth, it should be said that a debt diminishes the *ratio* of merit only to the extent that it diminishes the *ratio* of the voluntary, inasmuch as a debt implies a certain necessity.[400] But if a debt is paid back voluntarily, there will be as much merit in that act of repayment as there is the *ratio* of the voluntary.[401]

5. To the fifth, it should be said that nature is not contrary to grace. Hence, an admixture of nature with grace does not cause any lessening in the effects of grace, for such a lessening can be caused only by the admixture of grace's contrary.[402]

6. To the sixth, it should be said that an act has goodness both from the object and from the end; and the goodness that is from the object is

material with respect to the goodness that is from the end,[403] to which the will looks; and merit consists rather according to that [aspect, the end, than the former aspect, the object].

7. To the seventh, it should be said that in things that are related by the addition of one to the other, there is a consequence in the contrary, not a consequence in it, as is evident in "man" and "animal." For just as "man" is related to "animal," so "not-animal" is related to "not-man."[404] Hence, since the effort that is found in the love of enemies is related to the effort found in the love of friends as something added to it, it follows that, just as loving an enemy is of greater merit insofar as it takes a greater effort, so to dismiss the love of friends is more evil.

8. To the eighth, it should be said that that argument runs along the lines of the goodness an act has from the proper *ratio* of its species, which is from the object.

ARTICLE 4[a]   Whether to love one's neighbor is more meritorious than to love God

Objections:

Proceeding to the fourth, it seems that to love one's neighbor is more meritorious than to love God.

1. For we do not merit by doing natural things; but to love God is natural, since love of the highest good is naturally in all, as Dionysius says in chapter 4 of *On the Divine Names.*[b] Therefore to love God is less meritorious than to love one's neighbor, which is not so natural.

2. Further, what is more fruitful and laborious seems to be more meritorious. But those things that pertain to the active life are more laborious and fruitful than those which pertain to the contemplative life; therefore they are more meritorious. But love of one's neighbor pertains to the active life, whereas love of God pertains to the contemplative. Therefore it is more meritorious to love a neighbor than to love God.

3. Further, just as loving one's enemy is placed in the ultimate degree of charity, so loving God is placed in the first degree. But loving one's enemy is more meritorious than loving a friend. Therefore, by the same reasoning, it is more meritorious to love one's neighbor than to love God.

4. Further, that which presupposes another, and not conversely,

a. Parallel: *ST* II-II, q. 27, a. 8.
b. Pseudo-Dionysius, *On the Divine Names,* ch. 4, n. 10 (PG 3:707).

seems to be more perfect. But love of one's neighbor presupposes love of God, since God is the reason for loving one's neighbor. Therefore love of one's neighbor is more meritorious than love of God.

5. Further, an act for which a greater effort is required must be more meritorious. But a greater effort is required to love an enemy than to love God. Therefore love of one's neighbor, at least with respect to love of enemies, is more meritorious than love of God.

On the contrary:

1. "That on account of which anything is such, is itself more such."[a] But love of one's neighbor is not meritorious except insofar as it is ordered, either actually or habitually, to God. Therefore love of God is more meritorious.

2. Further, when charity is more intense, it seems to be more meritorious. But charity loves God more intensely than it loves the neighbor. Therefore in this [difference of intensity], it merits more.

3. Further, a virtue works more efficaciously concerning its own object, the more that object is proper to it and *per se*. But the *per se* object of charity is God, whereas the neighbor is not its object except secondarily,[b] just as magnitude is only a secondary object of sight, whose *per se* object is color. Therefore, since meriting is an effect of charity, it seems that, even as sight knows color better than magnitude, since it is not deceived about color as it can be about magnitude, so too charity merits more by the love of God than by the love of one's neighbor.

4. Further, what is more difficult seems to be more meritorious. But loving God seems to be more difficult than loving one's neighbor, for it is said in 1 John 4:20: "He who does not love the neighbor whom he sees, how can he love the God whom he does not see?" Therefore love of God is more meritorious than love of one's neighbor.

Response:

It should be said that love of God is the cause and reason for love of neighbor. Hence love of God is included in love of neighbor as a cause is in its effect by causal power,[c] and the love of neighbor is included in the love of God as an effect is in the power of its cause. Nevertheless,

a. Aristotle, *Posterior Analytics* I, ch. 2 (72b29).
b. *consequenter,* as something following after
c. The Moos ed. (p. 962, n. 61) has *includitur virtute in dilectione proximi,* while the Leonine has *includitur in dilectione proximi sicut causa in effectu est uirtute,* which parallels the conclusion of the sentence, *in causa potestate* (the same in both editions).

the motion of love that has its term in the neighbor is other than that which rests[a] in God, even as the acts by which principles and conclusions are considered are different acts, although in the aforesaid way they mutually include one another.

When therefore we compare these two motions from the two sides, as was said above, we find the love of God more powerful than the love of neighbor, viz., both with respect to the object, which more suits the nature of love,[b] and with respect to the will, which has a prompter and more intense affection for God than for the neighbor. As a result, the motion of love toward God is better and more meritorious than the motion of love toward the neighbor, unless the love of a neighbor should [in a given act] proceed from a greater love of God than a love borne immediately toward God in another act—which happens at times, but not always, since the least love of charity toward God is enough to extend one's affection toward the neighbor as well.[405]

Replies to objections:

1. To the first, therefore, it should be said that whatever things are purely natural are not meritorious, but whatever things proceed from nature perfected by charity and grace *are* meritorious; nor does nature diminish the *ratio* of merit, as was said above.[c]

2. To the second, it should be said that, even supposing that the activity of the active life is more meritorious than the activity of the contemplative life—which perhaps is not true, as will be said below[d]—still the love of neighbor need not be more meritorious than the love of God, since the love of God is the source of whatever pertains to *each* life, as was said. Or otherwise it could be said that, as regards the *interior* act, love of God and love of neighbor pertain to the contemplative life (for which reason Gregory, commenting upon Ezechiel, says that the contemplative life perseveres in the love of God and neighbor),[e] but that, as regards *exterior* acts, each pertains to the active life, although an act of this sort is expended[f] only toward neighbors because God does not need our works.

3. To the third, it should be said that love of enemies was not earlier

a. *sistit*   b. *competentius dilectioni*
c. In article 3.
d. *In III Sent.* d. 35, q. 1, a. 4, qa. 2, solutio.
e. Gregory, *Homilies on Ezekiel,* Book II, Homily 2, n. 8 (CCSL 142:230). For "perseveres in" Thomas has *insistit,* which could also be rendered "continues in," "pursues," "holds fast to," "applies itself to," or "holds fast to." In Gregory's text, however, the verb employed is *retinere.*
f. Leonine: *expendatur;* Moos: *extendantur*

argued to be more meritorious than love of friends except insofar as it was posited to have proceeded from a stronger force, which strength was viewed according to how much more intensely the will adhered to God.[a] Hence it does not follow that love of neighbor is more meritorious than love of God, unless the one who loves his neighbor should at the same time love God more.

4. To the fourth, it should be said that love of neighbor presupposes love of God, not as the more perfect presupposes the less perfect, as was the case in the other degrees, but rather as an effect presupposes the cause; and therefore the argument does not follow.

5. To the fifth, it should be said that the effort of will in question is not to be taken as referring to anything else but this: that the will have more vehement affection for God, as was said before, since whoever strives toward anything does so only to the extent that he desires the end.[b]

However, what is given as an argument to the contrary—viz., that it is more difficult to love God than neighbor—is to be understood not of natural love, by which all love him, but of freely given love [i.e., charity]; and even this is called more difficult not as if it were more laborious (for it is sweeter), but because it more greatly exceeds the powers of nature, since it is directed toward a loftier object.

ARTICLE 5[c, 406]   Whether merit consists chiefly in charity

Objections:

Proceeding to the fifth, it seems that merit does not consist chiefly in charity.

1. For grace is said to be the principle of meriting. But charity is not the same as grace. Therefore merit does not consist chiefly in the force of charity.

2. Further, no one merits unless he is justified. But to justify is the

---

a. The tenses of the verbs in this sentence plainly indicate that Thomas is referring back to his earlier arguments, although he does not expressly say so: *dilectio inimici non erat magis meritoria nisi in quantum procedebat ex fortiori uirtute, que fortitudo attendebatur secundum quod uoluntas intensius Deo adherebat.*

b. *nullus conatur ad aliquid nisi secundum desiderium finis*

c. Parallels: *In II Sent.* d. 29, a. 4 and d. 40, q. 1, a. 5, esp. resp. & ad 3; *In IV Sent.* d. 49, q. 1, a. 4, qa. 4 (see below) and q. 5, a. 1; *ST* I-II, q. 114, a. 4; *De ueritate* q. 14, a. 5, ad 5; *De potentia* q. 6, a. 9; *Super Rom.* c. 8, lec. 5; *Super I Tim.* c. 4, lec. 2; *Super Heb.* c. 6, lec. 3.

function of faith, as is evident from Romans 5. Therefore the power of meriting is especially to be found in the presence of faith.[a]

3. Further, an act is meritorious as well as praiseworthy through order to its rightful end. But it belongs to any virtue to make an act praiseworthy—and therefore to make it meritorious, too. And thus it seems that merit does not consist [uniquely] in the force of charity.

4. Further, that which makes for a lessening of merit does not seem to be the root of meriting. But charity makes for a lessening of merit, since it makes all things easy, not only on account of its being a habit, but also just because it is love, as is evident from the aforesaid. Since therefore difficulty makes for merit, it seems that charity is not the root of meriting.

5. Further, if charity were the root of meriting, there would be equal merit wherever there was equal charity. But sometimes a person with little charity does some act in which he merits more than does another, who has great charity, in a small act that *he* does. Therefore charity is not the root of meriting.

On the contrary:

1. That without which no merit avails seems to be the root of meriting. But charity fits this description, as is evident from 1 Corinthians 13. Therefore charity is the root of meriting.

2. Further, that which is opposed to every demerit seems to be the root of meriting. But charity fits this description. Therefore it is the root of meriting.

3. Further, we merit from the fact that we are conjoined to God. But this conjunction is brought about by charity. Therefore charity is the root of meriting.

Response:

It should be said, as was said above,[b] that merit properly signifies what someone exhibits so that he might make something, viz., the reward of merit, his own.[c] Hence, for merit two things are chiefly required: one is that what is exhibited be [merely] exhibited and not extorted; and since nothing can be exhibited except what is in the power of the one exhibiting, therefore what is exhibited must be voluntary,

---

a. *apud ipsam precipue est uirtus merendi.* The order of the second and third objections is given as found in the provisional Leonine edition; in the Moos ed. the order is the reverse.

b. *In III Sent.* d. 18, a. 2.

c. *meritum proprie dicitur quod exhibet ad hoc quod faciat aliquid suum quod est premium meriti*

since it is the will that makes us lords of our acts. The other thing required is that what is exhibited be sufficient for making one's own that for which it is exhibited.[a]

And from each side, the preeminent principle of meriting is from charity.[b] For charity is in the will as in a subject, perfecting it with respect to its first and chief act;[c] and again, since it is the love of God, it makes the very beloved, who is the reward, to be its own, insofar as it brings about union with the beloved.[407] And therefore the preeminent principle of merit is found in charity, while in other things [a principle of merit is found] insofar as they are informed by charity.

Replies to objections:

1. To the first, therefore, it should be said that grace causes merit as the remote principle that constitutes us in spiritual being, without which we cannot merit anything spiritual; but charity is as the proximate principle.[408]

2. To the second, it should be said that faith does not justify unless it is informed by charity. But justification is especially *attributed* to faith, since the first thing in which a just man is distinguished from an unjust man is the act of faith, even as the first thing in which a living creature is distinguished from a non-living creature is the act of the nutritive power; and therefore "living" is said according to the presence of that power, and "sensing" is said according to the presence of the sense of touch, which is the first sense, as is said in *On the Soul* II.[d]

3. To the third, it should be said that acts of other virtues are not meritorious except insofar as they are informed by charity, just as neither are acts of virtues praiseworthy except insofar as they are voluntary.[409]

4. To the fourth, it should be said that difficulty does not make for merit, except perhaps in the sense that enduring it can lessen one's punishment for sins in the manner of a certain exchange.[e, 410] But difficulty does not contribute to the merit that is ordered precisely to the attainment of the *good* in relation to which merit, properly speaking, exists,[f] except insofar as some difficulty causes the need for greater ef-

a. In the present case, "that for which" is eternal life, perfect union with God.

b. *principalitas merendi est ex caritate*

c. Namely, to love, which is the first act of appetite as such. See *In III Sent.* d. 27, q. 1, a. 1 (above).

d. Aristotle, *On the Soul* II, ch. 2 (413b4).

e. This is an interpretive translation of *quod difficultas non facit ad meritum nisi forte dimissionis pene per modum cuiusdam commutationis.*

f. *ad meritum quod ordinatur ad consequutionem boni, ad quod proprie ordinem habet, non facit*

fort, which can result only from a greater inclination of the will to that good. And since habit and love bring about facility in acting from the fact that they cause a greater inclination of the will, therefore such facility does not diminish the *ratio* of merit.[411]

5. To the fifth, it should be said that virtuous habits, although they incline the will, do not compel it. And therefore it can happen that one who has a greater habit sometimes produces less intensity in an act, even as he may sometimes produce no act at all. And then a less intense act proceeding from a greater charity is less meritorious with regard to the accidental reward (which is given in view of the act itself), but more meritorious with regard to the essential reward (which is given in view of the capacity for acting, which is from the habit of charity).[a]

Notes on the text of Lombard

Whether one and the same motion is therefore extended toward a friend and toward an enemy.

This is impossible, unless the one be loved on account of the other, and is referred to that other by actual consideration.

Therefore the friend is loved more fervently.

This statement is to be understood with respect to the object itself; but with respect to the end, the one who acts with greater effort, pre-

---

a. The "essential reward" is that in which beatitude is essentially found, viz., God; the "accidental reward" is the possession of some good other than God but in relation to him (e.g., the condition of the blessed as regards their bodies or their knowledge of separated substances or worldly events). The text as edited by both Moos and the Leonine editors reads *Et tunc actus ex maiori caritate procedens minus intensus est magis meritorius respectu premii accidentalis, quod respicit ipsum actum, set minus respectu premii essentialis, quod respicit capacitatem que est ex habitu caritatis.* There must be a mistaken reversal of words either in what Thomas himself wrote or in the early manuscript tradition, for the argument makes sense only if one reads *minus* first and *magis* second. An explanation of the argument: John does a greater act but has a lesser habit of charity. Joseph does a lesser act but has a greater habit of charity. What essential reward did each merit by their acts? According to the perspective of the *Scriptum*, Joseph merits an essential reward in proportion to the habit (in the *Summa* the idea of a strict proportion is abandoned), and so he merits a greater essential reward than John does, whose habit is lesser. The accidental reward, however, is in relation to the kind and intensity of an act; and so, in this case, John merits an *accidental* reward in proportion to his *act*, which was greater than Joseph's.

cisely as having such effort, is more fervent[a] [in loving the object, be he friend or foe].

When it is said in the Lord's Prayer: "Forgive us our debts, even as we forgive our debtors . . ."

It seems that whoever holds a grudge sins by saying this prayer. In response, it should be said that such a man does not sin, because he does not say the prayer in his own person but in the person of the Church; or if in his own person, he says it not in respect to what he does, but in respect to that at which he desires to arrive.

a. *respectu finis, ille qui habet maiorem conatum, in quantum huiusmodi, est feruentior*

DISTINCTION 31[a]
[CHARITY'S DURATION]

Division of the text

"Nor should we omit to discuss the view [of certain ones who assert that charity once had cannot be cut off]." After the Master has determined about charity, here he determines about its duration.

This consideration is divided into two parts. In the first, he determines about the duration of charity in regard to its essence; in the second, about its duration in regard to its order, showing how it was in Christ and how it will be in the blessed, where he says: "Now, however, it remains to investigate [if Christ, as man, fulfilled the commanded order of love]."

The former is divided into two parts. In the first, he determines about the duration of charity; in the second, about the duration of other habits, where he says: "Attention should also be paid [to the manner in which faith, hope, and knowledge are said to be emptied out . . . but not charity]."

Concerning the former, he does three things. First, he lays down a false opinion of some [authors], who said that charity cannot be lost, and the reasons for that opinion; second, he brings in objections to the contrary, where he says: "This opinion is overthrown by reason [and by authority]"; third, he responds to the arguments advanced in favor of this opinion, where he says: "Indeed, the Apostle's statement [that 'charity is never cut out' offers no support to their opinion]."

Here, there are two questions for discussion: the first, on the emptying out of charity through sin; the second, on its emptying out through glory.

---

a. Latin text: provisional critical ed. of the Leonine Commission; cf. Moos ed., 968–98.

QUESTION 1   On the emptying out of charity through sin

Concerning the first, we will inquire into four things: (1) whether charity once had can be lost; (2) whether someone can be erased from the Book of Life;[a] (3) whether the least charity can resist any temptation whatsoever; (4) of the quantity of charity in those who rise up from sin.[b]

ARTICLE 1[c]   Whether one who has charity can lose it

Objections:

Proceeding to the first, it seems that one who has charity cannot lose it.

1. For everyone who has charity is born of God, since charity makes men sons of God. But everyone who is born of God does not sin, as is said in 1 John 3. Therefore everyone who has charity does not sin; and so charity once had cannot be lost.

2. Further, there is merit of eternal life in whosoever has charity, since charity is the principle of meriting, as was said.[d] But someone is unjustly treated if what he merited is not returned to him, since it is owed to him. Therefore eternal life will be given to whosoever has charity at some time. But eternal life will be given to no one unless he has charity in the end.[e] Therefore whosoever has charity will have it in the end; and so it cannot be lost, at least as regards having it in the end, as it seems.[412]

3. Further, what is most powerful cannot be conquered by what is

a. When we actually come to the second article, we discover that it takes into its purview much more than merely the question of whether erasure from the book is possible. It first addresses whether the Book of Life is something created; second, whether it is about God; third, whether anything can be erased from it.

b. *in resurgente.* The meaning of this question will become clearer below; see the note affixed to the title of that article for further explanation.

c. This article of the *Scriptum* combines inquiries that St. Thomas sometimes treats separately: whether charity, once had, can be lost; whether charity is lost through one mortal sin. Parallels to the former inquiry: *ST* II-II, q. 24, a. 11; *SCG* 4, ch. 70; *Super I Cor.* 13, lec. 3; *Super Rom.* 8, lec. 7; *De caritate*, a. 12. Parallels to the latter inquiry: *In I Sent.* (Paris version) d. 17, q. 2, a. 5 (see above); *In I Sent.* (*Lectura romana*) d. 17, q. 2, a. 4 (see above); *ST* II-II, q. 24, a. 12; *De caritate* aa. 6 & 13.

d. In the article immediately preceding this one: *In III Sent.* d. 30, a. 5 (see above).

e. *finaliter,* i.e., at the moment of death.

weakest. But charity is the most powerful, since it is "strong as death," as is said in the last chapter of the Song of Songs.ª Sin, however, is the weakest, since "evil is weak and sluggish," as Dionysius says in chapter 4 of *On the Divine Names*.ᵇ Therefore charity cannot be expelled through sin. Yet there is in no other way in which it can be lost. Therefore charity, once had, cannot be lost.

4. Further, "cupidity is the root of all evil" (1 Tim. 6:10). But charity—at least perfect charity—is not compatible with cupidity, as Augustine says in *The Book of Eighty-Three Questions*.ᶜ Therefore one who has charity cannot fall into something evil; and thus he cannot lose it.

5. Further, if sin expels charity, the sin that does so must be either a sin that already is, or a sin that has not yet come to be. But it is not a sin which already is, since that does not conquer charity;[413] nor a sin that has not yet come to be, since what does not exist cannot act. Therefore sin in no way expels charity.

6. Further, what is or occurs for the lesser part stands further from what is or occurs for the most part than it does from what is indifferent to alternatives. But from that which is indifferent, nothing can proceed, as the Commentator says in *Physics* II; therefore much less can something proceed from what is or occurs for the lesser part.ᵈ﹐[414] But charity, although it does not bring it about of necessity that good always be done, nevertheless brings about an inclination for good to be done in most cases. Therefore one who has charity cannot do evil, to which he has no relation, except for the lesser part;ᵉ and thus he cannot sin or lose charity.

7. Further, charity's love is stronger than natural love. But natural love is not lost through sin; therefore neither is charity's love.

8. Further, charity is greater than faith; and each is a gift of God. Since therefore faith is not taken away through mortal sin, it seems that neither is charity.

---

a. The full verse reads: "Put me as a seal upon thy heart, as a seal upon thy arm, for love is strong as death, jealousy as hard as hell, the lamps thereof are fire and flames" (8:6, Douay-Rheims).

b. Pseudo-Dionysius, *On the Divine Names*, ch. 4, n. 32 (PG 3:731).

c. Augustine, *The Book of Eighty-Three Questions*, Q. 36, n. 1 (CCSL 44A:54).

d. As the argument is extremely condensed, it has been expanded in translation: *Illud quod est in minori parte magis distat ab eo quod est in pluribus quam ab eo quod est ad utrumlibet. Set ex eo quod est ad utrumlibet non potest aliquid procedere, ut dicit Commentator in II Phisicorum. Ergo multo minus ab eo quod est in minori parte.*

e. *ad quod non se habet nisi sicut in minori parte*

On the contrary:

1. It says in Revelation 2:4: "I have a few things against you, since you have abandoned your first charity." Therefore charity can be lost.

2. Further, there is no need for caution in him who cannot fall. But caution is [taught as] necessary for one who is standing through charity: "The one who stands, let him take care that he not fall" (1 Cor. 10:12). Therefore charity can be lost.

3. Further, David had charity at first, for otherwise he would not have begged that the joy of salvation be given back to him; and nevertheless [the same verse indicates that] he sinned and lost the charity whose restoration he was begging.[a] Therefore charity once had can be lost.

4. Further, whoever cannot sin has a free will confirmed in good.[b] But not everyone who has charity has a free will confirmed in good.[415] Therefore someone who has charity can sin, and thus lose charity.

Response:

It should be said that the opinion of those who held that charity, on account of its firmness, cannot be lost, is similar to the opinion of Socrates who held that one who has knowledge,[c] on account of its nobility and certainty, cannot go astray,[d] as the Philosopher says in *Ethics* VII;[e] and so there is a similar proof and disproof of each, as well as a refutation of the proof. For each position is most powerfully disproved through experience, but is "proved" through the firmness of knowledge and charity.

Now the Philosopher refutes the just-mentioned proof regarding knowledge by pointing to the fact that knowledge chiefly consists in the universal, whereas actions are concerned with singulars. And therefore concupiscence, which tends to the particular good unless it be restrained, impedes the application of universal knowledge to the particular,[f] absorbing the consideration of knowledge in a particu-

a. In Ps. 51[50]:14 we read: *redde mihi laetitiam salutaris tui*—"restore unto me the joy of thy salvation" (Douay-Rheims), implying that he had had this joy but lost it, otherwise it could not be given back.

b. *liberum arbitrium confirmatum,* a technical expression meaning a will that is unable to deviate from the divine good owing to the will's perfect adherence to it by a gift of grace or of glory.

c. "Knowledge" translates *scientia* throughout this response.

d. *peccare*

e. Aristotle, *Ethics* VII, ch. 2 (1145b25).

f. *deductionem scientie uniuersalis ad particulare impedit*

lar matter of action,[a, 416] so that although a morally incontinent man[b] seized by the fervor of conscupiscence considers rightly (and not merely holds by habit) some universal, for example that all fornication is to be fled, nevertheless when he descends to this particular good by the force of concupiscence, the habit of right reason is bound, so that he cannot carry through an act of right consideration about the particular.[417]

In a similar way, too, charity is chiefly concerned with the eternal good, so that it makes one have the universal conception that nothing is to be done against God; but when a man descends to the particular, some temptation absorbs the aforesaid inclination of charity, as was said about knowledge. But since charity loves God more vehemently than any concupiscence loves any mutable good, if someone should extend the affection that he has toward God to the particular work he is engaged in, using this as a rule for his work, he would never fall into sin.[418] But because it is in our power to use or not use the act of charity (for charity does not compel the will), affection for a mutable good can therefore prevail and induce a sin. And on account of this, it is evident that every sin comes from error and from contempt, in other words, negligence [of charity's rule of working].[c] Hence Boethius says: "Such weapons we brought you as would keep you safe by their unconquered strength, if you had not earlier thrown them away."[d]

Thus, the man who has fallen into [mortal] sin loses charity, since by sin he is divided from God, and this is because he sets for himself another end and there cannot be two ultimate ends.[419] Hence, since charity has for its cause conjunction with God,[e] it is immediately lost by one act. And this immediate loss may be found in all accidents that have a cause *outside of* the subject in which they exist, because nothing can remain in being once it has been separated from its essential cause, as is evident with light.[420] However, it is otherwise with habits that have their cause *in* the subject itself, because they are not totally destroyed through one act of sin.[421]

---

a. *considerationem scientie in particulari operabili absorbens*

b. A person unable to contain or control himself when under the influence of desire.

c. *ex contemptu negligentie*

d. Boethius, *On the Consolation of Philosophy*, Book I, prose 2 (CCSL 94:4). In the Leonine text, the citation is given as *Atqui talia arma contuleramus tibi que, nisi ea prior abiecisses, inuicta te firmitate tuerentur.*

e. *cum caritas habeat causam coniunctionem ad Deum*

Replies to objections:

1. To the first, therefore, it should be said that this statement is to be understood thus: as long as he wishes to *use* grace, through which he is a son of God, he will not sin; for by this grace he is able to resist sin.[a]

2. To the second, it should be said that certain ones said that only final charity, and no other, merits [eternal life].[b] But this is false, since only the charity that is in the last moment of life can be called "final," and perhaps at that moment a man merits nothing, but instead sleeps. Hence, it should be said that *any* act of charity merits eternal life and makes this something owed to it. But when a man sins, he now becomes, in a way, *other* than he was before, as the Philosopher says in *Ethics* IX,[c] since he is changed from what was fitting for him according to his nature to what is against that nature.[d] And therefore it is not necessary that eternal life should be given to him as something owed, even as something the return of which is owed to a person in his right mind is not to be returned to a person gone mad.[e, 422]

3. To the third, it should be said that it is not owing to any defect in charity that it is conquered by sin, but rather owing to a defect in the one who has charity,[f] who[g] does not make use of it [in order to avoid sin], as was said.

4. To the fourth, it should be said that although cupidity is not actually present in him who has charity, still the root of it remains in the soul,[h, 423] and through charity it can be blocked so that it does not rush forward into act.[i] And when cupidity is not blocked, it starts germinating, and expels charity.

---

a. *dicendum, quod hoc intelligendum est: si uelit uti gratia per quam filius Dei est; per eam enim potest peccato resistere*

b. Thomas does not provide the direct object of the sentence (eternal life), but in the context it is plainly intended.

c. Aristotle, *Ethics* IX, ch. 3 (1165b22).

d. *secundum naturam . . . preter naturam.* Though *praeter* often means besides or beyond, it can also mean contrary to or against.

e. *illud quod est debitum reddi sano non redditur furioso.* At times Thomas uses *furiosus* to indicate a condition of raving or fury, but at other times it serves more generally as a description of mental imbalance or abnormality. Similarly, *sanus* can mean sane, in one's right mind, or more broadly, healthy, normal.

f. *non ex defectu caritatis . . . set ex defectu habentis caritatem*

g. Leonine: *qui;* Moos: *quia*

h. *quamuis cupiditas non sit in actu in eo qui habet caritatem, tamen est in radice*

i. The Moos ed. reads: *et caritatem potest impedire ne in actum prorumpat,* "it [viz., cupidity] can impede charity so that it [viz., charity] does not rush forward into act." The Leonine editors establish: *et per caritatem potest impediri ne in actum prorumpat,* "and it can be impeded through charity, so that it [viz., cupidity] does not

5. To the fifth, it should be said that charity is expelled in the very instant in which sin comes to be; and just as that instant is the first in which sin begins to be, so it is the first in which charity begins not to be, as is evident in the case of natural things when there are two contrary forms.[424]

6. To the sixth, it should be said that what is indifferent to each outcome is determined to one outcome insofar as it is moved from another extrinsic[a] cause, and thus [when it is determined in this way] an effect can proceed from it. But when it is not made wholly determinate by a single thing,[b] it remains able to be determined to the opposite as well. And in this way, from that thing [e.g., the will] which stands to something [e.g., evil] for the lesser part insofar as it is already determined by a first cause [e.g., charity], the contrary [of that to which it is already determined by the first cause] can occur for the lesser part on account of some determining cause [e.g., sensible affection] contrary to that first cause determining it for the most part.[c, 425] And so it is likewise with the topic at hand: for just as charity, as far as lies in it,[d] inclines [a man] for the most part to what is good, so sensible affection inclines [a man] for the most part to what is pleasant to sense, and from this inclination, as from a kind of habit, the will is inclined to sin.[426]

7. To the seventh, it should be said that natural love is, at the level of the will,[e] entirely determined to one [end]. But it is not the same with the love of charity, except in the blessed who are now confirmed in good.[f]

8. To the eighth, it should be said that a man is not *totally* separated from God by sin, for if he were, he would simply cease to exist; but he is separated from God with respect to the ultimate and perfect conjunction with him that charity brings about. And therefore it is not necessary that faith be taken away by sin, as charity is—even as the air loses the sun's rays when clouds come in between but does not lose every sort of brightness, for instance that which comes from reflection,[g] the sort that appears even where there are no direct rays of sun.

---

rush forward into act." The latter reading fits the context better, but both make sense.

    a. Leonine: *extrinseca*; Moos: *intrinsica*

    b. *ab aliquo uno*

    c. *Et sic ab eo quod est ut in paucioribus respectu ipsius iam determinati per primum, potest contrarium accidere ut in paucioribus propter aliquod aliud determinans quod est contrarium illi determinanti ut in pluribus*

    d. *quantum est in se*   e. *secundum uoluntatem*

    f. *nisi in illis qui iam confirmati sunt*   g. *ex reuerberatione*

ARTICLE 2   On the Book of Life[a]

Proceeding to the second, [we divide the article into three subquestions: (1) whether the Book of Life is something created; (2) whether the Book of Life is about God; (3) whether anything can be said to be erased from the Book of Life].

SUBQUESTION 1[b]   Whether the Book of Life is something created

Objections:

It seems that the Book of Life is something created.

1. For on Ecclesiasticus 24:32, "All these things are the Book of Life,"[c] a gloss says: "The Book referred to here is the Old and New Testament." But that is something created; therefore so is the Book of Life.

2. Further, on Revelation 20:12, "Another book was opened, which is of life,"[427] the gloss says: [the book is] "Christ, who will then appear manifest to all."[d] But he will not appear to all except according to his human nature.[428] Since therefore human nature in Christ is created, it seems that the Book of Life is something created.

3. Further, a book, insofar as things come to be written in it, is receptive of impressions from without. But uncreated things are not susceptible to alien impressions. Therefore the Book of Life is not something uncreated but something created.

4. Again, it seems that the Book of Life is proper to the Son. For the gloss interprets Psalm 40:7, "In the head of the book it is written

---

a. At the start of question 1 where St. Thomas lists the articles, he identifies the second article as being concerned with erasure from the Book of Life. In the Parma ed., a different title is proposed at this point, namely: "Whether the Book of Life is something created." Neither description covers all the subquestions, so we have simply called it "On the Book of Life." However, the reader should note in the parallel texts that Thomas has already spoken somewhat of the Book of Life in Book I, in the discussion of predestination. The listing of subquestions has been added for clarity.

b. Parallels: *In I Sent.* d. 40, q. 1, a. 2, ad 5; *ST* I, q. 24, a. 1; *De ueritate*, q. 7, aa. 1 and 4; *Super Philip.* 4, lec. 1.

c. In the Vulgate: *haec omnia liber vitae testamentum Altissimi.* Versification and wording in the Book of Ecclesiasticus (or Sirach) vary considerably in the MS tradition. In the RSV the verse cited by Thomas is Sir. 24:23, with no explicit mention of life: "All this is the book of the covenant of the Most High God."

d. Strabo, *Glossa ordinaria* on Rev. 20:12 (PL 114:745).

of me,"[a] to mean this: "In the Father, who is my head."[b] But in the Divinity, that whose head is the Father is the Son. Therefore the Book of Life is the Son.

5. Again, it seems that the Book of Life is the Holy Spirit. For "life-giving" is attributed to the Holy Spirit both in the Creed[c] and in John 6:64: "It is the Spirit who gives life." Therefore since the Book of Life is ordained to life, it befits the Holy Spirit, whether properly or by appropriation.

On the contrary:

Augustine says in Book XX of *On the City of God*: "The Book of Life is the foreknowledge of God, which cannot fail."[d] But foreknowledge is something essentially uncreated and is appropriable to the Son; therefore, so is the Book of Life.

Response:

It should be said that the "Book of Life" of which we now speak is said metaphorically. Hence its meaning must be grasped according to its likeness to a material book, the *ratio* of which seems to be that it contains some figures that function as though likenesses of the things known by means of that book. Hence what we are speaking of is called the Book of Life because it contains likenesses by which life can be known. It would not, however, be the Book of Life in a sufficient way—that is, as though producing perfect knowledge about life—unless it should contain likenesses of every life[e] in particular, since knowledge at the universal level is imperfect and still in potency to particulars.[f] But to have in just this way the likenesses of all things that have life, and to have these likenesses determinately, belongs only to the divine mind, in which are the proper exemplars of all things. And for this reason the Book of Life is not something created, but is the di-

a. "Then I said: 'Lo, I come; in the roll of the book it is written of me: I delight to do thy will, O my God; thy law is written within my heart'" (Ps. 40:7–8, RSV). The Latin expression *in capite libri* is here interpreted in light of 1 Cor. 11:3, "the head of Christ is God."

b. Strabo, *Glossa ordinaria* on Ps. 40:7 [39:9 iuxta Vulg.] (PL 113:903).

c. "Life-giving": *uiuificatio*; "in the Creed": *in Simbolo*. A reference to the Niceno-Constantinopolitan symbol or profession of faith agreed upon at the First Council of Constantinople (381), which expanded on the original Nicene profession particularly as regards the Person of the Holy Spirit, whom it described as "Lord and giver of life."

d. Augustine, *On the City of God* XX, ch. 15 (CCSL 48:726).

e. Moos: *de vita cujuslibet*; Leonine: *de uita cuiusque*

f. *quia cognitio in uniuersali est imperfecta et in potentia*

vine knowledge[a] about life, not only at the universal level but down to the particular, with respect to everything in which life is found. And since knowledge is essential [to the divine nature] and is appropriated to the Son, therefore the Book of Life is something essential in God[b] and is appropriated to the Son.

Replies to objections:

1. To the first, therefore, it should be said that the Old and New Testament is called[c] the Book of Life as though producing knowledge about life at the universal level and teaching commandments by which life is attained; but nevertheless it does not produce knowledge about the life of each one in particular. And therefore it can be called the Book of Life in some sense, but not according to the full *ratio*.[429]

2. To the second, it should be said that Christ according to his human nature is called the Book of Life as though the universal exemplar of life, not as though he were a likeness causing one to know particularly the life of each one.

3. To the third, it should be said that the likenesses or figures in that Book are not something added to its essence, since the exemplar *rationes*, as was said in Book I,[d] are the divine essence itself; and therefore it is not necessary that it should receive alien impressions.[e]

4. To the fourth, it should be said that the Father is called "head of the book," i.e., of the Son, insofar as "book" is appropriated to the Son.

5. To the fifth, it should be said that while life may be appropriated to the Holy Spirit, *knowledge* about life is appropriated to the Son.

SUBQUESTION 2[f]   Whether the Book of
Life has to do with God

Objections:

Furthermore, it seems that the Book of Life has to do with God.[g]

1. For on Psalm 69:28, "May they be erased from the book of the liv-

---

a. *diuina notitia.* In these subquestions, "knowledge" generally translates *notitia.*

b. *in diuinis*

c. Thomas speaks of the Old and New *Testament*, not *Testaments*; hence his use of the singular verb *dicitur.*

d. *In I Sent.* d. 36, q. 2, esp. a. 2.

e. *peregrinas impressiones*

f. Parallels: *ST* I, q. 24, a. 2; *De ueritate,* q. 7, aa. 5–7.

g. *in respectu Dei*; elsewhere in the subquestion the phrase is *respectu Dei.*

ing," the gloss says: "The book of the living is the knowledge of God."[a] But God has maximal knowledge of himself. Therefore the Book of Life has to do with God.

2. Further, he is the font of any life whatsoever. If therefore the Book of Life is about others who have life by way of participation, much more is it about himself who has life in the way of the origin.[b]

Again, it seems that it is about all creatures.

3. For foreknowledge extends to all creatures. But the Book of Life is the divine foreknowledge, as was said above. Therefore it will be about all things.

4. Further, it is said in John 1:3: "What was made, in him was life."[c] But every creature is made; therefore every creature is written in the Book of Life.

Again, it seems that the Book of Life is also about the wicked.

5. For on Luke 10:20, "your names are written in heaven," the gloss says: "Whether someone performs heavenly or earthly works is eternally fixed within the memory of God, being annotated in this quasi-text."[d] But performing earthly works is characteristic of those who are wicked. Therefore, since the Book of Life is nothing other than the reservoir of the divine memory,[e] it seems that the Book of Life is also about the wicked.

6. Again, the Book of Life is ordained to life. But the life of nature is common to the good and the wicked, and the life of grace, moreover, is common in this life to those who are foreknown but not predestined and those who are predestined to eternal life.[f] Therefore the Book of Life is about the good and the wicked, the predestinate and the fore-known.

a. Strabo, *Glossa ordinaria* on Ps. 68:29 [69:28 iuxta Heb.] (PL 113:950), derived from Augustine, *Expositions of the Psalms*, Ps. 68, Serm. 2, n. 13 (CCSL 39:927).

b. *participatiue . . . originaliter*

c. The Leonine editors punctuate as follows: *"Quod factum est. In ipso uita erat."* Even if this is what St. Thomas's Vulgate text may have had, he ignores the punctuation and reads the phrases as if the former led immediately into the latter. Thomas is aware of several ways of punctuating these verses, so pregnant with metaphysical meaning; see *Super Ioan.* 1, lec. 2, where the exegetical approaches of Augustine, Origen, Hilary, and Chrysostom are discussed.

d. Strabo, *Glossa ordinaria* on Lk. 10:20 (PL 114:286). In the Migne ed.: *Si quis coelestia sive terrestria opera gesserit, per haec quasi litteris adornatus apud Dei memoriam aeternaliter est affixus.* As Thomas cites it: *Siue terrestria siue celestia opera gesserit quis, per hec quasi litteris annotatus, apud Dei memoriam eternaliter est affixus.*

e. *reseruatio diuine memorie*

f. *uite gratie communis prescitis et predestinatis*—a shorthand way of saying what the translation spells out.

On the contrary:

7. Something is said to be "written in God" which has an exemplar in him. But evil things, insofar as they are evil, have no exemplar in him. Therefore they are not written there.[a]

Response:

It should be said that God's knowledge is called the Book of Life. Since, however, a book is properly about those things of which it produces knowledge through figures and likenesses existing in the book, therefore only the knowledge of those things that God knows through a likeness can be called a book.

Now God does not know evils through likenesses of evils existing in himself; they are rather known in the manner of privations.[b] In like manner, too, God does not know himself through a likeness of himself, but rather by the fact that he is present to himself according to his own essence. Hence neither the knowledge God has of himself nor the knowledge he has of evils can be called a book,[c] except when it comes to the punishments of the wicked insofar as these punishments are just and good, for, from this vantage, God's knowledge may be called the Book of Death.[d]

Life, however, is counted among good things. Hence the Book of Life must be understood with respect to the life found in creatures; and although God has knowledge about the life of nature, of grace, and of glory—so that with respect to any of the aforesaid lives God's knowledge could be called the Book of Life—nevertheless the perfect *ratio* of life is found only in the life of glory, which suffers no admixture of death. And therefore the Book of Life, according to its proper sense, is the knowledge of God that he has about the life of glory of each one [who can receive it].

In this way, the Book of Life differs: (1) from God's knowledge, which is about both temporal and eternal things; (2) from God's foreknowledge, which is about both the good and the wicked; (3) and also from predestination, since predestination, properly speaking, is about future things and implies providential direction to an end, since it is the purpose to have mercy.[e] But the Book of Life implies sim-

a. The Leonine editors identify the *sed contra* as a seventh argument, because Thomas's reasoning in the response also applies to it.

b. *per modum priuationis*

c. Leonine: *liber*; Moos: *liber vitae*

d. *nisi de malis pene, in quantum sunt iusta et bona, secundum quod dicitur liber mortis*

e. *cum sit propositum miserendi.* The use of *propositum* here echoes the uses of

ple knowledge about life, leaving the time undetermined;[a] hence both those who already have life and those who are going to have it are said to be written in the Book of Life.

And through this response, the solution to all the objections (1–7) is evident.

SUBQUESTION 3[b]   Whether anything can
be said to be erased from the Book of Life

Objections:

Furthermore, it seems that nothing written there ought to be said to be erased from it.

1. For the Book of Life is divine predestination, as the gloss says on Philippians 4:3.[c] But no one is said to fall away from predestination; therefore neither should anyone be said to be erased from the Book of Life.

2. Further, a book in which something can be written down and erased is changeable. But the Book of Life is unchangeable, since it is something uncreated. Therefore no one can be erased from it.

3. Further, what is taken for true according to mere opinion, since it is true only in some respect, should not be spoken of as though it were simply so.[d] But on Psalm 69:28, "May they be erased from the book of the living," the gloss says that this is to be taken[e] only in respect to the hope of those who suppose themselves to be written there.[f] Therefore it seems that [properly speaking] no one ought to be said to be erased from it.

---

the term in Scripture in the context of predestination; it is usually rendered into English as "purpose." The Moos ed., reading *providentia* (p. 977, line 14), makes of providence a fourth item to be distinguished from the Book of Life, whereas the Leonine ed., reading *providentie,* makes the phrase explanatory of predestination.

a. *et non determinat aliquod tempus*

b. Parallels: *In I Sent.* d. 40, q. 1, a. 2, ad 5 and q. 3, ad 3; *ST* I, q. 24, a. 3; *Super Philip.* 4, lec. 1.

c. Strabo, *Glossa ordinaria* on Phil. 4:3 (PL 114:607).

d. *Illud quod est secundum opinionem tantum, cum sit secundum quid, non debet enuntiari simpliciter*

e. Leonine: *hoc accipiendum fore*; Moos: *hoc accipiendum forte*

f. In other words, they were never written there in reality, but only reputed themselves written there; hence the Psalmist prays that God may punish them by exposing their pretense.—Strabo, *Glossa ordinaria* on Ps. 68:29 [69:28 iuxta Heb.] (PL 113:950), derived from Augustine, *Expositions of the Psalms,* Ps. 68, Serm. 2, n. 13 (CCSL 39:927).

On the contrary:

1. "The one who has sinned against me, I will erase him from my book" (Ex. 32:33). But many sin; therefore many are erased.

2. Further, no one is both written in the Book of Life and damned. But many who earlier were written in the Book of Life are afterwards damned, as is clearly seen among the disciples of Christ to whom it was said: "Rejoice, for your names are written in the Book of Life" (Lk. 10:20), even though from their number many turned aside and fell away, as is said in John 6:67. Therefore some who were written there earlier are erased.

Response:

It should be said that the Book of Life, as was said, is God's knowledge about the life of glory of any man. Now a thing has being in a twofold manner: in itself and in its cause. In itself, indeed, it *is* simply, while in its cause, it has being in a certain respect. But grace, just in itself, is a sufficient cause of glory, so that he who has grace has now, in a certain respect, the life of glory.

Therefore God has knowledge about the life of glory of anyone in two ways: in one way, insofar as God knows the very life of glory to be in that one [right now], or to be in him in the future, *simply*; and then such a man is said to be written in the Book of Life *simply* (or, as certain ones put it, "enrolled,"ª from a likeness to those who are enrolled in the military or in some office); in another way, insofar as God knows the life of glory to be in that one, or to be in him in the future, *in its cause,* which is grace; and such a man is said to be written in the Book of Life in a certain respect (or, as certain ones put it, "noted down").ᵇ

Since therefore it is impossible that the knowledge of God should fail, it follows that whosoever he knows is to have eternal life will in fact have it. Hence that man who is written simply (or "enrolled") in the Book of Life cannot be erased from it.

But since grace, which is the cause of glory in a man who has present justice, ceases to be a cause of glory in him when he falls away from justice by sin, therefore God's knowledge about that man's grace is not a knowledge of grace *as cause of glory*. Hence the knowledge God has of that grace[430] does not now pertain to the book of the life of glory. And according to this, he is said to be erased from the Book of

a. *ascriptus*
b. *annotatus*

Life not by some change made in the book itself, but rather by some change in the one in whom it happens that grace is not now the cause of glory. And God is said to erase someone from the Book of Life insofar as God permits him to fall away from justice by sin.[431]

Replies to objections:

1. To the first, therefore, it should be said that "pre-destination" implies direction to an end, which "Book of Life" does not imply, as was said. And so, the one who has only present justice cannot be called predestined, but he can be said in some way to be written in the Book of Life, as was explained.

2. To the second, the solution is evident from what was said above.

3. To the third, it should be said that the gloss is speaking there about the writing by which someone is written in the Book of Life simply.

ARTICLE 3[a]   Whether any charity can
resist any temptation[b]

Objections:

Proceeding to the third, it seems that not any charity whatsoever can resist any temptation whatsoever.

1. For just as charity is an obstacle to sin, so also is reason, as was said above.[c] But not any [power of] reason whatsoever is capable of resisting temptation, as can be seen in the morally incontinent, who have right reason and yet are overcome, as the Philosopher says.[d] Therefore not any charity is capable of resisting any temptation.

2. Further, there is greater difficulty in resisting evil than in doing good, simply speaking. But the least [amount of] charity cannot do any and every good work; therefore neither can it resist any and every temptation.

3. Further, in resisting the greatest temptation, there is the greatest merit, since in that case there is the greatest fight that merits a crown. But the least charity cannot bring about the greatest reward; therefore neither can it resist the greatest temptation.

a. Parallels: *ST* III, q. 62, a. 6, ad 3 and q. 70, a. 4; *De caritate*, a. 10, ad 4.

b. In this article Thomas at times speaks of resisting temptation, at times of conquering or overcoming it; the verbs are *resistere* and *uincere.*

c. Thomas is probably referring back to article 1 of the present question, though there are also other places in the *Scriptum* where he stresses how right reason, as such, is contrary to sin (e.g., *In II Sent.* d. 21, q. 2, a. 3; d. 24, q. 3, a. 3).

d. Aristotle, *Ethics* VII, ch. 8 (1151a20–25).

4. Further, imperfect charity does not resist venial sins. But the on-slaught of mortal sins[a] is greater than that of venial sins. Therefore imperfect charity does not resist the greatest temptations.

5. Further, it is said in 1 Corinthians 10:13: "God is faithful, who does not permit you to be tempted beyond what you are able to bear." But those to whom that verse was written had grace, as is evident from the beginning of the Epistle.[432] Therefore some temptation is beyond the power of the one who has grace or charity.

On the contrary:

1. It is impossible to avoid every sin unless every temptation to sin is resisted. But the least charity can avoid every sin, since even a man existing in a purely natural state would have been able to do this.[433] Therefore any charity is capable of overcoming every temptation.

2. Further, "charity loves the law of God more than cupidity loves thousands of gold and silver pieces," as a gloss says on Psalm 119.[b] But a greater love can resist a lesser love.[c] Therefore any charity is capable of resisting any temptation.

3. Further, no one commits a sin in something he is not capable of avoiding, as Augustine says.[d] If therefore the one who has charity were not able to resist *any* temptation, it seems that he would not commit sin by consenting to [at least *some*] temptation.

Response:[434]

It should be said that "resisting temptation" is said in two ways: in one way, it means that someone is not conquered by temptation; in another way, that someone conquers temptation. For someone is said to be conquered by temptation when, by a temptation, he is drawn away from a good he proposes to follow and into consenting to sin, as occurs in the morally incontinent man who has right reason but is led astray [by some sensible good]; for someone who never even proposes to follow the good, e.g., the intemperate or lustful man,[e] is not "con-

a. *impugnatio mortalium*

b. Ps. 119:72 (Ps. 118:72, iuxta Vulg.): "The law of thy mouth is better to me than thousands of gold and silver pieces." The gloss is that of Augustine, *Expositions of the Psalms*, Ps. 118, Serm. 17, n. 10 (CCSL 40:1722).

c. Leonine: *Set maior dilectio minori resistere potest*; Moos: *Sed major dilectio minori tentationi resistere potest.* The argument is that temptation is always based on some love other than charity, and since charity is the greater love, it can resist the temptation toward something less loved.

d. Augustine, *On Free Choice of the Will* III, ch. 18, n. 50 (CCSL 29:304).

e. "lustful": *luxuriosus.* For Thomas *luxuria* signifies an inordinate habit, act, or pleasure regarding sex; normally synonymous with "lust."

quered by" temptation, since he freely gives in to it. That man is said to *conquer*, however, who not only is not led into an act of sin from a temptation coming upon him, but also, owing to the greatness of his virtue, esteems the temptation as though it were nothing; whereas the man who suffers difficulty from a temptation but is not led away by it, does indeed *resist* temptation by not consenting to it, but does not conquer, properly speaking.

Speaking therefore in the first way about resisting sin [i.e., not being conquered], in this manner any charity is capable of resisting [any] sin, on account of a free will freed from the slavery of sin, although it suffers difficulty under the incitement of temptation;[a] whereas speaking of temptation in the second way [i.e., as a prey of conquest], in this manner a charity that is small when the temptation begins is capable of resisting any temptation,[b] because [when made use of] it becomes great by the time the temptation has ended, since God will always administer help to one who is fighting. Yet on the hypothesis that a certain charity were always to remain small, it would not be capable of resisting temptation in the second way.

Replies to objections:

1. To the first, therefore, it should be said that the case of the morally incontinent and the case of one who has charity are not parallel, since the one who has charity really has the habit of virtue right now, which the incontinent one does not have. And further, even the incontinent man is not overcome as though unable to resist, since if he wanted to use the right reason he has, he could,[c] as was said above.

2. To the second, it should be said that although [in resisting evil] there is greater difficulty in regard to labor [than in doing good], still there is not greater difficulty considered in terms of an excess of the work vis-à-vis the power; and this is what one looks to when it comes to virtues, as was said.[d, 435] Or it can be said that even the least charity is capable of attaining the greatest object, but not of positing a greatest act in regard to intensity.[e]

3. To the third it can be said that a small charity[f] is capable of lead-

---

a. *propter temptationis impulsum*

b. Leonine: *potest temptationi cuilibet resistere*; Moos: *potest tentationibus resistere*

c. *si uellet ratione recta quam habet uti*

d. See *In III Sent*. d. 23, q. 1, a. 3, qa. 1.

e. The Moos ed. lacks this final sentence, supplied in the Leonine: *Vel potest dici quod etiam minima caritas potest in maximum obiectum, non autem in maximum actum quantum ad intensionem.*

f. Leonine: *parua caritas*; Moos: *etiam minima caritas*

ing to great merit with respect to the accidental reward, but not with respect to the substantial reward, as was said above.[a]

4. To the fourth, it should be said that imperfect charity could even resist venial sins, if someone made use of charity against the temptation to commit venial sins—not as though he would avoid all of them, but because he is able to avoid any given one.[b, 436]

5. To the fifth, it should be said that the Apostle speaks with respect to what a man can endure without disturbance of soul; and only perfect charity can bring it about that a man preserve equanimity in the midst of great tribulations.[c]

ARTICLE 4[d]   On the charity with which a
man rises up from sin[e]

Proceeding to the fourth, [we divide the article into three subquestions: (1) whether a man always rises up from sin to a lesser charity than he had before he sinned; (2) whether a man always rises up from sin into a greater charity than he had before he sinned; (3) whether a man rises up from sin into a charity at least *equal* to the charity he had before he sinned].

a. See *In III Sent.* d. 30, a. 5, ad 5 (above).

b. *set quia potest singula uitare*

c. *Apostolus loquitur quantum ad id quod homo potest sustinere sine animi perturbatione, quod non potest nisi caritas perfecta, ut in magnis tribulationibus equanimitatem seruet*

d. Parallel: *ST* III, q. 89, aa. 2–3.

e. At the start of question 1, Thomas identifies the fourth article as being concerned with "the quantity of charity in those who have risen up," and as it is clear from the arguments that he means rising up *from sin* (i.e., returning to grace after having sinned), we have added "from sin." The question is then subdivided into the three logical possibilities: when a sinner repents, does he return to a lesser charity than he had when he fell, a greater, or at least an equal? The Parma ed. entitles the article "Whether a man always rises up in a lesser charity," but in view of the contents this is not accurate. We have supplied a title as well as the listing of subquestions. The phrases "than he had before falling" and "than before" are added for clarity.

The subquestions here cannot be rearranged as wholes, as we have done elsewhere, by grouping together the objections, response, and replies, because the response to the first subquestion presupposes that one is aware of the questions raised in the *other* subquestions, and the objections in the second and third subquestions presuppose that one has not yet read the response to the first. There is in fact just one overall question here, viz., "Whether the charity recovered by the one who rises up from sin always has the same relation to the charity that he had before his sin." St. Thomas might have simply grouped all the objections together, voicing the various logical possibilities, and then presented his

SUBQUESTION 1   Whether a man always rises up from
sin with less charity than before

Objections:

It seems that he always rises up from sin with *less* charity.

1. For on Amos 5:2, "Fallen, no more to rise, is the virgin Israel,"[a] the gloss says: "It is not denied that she might rise, but rather that she can rise as a virgin, since one who has gone astray, even if he be carried back on the shepherd's shoulders, does not have as much glory as if he had never strayed."[b] But glory is commensurate with charity. Therefore a man after sinning does not have as much charity when he rises, as he had at first.

2. Further, Ezekiel 44 says: "The Levites who went away from me . . . shall never come near to me that they might once again exercise the priesthood."[c] But as regards the spiritual priesthood of the faithful, someone comes near to God through charity.[d, 437] Therefore the one who at some time went away from God by sin does not have as much charity as he had before.

3. Further, beginning charity is never as much as advancing and perfect charity. But sometimes when someone falls, he had until that moment advancing or perfect charity; whereas when he rises up from sin, he has beginning charity [since he appears to be starting over again]. Therefore he does not have as much charity as before.

4. Further, that which is without charity can never dispose to receiving the influence of divine light as much as charity can do.[e] But in-

---

answer in a single response, followed by all the replies. A sign that he should have done so is the fact that the first response does not stand well by itself, but requires the second and third responses to be complete. This article displays the potential for confusion inherent in "subquestion" structuring, which Thomas, ever aspiring to formal and material clarity, wisely abandoned in works after the *Scriptum.*

a. According to the RSV. Thomas quotes only three words: *Virgo Israel cecidit.*

b. Derived from Jerome, *Commentary on Amos*, Bk. II, 5:1–2 (CCSL 76:273).

c. A quotation joining the beginning of Ezek. 44:10 with the beginning of 44:13.

d. Thomas does not write "of the faithful," but his phrase *spirituale sacerdotium* is a reference to this doctrine, which he teaches elsewhere (see *In IV Sent.* d. 4, q. 1; *ST* III, q. 63).

e. Leonine: *Numquam potest tantum disponere ad recipiendum diuini luminis influentiam quod est sine caritate quantum caritas;* Moos: *Nunquam potest tantum disponere se ad recipiendum divini luminis influentiam qui est sine caritate, quantum cum caritate—* someone who is without charity can never dispose himself to receiving the influence of divine light as much as someone with charity can do.

sofar as someone disposes himself to grace, God infuses grace into him. Therefore someone remaining in charity always receives more of the influence of grace than one receiving charity anew; and so the same conclusion follows as before.

On the contrary:

"The sacrifice of Judah and Jerusalem shall please God, as in the former days and the ancient years" (Mal. 3:4). But charity makes everything of ours to be accepted by God. Therefore someone rising after a fall can have as much charity as he had at first.

SUBQUESTION 2   Whether a man always rises up from sin
with greater charity than before

Objections:

Furthermore, it seems that he always rises up from sin with a *greater* charity.

1. For on Genesis 1:5, "There came to be evening and morning, one day," a gloss says: "The evening light is that from which someone falls; the morning light, that in which he rises." But morning light is greater than evening light. Therefore, too, the grace or charity in which someone rises is greater than that which he had before he fell.

2. Further, Romans 5:20 says: "Where offense abounded, grace superabounded." But where grace superabounds, there is greater charity. Therefore, [the same conclusion follows].

3. Further, sin conquers the first charity, but [when a man rises up] it is then conquered by the second charity. Therefore the latter charity is stronger and greater than the former.[a]

On the contrary:

An innocent man is not less apt for receiving grace than a sinner. But the man who received the first grace as an innocent man, receives the second grace as a sinner.[b] Therefore it need not be the case that the second grace is greater than the first.

---

a. Thomas speaks of *prima* and *secunda caritas,* which mean the charity had before the sin and the new charity had afterwards.

b. *Set primam gratiam accepit innocens, secundam accipit peccator*

SUBQUESTION 3   Whether a man rises up from sin with a
charity at least equal to that which he had before

Objections:

Furthermore, it seems that the charity of the one rising up from sin
is at least always *equal.*

1. For on Romans 8:28, "To those who love God, all things work
together for good," a gloss says: "Even a fall into sin." But this would
not be so, if the sinner were to rise with less charity. Therefore he never rises up with less charity, but always with charity [at least] equal to
what he had before.

2. Further, Ambrose[a] says that penance restores everything that has
been taken away. But this would not be so, if the penitent were not
to rise up in a charity at least equal to what he had before. Therefore
someone always rises up with [at least] an equal charity.

3. Further, contrition ought to be proportionate to the preceding
sin. But sin is proportionate, in a certain way, to the grace that it expels. Therefore the grace or charity through which a man has contrition for sin ought to be equal to the preceding grace that the sin expelled. [And so the charity out of which this contrition emerges has to
be at least equal to the charity expelled by the sin.]

4. Further, penance restores life to merits deadened by sin. Therefore the penitent will have as much glory as he merited before his sin.
But he merited as much as he had of charity. Therefore the glory the
penitent will have is proportionate to the charity he had *before* his sin.
Yet this glory is proportionate to the charity in which, *after* his repentance, he is found at the moment of death, since "in whatever place
the tree shall fall, there it shall remain" (Eccles. 11:3). Therefore the
charity with which the penitent rises up from sin is equal to the charity from which he falls.[438]

On the contrary:

The least contrition is enough to blot out all sins. But the quantity
of charity in which someone rises up after sinning is gauged according to the quantity of contrition for that sin. Since, therefore, when he
had grace earlier on, he might have received that grace due to a great
preparation, it seems possible that he should receive a lesser grace and
charity than he had before [due to a lesser preparation].

a. According to Moos, these words are not found verbatim in Ambrose, but
can be gathered from *Libri Hypognosticon* III, ch. 9 (PL 45:1631), where we read:
Poenitentia ergo res est optima et perfecta, quae defectos revocat ad perfectum.

RESPONSES TO SUBQUESTIONS 1–3
AND THEIR OBJECTIONS

Response to the first subquestion:

It should be said that the measure of charity is pre-fixed by God according to his will, and in some way is [also] commensurate with the effort of the one who receives grace. Hence, because someone after sinning can expend more or less effort to recover charity,[a] and by sin no limit is imposed upon divine liberality—since, as far as lies in him, he is prepared to blot out all sins entirely[b]—it must be said, as is commonly said, that someone can rise up after sin with charity greater than, less than, or equal to that which he had before.

Replies to the first set of objections:

1. To the first, therefore, it should be said that the gloss is speaking about the glory of the accidental reward, which is commensurate not with charity but with an act or state: for after sin, a virgin will not have an aureole;[439] and similarly, neither will a sinner rising up after a fall have the joy of continual innocence.

2. To the second, it should be said that someone is driven from an office of dignity on account of the sin committed, even if he should repent, as, e.g., he is driven from the priesthood on account of having committed homicide; and this is because he is not restored [by penance] to a state of such dignity, even though he might be restored to an equal charity.

3. To the third, it should be said that it is true, speaking of one and the same charity, that beginning charity is less than advancing or perfect charity; but a given beginner can be greater in quantity of charity than another person who is in the state of one advancing, just as a newborn animal can be greater in size or strength than another animal, even a fully grown one.[c]

4. To the fourth, it should be said that, other things being equal, the one who has charity always receives more of the influence of divine light; but one who does not have charity can yet strive for it more[d] and will receive it more.

---

a. Leonine: *ad recuperandum caritatem*; Moos: *ad recipiendum caritatem*

b. *cum ipse, quantum in se est, sit paratus omnia peccata totaliter delere*

c. The phrases "in quantity of charity" and "in size or strength" have been added for clarity.

d. *plus conari*

Response to the second subquestion:

It should be said that it need not be the case that a man should always rise up with a greater charity, since even a lesser or an equal preparation is a sufficient condition for the infusing of grace.[a]

Replies to the second set of objections:

1. To the first, therefore, it should be said that the likeness mentioned in that gloss is not to be evaluated with respect to the quantity of light, but with respect to the order of light to darkness.

2. To the second, it should be said that the Apostle is speaking in that passage of the grace of redemption, which superabounded in regard to the offense of the first man; he is not speaking universally.[440]

3. To the third, it should be said that sin does not conquer charity on account of a weakness in charity itself, but because he who sins does not make use of the help that charity affords; and therefore the argument does not follow.

Response to the third subquestion:

It should be said that a man can rise up from sin even with less charity than he had before, since, however little he sorrows about sin and prepares himself for grace, as long as he comes to that extent of contrition by which it more displeases him to have gone away from God than any temporal good pleases him,[b] then he will have grace—even if he does not prepare himself for this gift of grace as much as he prepared himself earlier on, when he was innocent.

Replies to the third set of objections:

1. To the first, therefore, it should be said that this [i.e., the fact that we can benefit from a fall] is not understood to refer always to a greater quantity of charity in the one rising up, but [in any event] to the greater diligence or humility, at least actual, in which the penitent sinner rises up. It is less evil, however, that charity should be diminished than that it should be entirely lost; and the lesser evil is reckoned the

---

a. *sufficit ad hoc quod gratia infundatur.* The *preparatio* refers to the ultimate disposition for receiving grace, which in the case of a sinner would mean the contrition that suffices for receiving God's forgiveness—imperfect contrition if sacramental confession is availed of; otherwise, perfect contrition. See the response to the third subquestion.

b. *dummodo ad terminum contritionis perueniat qua plus displicet ei a Deo recessisse quam aliquod temporale commodum <placet>*

greater good, as is said in *Ethics* V.[a, 441] And therefore sin can turn out to be for the *good* of one who loves God, even if he should rise up with less charity than he had before, in the sense that, through the humility and caution he learns, he is protected[b] from all sorts of loss of grace.

2. To the second, it should be said that penance does restore all things, but the things restored need not be equal to what they were before.

3. To the third, it should be said that the quantity of sin is *not* proportionate to the grace that it excludes, because a small sin can expel the greatest charity, just as conversely a small charity is capable of blotting out the greatest sins,[c] since this [effect] depends upon a man's effort rather than the habit's quantity.

4. To the fourth, it should be said, as is evident from what has been said before,[d] that he merited by prior merits so much glory as he had of charity. But through sin he became other than he was, and is not fully restored to the pristine degree he occupied. And therefore he will not fully receive the effect of prior merits, except with respect to the accidental reward, which is measured by acts of charity more than by the habit of charity.[442]

QUESTION 2   On the emptying out of charity through glory

The next subject for inquiry is the emptying out of charity through glory. Concerning this, we will inquire into four things: (1) whether faith and hope are emptied out at the advent of glory; and whether (2) charity, (3) the order of charity, and (4) knowledge, are [likewise] emptied out at the advent of glory.

ARTICLE 1   Whether faith and hope are emptied out in the fatherland[e]

Proceeding to the first, [we divide the article into three subquestions: (1) whether faith is emptied out in the state of glory; (2) wheth-

a. Aristotle, *Ethics* V, ch. 2 (1129b12).

b. Leonine: *tueatur;* Moos: *curatur*

c. Leonine: *caritas potest . . . delere;* Parma: *caritas dicitur . . . delere;* Moos: *caritas . . . delere,* with *potest* being understood from an earlier phrase.

d. See *In III Sent.* d. 30, a. 5 (above).

e. The title as well as the listing of subquestions is our editorial addition.

er hope is emptied out in the state of glory; (3) whether something of the substance of the habits of faith and hope remains in the state of glory].

SUBQUESTION 1ª   Whether faith is emptied out in the state of glory

Objections:

It seems that faith will not be emptied out.

1. For faith is the foundation of the spiritual building. But the foundation remains unmoved, whatever is built upon it. Therefore faith is not emptied out at the advent of glory.

2. Further, nothing is expelled except by its contrary. But glory is not contrary to faith. Therefore faith is not emptied out at the advent of glory.

3. Further, in regard to things different in species, the perfect and the imperfect can certainly exist together in the same subject, e.g., that a man might have perfect geometry and imperfect grammar. But faith and the vision of glory are other in species. Therefore the vision of glory does not expel faith.

4. Further, opinion and science are related as imperfect and perfect knowledge; and in like manner, the "morning" and "evening" knowledge in angels.[443] But in men science and opinion remain together at the same time, and in the angels morning and evening knowledge remain together at the same time. Therefore faith remains together with the vision proper to the fatherland.[b]

On the contrary:

1. Against this is what the Apostle says in 1 Corinthians 13.[c]

2. Further, faith is of things that are not apparent to us. But in the fatherland, none of the things about which faith is had will be not apparent. Therefore faith will not be there.

a. Parallels: *ST* I-II, q. 67, a. 3; II-II, q. 4, a. 4, ad 1; III, q. 3, a. 3, ad 3; q. 18, a. 2; *De spe,* a. 4, ad 14; *De uirt. card.,* a. 4, ad 10.

b. *uisio patrie* has been rendered "vision proper to the fatherland" to avoid conveying that the *object* of the vision is the fatherland, as "vision of the fatherland" may suggest.

c. 1 Cor. 13:9–12 (RSV): "For our knowledge is imperfect and our prophecy is imperfect; but when the perfect comes, the imperfect will pass away. When I was a child, I spoke like a child, I thought like a child, I reasoned like a child; when I became a man, I gave up childish ways. For now we see in a mirror dimly, but

Response:

It should be said that in faith there is a certain sort of knowledge as well as a mode of knowing, because it knows "in a mirror and in an enigma."[a] Now, this mode is one of imperfection, and implies obscurity. Hence, since glory, at its advent, takes away all imperfection and obscurity, it will take away faith's *mode* (that is, it will take away faith as regards its mode of knowing),[b] but the *knowledge* of those things with which faith is concerned will remain—indeed, it will not then be enigmatic, but clear.

Replies to objections:

1. To the first, therefore, it should be said that faith is the foundation [of the spiritual building] with regard to what it has of knowledge, not with regard to what it has of enigma. Hence, with regard to that which is foundational,[c] it will remain.

2. To the second, it should be said that although the vision of glory is not contrary to faith with regard to what faith has of knowledge, it is nevertheless contrary to it with regard to what it has of enigma; and in reference to this aspect,[d] it expels it.

3. To the third, it should be said that perfection and imperfection of knowledge can go along well with each other about different things, but not about the same thing; and therefore someone can have simultaneously an imperfect knowledge about what pertains to one thing, and a perfect knowledge about what pertains to another, but there is no parallel in the case at hand, since faith and the vision of glory are about the same thing.

4. To the fourth, it should be said that, although there can be opinion and knowledge of the same thing, nevertheless they are of it, not according to the same middle term, but according to different middle terms; and therefore they can co-exist. But faith and the vision prop-

---

then face to face. Now I know in part; then I shall understand fully, even as I have been fully understood."

a. *in speculo et in enigmate,* a reference again to 1 Cor. 13:12. *Enigma* can be rendered "puzzle, riddle, obscure saying," whence *enigmatica* comes to mean "dim, dark, obscure." Since Thomas sees obscurity as the property that attaches to what is enigmatic (see the response to qa. 3), we have refrained from translating *enigma* by some other word.

b. *tollet quidem modum fidei quantum ad modum cognoscendi*

c. More literally, "with regard to that which is the foundation," *quandum ad id quod est fundamentum.*

d. *ex hac parte*

er to the fatherland are of the same thing *and* according to the same middle term, since faith assents to the first Truth on account of the first Truth itself, and similarly so does the vision of glory. And therefore the latter's perfection is not compatible with the former's imperfection. But morning and evening knowledge, although they are of the same thing in reality, are nevertheless not of the same thing according to the same [mode of] being, since morning knowledge is of a thing insofar as it has being in the Word, whereas evening knowledge is of a thing insofar as it has being in its own nature[a]—and therefore there is no parallel with faith and the vision of glory.

SUBQUESTION 2[b]   Whether hope is emptied out
in the state of glory

Objections:

Furthermore, it seems that neither will hope be emptied out.

1. For just as hope stands to good things, so fear stands to evil things. But servile fear will always remain in the damned. Therefore, similarly, hope will remain in the blessed.

2. Further, it is said in Ecclesiasticus 24:29: "They that eat me, shall yet hunger";[444] and the text is speaking of the enjoyment of divine wisdom that will take place [not only in this life but] also in the fatherland. But one who hungers looks forward to something in the future. Therefore the saints will look forward to something in the future, even in regard to the substantial reward.[c]

3. Further, in the faith that is emptied out, something common to faith and glory is found, namely vision. But in hope is found nothing that could remain in the fatherland, since the very substance of hope is expectation, which will not remain in the fatherland. Therefore it seems that hope will not be *emptied out* [but instead will be simply cancelled out].[445]

On the contrary:

1. "Who hopes for something he sees?" (Rom. 8:24). But the saints in the fatherland see whatever they looked forward to. Therefore hope will not be in them.

---

a. *esse in Verbo . . . esse in propria natura*

b. Parallels: *In III Sent.* d. 26, q. 2, a. 5, qa. 2, solutio (Moos, 845–46); *ST* I-II, q. 67, a. 4; II-II, q. 18, a. 2; *De spe*, a. 4; *De uirt. card.*, a. 4, ad 10.

c. "Look forward to" translates the verb *expectare*, but the noun is translated "expectation."

2. Further, hope is the expectation of *future* beatitude. But in the fatherland beatitude will not then be something of the future. Therefore neither will hope be there.

Response:

It should be said that judgment about habits must be taken from the acts of which they are the source. Now there are two kinds of acts:[a] an act that is of the imperfect *as* imperfect, such as motion; and an act that is of the perfect *as* perfect, such as an operation that follows upon a form.

It sometimes happens, however, that an act of the perfect is found in the imperfect, insofar as it is now participating in something of perfection, even as something of the act of the white is in the pallid. When therefore the imperfect arrives at perfection, the act of the imperfect, insofar as it has something of the perfection into which it was tending, remains with regard to what is of the *substance* of the act, but is taken away with regard to what belonged to the act's imperfection, as the stammering speech of a boy when he reaches a more mature age[b] is taken away with regard to what was of imperfection in that speech, while there remains whatever was of the perfection and substance of speech. But motion, which is an act of the imperfect [as such], when it attains the motion's terminus, does not remain with regard to anything that belongs to the substance of the act, but only with regard to the root according to which it was in motion to begin with[c]—which [root] was a certain proportion and order of the imperfect to perfection.

Now knowledge, as such, implies an act of the perfect; and therefore knowledge had in the state of imperfection remains [in the state of perfection] with regard to what belongs to knowledge itself, the imperfection being taken away.

Hope, however, insofar as it tends toward a difficult [good] as yet unpossessed and looked for in the future, is like an act of the imperfect, since it is, as it were, a certain motion. And therefore when it arrives at the perfect possession of good, that which belongs to expectation or hope, precisely as such, does not remain, but only that in which this expectation was rooted—viz., the order and proportion of that man to those goods now possessed, which were the same goods that hope was about, when they were not yet possessed. And therefore there is not

---

a. *est autem duplex actus*

b. *sicut loquela balbutientis pueri tollitur quando uenit ad perfectam etatem*

c. *quantum ad radicem secundum quam motus inerat*

set down anything the same in species with hope succeeding to it after this life, but rather what succeeds to it is simply the taking hold of,
or "comprehension," proper to beatitude, which bespeaks a *now actually possessed* order of man to God—the same order that hope was about
when it was not yet actually possessed. Hence that order is common to
both; and with regard to this order hope remains, but it passes away
with regard to the nature of its proper act.[a]

Replies to objections:

1. To the first, therefore, it should be said that those who will be
suffering punishments, since they are removed from the participation
of eternity, will always be in motion and succession, and on account of
this the fear of future evil can continue to be in them. But those who
will be in the fatherland will be supremely in the participation of eternity with regard to the substantial reward they receive; and therefore,
according to this participation, there will not be in them anything of a
reward still to come in the future, but they have the whole all at once;
hence hope does not remain in them.

2. To the second, it should be said that the "hunger" spoken of in
that text does not imply expectation of something still to come in the
future, but rather removes the notion of disgust about what is already
amply possessed.[b, 446] Hence with regard to the substantial reward,
there will not be any expectation in heaven, but only full enjoyment;
but with regard to some accidental things, or even about the robe of
the body,[c] there can be expectation there—yet not hope, as was said
above.[d]

3. To the third, it should be said that even in hope is found something that remains in the fatherland, namely, order and proportion
to a looked-for good. But that order will be perfect in the fatherland,
whereas in the wayfaring state it is imperfect due to the absence of the
good to which it is directed.

---

a. *Et ideo, cum ad perfectum uenerit, non manet id quod expectationis aut spei est, set
hoc tantum in quo hec expectatio radicabatur, scilicet ordo et proportio ipsius hominis ad
illa iam habita, quorum, dum non habebantur, erat spes. Et ideo non ponitur aliquid spe-
ciale succedens spei, set tentio siue compreensio beatitudinis, que dicit ordinem hominis ad
Deum iam habitum, cuius non habiti erat spes. Vnde ordo iste communis est utrobique.
Quantum ad hunc ordinem spes manet, set quantum ad naturam actus sui transit.*

b. *Ad secundum dicendum, quod illa fames non importat expectationem futuri, set
aufert fastidium iam habiti*

c. *stole corporis*

d. *In III Sent.* d. 26, q. 2, a. 1, qa. 2.

SUBQUESTION 3[a]   Whether anything of faith
and hope remains in the state of glory

Objections:

Furthermore, it seems that something of the substance of the habits of faith and hope will remain numerically the same.

1. For in every change there must be something common to both terms.[447] But faith and hope are changed into the goods of glory. Therefore *something* of the substance of the habits of faith and hope must remain numerically the same.

2. Further, just as the advent of charity is opposed to unformed faith not in regard to the substance of faith but in regard to its being unformed, so the advent of glory is opposed to faith not in regard to the substance of the vision, but only in regard to its imperfection. But the advent of charity takes away the unformedness of faith, which remains numerically the same habit of faith with respect to its substance, as was said above.[b] Therefore in like manner, the advent of glory takes away only imperfection, leaving the habit's substance numerically the same.

3. Further, when imperfect knowledge grows into perfect knowledge, the substance of knowledge is not taken away, just as the body's substance is not taken away when a child grows into an adult,[c] for the man remains numerically the same. But the Apostle compares the emptying out of faith to the perfection of knowledge and of age.[d] Therefore the substance of faith remains numerically the same.

On the contrary:

1. Forms, even as they are brought into being entirely from nothing, tend entirely into nothing when destroyed.[e] But because they are habits, faith and hope are certain forms. Therefore when they are destroyed at the advent of glory, as the Apostle says they are, it seems that nothing of them remains numerically the same.

2. Further, it is impossible that anything be the same in number which is not the same in species, as the Philosopher says about belief and opinion in *Topics* IV.[f] But faith and the vision proper to the father-

a. Parallels: *ST* I-II, q. 67, a. 5; II-II, q. 18, a. 2; *De uirt. card.,* a. 4, ad 10.

b. *In III Sent.* d. 23, q. 3, a. 4, qa. 1 (see above).

c. *quando ex puero fit uir*

d. See 1 Cor. 13:9–12.

e. *Forme quando destruuntur, sicut ex nichilo totaliter sunt, ita totaliter in nichilum tendunt*

f. *de fide et opinione.* To translate Aristotle's term as "faith" would, however, be

land differ in species much more than belief and opinion differ. Therefore the vision of faith and the vision proper to the fatherland[a] are not
numerically the same.

Response:

It should be said that the removal of anything that is of the substance of a thing induces the corruption of that thing, but the same
does not occur upon the removal of something related accidentally to
that thing. Now the precise imperfection that glory takes away from
faith is of the very substance of faith, pertaining to its species—which
is apparent if one considers the *ratio* of the object from which faith receives its species; for obscurity, which enigma implies, pertains to the
genus of knowledge. It is therefore necessary that as soon as that imperfection is removed, the substance and species of faith be destroyed,
just as if irrationality should be removed from a donkey,[b] the donkey
as such would be destroyed.[448]

Now, since faith is a simple accidental form not composed out of
matter and form, when it is destroyed nothing of faith remains the
same in number, but something remains the same in genus—as is evident when something white becomes black or conversely, where that
which pertains to color remains, yet the color is not the same in number but only the same in genus; whereas light [which makes color actually visible] remains the same in number whether it be perfect or
imperfect, since that imperfection or perfection does not pertain to the
species of light, but is accidental to it.

And one should speak in a similar way about hope, where the application of what was just said is even more apparent.[449]

Replies to objections:

1. To the first, therefore, it should be said that the common thing
that remains numerically the same in changes is the subject, whereas
the nature of the genus remains generically the same.[450] And thus, in
this transmutation [from wayfarer to comprehensor], the soul remains
numerically the same, but vision or knowledge remains only generically the same.

2. To the second, it should be said that the unformedness in ques-

---

misleading, given the subsequent history of the word. The reference is to *Topics*
IV, ch. 5 (125b36).
    a. *uisio fidei et patrie*
    b. *sicut si ab asino remouetur sua irrationalitas*

tion is not among the things pertaining to the species of faith, as enigmatic knowledge[a] is; and therefore no parallel can be drawn.

3. And a similar response should be made to the third.

ARTICLE 2[b]   Whether the charity of the wayfaring state will be emptied out in the fatherland

Objections:

Proceeding to the second, it seems that the charity of the wayfaring state will be emptied out.

1. For it says in 1 Corinthians 13:10: "When what is perfect shall come, what is in part will be emptied out." But the charity of the wayfaring state[c] is in part, since the commandment "Love the Lord your God with your whole heart," is not entirely fulfilled in this state, as was said above.[d] Therefore [such] charity will be emptied out in the fatherland.

2. Further, when the cause is destroyed, the effect is destroyed. But faith generates charity, as is said in a gloss on Matthew 1. When therefore faith is emptied out, charity too will be emptied out.

3. Further, just as faith is enigmatic, so too is charity, since the charity of the wayfaring state moves the affection toward what is not seen as it is in itself.[e] But faith, because it is enigmatic, will be emptied out in the fatherland; therefore charity too.

4. Further, motion ceases when it arrives at its terminus. But charity is a certain motion of the mind toward God.[f] When therefore it arrives at its terminus, charity will cease.

5. Further, in things that have a single *ratio,* progress can be made from the one to the other if they differ according to perfect and imperfect.[g] But the charity of the wayfaring state, although it can increase, can never attain to the mode charity has in the fatherland.

a. Noting many discrepancies among the MSS, Moos reads: *cognitio aenigmatica,* which makes sense in the context. The Leonine editors read *perfectio enigmatica,* which would have to be taken as a paradoxical expression: faith is a genuine perfection, yet enigmatic in mode.

b. Parallels: *ST* I-II, q. 67, a. 6; *De ueritate,* q. 27, a. 5, ad 6; *De spe,* a. 4, ad 7, 13, et 14; *De uirt. card.,* a. 4, ad 10; *Super I Cor.* 13, lec. 3.

c. The phrases "of the wayfaring state" and "in the fatherland" have been added for clarity here and in the third objection; they are implicit in both arguments.

d. *In III Sent.* d. 23, q. 3, a. 4 (see above).

e. *per speciem*   f. *quidam motus mentis in Deum*

g. *Ea que sunt unius rationis, unum potest in alterum proficere, si differant secundum perfectum et imperfectum*

Therefore it follows that the charity of the wayfaring state and the charity of the fatherland are not of a single species; and thus, it seems that charity is emptied out [at the transition from this-worldly to heavenly charity].

On the contrary:

1. "Charity never falls away" (1 Cor. 13:8).[a]

2. Further, the beloved's presence does not take away love, but increases it. Now charity is the love of God. Therefore, when we shall see God present, charity will not be taken away but rather increased.

Response:

It should be said that love, according to the *ratio* of its essence, does not imply anything of imperfection, but rather implies simply perfection, inasmuch as it implies affection's having a terminus of rest, and a certain transformation of the lover into the one loved.[b] Hence glory, at its advent, will take away nothing of those things that pertain to the essence of charity. And therefore charity will not be destroyed.

Replies to objections:

1. To the first, therefore, it should be said that that imperfection is accidental to charity; and therefore, when it has been removed, charity will nonetheless remain the same in number.

2. To the second, it should be said that faith is a cause of charity by reason of the *knowledge* faith imparts, but such knowledge will remain,[c] as was said.

3. To the third, it should be said that [the condition signified by the word] enigma is essential to faith, since it pertains to the *ratio* of faith's proper object; but this condition is accidental to charity, and so the same argument cannot be made.

4. To the fourth, it should be said that "to love" bespeaks, not a motion that is an act of the imperfect, but a motion that is an act of the perfect, like sensing and understanding, as the Philosopher says in *On the Soul* III.[d] Therefore the argument does not follow.

a. *Caritas numquam excidit,* as translated in the Douay-Rheims; the RSV has "Charity never ends."

b. *amor secundum rationem sue speciei non importat aliquid imperfectionis, set magis perfectionem, in quantum importat terminationem affectus et quandam informationem in re amata.* For discussion of this notion, see *In III Sent.* d. 27, q. 1, a. 1 (above).

c. *fides est causa caritatis ratione cognitionis, cognitio autem manebit.* The reference is to the preceding article, qa. 1.

d. Aristotle, *On the Soul* III, ch. 7 (431a4ff.).

5. To the fifth, it should be said that a wayfarer's charity, so long as he remains a wayfarer, cannot attain to the perfect charity of the fatherland because of his present condition, insofar as he does not perfectly possess what he loves—*not* so far as that which is proper to the *ratio* of charity is concerned.[a]

ARTICLE 3[b]   Whether the order of love obtaining in this life[c] is also to be found in Christ or in the saints who are in the fatherland

Proceeding to the third, [we divide the article into three subquestions: (1) whether the order of love obtaining in this life with regard to love of enemies is also to be found in Christ and the saints in the fatherland; (2) whether the order of love obtaining in this life with respect to love of self and neighbor is also to be found in the saints in the fatherland; (3) whom Christ loved more, Peter or John].[d]

SUBQUESTION 1   Whether the order of love obtaining in this life with regard to love of enemies is also to be found in Christ and the saints in the fatherland

Objections:

It seems that the order of love obtaining in this life with regard to love of enemies is neither in Christ nor in the saints who are in the fatherland.

1. For the only enemies of the saints, at least after the day of judgment, will be demons and the damned. But charity is not had toward those, as was said above.[e] Therefore the saints will not love enemies.

2. Further, in them there will be the highest conformity of the will to God. But God does not love the enemies of the saints, but hates them. Therefore neither Christ nor the blessed will love their enemies.

3. Further, whosoever loves anyone from charity wishes the good of eternal life for him. But Christ did not wish this to enemies, nor do the

---

a. *hoc quod caritas uie, manens in uia, non potest peruenire ad perfectionem caritatis patrie est propter statum uiatoris, et non quantum ad id quod est de ratione caritatis, in quantum uiator non possidet perfecte quod amat*

b. Parallels to subquestions 1 and 2: *ST* II-II, q. 26, a. 13; *De caritate* a. 9, ad 12.

c. *ordo dilectionis qui modo est,* literally "the order of love that now is," that holds in this life.

d. The listing of subquestions is our editorial addition.

e. *In III Sent.* d. 28, a. 5 (see above).

blessed wish it to them; since if they had wished it, it would surely have come to be.[451] Therefore they do not love their enemies from charity.

On the contrary:

4. To love one's enemy pertains to the perfection of charity. But in Christ and in the blessed there is the fullest and most perfect charity. Therefore they love enemies.

5. Further, Christ loved from charity those for whom he died: "No greater love has a man than this, that he should lay down his life for his friends" (Jn. 15:13). But [we are taught expressly that] he died for enemies (Rom. 5:6–10). Therefore he loved enemies; and for the same reason, the blessed love them.[452]

Response:

It should be said that "enemies of Christ" can be taken in two ways: either with respect to their final departure from him, as with those who are damned (either actually or in the divine foreknowledge); or with respect to their present state of enmity only, as Saul was at a certain time.[453]

With respect to the former kind of enemies, there is in Christ the same *ratio* of love as there is in us toward those whom we know to be damned, because we love their nature. And the nature alone being considered, we would wish eternal life for them; but taking into consideration divine justice as well as their merits, we do not will this good for them, because we love the divine justice more than their nature. The first will [which looks to the nature alone] is antecedent will, while the second [which looks to their merits] is consequent will. And so, [equipped with this distinction, we may say that] Christ loved enemies who were really damned or were going to be damned [in the sense that he was] willing good for them by his antecedent will, which is not always fulfilled, but not [in the sense that he was] willing good for them by his consequent will, as neither does God. And the same *ratio* holds for the other blessed concerning those who are actually damned; but concerning those who are going to be damned, perhaps they do not know who all of them are.[a]

But with respect to the other kind of enemies—those, that is, who are enemies only at the present time but who will later become his friends—Christ loved them by both antecedent and consequent will,

---

a. *de dampnandis forte nesciunt de omnibus qui sunt*

and wrought good things for them, because the death he endured was efficacious for them.ᵃ

And from this, the response to the objections (1–5) is evident.

SUBQUESTION 2   Whether the order of love obtaining in this life with respect to love of self and neighbor is also to be found in the saints in the fatherland⁴⁵⁴

Objections:

It seems that the order of charity obtaining in this life with respect to love of self, neighbor, those who are close to us, and outsiders,ᵇ is not in the saints.

1. For Augustine, in the book *On the True Religion,* says: "Perfect charity is when we love more strongly what is more good, and love less what is less good."ᶜ But there will be perfect charity in the fatherland. Therefore anyone in that state will love a neighbor who is better than himself more than he will love himself, and similarly he will love an outsider more than he will love someone close according to the flesh, if the former is better than the latter.ᵈ

2. Further, in the fatherland there will be perfect conformity of the human will to God. But God loves the better ones more. Therefore, too, each one there will love the one who is better than himself more than he will love himself.

3. Further, he for whom a greater good is desired is the one more loved. But in the fatherland, each man wills a greater good for the one who is better than himself than he wills for himself, since each one wills the good that he himself has, nor does he seekᵉ for anyone what

a. *Set quantum ad alios inimicos, secundum presentem statum tantum, diligebat et ad eos bona operabatur quod pro eis mortem subiit.* As this sentence could be misunderstood in a Jansenistic way, which would not be consistent with Thomas's theology of grace, we have expanded the phrases as he might have done.

b. *quantum ad se et proximum et propinquos et extraneos.* The latter two could also be rendered "those who are closer and those who are distant," but the emphasis in such discussions is usually placed on the main examples of these categories—namely, those who belong to the family (parents, siblings, spouses, children) and those who are outside the family. "Outsiders" preserves a desirable vagueness that can range from the man across the street, who is not a part of my family circle, to "perfect strangers" across the globe whom I will never meet in this life.

c. Augustine, *On the True Religion,* ch. 48 (PL 34:164).

d. *Ergo proximum meliorem se plus diliget aliquis quam se ipsum, et similiter extraneum quam propinquum secundum carnem*

e. "seek": *appetit*

that one does not have, for if he did, his desire would not be at rest.[455] Therefore he loves the one better than himself more than he loves himself.

On the contrary:

1. Glory perfects nature. But that a man should love himself more than he loves another is an order proceeding from the nature of man. Therefore glory does not remove this order.

2. Further, were someone to neglect his own salvation for the salvation of another, he would commit a sin. But in the fatherland there will be nothing disordered. Therefore a man there will always love his own salvation more than that of another; and thus he will love himself more than another.[456]

Response:

It should be said that there is a twofold opinion about this matter.

For certain ones say that in the fatherland God will be all in all, and the whole mind, resting in God, will have God as the whole *ratio* of love; and so it will love God above all things, and others so much the more as they are nearer to God—even others more than itself, if they are better.

But that position does not seem reasonably said. For each one will love to enjoy God as much as he will love God himself; and since he will love God above all things, above all things he will want to enjoy God; and therefore he will wish this enjoyment of God more for himself than for another. Hence it seems that he will love himself more than another. Moreover, the affection of love does not rest in anything except its proper object. But just as the proper object of love is the good, so the proper object of a particular man's love is that man's good. Hence it follows that he will love God supremely, insofar as God is that man's highest good.[a, 457] Thus it is not necessary that one love someone else more to the extent that he is simply nearer to God, but rather, he should love someone more to the extent that he is nearer to God insofar as God is one's own good.

And therefore what others say seems more probable—namely, that each one in the fatherland will love himself more than he loves his neighbor.

a. *Affectus dilectionis non quiescit in aliquo nisi in proprio obiecto. Sicut autem proprium obiectum amoris est bonum, ita proprium obiectum amoris istius hominis est bonum istius. Vnde et Deum summe diliget, in quantum est summum bonum suum.* See earlier discussions of this topic: *In III Sent.* d. 28, a. 6 (above); d. 29, aa. 1, 3, 4, and 5 (above).

But as to the comparison of those who are close to us and outsiders, I believe that, simply speaking, each one will love an outsider who is better more than a blood relative who is not as good, because in the fatherland the order of love is looked to more as regards nearness to God than as regards nearness to self, although it is necessary that both be looked to. Hence among those who are equally good, one will love those who are nearer to oneself more than those who are more distant, but among the unequally good, one will love those who are better more than one loves those who are nearer.[a]

Replies to objections:

1. To the first, therefore, it should be said that [in explaining this statement of Augustine's] one ought to understand that a man loves more the greater goods that are also greater for himself, just as he loves spiritual goods more than bodily goods.[b]

2. To the second, it should be said that our will, precisely by following the motion naturally established in it by God, will be conformed to the divine will.[c, 458]

3. To the third, it should be said that by consequent will, he [viz., the saint in heaven] wills a *greater* good for another than for himself, whereas he wills the good for himself *more intensely*; but by antecedent will, he wills a greater good for himself. Yet this difference does not impede the resting of desire, since the antecedent will is not will simply but conditionally, or a sort of "willingness,"[d] as certain ones say.

SUBQUESTION 3[e]   Whom Christ loved more, Peter or John

Objections:

It is asked whom Christ loved more, Peter or John; and it seems that it was John.

a. *Vnde de equaliter bonis plus diliget proximiorem, set de inequalibus diliget meliorem*

b. On the point being made here, see, among other texts, *In III Sent.* d. 29, a. 5 (above).

c. *in hoc ipso uoluntas nostra uoluntati diuine conformabitur, quod sequetur motum naturaliter sibi impositum a Deo*

d. *uelleitas quedam*

e. Parallel: *ST* I, q. 20, a. 4, ad 3. In the *ST* text, having nicely summarized the arguments, an older Thomas concludes with a touch of hesitation: "Nevertheless, it may seem presumptuous to pass judgment on these matters; since the Lord, and no other, is the weigher of spirits, as it says in Proverbs 16:2."

1. For we read in the last chapter of John (21:20): "Peter turned and saw following them the disciple whom Jesus loved." But this remark is not said as if he loved only that one and no other. Therefore it was said on account of the eminence of Jesus' love for John.

2. Further, a love in which affection does not correspond to the effect or signs of love is a feigned love. Now, since Christ showed a greater familiarity to John than to Peter, and his love was in no way feigned, it seems that he loved John more than Peter.

On the contrary:

"I love them who love me" (Prov. 8:17). But Peter loved more, as is evident from the last chapter of John.[a] Therefore he too was more loved.

Response:

It should be said, as is said by others who take up the question,[b] that Peter loved Christ more by the love that is poured out from Christ into the members [of his mystical body], but John loved him more by the love that rests in Christ himself.[c] To Peter, therefore, the Lord committed the care of the members, while to John he committed the care of his mother—a care that concerned more directly his own person.[d]

Hence Peter, too, was more loved by Christ with regard to interior effect,[e] since a greater gift of charity was then bestowed upon him,[f] whereas John was more loved with regard to signs of exterior familiarity—and this, on account of four causes: first, because John symbolizes the contemplative life, which involves a greater familiarity with God, although the active life that Peter symbolizes is more fruitful and more laborious; second, on account of age, because John was a youth; third,

---

a. See Jn. 21:15–17, where Jesus asks Peter pointedly, three times: "Simon . . . do you love me more than these?" and receives three times the answer: "Yes, Lord."

b. *dicendum, quod, sicut dicitur:* implied is a reference to other discussions of the same question in Thomas's predecessors.

c. *in Christo sistit*

d. *Iohanni autem curam matris, que ad personam ipsius specialius spectabat*

e. Leonine and Moos: *ad effectum interiorem;* Parma: *ad affectum interiorem*

f. *donum maioris caritatis erat ei tunc collatum.* St. Thomas is speaking of Jn. 21, which many of the Fathers and schoolmen understood as a scene that displayed the actual bestowal or conferral of the papal office promised in Mt. 16. Thus it seems best to interpret this remark as a reference not to the habit of charity (as if *donum caritatis* meant the gift of the infused virtue itself), but to the special office conferred upon Peter out of Christ's generosity (taking *caritatis* as pointing to the origin or cause of the *donum*).

on account of his chastity; fourth, on account of his inborn gentleness.

And through this response, the solution to the objections is evident, since each one loved Christ more [in some respect], and in a certain way was more loved by him.

ARTICLE 4[a, 459]   Whether the knowledge that we have here below will be entirely taken away in the fatherland

Objections:

Proceeding to the fourth, it seems that the knowledge that we have here below will be entirely taken away in the fatherland.[b]

1. For it says in 1 Corinthians 13:8: "Knowledge will be destroyed." But an accident that is destroyed is entirely taken away. Therefore knowledge will be entirely taken away.

2. Further, faith is more spiritual than [other] knowledge.[460] But faith will be taken away; therefore knowledge too.

3. Further, the actual consideration of knowledge is the most delightful of delightful things.[c] If therefore the knowledge acquired here remains, some cleric great in learning will have more joy in heaven than some old woman whose charity will be greater[d]—which seems to be impossible.

4. Further, those who are in the fatherland know everything in the Word of which they had knowledge here, and many more things and much more perfectly. If therefore knowledge has no other reason to be except for knowing, in vain would past knowledge remain in the blessed.

5. Further, habit is ordered to act. Where the act does not remain, therefore, neither can the habit remain, since in vain would it remain. But the act of knowledge that takes place here below will not remain in the fatherland, since the consideration of various kinds of knowledge[e] consists in understanding with the aid of a phantasm, not only in acquiring knowledge to begin with, but also in considering things

a. Parallels: *In IV Sent.* d. 50, q. 1, aa. 1 and 2; *ST* I, q. 89, a. 1 and a. 5; I-II, q. 67, a. 2; *SCG* II, ch. 81; *De ueritate*, q. 19, a. 1; *De anima*, a. 15; *Quodl.* III, q. 9, a. 1 and XII, q. 9, a. 1; *Super I Cor.* ch. 13, lec. 3.

b. *Videtur quod scientia quam modo habemus totaliter tolletur.* The question asks whether the *scientia* (translated throughout as "knowledge") that we acquire "here below," in this life, will be canceled out in the state of glory.

c. *Consideratio scientie est de delectabilibus maxime*

d. *aliquis magnus clericus habebit plus de gaudio quam aliqua uetula que erit maioris caritatis*

e. *consideratio scientiarum*

we have already learned. Hence, when the organ of imagination is harmed, the intellect's operation is impeded, even as to things one already knew. Therefore [since the act of understanding with a phantasm will not be in the fatherland, at least before the resurrection of the body,] neither will the habit of knowledge remain.[a, 461]

6. Further, the consideration of knowledge as we now have it is collative.[462] But that mode, where knowledge has to be *gathered*,[b] will not be in the fatherland, since if it were, it would follow that study and disputation would take place there, which is absurd. Therefore knowledge acquired here will not remain in the fatherland.

On the contrary:

1. The Master in Distinction 1 of Book II said—and many philosophers also say—that the soul is placed in the body so that by means of this union, it might be perfected by various kinds of knowledge.[c] But in vain would the soul be placed in the body with a view to that purpose, unless knowledge [acquired here below] remained in it after the body perished. Therefore [such] knowledge will remain.

2. Further, it is beyond doubt that those who are in hell continue to know something of what they once knew, as is evident from the rich man, who in his torments remembered what had belonged to him in this life.[d] But beyond the knowledge they had here, no new knowledge will be added to the damned.[e, 463] Therefore prior knowledge will remain in them.

3. Further, if knowledge is destroyed with the body, it will be shown to be a temporal good.[f] And so the pursuit of knowledge will be reckoned as a case of solicitude for temporal things, which seems absurd.

---

a. *Ergo nec scientia remanebit*

b. "collative": *collatiua;* "that mode, where knowledge has to be gathered": *iste modus conferendi*

c. *anima posita est in corpore, ut scientiis perficiatur,* i.e., in order that the many kinds of knowledge can be learned by the soul, so as to perfect its capacity.

d. *Constat quod illi qui sunt in inferno aliquid cognoscunt etiam de his que prius cognouerunt, sicut patet de diuite, qui suorum memoriam habebat.* The allusion is to Lk. 16:19–31, where the rich man after his death remembers clearly who Abraham and Lazarus are, who his family members are, all the good things he received in his life, and the poor treatment he gave to Lazarus.

e. *Set eis non addetur alia cognitio quam hic habuerunt*

f. The text says *erit bonum temporale,* but the sense is: the destruction will show what it really is, namely a good essentially immersed in matter and motion.

Response:

It should be said that in the knowledge we have in our present state, there are three things to consider: the habit, the act, and the mode of acting. The *mode* of acting is that we understand[a] with a phantasm, since in the wayfaring state the doctrine of the Philosopher in *On the Soul* III is true,[b] namely that the soul would never understand without a phantasm—not only with respect to acquiring knowledge, but also for the consideration of things already known, since the phantasms stand to the intellect as sensible things to the senses.[464] It is characteristic of the *act* of knowledge that [in our present state] we know conclusions by tracing them back to first principles known *per se*; while finally the *habit* of knowledge is a certain quality of a man, fitting him to perform this act.

Now the aforesaid *mode* of understanding comes to be that of the human soul for two reasons. One reason[c] is that the human soul is, in the order of nature, last among grades of intellect. Hence, its possible intellect stands to all intelligible things as prime matter stands to all sensible forms; and on account of this it cannot proceed into act before it receives the species of things, which comes about through sense and imagination. The other reason is that the human soul is the form of the body. Hence, its operation must be the operation of the whole man; and therefore in man the body communicates with the intellective soul not merely as an instrument by which the latter carries out an operation, but as representing an object (namely, the phantasm) to the soul; and so it happens that the soul [in our present state] is incapable of understanding without phantasms even the things it already knows.[d, 465]

a. Thomas phrases this discussion abstractly: *ut intelligat cum phantasmate,* as if the knowledge is the subject of the sentence, but in fact he is describing the way *we* know in the wayfaring state. Similarly, in the next sentence he writes: *Actus autem scientie proprius est ut cognoscat conclusiones,* again as if the subject were the knowledge.

b. Aristotle, *On the Soul* III, ch. 7 (431a16ff.).

c. "for two reasons. One reason" translates: *ex duobus. Vno modo,* etc. Though Thomas is saying "In one way . . . In another way," he is talking about the "reasons why" the mode of understanding just described belongs to the human soul; he will then show how, and to what extent, they are affected by the separation of soul and body.

d. *Vnde oportet quod operatio eius sit operatio totius hominis. Et ideo communicat ibi corpus, non sicut instrumentum per quod operetur, set sicut representans obiectum, scilicet phantasma. Et inde contingit quod anima non potest intelligere sine phantasmate etiam ea que prius nouit.* (The last phrase could also be: "the things it previously learned.")

Accordingly, in the soul separated from the body, the soul's *nature* will remain, but its actual union with the body will not remain; and therefore, the soul being considered just in its own nature, it will not need the phantasms with respect to the consideration of what it knew before, but only with respect to the consideration of what it is obliged to know for the first time; and thus, it will be able to consider what it knew before, not indeed by using a phantasm, but out of the habit of science previously had. But it will not be able to know things that it did not know before, except to the extent that they can be elicited from what it already knows, or insofar as other species are divinely infused into it. For to say that the soul, according to what it now has in its nature, cannot understand in any way without the body, is very much akin to [what is said by] those who maintain that the soul perishes with the body, since, as is said in *On the Soul* I,[a] if none of the operations it has can be without the body, neither can it itself be without the body, for natural operation follows upon nature.

Now in the aforesaid *act* of knowledge, there are two things to be considered: the motion of inquiry and of discursive reason, and the terminus, viz., the certainty had about conclusions insofar as they have been traced back to first principles. However, such motion is a thing of imperfection with regard to the need for discoursing in order that certainty be brought about.[b, 466] And therefore in the blessed the act of knowledge will not remain with respect to the necessity of such motion, but with respect to the certainty alone.

And therefore it seems it should be said, according to what certain ones say, that in the fatherland there will be another *mode* of understanding for the separated souls, since they will exercise their knowledge without having recourse to phantasms.[c] But after the resurrection it will be possible for both modes of knowing to coexist, insofar as the soul will not then be in subjection to the body but will rule it completely.[d, 467] Yet in the saints the *act* will be changed, since it will remain with respect to its terminus but not with respect to the discoursing [that now goes along with achieving that terminus]. (In the damned, however, this [discoursing] is not removed, so that a need for collation remains.) And thus, the *habit* of science remains in them with

a. Aristotle, *On the Soul* I, ch. 1 (403a1).

b. *Motus autem ille imperfectionis est quantum ad necessitatem discurrendi ut causetur certitudo*

c. *quia sine phantasmate considerabunt*

d. *Set post resurrectionem poterit esse uterque modus, in quantum anima non subiacebit corpori, set ex toto ei dominabitur*

respect to its substance; for it seems absurd to say that a habit might remain when its act in no way remains, since a habit is nothing other than a making-able for acting.ᵃ

Replies to objections:

1. To the first, therefore, it should be said that knowledge will be destroyed with respect to *mode* and will be changed with respect to *act*, but will remain with respect to *habit*, as was said.

2. To the second, it should be said that the mode of imperfection is of the essence of faith and belongs to its *ratio*, whereas the mode of knowing by means of phantasms does not belong to the *ratio* of knowledge, but attaches to it owing to the condition of a given subject.ᵇ

3. To the third, it should be said that it is not unfitting that one who has less charity has more joy with respect to some act of his soul, since nevertheless he has less joy about God, which is the essential reward.

4. To the fourth, it should be said that to know something in many ways is not in vain, even as Christ too had natural knowledge of things he knew in the Word.

5. To the fifth, it should be said that this mode of knowing [viz., turning to phantasms] attaches to knowledge owing to the state of the one in whom that knowledge is, for the phantasm, since it is intelligible in potency and not in act, is *not* the proximate and proper object of the intellect, whose *per se* object is rather the actually understood species.

6. To the sixth, it should be said that in the blessed there will be the act of knowledge not in regard to the activity of discourse, but only in regard to the terminus of knowledge, namely certainty.ᶜ Moreover, there would be no need for study or discussion among the blessed,ᵈ since of all the things they might wish to consider, they could draw their knowledge from the Wordᵉ or have it by way of direct illumination from superiors. The damned, however, will have no leisure for discussion due to the weight of punishment bearing down on them.ᶠ

---

a. *habitus nichil est aliud quam habilitas ad actum.* The word play is impossible to capture.

b. *set accidit ei ex conditione subiecti*

c. *non erit actus scientie quantum ad discursum, set quantum ad terminum certitudinis*

d. Leonine: *beatos*; Moos: *bonos*

e. *omnium illorum que considerare uellent in Verbo cognitionem possent accipere*

f. *Dampnatis autem non uacabit disputare, penarum pondere pressis*

Notes on the text of Lombard

*[Again, the statement] "a charity that can be forsaken never was true" [is not to be referred to the essence of charity, but to its efficacy, because a charity that is forsaken does not make man truly blessed, nor does it lead to the true good].*ᵃ

This assertion is true, if charity be forsaken on account of a weakness of love—in other words, such that someone would love God less than that thing for which he commits a sin. For in that case, there would not be true charity.⁴⁶⁸

*[Although this and the rest of the things that are said about charity] can be understood of the perfect, [i.e., the charity that only the perfect have. Which, once had, is not lost; however, the beginnings of charity at times grow to greatness, at times falter and fail].*ᵇ

That charity is called "perfect" which is in those who are confirmed in good, whether in the wayfaring state or in the fatherland.⁴⁶⁹ Or it is understood not that charity cannot be lost [by the perfect], but rather that it is difficult for it to be lost [by them].

a. From Lombard's text (Grottaferrata ed., 2:182.19–22): *Item quod dicitur, 'caritas nunquam fuisse vera, quae deseri potest', non ad essentiam caritatis refertur, sed ad efficientiam: quia non efficit caritas quae deseritur hominem vere beatum, non* [other MSS: *nec*] *perducit ad verum bonum.* Thomas is commenting simply on the words *caritas quae deseri potest,* but this phrase has to be placed in its context in order to make sense.

b. From Lombard's text (Grottaferrata ed., 2:183.1–3): *Potest tamen hoc, et cetera quae de caritate dicta sunt, de perfecta intelligi, quam soli perfecti habent. Quae semel habita, non amittitur; exordia vero caritatis aliquando crescunt, aliquando deficiunt.* In the Moos ed. (967, n. 3) these lines are punctuated somewhat differently: *Potest tamen hoc et cetera quae de caritate dicta sunt, de perfecta intelligi, quam soli perfecti habent, quae semel habita non amittitur. Exordia vero caritatis . . .*

DISTINCTION 32[a] [GOD'S LOVE FOR CREATURES]

Division of the text

"To the foregoing discussion, something should be added [concerning the love of God by which he himself loves us]." After the Master has determined about the love of charity by which we love God, here he determines about the love by which God loves us.[b]

And this consideration is divided into two parts. In the first, he shows how God loves every creature; in the second, he raises a question about the reprobate whom God does not seem to love, at the place where the text says: "Concerning the reprobate, however, [who are prepared not for life but for death, if inquiry is made whether it ought to be conceded that God loved them from eternity, we say that this is to be conceded simply about the elect alone]."

The former is divided into two parts. In the first, he determines about the love of God according to which God is said, absolutely [speaking], to love the creature; in the second, he determines about the degrees of divine love according to which he is said to love one thing more and another less, where the text says: "Now since the love of God is immutable [and therefore neither intensified nor diminished, if one inquires into the rationale for saying that he loves this more or less than he loves that. . .]."

And this part is divided into two parts. In the first, he determines about the order of love with respect to different objects; in the second, with respect to the same object, where he says: "If, however, inquiry be made [whether one and the same thing is loved by God more at one time than at another, a distinction needs to be made in how the statement is understood]."

About the former, he does three things. First, he raises the question.

---

a. Latin text: provisional critical ed. of the Leonine Commission; cf. Moos ed., 1000–1013.

b. Throughout this discussion, "love" nearly always translates *dilectio* and *diligere*. As the Brief Introduction explains (pp. xxi–xxiv; cf. the Full Introduction), Thomas is accustomed to using *amor* and *amare* to refer to the same thing, as he does in the first article here.

Second, he determines it, where he says: "Nevertheless it can be safely understood," etc. Third, he confirms the solution, where he says: "For [the love of God] is considered in two ways," etc.

Here, we will inquire into five things: (1) whether God loves the creature; (2) whether he loves every creature; (3) whether he loves [creatures] from eternity; (4) whether he loves them all equally; (5) what he loves more, what less or equally.[a]

ARTICLE 1[b]   Whether it accords with God's nature that he love a creature

Objections:

Proceeding to the first, it seems that loving a creature does not accord with God's nature.[c]

1. For love implies a certain passion of the soul. But other passions of the soul, such as anger and things of this sort, are not in God, except according to effect and by way of likeness.[470] Therefore neither is love in him.

2. Further, across a great distance there cannot be love. Hence, friends do not desire the greatest of goods for their friends, lest the friendship be dissolved, as the Philosopher says in *Ethics* IX.[d, 471] But there is no distance as great as that between Creator and creature. Therefore there cannot be a love of God for a creature.

3. Further, love bears the lover into the beloved, so that he now lives the life of the beloved, as Dionysius says in the book *On the Divine Names*.[e] But God is not borne into anything other, since he is unmov-

---

a. The Parma ed. lists only articles 1, 2, 4, and 5, numbering them 1, 2, 3, and 4, although in fact the text still contains five articles. The Moos and Leonine editions correct this mistake. The first and fifth articles are given more focused scopes when they are formulated in their own places: whether it *belongs to God* [*Deo competit*] to love the creature, and whether God loves more (a) the now-just man foreknown to be lost than a sinner predestined for eternal life, (b) the penitent than the innocent, (c) man than angel, (d) the human race than Christ.

b. Parallels: *ST* I, q. 20, a. 1; q. 82, a. 5, ad 1; *SCG* I, ch. 91; *In De div. nom.* 4, lec. 9.

c. It is difficult to get just the right word for the expression *competere* with the dative, as in the present inquiry: *Videtur quod Deo non competat creaturam amare.* Does it accord or agree with, suit or befit who or what God is, that he should love a creature?

d. "desire": *optant.*—The reference is to Aristotle, *Ethics* IX, ch. 7 (1159a6).

e. Pseudo-Dionysius, *On the Divine Names*, ch. 4, n. 13 (PG 3:711). The Areopagite is commenting on Paul's statement in Gal. 2:20: "I live, yet no longer I, but Christ lives in me." For further discussion of the idea that *amor transfert aman-*

ing; rather he draws all to himself, as is said in John 12:32.[a] Therefore he does not love the creature.

4. Further, the one loving is, in a way, subjected to the beloved, insofar as the lover's affection is informed by the beloved, as was said above.[b] But God is in no way subjected to a creature. In no way, therefore, does he love a creature.

5. Further, all our perfection has the divine perfection for exemplar.[c] But every virtue is a perfection of the mind. Therefore, since certain other virtues are not in God—for example temperance and things of this sort—it seems that neither is charity.

On the contrary:

1. Just as God's essence is the exemplar of every creature, so God's goodness[d] is the cause of all goodness in the creature. But God, in knowing his essence, knows all the things that have it for exemplar.[e] Therefore in loving his own goodness, he loves all the things that participate goodness from him.

2. Further, "God so loved the world [that he gave his only-begotten Son]" (Jn. 3:16).[f]

3. Further, Dionysius says that "divine love does not allow itself to be without seed."[g, 472]

Response:

It should be said that to each thing possessed of knowledge, its own proper good is lovable—not only by a natural love, but by an animal or an intellectual love. Hence, since in God there is perfect knowledge of himself, he loves his own goodness. Now the good of a thing refers not only to good present in it itself, but also to good present in another by way of that other's likeness to it.[h] Since, therefore, the goodness that is

---

tem in amatum, see *In III Sent.* d. 27, q. 1, a. 1 (above), and other articles in the same question.

a. "unmoving": *immobilis.* In Jn. 12:32 it is Jesus who says: "I, when I am lifted up from the earth, will draw all [men] to myself." Here the Latin does not say "all men" but simply *omnia,* all things.

b. See esp. *In III Sent.* d. 27, q. 1, a. 1 (above).

c. *Omnia nostra perfectio a diuina perfectione exemplatur*

d. *essentia sua . . . bonitas sua*　　　　　e. *omnia que ab ipsa exemplantur*

f. St. Thomas quotes only the beginning of the verse, since it establishes the point he wants to make: *Sic Deus dilexit mundum.* The Parma ed. cites the verse in its entirety.

g. Pseudo-Dionysius, *On the Divine Names,* ch. 4, n. 10 (PG 3:707).

h. *Bonum autem alicuius non solum dicitur secundum hoc quod in ipso est, set etiam secundum quod in alio est per similitudinem*

in creatures is a likeness of the divine goodness, it follows that he himself loves the creature.

Replies to objections:

1. To the first, therefore, it should be said that certain passions imply in their *ratio* some material transmutation, and for this reason they cannot be transferred to God except by way of likeness, such as anger, and in like manner, those that imply a defect, such as sadness, and anger again, insofar as it is caused by sadness. But there are certain passions that do not imply in their *ratio* anything material or any defect, such as pleasure or delight.[a] Hence, as the Philosopher proves in *Ethics* VII,[b] delight is found in intellectual activity, not just in bodily activity; and it is on account of this that delight can be posited in God—not indeed in the manner of a passion, but as (according to our mode of understanding) consequent upon his simple and motionless activity.[c] Hence, the Philosopher says in *Ethics* VII: "God rejoices in a simple activity."[d] And a like response is to be given concerning love in God.

2. To the second, it should be said that between those who are at a great distance, love can certainly exist, but not friendship, since they are not sharing a life together, which is the activity proper to friendship.[e] God, however, though he stands infinitely distant from the creature, nevertheless works actively in all things and exists in all things;[f] and therefore even the *ratio* of friendship can be preserved in his regard.

3. To the third, it should be said that, in a way, *every* love bears the lover into the beloved, yet in two different ways: in one way, insofar as the lover is borne into participating those things that belong to the beloved; in the other way, so that the lover communicates to the beloved those things that are his own.[473] In the former way, therefore, God is not borne into the creature loved by him,[g] but in the latter way [one can say that he is borne, by love, into the creature,] insofar as he com-

---

a. A single word in Latin, *delectatio,* but hard to convey with a single word in English, since "pleasure" leans more toward the sensual, and "delight" more toward the spiritual. Since the discussion moves in the direction of God's *delectatio,* the latter option has been chosen, but the former should not be forgotten.

b. Aristotle, *Ethics* VII, ch. 14 (1154a8ff.).

c. *operationem suam simplicem et sine motu consequens per modum intelligendi*—the point being that delight is really identical to God's activity and is a "consequence" of it only according to the way in which we conceive the notions.

d. *Deus simplici operatione gaudet.*—Aristotle, *Ethics* VII, ch. 15 (1154b26).

e. *quia non conuersantur simul, quod est proprium amicitie*

f. *operatur in omnibus et in omnibus est*

g. *in amatum quod est creatura*—literally, "into the beloved that is the creature."

municates his goodness to it. And this is the sense in which Dionysius says, in chapter 4 of *On the Divine Names*, that "even God himself suffers ecstasy through love."[a, 474]

4. To the fourth, it should be said that a passive power is informed by its object, but an active power places its own form upon the object, as is evident with the agent and possible intellect.[b, 475] Hence, just as the divine intellect is not informed by the things he knows through his essence, so neither is his will informed by the things he loves, since he loves them through his own goodness, and by loving, communicates his goodness to them.

5. To the fifth, it should be said that virtues that have determinate matter in connection with bodily acts and passions, or that imply some defect, such as faith, cannot have an exemplar in the divine nature in such a way that those virtues themselves are in God; but they do have [*some*] exemplar in the divine intellect, even as the rest of material things have.[476] And therefore, since charity implies neither defect nor anything material, it is found in God [i.e., predicated of God] before certain other virtues.[c, 477]

ARTICLE 2[d]   Whether God loves every creature

Proceeding to the second, it seems that God does not love every creature.

1. For whatever God loves, he loves from charity. But irrational creatures are not loved from charity, as was said above.[e] Therefore God does not love them.

2. Further, as the Philosopher says in *Ethics* VIII,[f] inanimate creatures are not loved except by a love of concupiscence, as is clear with love for wine. But God does not love anything by a love of concupiscence, since he does not need our goods.[g] Therefore in no way does he love inanimate creatures.

a. *etiam ipse Deus est per amorem extasim passus.*—Pseudo-Dionysius, *On the Divine Names*, ch. 4, n. 13 (PG 3:711).

b. *potentia passiua informatur ex obiecto suo, set potentia actiua ponit formam suam circa obiectum, sicut patet de intellectu agente et possibili*

c. *inuenitur in Deo pre quibusdam aliis uirtutibus*

d. Parallels: *In II Sent.* d. 26, a. 1; *ST* I, q. 20, a. 2; q. 23, a. 3, ad 1; I-II, q. 110, a. 1; *SCG* I, ch. 91; *De caritate*, a. 7, ad 2; *Super Ioan.* 5, lec. 3; *In De div. nom.* 4, lec. 9.

e. *In III Sent.* d. 21, q. 1, a. 2; *In III Sent.* d. 28, a. 2 (above).

f. Aristotle, *Ethics* VIII, ch. 2 (1155b3ff.).

g. An allusion to Ps. 15:2 (16:2 iuxta Heb.), in the Vulgate: *dixi Domino Dominus meus es tu quoniam bonorum meorum non eges.*

3. Further, intellectual love is a cause of choice.[a] But not everything is specially chosen by God, not even all men.[b] Therefore he does not love all creatures.

4. Further, whoever loves something wills good for it. But God does not will for the reprobate the one good that is the perfect good, namely eternal life, since, if he willed it for them, they would have it. Therefore God does not love every creature.

5. Further, there cannot be love and hatred from the same source toward the same object. But God hates some creature: "I have hated Esau" (Mal. 1:3). Therefore he does not love every creature.

On the contrary:

1. "You love all things that exist, and you hate none of the things you have made" (Wis. 2:25).

2. Further, Dionysius says that "divine love moves superior things to have providence for inferiors."[c] But God has providence over all things; therefore he loves all things.

3. Further, "God saw all the things that he had made, and they were very good" (Gen. 1:31); and Augustine says that by this verse it is signified that God approved of all things.[d] But nothing is approved of unless it is loved. Therefore God loves all things.

Response:

It should be said that friendship, as was said above,[e] adds something beyond love, since for the *ratio* of love it is enough that a man wish *any* good for someone, whereas for the *ratio* of friendship it is necessary

a. A favorite wordplay is concealed by the translation: *Dilectio est causa electionis. Set Deus non omnes etiam homines eligit. Ergo non omnes diligit.* Cf. *In I Sent.* d. 10, exp. text. (Mandonnet, 272): *Dilectio autem praesupponit electionem, sicut ipsum nomen ostendit; unde tantum rationabilium est.* The same point about the connection between the words is made at *In I Sent.* d. 41, q. 1, a. 2, *sed contra.* Cf. *ST* I-II, q. 26, a. 3: *Addit enim dilectio supra amorem, electionem praecedentem, ut ipsum nomen sonat.*

b. *Set Deus non omnes etiam homines eligit.* A too literal translation here would make the argument unintelligible. The argument: men are favored objects of God's attention because they are capable of enjoying friendship with him through a gift of grace, unlike irrational beings, who cannot reciprocate in any way. Yet not even all men are chosen (or "elected") for eternal life, and hence not all men are loved by God. *A fortiori,* God does not love all creatures.

c. Pseudo-Dionysius, *On the Divine Names,* ch. 4, n. 15 (PG 3:714). For Thomas's earlier discussion of this statement, see *In III Sent.* d. 27, q. 1, a. 1 (above).

d. Augustine, *On the Literal Interpretation of Genesis, an Unfinished Book,* n. 22 (PL 34:228). In fact Augustine makes this remark in connection with the creation of light.

e. *In III Sent.* d. 27, q. 2, a. 1 (see above).

that a person wish for someone the very good he wishes for himself—namely, that he wish to converse with him and share his company in the things he loves the most.[a]

So, then, if we speak about love in general, God loves all things insofar as he wills for them some good, namely, their natural good. But the good that he wills for himself, namely, the vision of himself and the enjoyment by which he is blessed, he wills indeed to every rational creature by his antecedent will, but only to the elect by his consequent will, which is will simply. And therefore he loves only the elect with love of friendship, while he loves all others, insofar as they are good, with love understood in the general sense of the word.[b]

Replies to objections:

1. To the first, therefore, it should be said that God loves all other things (that is, irrational creatures) from charity, not as though he has charity for them, but as ordering them to those for whom he does have charity.[c]

2. To the second, it should be said that although we do not love inanimate creatures with a love of benevolence, since their good does not come from us, God on the other hand loves them with a love of benevolence, since by the very fact that he wills good for them, they are and are good. Nevertheless, although God does not love anything with concupiscence as desiring it for himself, he loves it with concupiscence as desiring it for another—if we do not give full force to the term "concupiscence," which suggests not just what is proper to desire [as such], but an *anxiety* of desire.[d, 478]

3. To the third, it should be said that it is love of friendship that causes choice; and this kind of love God does not have toward all things.

4. To the fourth, it should be said that God wills for all irrational creatures the good proportionate to them and the good of which they are capable; and therefore it can be said that God loves them, simply speaking. But when it comes to the reprobate, God by consequent will (according to which he is said to will something simply) wills for them the good of nature, but he does not will the good of which they are ca-

---

a. *ut scilicet uelit conuersari cum ipso et conuiuere in illis que maxime amat*

b. *Et ideo solos electos diligit amore amicitie, alia autem diligit amore communiter dicto, in quantum sunt bona*

c. Cf. *In III Sent.* d. 28, a. 2 (see above).

d. *ut non fiat uis in uerbo concupiscentie, que anxietatem, non proprietatem, desiderii importat*

pable, namely grace and glory, except by antecedent will. And therefore in their case it is not to be said that God loves them simply speaking, but rather he loves them in a certain respect, namely insofar as they are creatures.

5. To the fifth, it should be said that God does not hate the reprobate insofar as they are his creatures, but insofar as they are evil; and that they are evil is not from him.[a, 479]

ARTICLE 3[b]   Whether God has loved creatures from eternity

Objections:

Proceeding to the third, it seems that God has not loved creatures from eternity.

1. For love is only of what is good. But creatures were not good from eternity [since they have not existed for eternity]. Therefore he has not loved them from eternity.

2. Further, love signifies the divine essence, and connotes an effect in the creature. But names that imply an effect in the creature are said of God from the vantage of time (i.e., owing to his causality in regard to things existing in time), for example "Lord," "Savior," and names of this sort. Therefore "to love creatures" is said of God temporally, since it, too, involves his causality in regard to things existing in time.[c, 480]

3. Further, love unites the lover to the beloved. But things could not be conjoined or united to God before they existed. Therefore they could not be loved by him from eternity.

4. Further, in things that have the same characteristic, there is a single *ratio* for love.[d] But before creatures existed, they were distinguished in nothing. Therefore in one [as yet uncreated thing] there was no reason why it should be loved more than there was in any other [as yet uncreated thing]. And so, from eternity God has not loved the elect, except perhaps just as he loved others.

5. Further, the lover wants the beloved to exist. But God was not

a. *in quantum mali sunt; quod ab ipso non est*

b. Parallels: *ST* I, q. 20, a. 2, ad 2; *SCG* IV, ch. 23; *Super Rom.* 9, lec. 2; *Super Ephes.* 1, lec. 1.

c. This is a much-expanded version of the original: *Dilectio significat diuinam essentiam et connotat effectum in creatura. Set ea que important effectum in creatura dicuntur de Deo ex tempore, sicut Dominus et Saluator et huiusmodi. Ergo et diligere creaturas non dicitur de Deo nisi ex tempore.*

d. *Eorum que similiter se habent est una ratio amoris*

willing creatures to exist before they actually existed; since if he had wanted them to exist before, they would have existed before. Therefore he did not love them before they actually existed.[a]

On the contrary:

1. "He *chose* us before the foundation of the world" (Eph. 1:4). But that choice was from love.[b] Therefore he also *loved* creatures from eternity.

2. Further, Dionysius says in chapter 4 of *On the Divine Names* that "divine love was the reason why God made the things he made."[c] Therefore the love of things was in God before the things themselves existed; and so it was in him from eternity.

3. Further, affection for the good follows upon knowledge of the good. But God has known from eternity whatsoever good there is in creatures. Therefore from eternity he has loved creatures.

Response:

It should be said that certain names may be said of God only from the vantage of time—but only those that imply in the chief thing signified something that is not really in God,[d] such as names that imply in the chief thing signified a relation of God to the creature, e.g., "Lord" and others of the same sort. For indeed, while this relation is a real relation in the creature, in God it is a relation according to reason only. It is similar with names that imply in the chief thing signified a divine action having its term in something outside himself, e.g., "to create"[e] and others of the same sort. Now love, in the chief thing signified, does *not* imply relation but rather an activity of the will—the activities of which, as with the activities of the intellect alongside it and elicited by it,[f] remain in the one acting and do not pass over into the establishment of something in exterior matter. And therefore love [of creatures] belongs to God from eternity.

---

a. *Amans uult esse amatum. Set Deus non uolebat esse creaturas antequam essent, quia si uoluisset eas esse, fuissent. Ergo non amabat eas antequam essent.*

b. *Set electio erat ex dilectione*

c. *diuinus amor fuit causa quare res fecit.* Here, *causa* means more "the reason why" or "the motive."—The reference is to Pseudo-Dionysius, *On the Divine Names*, ch. 4, n. 10 (PG 3:707).

d. *aliquid quod in Deo secundum rem non est*

e. Moos: *sicut causare*; Leonine: *sicut creare*

f. *sicut et operationes intellectus proxime et ab eis elicite*

Replies to objections:

1. To the first, therefore, it should be said that although from eternity creatures were not good in their proper nature, nevertheless they were good in the foreknowledge of God.

2. To the second, it should be said that love connotes an effect not in act but in habit.[481] And this is because activities of the soul do not have their term in something outside the one acting; hence, they can be extended even to that which is not in act.[482]

3. To the third, it should be said that love does not always bring about a real union,[a] but is [essentially] a union of affection—a union that can be had even with what is absent or altogether non-existent.

4. To the fourth, it should be said that although [prior to being created] they did not differ according to that which (in their proper natures) they were not, yet they did have difference in God's foreknowledge,[b] according to which he foreknew their future diversities.

5. To the fifth, it should be said that God was eternally willing that creatures exist, but he was not willing that *they* exist from eternity, but rather, according to the order appointed by his wisdom.[c]

ARTICLE 4[d]   Whether God loves all things equally

Objections:

Proceeding to the fourth, it seems that God loves all things equally.

1. For providence, as Dionysius says, is an effect of love.[e] But "[God made the little and the great, and] he hath equally care of all" (Wis. 6:8). Therefore he loves all things equally.

2. Further, "God's love for creatures" signifies his relationship to creatures. But God relates equally to all things, as the Philosopher says,

a. *unit secundum rem:* the union of the lover with a really existing beloved, in the manner in which the two can be most fully present to each other. See *In III Sent.* d. 27, q. 1, ad 2 and ad 5 (above); d. 29, a. 3, ad 1 (above).

b. *tamen differentiam habebant in Dei prescientia.* It is important here not to translate as if Thomas had said: "yet they differed in God's foreknowledge." As contained in God's knowledge—as, indeed, identical to God—they are not really different from him or from his act of knowing. However, he knows creatable creatures as "having difference" in their *rationes.*

c. *Deus uolebat ab eterno creaturas esse, set non eas esse ab eterno, set secundum ordinem sue sapientie*

d. Parallels: *In III Sent.* d. 19, a. 5, qa. 1, solutio (Moos, 602); *In II Sent.* d. 26, a. 1, ad 2; *ST* I, q. 20, a. 3; *SCG* I, ch. 91.

e. Pseudo-Dionysius, *On the Divine Names,* ch. 4, n. 12 and n. 15 (PG 3:710, 714).

although all things are unequally related to him.[a] Therefore he loves all things equally.[483]

3. Further, just as God loves all things, so he knows all things. But he knows all things equally; therefore he loves all things equally.

4. Further, the same act cannot be more intense and more remiss, except according to different parts of it.[484] But God loves all things by the same *simple* act. Therefore he does not love one thing more than another.

5. Further, a lover loves one thing more than another for the same reason that he loves the same thing sometimes more, sometimes less: since just as one thing is better than another, so the same thing is better at some times than it is at other times.[b] But God does not love anything sometimes more, sometimes less, since in this way his love would be changeable, which is impossible. Therefore he does not love one thing more than another.

On the contrary:

1. "The Lord has made all things for himself" (Prov. 16:4);[c] and in like manner, too, it is said that he made all things for the sake of man.[d]

---

a. *Dilectio Dei ad creaturas significat habitudinem ipsius ad creaturas. Set Deus equaliter se habet ad omnia, ut Philosophus dicit, quamuis non omnia equaliter se habeant ad ipsum.* On the minor premise of the argument, see webnotes 11 and 33. The statement is not found verbatim in the works of Aristotle, but as Moos notes, the sense of it is found in the pseudo-Aristotelian *De mundo,* ch. 6 (e.g.: "[I]nasmuch as it is the nature of the divine to penetrate to all things, the things also of our earth receive their share of it in the same way as the things above us, according to their nearness to or distance from God receiving more or less of divine benefit" [397b32–35]; "enthroned amid the immutable, he moves and revolves all things where and how he will, in different forms and natures; just as the law of a city, immutable in the souls of those who are under it, orders all the life of the state" [400b11–15]; cf. Barnes, *Complete Works of Aristotle,* 1:634–39), and even more clearly in Proposition 24 of *The Book of Causes,* which at the time of the *Scriptum* Thomas did not yet know to be based on Proclus's *Elements of Theology,* as he was to discover later in his career (cf. Vincent A. Guagliardo, Introduction to *St. Thomas Aquinas's Commentary on The Book of Causes,* ix–xiii). Prop. 24 reads: "The first cause exists in all things according to one disposition, but all things do not exist in the first cause according to one disposition." For Thomas's commentary on this proposition, see ibid., 134–38. It is consistent with Thomas's earlier writings that the author of *The Book of Causes* be referred to as "the Philosopher."

b. *Qua ratione diligit unum plus altero, eadem ratione diligit aliquem quandoque plus, quandoque minus, quia sicut una res est melior altera, ita idem secundum diuersa tempora est melius se ipso.* The last phrase is literally: "so the same thing at different times is better than itself."

c. *Vniuersa propter se ipsum operatus est Dominus,* as translated in the Douay-Rheims.

d. Implicitly in both creation accounts (Gen. 1:28–29; 2:8–9, 2:15) and in oth-

But that for the sake of which something comes to be is loved more. Therefore God loves himself more than others, and among others, he loves one more than another.

2. Further, God's charity[a] is of the good precisely as good. Therefore, the more good something is, the more God loves it.[b]

3. Further, the order of charity pertains to its perfection. But God's charity is most perfect. Therefore, in accordance with order, he loves one more than another.

Response:

It should be said that love is measured in two ways. In one way, it is measured from its principle, so that something is said to be more loved when the will is more efficaciously inclined to loving it. And in this way, God loves all things equally, because in his love with respect to anything whatsoever he has an infinite efficacy in loving. In another way, love is measured in terms of its object; accordingly, someone is said to love more that for which he wills a greater good. And in this way, God is said to love one more than another, insofar as he wills for it a greater good. And through this willing of a greater good he also brings about a greater effect in the more favored object, because his will is the cause of things.[c]

Replies to objections:

1. To the first, therefore, it should be said that the care of all things belongs to him equally as regards his solicitude for all, but not as regards the things provided for them.

2. To the second, it should be said that love implies not only what exists on the part of God, but also what exists on the part of the creature, whose [actual] good,[485] insofar as it too is willed by God, is included in God's love. And since creatures are not equally related to God, nor can they equally participate his goodness, therefore he does not love all things equally.

3. To the third, it should be said that, whereas knowledge involves a thing's motion into the soul, love involves the soul's motion toward things;[d] and therefore knowledge takes its measure only from the side

---

er texts that underline the gift of all things to man (e.g., Gen. 9:1–3, Ps. 8:6; Wis. 9:1–3; 1 Cor. 3:21).

a. Leonine: *caritas Dei*; Moos: *caritas*

b. *magis bonum, magis amat,* which may also be translated: "it [God's charity] loves more the more good."

c. *Et ex hoc etiam habet maiorem effectum in illo, quia uoluntas eius est causa rerum*

d. *cognitio est secundum motum rei ad animam, amor autem secundum motum anime ad res*

of the knower, whereas love takes its measure from both sides. For one is not said to know more just because he knows a greater thing to exist in anything, in the way that one *is* said to love more the one in whom he wishes a greater good to exist. Hence no parallel can be drawn in this regard between love and knowledge.

4. To the fourth, it should be said that he is said to love something more, not because he loves it more intensely, but because he wills a greater good for it.

5. To the fifth, it should be said that, with respect to the affection[a] of love, he always loves the same thing equally, since, when all is said and done, he always wills for it the same good, even though he does not wish that it always have an equal or the same good.[b] And so, as regards the effect, there is not an equal love.[c]

ARTICLE 5[d]   On the comparison of things loved by God[e]

Proceeding to the fifth, [we divide the article into four subquestions: (1) whether God loves the now-just man foreknown to be lost more than the sinner predestined to be saved; (2) whether God loves the penitent more than the innocent; (3) whether God loves man more than angel; (4) whether God loves the human race more than Christ].

a. Leonine and Moos: *affectum*; in at least one MS is found the miscopy *effectum*.

b. *semper uult ei idem bonum finaliter, quamuis non uelit quod semper habeat equale bonum uel idem.* This phrase seems to mean: "when all is said and done [*finaliter*] he always wishes for it whatever good it has at a given time, even though he does not wish that it should have an equal or the same good at all times." Hence, his affection remains constant, for he wills these different goods at different times with the same affection, knowing what is best for the creature or for the whole order of creation; but the particular *effects* of this constant love vary.

c. Leonine and Moos: *et ideo secundum effectum non est equalis dilectio.* Some manuscripts mistakenly read *affectum* for *effectum*, while others omit *dilectio*.

d. Parallel: *ST* I, q. 20, a. 4, an article where three of the four objections are concise versions of three of the four subquestions found in the *Scriptum*, as follows: obj. 1 concerns the comparison of Christ and the human race (qa. 4); obj. 2 concerns the comparison of angel and man (qa. 3); obj. 4 concerns the comparison of the penitent and the innocent (qa. 2); obj. 5 concerns the comparison of the just man foreknown to be lost and the sinner predestined for salvation (qa. 1). One notes that the order of arguments has been exactly reversed; arguably the *Summa*'s order is the more appropriate, given that it goes from the more obvious and potent objections against the thesis to those that are more subtle. Obj. 3 takes up the comparison of Peter and John, which has already been considered at *In III Sent.* d. 31, q. 2, a. 3, qa. 3 (see above).

e. For clarity we have supplied the title and the listing of subquestions.

SUBQUESTION 1   Whether God loves the now-just
man foreknown to be lost more than the sinner
predestined to be saved[a]

Objections:

It seems that God loves the now-just man more than the sinner
predestined to be saved.

1. For it is said in Proverbs 8:17: "I love those who love me." But
[insofar as he is presently a sinner,] that sinner predestined to be saved
does not love God, whom the now-just man presently loves. Therefore he loves the now-just man more than the sinner predestined to
be saved.

2. Further, God loves more that which is better. But [compared simply, as they now are in themselves,] that just man is better than that
sinner. Therefore he is more loved by God.

3. Further, in the text of the Master it is said that God loves the
members of his only-begotten Son more than others. But the sinner predestined to be saved is not [now actually] a member of Christ.
Therefore he is loved less by God than the now-just man who is [now
actually] a member of Christ.

On the contrary:

4. Intellectual love is a cause of choice.[b] But God chooses [for salva-
tion] the sinner predestined to be saved. Therefore he loves him more
than he loves a now-just man whom he does not choose for salvation.

5. Further, he loves more the one for whom he wills a greater good.
But he wills a greater good, namely eternal life, for the sinner predestined to be saved. Therefore he loves him more.

---

a. *Iustus praescitus* and *peccator praedestinatus* are scholastic abbreviations for "a
man who is now just but is foreknown to be lost" and "a man who is now a sinner but is predestined to be saved." In the remainder of the text we will translate
iustus praescitus as "the now-just man" and *peccator praedestinatus* as "sinner predestined to be saved." In theory, "predestined sinner" would suffice for a translation, since for Aquinas "predestined" always refers to God's election of souls for
eternal life, but as the modern reader may perhaps be confused by the Calvin-
ist theory of so-called "double predestination," it is helpful to take precautions
against any misunderstanding. The verb opposite to *praedestinare* is *reprobare* and
the noun, *reprobatio.*

b. *Dilectio causa est electionis;* "intellectual" because not every kind of love
causes choice.

Response:

It should be said that, simply speaking, God wills a greater good for the sinner predestined to be saved than he wills for the now-just man; but as for what is the case right now,[a] he wills a greater good for the just man foreknown to be lost. But this determination—"what is the case right now"—falls not on love's side but more on the object's side, because God's love is not changed over time, for from eternity he willed a greater good for that predestined man. Hence, it is to be conceded, simply, that he loves the one predestined more than the one foreknown to be lost.

And from this, the response to the objections (1–5) is evident, since they argue concerning what is the case right now.[486]

SUBQUESTION 2   Whether God loves the penitent
more than the innocent

Objections:

Furthermore, it seems that he loves the penitent more than the innocent.

1. For joy follows upon love; but God rejoices more about a penitent, as is clear from Luke 15.[b] Therefore he loves him more.

2. Further, where a person does more work, he loves more—on account of which, as the Philosopher says,[c] mothers love their children more than fathers do. But God *does* more (since he cannot "work") for the salvation of a penitent than for the salvation of an innocent.[d] Therefore he loves him more.

3. Further, love's affection is gauged from love's effect.[e] But it seems to be a greater effect of love to call an enemy back to friendship than

a. *ut nunc*

b. Lk. 15 contains three parables that make the same point: the parable of the lost sheep (vv. 1–7), the parable of the lost coin (vv. 8–10), and the parable of the prodigal son (vv. 11–32). In each, the character who represents God (the shepherd, the woman, the father) rejoices more over the recovery of the thing that was lost than over the maintenance of the remaining goods. This point is driven home especially in v. 7: "Just so, I tell you, there will be more joy in heaven over one sinner who repents than over ninety-nine righteous persons who need no repentance" (RSV).

c. Aristotle, *Ethics* IX, ch. 7 (1168a25).

d. *Set Deus plus operatur—quia laborare non potest—ad salutem penitentis quam innocentis.* Moos evidently did not encounter the set-apart phrase among the manuscripts he consulted, but the phrase has been recovered by the editors of the critical text.

e. *Affectus amoris ex effectu pensatur*

to preserve a friend in friendship. [And since a penitent is an enemy whom God called back to friendship while an innocent is a friend preserved in friendship,] therefore he loves more a penitent than an innocent.

On the contrary:

1. What is more lasting is more worthy of being chosen and being loved. But the good of an innocent is more lasting. Therefore it is more loved by God.

2. Further, it was said above[a] that the one rising up from sin never returns to as much dignity, although he can return to as much charity. Therefore God loves an innocent more than a penitent.[487]

Response:

It should be said that, with respect to the good of the essential reward, God loves the penitent and the innocent equally if they have equal charity, or else he loves that one more who has the greater charity. But with respect to the accidental reward, he loves the innocent more, on account of the dignity of innocence—a dignity that the penitent cannot attain.

Replies to objections:

1. To the first, therefore, it should be said that even if a penitent rises up after a fall with a charity equal to that which he had before, and thus the good willed for him by God is equal considered in itself, nevertheless this good is greater in comparison to the man to whom it is given, just as when someone is needy, a benefit given to him is reckoned *more* of a benefit than were he not so needy. And on account of this it is said that God and the angels rejoice more over his conversion, even as a person rejoices more over a small sign of health appearing in a sick man than that person does over the full bloom of health the sick man once had. Or it may be said that this [viz., that God and the angels rejoice more over the recovery of one than the safety of the others] is said because of the fact that a penitent frequently rises up after a fall more humble and fervent and cautious.[b]

2. To the second, it should be said that God is not more active in him in whom he newly infuses grace than in him in whom he continues to sustain it, even as neither is the sun more active in illuminating dark air than in continuing its light in air already illuminated. For

a. *In III Sent.* d. 31, q. 1, a. 4, qa. 1, ad 2.
b. Cf. *In III Sent.* d. 31, q. 1, a. 4, qa. 3, ad 1 (see above).

nothing is able to subsist unless the activity of God be continued in it.

3. To the third, it should be said that, although the effect of love in question may be greater with respect to the one who is freed from the guilt of sin, nevertheless it is not greater simply speaking.[a]

SUBQUESTION 3   Whether God loves man more than angel[b]

Objections:

Furthermore, it seems that he loves man more than angel.

1. For "he never took hold of the angels, but he took hold of the seed of Abraham" (Heb. 2:16);[488] and thus, he did more for men than for angels. Therefore he loves them more.

2. Further, men are members of Christ in more ways than angels are, namely [not only with respect to grace but also] with respect to a conformity of nature. But God loves more those who are members of Christ, as is said in the text of the Master. Therefore he loves men more than angels.[489]

3. Further, God placed certain individuals of the human race—namely, Christ and the Blessed Virgin—above all the angels.[c] Therefore he loves men more than angels.

On the contrary:

4. Love is caused by a fittingness or agreement between lover and beloved.[d] But angels are more like unto God, as Gregory says.[e] Therefore he loves angels more than men.

5. Further, in the beginning he bestowed glory (as it were) upon the angels, but not upon men.[f, 490] Therefore he loves angels more than men.

a. *quamuis sit maius respectu illius qui liberatur, non tamen est maius simpliciter*

b. The title of the question speaks in the singular (*plus hominem quam angelum*), as if to ask whether God loves human nature more than angelic nature. At other points in the same subquestion, Thomas phrases the issue in the plural: does God love *men* more than he loves *angels*? In accord with traditional English, *homo, homines* is translated "man, men," except in the third objection.

c. *Homines supra angelos collocauit, scilicet Christum et Beatam Virginem*

d. Moos: *conuenientia amantis cum amato*; Leonine: *conuenientia amati cum amato*. Although the Moos reading seems to make more sense, the Leonine could be rendered as follows: "[Mutual] love is caused by a coming-together of [one] beloved with the [other] beloved," or "Love is caused by a coming-together of the beloved with what is [first] loved."

e. Gregory, *Morals on the Book of Job* XXXII, ch. 23 (CCSL 143B:1666).

f. *Angelis in principio quasi gloriam contulit, non autem hominibus*

Response:

It should be said that God loves angel more than man as regards the good of nature, but as regards the good of glory, angels are related to men as both exceeding and exceeded, because God will love certain men more than some angels, certain angels more than some men, and certain angels and men equally; for men will then be equal to the angels [as regards the essential reward, enjoyment of God in the beatific vision], and certain men will even be superior to the angels; and God has provided for each one in accordance with the needs and demands of his nature and of his state.[a, 491]

And through this answer the response to the objections (1–5) is clear. For it does not follow that a father loves a sick son more than a healthy one just because he gives to him remedies that he does not give to the one who is healthy.

SUBQUESTION 4   Whether God loves the human race more than he loves Christ

Objections:

Furthermore, it seems that God loves the human race more than he loves Christ.

1. For, as is evident from John 3, he gave Christ for the redemption of the human race.[b]

2. Further, "the common good is more divine than the good of one."[c] But the good of the human race is a common good, whereas the good of Christ is the good of a single person. Therefore God loves the human race more than he loves Christ.

On the contrary:

1. It is through Christ that the whole human race comes to be accepted by God. Therefore he loves Christ more.

a. *quantum ad bonum nature plus diligit Deus angelum quam hominem, set quantum ad bonum glorie se habent ut excedentia et excessa, quia quosdam homines plus et quosdam angelos plus et quosdam equaliter, quia homines erunt equales angelis et quidam etiam superiores angelis, et unicuique prouidit secundum exigentiam nature et status sui*

b. *Quia ipsum pro redemptione humani generis dedit, ut patet Io. III.* The reference is to Jn. 3:16–17 (RSV): "For God so loved the world that he gave his only-begotten Son, that whoever believes in him should not perish but have eternal life. For God sent the Son into the world, not to condemn the world, but that the world might be saved through him."

c. Aristotle, *Ethics* I, ch. 1 (1094b9–10).

2. Further, the Spirit is given to Christ without measure (Jn. 3:34). Therefore God loves him more [than all others, who receive the Spirit up to a certain measure].

Response:

It should be said that God loves Christ not only more than men, but also more than creation in its totality[a]—[and he loves him more] not only with respect to his divine nature, but even with respect to his human nature, insofar as he predestined it to a greater good, namely to union with a divine Person.

Replies to objections:

1. To the first, therefore, it should be said that even in Christ's being given on behalf of men, the greatest good redounded to Christ himself, inasmuch as through this giving of himself his virtue was manifested and he became the cause of human salvation, which makes him exceedingly honorable.[b]

2. To the second, it should be said that, although he be a single Person, Christ is nevertheless the universal cause of salvation to the human race: and the cause has preeminence over the caused.[c]

Notes on the text of Lombard

"To the aforesaid is to be added [the treatment] about the love of God by which he loves us."

It seems that the Master ought to have determined about this matter in the first Book. And it should be replied that it could have been suitably placed in the first Book, too, insofar as the divine love is the divine essence; and it can be fittingly placed here, insofar as God's love is the exemplar of our love.

---

a. *totam creaturam,* meaning all *mere* creatures, which excludes the created human nature of Christ, as is evident from Thomas's response.

b. *in hoc etiam quod Christus pro hominibus fuit datus, maximum bonum ipsius Christi fuit, secundum quod in hoc uirtus sua manifestata fuit, et causa fuit salutis humane, quod est sibi ualde honorificum*

c. *causa prestantior est causato*

"God's love is the divine ousia."

(That is, essence.) This is said because essence and love in God are one and the same thing, differing only in *ratio,* as was said in the first Book.[a]

a. In Book I there is much discussion of love in God and the Holy Spirit as love, so the reference is not immediately clear; two candidates would be d. 10, q. 1, a. 2, ad 4, and d. 32, q. 1, a. 2, ad 4—both discussions of the threefold meaning of "love" *in divinis,* namely, essential, personal, and notional.

DISTINCTION 36

ARTICLE 6[a, 492]   Whether a commandment contains the
requirement that it be fulfilled charitably[b]

Objections:

It seems that any commandment contains the requirement that it
be fulfilled out of charity.[c]

1. For just as virtues are connected to each other in charity, so too
are all commandments reduced to charity. But the virtues are thus
connected to each other in charity because they are formed through
charity.[d] Therefore the commandments, too, are reduced to charity because a charitable way of acting falls within a commandment.[e]

---

a. Latin text: provisional critical ed. of the Leonine Commission; cf. Moos ed.,
1226–29. Parallels: *ST* I-II, q. 100, a. 10; *De ueritate*, q. 23, a. 7, ad 8, and q. 24, a. 12,
ad 16; *De malo*, q. 2, a. 5, ad 7. There is some common ground between matters discussed in this article and those discussed in an earlier article: whether a man without grace can fulfill all the commandments of the law (*In II Sent.* d. 28, a. 3).

b. Distinction 36 as a whole is dedicated to questions concerning the connection of the virtues, of the gifts, and of the vices. After inquiring into the connection of political (i.e., acquired) virtues, gratuitous virtues, and the gifts of the
Holy Spirit, the equality of the virtues, and the paralleling of vices, Thomas turns
in the sixth article to a question he announces initially as *utrum precepta connectan-
tur in caritate, ita quod modus sit in precepto*. The first objection explains why this
question is posed in this context. The Master has been speaking at length about
how all virtues are bound up with charity and how active charity is the fulfilling of the law. This suggests a further step: all commandments contain a reference to charity, such that obeying the commandment *requires* having charity—
any particular commandment must be fulfilled out of charity. Thus, the question
at hand actually means: Does each and every commandment given to man contain within itself a condition or requirement that it be done by means of charity
or in a charitable manner (i.e., the *modus caritatis*)? Here, charity cannot be anything other than the infused gratuitous virtue. Hence, one result of answering in
the affirmative would be to say that a man lacking charity is simply powerless to
act according to any of the commandments, which seems counterintuitive, to say
the least.

c. *Videtur quod modus caritatis sit in precepto.* A too-literal translation is likely
to be unhelpful in this situation; see the preceding note on the meaning of the
question.

d. See *In III Sent.* d. 27, q. 2, a. 4, qa. 3 (above).

e. *modus caritatis sub precepto cadit.*—Throughout the question, this phrase and
others like it will be expanded as here.

2. Further, in Deuteronomy 6:5 it is said: "You shall love the Lord your God with all your heart, and with all your soul, and with all your strength." And it is obvious that *here* an act of charity is commanded. But works that fall under commandment receive from the act of charity itself their appropriate manner of being done.[a] Therefore the manner of acting mentioned in the text ("with all your heart," etc.) is contained *in* the very commandment.[493]

3. Further, in Matthew 19:17 it is said: "If you wish to enter into life, keep the commandments." But no one can enter into life without charity. Therefore contained in a commandment is the requirement that it be done out of charity.

4. Further, as moral deformity in works is opposed to a right formation of works, so prohibition is opposed to commandment. But deformity in works falls under prohibition; therefore a right formation, which comes to be through a charitable way of acting, falls under commandment.[b]

5. Further, it is through charity that acts of commandments are ordained to their due end. But this ordination itself falls under commandment, as is evident from what the Apostle says in 1 Corinthians 10:31: "Do all things for the glory of God."[494] Therefore to do acts out of charity, too, falls under commandment.

On the contrary:

1. Nothing falls under commandment except what is in our power. Hence Jerome anathematizes those who say that God has commanded something impossible for man.[c] But to have charity is not in our power. Therefore doing acts out of charity does not fall under commandment.

2. Further, whoever omits what belongs to the substance of a commandment commits a sin. But someone who loves God by natural love, or who does works of mercy[d] yet lacks charity, does not commit a sin in the positing of this very act. Therefore acting from charity does not fall under commandment.

3. Further, man in the state of innocence, even if he had not been given grace, would still have had the wherewithal to stand firm in the

a. *Set ex actu caritatis modificantur opera que sunt in precepto*

b. *Sicut deformationi opponitur formatio, ita prohibitioni opponitur preceptum. Set deformatio operum cadit sub prohibitione. Ergo formatio, que fit per modum caritatis, cadit sub precepto.*

c. In fact, this statement is not from Jerome, but from Pelagius (PL 45:1718, n. 10).

d. *opera pietatis*

good allotted him. But this would not be so if acting from charity fell under commandment, since he would then fall into sin whenever he fulfilled commandments without fulfilling that condition.[a] Therefore acting from charity is not *in* a commandment.

Response:

It should be said that there are four opinions about this matter.

The first opinion is that the mode in question—acting from charity—*does* fall under commandment, but in the following way: since that commandment is affirmative, it does not oblige one to act all the time, although it is always obligatory; and so a man is not bound to fulfill the commandment from charity except for that time in which he has charity. In this way, he is not obliged to do something impossible. But this opinion does not seem sufficient [for avoiding the problem], since if acting from charity belongs to the *substance* of the commandment, the obligation to do a certain act and the mode according to which the act is to be done will run parallel. Yet it happens that there will be a time for a man to honor his parents even when he does not have charity. Hence it seems that he will then be bound to fulfill it from charity.[495]

And therefore others say that the obligation of a commandment and the mode of acting from charity keep an equal step—in other words, that whenever a man is bound to fulfill a commandment, he is bound to fulfill it from charity; and [they say, moreover] that it does not follow, on this account, that God commands something impossible, since although man by himself cannot have charity, nevertheless he can do something whence he will receive charity from God (for, according to the Philosopher in *Ethics* III, "the things we do through our friends are in a way possible for us to do").[b] But this opinion cannot stand, since if it were true, it would follow that someone in a state of mortal sin, in doing any act whatsoever of the genus of good acts by which he would fulfill a commandment with respect to the *substance* of the work done, would in fact be committing a sin of omission precisely insofar as he would be omitting the aforesaid mode—which is false.[496]

And therefore still others say that the mode of acting from charity in no way falls under commandment, and that a man without charity really fulfills a commandment of the Law. But this opinion seems to border on the Pelagian heresy, which claimed that all commandments could be fulfilled without grace.[497]

a. *Homo in statu innocentie, etiam si gratiam non habuit, habebat unde poterat stare. Quod non esset si modus esset sub precepto, quia caderet si sine modo precepta seruaret.*

b. Or: "What we can do through our friends in some way we ourselves can do."—The reference is to Aristotle, *Ethics* III, ch. 5 (1112b27).

Therefore others hold a middle way, and say that the mode of acting from charity in a certain way falls within the commandment,[a] and in a certain way does not. For we are said to be "bound to the commandments" in two ways. In one way, we are bound such that unless we fulfill that to which we are bound, we are guilty of an omission of or a transgression against the thing commanded; and from this vantage, we are bound only to the *substance* of the commandment, not to the *mode* in which it is carried out. In another way, we are bound such that if we do not fulfill that to which we are bound, we do not receive the *fruit* of the commandment; and so, from this vantage, we are bound to the substance of the work *as well as* the mode in which it is carried out, without which mode a man will not arrive at life, howsoever much he carries out the substance of the work.[498]

And this opinion seems more reasonable than the others. For evidently a commandment may be considered in two ways. In one way, it may be considered insofar as it is imposed on someone as something he must necessarily fulfill; and in this way, nothing ought to be imposed on anyone except what he is capable of fulfilling immediately— and if he does not fulfill this he is punished, since it is within this perspective that law has coercive force, according to the Philosopher in *Ethics* X.[b] In another way, a commandment may be considered with respect to the intention of a lawgiver who intends to lead men to virtue through the law's commandments, as is said in *Ethics* II.[c] Hence, that something be done *virtuously* does fall under commandment as far as the lawgiver's ultimate intention is concerned, but this manner of acting does not fall under commandment specifically with respect to the binding force of the law.[d, 499]

Replies to objections:

1. To the first, therefore, it should be said that, in a way, the commandments are interconnected through charity as in an end common to them all,[e] since it is through charity that someone receives the *fruit* of a commandment that he has kept.

a. *in precepto cadit*; more often in this article, the phrase is *sub precepto cadit.*

b. Aristotle, *Ethics* X, ch. 10 (1180a21).

c. Aristotle, *Ethics* II, ch. 1 (1103b3).

d. *Vno modo in quantum imponitur secundum necessitatem quandam implenti. Et sic nichil debet imponi alicui nisi quod statim est in ipso ut impleat, quod, si non implet, punitur, quia sic lex habet uim coactiuam, secundum Philosophum in X Ethicorum. Alio modo quantum ad intentionem legislatoris, qui per legis precepta intendit ad uirtutem perducere, ut dicitur in II Ethicorum. Et sic quantum ad intentionem legislatoris modus uirtutis cadit sub precepto, non quantum ad obligationem legis.*

e. *sicut in fine*

2. To the second, it should be said that by this commandment an act of charity is commanded—not meaning an act that is *from* charity, but an act *similar* to that of charity, as is an act of natural love.[a] Or if an act of charity [in the proper sense] *is* commanded, then [it should be said that] this commandment exists more for showing what we ought to tend to than for laying us under an obligation to do it, as was said above in Distinction 26.[b]

3. To the third, it should be said that this argument runs more along the lines of the lawgiver's intention than of a law's binding force.

4. To the fourth, it should be said that, while it is within our power either to do a morally deformed act or to refrain from doing it, it is *not* without our power to do a rightly formed act. And therefore the same argument cannot be used for both.

5. To the fifth, it should be said that the mode of acting from charity implies more than a mere relation of a given work to the due end; for it implies that this act proceeds from the habit of charity, which is lacking in many who nevertheless refer their particular acts to God.[500]

a. *illo precepto precipitur actus caritatis, non qui sit a caritate, set qui est similis actui caritatis, sicut est actus naturalis dilectionis*

b. Leonine: *distinctione XXVI*; Moos: *distinctione XXVII* (Moos notes, however, the alternate reading adopted by the Leonine editors). Nevertheless, I can find nothing in d. 26 that would be immediately relevant, whereas a passage expressly relevant is found at d. 27, q. 3, a. 4, in the response (see above). One may conclude that if Thomas actually referred to d. 26, this was a slip of the pen; he meant to refer to d. 27.

IN IV SENTENTIARUM

DISTINCTION 49[a]

QUESTION 1   On beatitude

ARTICLE 1   On that in which beatitude consists

SUBQUESTION 1[b, 501]   Whether beatitude[c] consists in goods of the body

Objections:

Proceeding to the first, it seems that beatitude consists in goods of the body.

a. The commentary on Book IV, Distinction 49—the penultimate Distinction of the *Sentences*, and one of the lengthiest and most complex in the entire commentary—is divided into five questions, as announced in the *divisio textus*: first, on beatitude; second, on the vision of God, in which beatitude chiefly consists; third, on delight, which formally completes beatitude; fourth, on the "dowries" that are contained in beatitude; fifth, on the aureoles with which beatitude is perfected and adorned. The first question is divided into four articles, which can be summarized as: 1. On that in which beatitude consists; 2. On beatitude as created and uncreated; 3. On appetite for beatitude; 4. On participation in beatitude. Each of these is further divided into several *quaestiunculae*, for a total of 17 subquestions. These are what we have translated here. Since the Moos ed. of Book IV ends at d. 22, for the Latin text of d. 49, q. 1 we have used the Parma ed., as found in Busa's *Index Thomisticus* and now available through Enrique Alarcón's *Corpus Thomisticum*; the printed edition is *Sancti Thomae Aquinatis Opera omnia,* vol. 7/2: *Commentum in quartum librum Sententiarum magistri Petri Lombardi* (Parma: Typis Petri Fiaccadori, 1858), 1180–96. Information on authorities cited by Thomas has been supplied wherever feasible.

b. Parallels: cf. similar discussions at *ST* I-II, q. 2, aa. 1–5; *SCG* III, chs. 28–32; *Sent. Eth.* I, lec. 5.

c. Throughout these articles, Thomas speaks almost exclusively about *beatitudo,* a conception for him broad enough to include all that the pagan philosophers argued about man's ultimate perfection, but carrying the unmistakable note of a revealed destiny that makes man truly "blessed," *beatus,* as Christ promises to his disciples. In contemporary English, the word "happiness" does not function very well to describe the "blessedness" Thomas has in mind—a timeless ecstasy of contemplative communion with the eternal, all-lovable God. (There are additional difficulties: to most, "happiness" immediately suggests something emotional, a matter of feelings; and the strong echo of "happens" makes it, like the related word "fortunate," seem more a matter of luck than of virtue.) Yet in its favor, "happiness" is a familiar word, readily responded to, while "beatitude" is (for many, at any rate) an ethereal, exotic word, possibly a cold word. To make

1. For it is impossible that that which is asserted by most people is totally false, as the Commentator says in the book *On the Soul*; and the Philosopher says in *Ethics* VII, "a saying generally expressed among the people never dies completely."[a] But the greater number of people are inclined to seek bodily pleasures and bodily goods as their end. Therefore the end of human life consists in bodily goods. But we call the end of human life beatitude. Therefore beatitude is to be sought for in goods of the body.

2. Further, the more ultimate an end is in the line of attainment, the more prior it is in the line of intention and appetite. But man has appetite for bodily good before he has appetite for spiritual good, since we are led, as by the hand, from the love of bodily things to the love of invisible things, as Gregory says.[b] Therefore bodily good is our ultimate end. But such an end is beatitude. Therefore beatitude is to be sought for in bodily goods.

3. Further, the more common a good is, the more divine it is, as is clear from *Ethics* I.[c] But bodily good is more common than spiritual good, because bodily good extends itself even to plants and brute animals, while spiritual good does not. Therefore bodily good is superior to spiritual good; and so beatitude is to be sought more in bodily goods than in spiritual ones.

4. Further, beatitude is set down by all as the end of virtue. But virtue has its end not only in spiritual goods, but also in bodily ones; for through the virtue of temperance and other [such] virtues man is preserved from harmful things even in regard to his body. Therefore beatitude is to be sought not only in spiritual goods but also in bodily ones.

5. Further, according to the Philosopher in *Physics* II, happiness and fortune seem to be about the same affairs.[d] But the goods of fortune have to do with bodily things. Therefore the goods in which beatitude and happiness consists[e] are bodily.

things still more vexed for the translator, Thomas occasionally uses the term *felicitas*, which seems to have something of the worldly character of "happiness." So, being faced with a wholly unsatisfactory set of alternatives, the translator can only do his job well if he tries to be intelligently consistent in his choices. Here, *beatitudo* and *beatus* will always be rendered "beatitude" and "blessed," whereas *felicitas* will be rendered "happiness."

a. Aristotle, *Ethics* VII, ch. 13 (1153b27).

b. Gregory the Great, *Homilies on the Gospels*, Homily 11, n. 1 (CCSL 141:74).

c. Aristotle, *Ethics* I, ch. 2 (1094b6–10). In context, this statement is not set down as a general principle but is asserted to be true of the state or political society.

d. Aristotle, *Physics* II, ch. 6 (197b4).

e. Though Thomas mentions both *beatitudo et felicitas*, he uses a singular verb, *consistit*, as if the two were meant to be synonymous.

6. Further, man is constituted from soul and body. Therefore man's good ought to be common to soul and body. But spiritual good cannot be common to the body, whereas bodily good *can* be common to the soul, inasmuch as the soul takes pleasure in bodily things. Therefore beatitude, which is man's good, consists more in bodily goods than in spiritual ones.

On the contrary:

1. That which belongs to man in terms of his body can be common to him and to the other animals. But beatitude cannot accord with the nature of the other animals.[a] Therefore beatitude is not to be sought in goods of the body.

2. Further, beatitude is man's highest good. Therefore it is to be sought among the foremost goods of man. But goods of the soul are nobler than goods of the body, even as the soul itself is nobler than the body. Therefore beatitude is to be sought in goods of the soul.

3. Further, that which is the ultimate measure is not measured in any way. Therefore that which cannot be good unless it be measured cannot be the ultimate measure in human affairs, nor can it be the ultimate end, which is beatitude, since the end is the measure that imposes due limits on things ordered to an end.[b] But bodily goods are praiseworthy or good only to the extent that they receive the measure of virtue, as is evident from what the Philosopher says in *Ethics* II.[c] Therefore beatitude cannot be [located] in bodily goods.

Response:

It should be said that "beatitude," since it is naturally desired by all men, designates the ultimate end of human life.[502] Now the end of anything whatsoever is its proper activity, or it arrives at its end through its proper activity. Now, since the principle of the proper activity of anything is its proper form, and the proper form of man, as man, is the rational soul, it necessarily follows that man's beatitude consists either in the very acts of the rational soul, or in those things to which man is related through acts of the rational soul. But these things are called goods of the soul; hence, even according to the [pagan] philosophers, it is necessary to locate beatitude in goods of the soul. However, that some located their beatitude in goods of the body comes from

a. *beatitudo aliis animalibus non potest competere.* What we mean by "beatitude" is not something that comports with or suits the activities of other animals; hence it cannot principally have to do with something they have in common with us.

b. *cum finis sit mensura imponens modum his quae sunt ad finem*

c. Aristotle, *Ethics* II, ch. 2 (1104a11–18).

the fact that they were ignorant of what they themselves really are; for they did not perceive themselves in terms of that which is better in them, which formally completes their being,[a] but in terms of that aspect of themselves which appears on the outside [viz., the bodily aspect]; and accordingly they sought their beatitude in external goods.

Replies to objections:

1. To the first, therefore, it should be said that it is not necessary for the opinion of many to be true simply speaking, but only that it be true in part. And indeed the multitude of men, who locate their beatitude in goods of the body, have true opinion in regard to one point: whatever they judge best for themselves, they reckon their beatitude to be; and there is truth to that opinion of theirs, namely that the best for man is beatitude. However, their opinion need not be true in regard to the locating of beatitude in goods of the body, since this opinion proceeds from a false root, because they judge them*selves* chiefly to be that which they are according to the· *body.*

2. To the second, it should be said that it happens only *per accidens* that bodily good is desired before spiritual good. For our knowledge proceeds from the more general to the particular,[b] as is clear from *Physics* I;[c] and so in the beginning [of our lives] we know nothing about the end of man except something general—that it is a certain best [to aim for]. And as we know, so do we desire. Thus, we judge that good to be among those goods that first come within range of our knowledge. However, what is first in our knowledge are sensible things; hence in the beginning we judge sensible goods as the highest goods, but eventually, when our knowledge is more mature,[d] we come to have a distinct knowledge of man's end, by discerning it clearly from other [rivals]; and at that point we hunger for the highest good where it is truly to be found, namely in spiritual realities.[e] But the argument went as if appetite for bodily good preceded appetite for spiritual good due to the nature of these things, [rather than due to our knowing bodily good before spiritual good].[f, 503]

---

a. *ex hoc provenit quod seipsos quid essent ignorabant; non enim agnoscebant se secundum id quod est in eis melius, quod eorum esse formaliter complet*

b. *ab universalioribus ad specialia*

c. Aristotle, *Physics* I, ch. 1 (184a16–b13).

d. *in fine quando cognitio nostra perficitur*

e. *et tunc appetimus summum bonum ut est, scilicet in spiritualibus*

f. *Ratio autem procedit, ac si per se loquendo appetitus boni corporalis praecederet appetitum boni spiritualis*

3. To the third, it should be said that something can be said to be common in two ways. In one way, by predication; but what is common in this way is not found numerically the same in the different things [to which it is common]; and it is in this way that the body's good has commonality. The other way is something common according to a participation of numerically one and the same thing; and this commonality can most of all be found in those things that pertain to the soul, since through the soul is touched that which is the common good of all things, namely God; and so the argument does not follow.

4. To the fourth, it should be said that end is twofold: the end of an activity and the end of an intention. So, then, the body's good can be the end of virtue, in the sense of a certain terminus or effect of virtuous activity; but it cannot be the end in which the *intention* of virtue resides. The reason is that virtue is a perfection of the soul, which is nobler than the body, and nothing acts for the sake of what is baser than itself; thus it cannot be that the intention of virtue rests in the body's good.

5. To the fifth, it should be said that happiness and fortune are said of something in two ways. In one way, as of a subject; and in this way happiness and fortune belong to the same, because neither can exist except in rational beings. The other way, as of an object or matter; and taken thus it is impossible that happiness and fortune be of the same, because fortune takes place in things done for the sake of something, when something unintended happens,[a] whereas happiness or beatitude is intended by all, nor is it ordered to another. And therefore although bodily things are called goods of fortune, materially speaking, it does not follow that happiness consists in bodily goods.

6. To the sixth, it should be said that although man consists of soul and body, he has his specific being from the soul, not from the body, because the form of anything whatsoever is the principle of its specific being.[b] Hence man's beatitude consists, both chiefly and in point of origin, in goods of the soul. For just as the body is for the sake of the soul as for an end, and matter for the sake of form, as is clear from *On the Soul* II,[c] so too goods of the body are ordered to goods of the soul as to an end; hence beatitude cannot chiefly consist in goods of the body.

---

a. *aliquid praeter intentionem accidit*
b. "Being" in both instances is *esse*.
c. Aristotle, *On the Soul* II, ch. 4 (415b15–20).

SUBQUESTION 2[a]   Whether beatitude consists more in things
    belonging to will or in things belonging to intellect

Objections:

It seems that beatitude consists more in things belonging to will
than in things belonging to intellect.

1. For beatitude is the highest good. But good, precisely as good, is
the object of will, not of intellect. Therefore beatitude consists more in
an act of will than an act of intellect.

2. Further, delight is required for beatitude, according to the Philosopher in *Ethics* VII;[b] hence in Greek the very word for beatitude is tak-
en from the word for joy. But delight is in the will or affection. Therefore so is beatitude.

3. Further, as the Philosopher says in *Ethics* X, happiness or beatitude consists in the act of the noblest virtue.[c] But charity is the most
excellent of all virtues, as is clear from the Apostle in 1 Corinthians 13.
Since therefore charity is in the will, that is where one should look for
beatitude.

4. Further, as the soul commands the body, so the will commands
the intellect, and, as a consequence, is superior to it. But beatitude is
set down more among goods of the soul than among those of the body,
because the soul is superior to the body. Thus, for the same reason, it
ought to be set down more on the side of will than on the side of intellect.

5. Further, man's beatitude consists in perfect union with God. But
man is conjoined to God more perfectly through will than through intellect; hence Hugh of St. Victor, commenting on the phrase "mobile
and acute," etc. from chapter 7 of *The Celestial Hierarchy,* says: "Love
towers above knowledge, and is greater than understanding. For God
is more loved than understood; love enters in, where knowledge remains outside."[d] Therefore beatitude consists in love more than in
knowledge, and in will more than in intellect.

---

a. Parallels: *ST* I-II, q. 3, a. 4; *ST* I, q. 26, a. 2, ad 2; *SCG* III, ch. 26; *Quodl.* VIII,
q. 9, a. 1; *Comp. theol.* I, ch. 107.

b. Aristotle, *Ethics* VII, ch. 13 (1153b9–21).

c. Aristotle, *Ethics* X, ch. 7 (1177a11).

d. Hugh of St. Victor, *Commentary on* The Celestial Hierarchy *of Saint Dionysius
the Areopagite,* Book VI, exp. of ch. 7 (PL 175:1038). "Understanding": *intelligentia.* When Thomas cites this text earlier (*In III Sent.* d. 27, q. 1, a. 4, arg. 10) the
wording follows what is found in the PL ed.: *Plus enim diligitur quam intelligitur.*
Here, at least in the Parma ed., the wording differs: *Plus enim Deus diligitur quam
intelligatur.*

On the contrary:

1. Stands what is said in the Gospel of John: "This is eternal life, that they may know you, the true God, and him whom you have sent, Jesus Christ" (17:3). But eternal life is beatitude itself. Therefore beatitude consists in knowledge.

2. Further, on 1 Corinthians 15:24, "when he delivers the kingdom to God the Father [after destroying every rule and every authority and power]," a gloss says: "This means, when he shall have conducted the faithful to the contemplation of God the Father, in which is found the end of all, everlasting rest and joy."[a] But this is [a description of] beatitude. Therefore beatitude consists in intellectual contemplation.

3. Further, the Philosopher in *Ethics* X shows that man's beatitude consists in the act of a contemplative virtue.[b] But this pertains to intellect. Therefore beatitude most of all consists in intellect [i.e., intellectual activity].

4. Further, according to the Philosopher in *Ethics* I, the good in which sufficiency is *per se* found, is happiness or beatitude.[c] But this is found in knowledge, as is clear from John 14:8: "Lord, show us the Father, and that will be sufficient for us." Therefore the same conclusion follows.

Response:

It should be said that [the assertion] "beatitude is in the will" can be understood in two ways. In one way, it can be understood to mean that beatitude is the will's *object*; and so regarded, beatitude—since it is indeed the ultimate end, and from the end is taken the *ratio* of the good, which is the will's object—must be held to be in the will. In another way, it can be understood to mean that beatitude is an *act* of the will; and so regarded, beatitude cannot be in the will, for beatitude implies man's ultimate end. Now man's ultimate end can be taken in two ways: an end within himself, and an end outside himself.[d] [There is an end] *within* him, as a thing's activity is said to be its end, since every thing exists for the sake of its activity. On the other hand, the end *outside* him is that to which he attains through his activity.

Now, it is not just any activity that can be called an end, but that one which first conjoins the agent to the end outside of it; and I say

---

a. Derived from Augustine, *On the Trinity* I, ch. 10 (CCSL 50:56).

b. Aristotle, *Ethics* X, chs. 7–8 (1177a11ff.).

c. Aristotle, *Ethics* I, ch. 7 (1097b14–16).

d. *unus in ipso, et alius extra ipsum*

this is so whenever a thing has an end outside itself, for then it is necessary that the end within be ordered to the end outside, so that the end outside is as the ultimate end; and the end within, which is activity, is ordered to that, even as we see that natural things, through the activities they have, attain (according to a certain assimilation) to the divine goodness, which is their end outside.

But it is not possible that the act of the will itself be the ultimate end of anyone, because since the will's object is the end, this very act (namely, to will), and any other act of will, are nothing other than to order some things to an end; hence such an act presupposes another end, and so, if the willing itself may be said to be willed, one must presuppose that something is willed before this. For one cannot understand there to be in any power reflection upon its own act unless its own act, toward which reflection comes to be, has its term first in its proper object, which is other than the very act of that power; otherwise it would be necessary to proceed to infinity. For if the intellect understands itself to understand, it must understand itself to understand *something;* and if you say that it understands itself to understand the act of "understanding itself," it will be necessary to posit still another act [of the same sort], and so on, to infinity.

It is evident therefore that the very act of understanding cannot be the intellect's first object, and for the same reason, neither can the very act of willing be the will's first object. Since therefore the will's first object is the ultimate end, it is impossible that any act of will be the will's ultimate end. Nor can it even be said that the attainment of the end outside is immediately through an act of will; for there is understood to be an act of will before the attainment of the end, as a certain motion toward the end, and an act of will after the attainment, as a certain resting in the end. But it cannot be that the will is now at rest in the end toward which it was previously tending, except because the will stands related in a different way to the end than it previously did, or the converse [i.e., the end changes relative to the will]. Therefore that which makes the will to stand related to the end in such a way as to be at rest in it is the ultimate end *within,* which first brings about union with the end outside—for example, if someone's end outside is money, the end within will be *possession* of money, through which the man stands related to the money such that his will is at rest in it.

Since therefore the ultimate end, quasi-external, of the human will is God, no act of will can be the end within; but what will be the ultimate end within is that act by which the will first stands related to God in such a way as to be at rest in him. But this is the vision of God according to intellect, because through this act there comes to be a sort of quasi-contact of God to the intellect—since every object of knowledge is *in* the knower insofar as it is known—[and thus it brings the will to rest in him,] even as bodily contact with a pleasant body leads to the being at rest of affection. And therefore man's ultimate end is in an act of the intellect; and so beatitude, which is man's ultimate end, consists in the intellect. Nevertheless, that which is on the part of the will—namely, its being at rest in the end, which can be called delight— is a quasi-formal completion of the *ratio* of beatitude, as being something additional to, yet consequent upon, vision,[a] in which the substance of beatitude consists; thus to the will is attributed both the *first* stance to the end, insofar as it has appetite for the attainment of the end, and the *last*, insofar as it is now at rest in the end attained.

Replies to objections:

1. To the first, therefore, it should be said that this argument shows that beatitude is in the will as the will's *object,* but not as if beatitude were an activity of will.[b]

2. To the second, it should be said that delight is required for beatitude as if a form completive of beatitude, because delight perfects activity as an additional end consequent upon the activity, even as the beauty that youths have as a consequence of their youthfulness adorns their youthfulness,[c] as is said in *Ethics* X.[d]

3. To the third, it should be said that the reason why charity is said to be a virtue higher than others in the wayfaring state is that it is charity that orders all [of them] to God; and also, the ultimate resting in God in the fatherland will belong to charity. Nevertheless, this fact does not grant to charity that its act be the very substance of beatitude, but that it be either a certain inclination to beatitude, as in the wayfaring state, or the resting in beatitude, as in the state of the fatherland.

4. To the fourth, it should be said that the act of a body cannot reach the level of attaining a good of the soul, but the act of intellect can reach the level of attaining the good for which the will has appetite; and therefore the two cases are not parallel.

5. To the fifth, it should be said that man is more perfectly united

---

a. *Sicut superveniens visioni.* There is really no English term corresponding to this usage of *superveniens.* We do have the term "supervenient," but it corresponds to only some uses of the Latin *superveniens.* The meaning is that given in paraphrase. See also the replies to the second and fifth objections.

b. *beatitudo sit in voluntate sicut suum objectum, non autem quasi ejus actus*

c. *quia delectatio perficit operationem ut quidam finis superveniens; velut si juvenibus superveniat pulchritudo, quae juventutem decorat*

d. Aristotle, *Ethics* X, ch. 4 (1174b31–33).

to God through affection than through intellect, inasmuch as the conjunction that occurs through affection comes as an addition to the perfect conjunction that occurs through intellect,[a] perfecting it and adorning it; yet nevertheless it is necessary that the first conjunction always be through intellect.[504] For love inclines one to seek the perfect conjunction before intellect perfectly conjoins, though not before intellect knows [the conjunction] in some sort of way, because appetite cannot be had for something altogether unknown, and it is in this sense [just explained] that Hugh says "knowledge remains outside, where love enters in."

SUBQUESTION 3[b]   Whether beatitude consists in an act
of the practical or of the speculative intellect

Objections:

Moreover, it seems that beatitude consists in an act of the practical intellect rather than of the speculative intellect.

1. For the more common a good is, the more divine it is, as is clear from *Ethics* I.[c] But the good of the speculative intellect belongs solely to the one who contemplates,[d] whereas the good of the practical intellect can be common to many [through the execution of a practical plan]. Therefore beatitude consists more in the practical than in the speculative intellect.

2. Further, beatitude is man's ultimate perfection. But something's perfection is greater when it is the cause of another than when it exists perfect in itself; hence Dionysius, in chapter 3 of *The Celestial Hierarchy,* says that of all things the most godlike is to be made a co-worker with God in the governing of others.[e] Now, through the speculative intellect a man has perfection in himself, whereas the practical intellect is the cause of others [being perfected]. Therefore beatitude consists more in the practical than in the speculative intellect.

---

a. *conjunctio quae est per affectum, supervenit perfectae conjunctioni quae est per intellectum*

b. Parallels: *ST* I-II, q. 3, a. 5; *Sent. Eth.* X, lec. 10–12.

c. Aristotle, *Ethics* I, ch. 2 (1094b6–10).

d. *bonum intellectus speculativi est singulariter ejus qui speculatur*

e. *omnium divinius est Dei cooperatorem fieri in reductione aliorum.* In this line, *reductio* has to be taken as broadly as possible, to include the three tasks of purification, illumination, and perfection that Pseudo-Dionysius argues to be the work of God in creatures and the work he shares with creatures capable of undertaking it. See *The Celestial Hierarchy,* ch. 3, 165D–168A.

3. Further, the end has a conformity to those things that are toward the end.[a] But beatitude is the end and reward of virtue, as is said in *Ethics* I;[b] while virtues consist more in activity than in knowledge, because merely knowing does little or nothing for virtue, as is clear from *Ethics* II.[c] Hence beatitude consists more in the practical intellect than in the speculative.

4. Further, man's beatitude consists in that which is noblest in man. But the practical intellect is nobler than the speculative, since it lays down the law for the speculative intellect, for the legislator, acting from prudence, ordains by whom, and in what manner, the speculative disciplines ought to be learned, as is clear from *Ethics* I.[d] Therefore beatitude is more in the practical intellect than in the speculative.

On the contrary:

1. Beatitude, since it is the ultimate end, is sought for its own sake, not for the sake of something else. But practical knowledge is ordered to something other than itself as to an end, namely to a given work, as is said in *Metaphysics* II;[e] whereas it is not so with speculative knowledge, which is sought for its own sake, as is clear from *Metaphysics* I.[f] Therefore beatitude consists more in the speculative than in the practical intellect.

2. Further, our beatitude consists in being joined to God. But we are joined to God not through the practical intellect, but through the speculative. Therefore beatitude consists more in the speculative than in the practical intellect.

3. Further, the *ratio* of beatitude includes permanence, sufficiency, and delight. But in the act of the contemplative intellect man is more sufficient unto himself than in the act of the practical intellect, for which he requires many external helps; nor is there an action in which man is able to persist so steadily as in contemplation, owing to its distance from bodily instruments, whose weakness brings about weariness; nor is there any delight so pure as that of contemplation, because

a. *finis est conformis his quae sunt ad finem*

b. Aristotle, *Ethics* I, ch. 9 (1099b16–17).

c. Aristotle, *Ethics* II, ch. 4 (1105b6).

d. Aristotle, *Ethics* I, ch. 2 (1094a27–b1).

e. Aristotle, *Metaphysics* II, ch. 1 (993b20–23).

f. Thomas may not have a specific text in mind but more the general perspective of the first book, which concerns the distinctively human quest for answers to wonder-born questions. Cf. Aristotle, *Metaphysics* I, ch. 1 (980a22–27, 981b14–24); ch. 2 (982a14–16, 982a30–b8, 982b11–28); etc.

no contrary is admixed into it; for indeed, it does not even have a contrary. Therefore beatitude most of all consists in an act of the speculative intellect.

Response:

It should be said—as is clear from what was said just above—that man's beatitude is constituted in an act of intellect due to the fact that through such an act there comes about the first union of man to his ultimate end outside himself, to which end the intellect is joined insofar as it knows it. Now, that which is known by the practical intellect cannot be the ultimate end outside man. The reason is as follows: the knowledge of the practical intellect is ordered to what it knows as cause to effect.[505] The effect of something cannot be its ultimate end, however, because the perfection of a cause does not depend on its effect, but vice versa. And so, beatitude cannot consist in an act of the practical intellect, but only in an act of the speculative intellect; and hence it is that all practical knowledge is pursued for the sake of something else for which one has appetite, whereas one has appetite for speculative knowledge for its own sake.

Replies to objections:

1. To the first, therefore, it should be said that the good to which the speculative intellect is joined through knowledge is more common than the good to which the practical intellect is joined, insofar as the speculative intellect is more separated from the particular than the practical intellect, whose knowledge is perfected in activity, which has to do with singulars. But it is true that the *attainment* of the end, to which end the speculative intellect arrives, is, as such [i.e., as that act of knowing *by which* the intellect is united to the object that it knows], proper to the one attaining it, whereas the attainment of the end intended by the practical intellect can be proper as well as common, inasmuch as someone, by practical intellect, directs both himself and others to an end, as is evident in the governor of a multitude; whereas someone, from the simple fact that he contemplates, directs himself alone to the end of his contemplation. However, as much as the very end of the speculative intellect is superior to the good of the practical intellect, so much does its singular attainment exceed the common attainment of the good of the practical intellect; and therefore the most perfect beatitude consists in the speculative intellect.[506]

2. To the second, it should be said that it is more perfect to have a perfection and to pour it from oneself into another than to have it in oneself alone. For the comparison of the aforesaid perfections can-

not be understood in another way, because something cannot have the perfection of being a cause unless at the same time it have in itself that perfection of which it is the cause. It happens, however, that something is of greater perfection insofar as it is perfect in itself than according to its being a cause of another. This is true when it either does not communicate to another the *same* perfection that it has, or communicates the same perfection but not to the same extent as it has it, even as the perfection that is considered in God, according as he exists in himself, is greater than his perfection considered insofar as he is the cause of others. And so, the perfection of the contemplator, inasmuch as he is perfect in himself in contemplating, is greater than that of an artisan inasmuch as he makes a knife. But the one who, by his contemplating, would establish other contemplatives equal to himself would be more perfect than he who could only contemplate by himself alone.

3. To the third, it should be said that an end and the things ordered to an end do not need to be conformed as if they were of a single genus; but there must be between them a conformity of proportion, such that the things ordered to an end be proportioned to leading one into the end; and in this way the virtues are conformed to beatitude, since they lead into beatitude by way of disposition and merit.

4. To the fourth, it should be said that the speculative intellect is nobler, simply speaking, than the practical, since it is on account of itself, whereas the practical is on account of its work; nor does the practical intellect lay down a law for it, for the speculative intellect is not directed in judging of the truth of things according to some law laid down by the practical intellect; but, as the Philosopher says in *Ethics* VI,[a] the practical intellect lays down a law for the sake of the speculative intellect when it ordains in what manner someone ought to arrive at the perfection of the speculative intellect; and by this very fact, the practical intellect is shown to be at the assistance of the speculative.

SUBQUESTION 4[b]   Whether beatitude can be had in this life

Objections:

Moreover, it seems that beatitude can be had in this life.

1. For Matthew 5:3 says: "Blessed are the poor in spirit, for theirs is the kingdom of heaven," and similarly: "Blessed are they who suffer

a. Aristotle, *Ethics* VI, ch. 1 (1138b26–28).
b. Parallels: *In IV Sent.* d. 43, a. 1, qa. 1; *ST* I-II, q. 5, a. 3; *SCG* III, ch. 48; *Sent. Eth.* I, lec. 10 and 16.

persecution"; and other sayings of this kind. But all these things can be had in this life. Therefore beatitude is [able to be had] in this life.

2. Further, if beatitude were not possible in this life, no one would know about it unless he had some knowledge of the other life.[a] But many philosophers wholly ignorant of the future life have yet treated of beatitude. Therefore beatitude is possible even in this life.

3. Further, man's present life is more perfect than the present life of any other animal. But the present life of other animals includes [the attainment of] their ultimate end. Therefore man's present life, too, includes beatitude, which is man's end.

4. Further, each and every thing naturally desires its end. But from the desire for the end arises a desire for the things that lead to the end. Now, especially ordered to an end are those things without which one cannot arrive at that end. Thus man's death would be ordered to beatitude, if man could not have beatitude in this present life. Therefore man would naturally desire death; which is perceived to be false by experience, and contradicts the authority of the Apostle, who says in 2 Corinthians 5:4: "Not that we wish to be unclothed, but further clothed." Therefore man's beatitude is [able to be had] in this life.

On the contrary:

1. No one can be blessed who does not have that which he wills well [i.e., as he ought to will it]. But any blessed person wills well and ordinately never to be able to be deprived of his beatitude. Therefore whosoever does not have this [security] is not truly blessed. But no one in his life has this [security], since the very happiness that one *can* have in this life must be taken away at least by death. Therefore beatitude cannot be had in this life.

2. Further, no one has already arrived at the ultimate [degree] of life if there remains anything for him to desire, since beatitude has sufficiency in itself, as even the Philosopher says.[b] But no matter how much someone in this life is perfect in knowledge or virtue or any other perfection, still there remains something for him to desire, such as knowing many things that he does not know; indeed, even the goodness of his [present] perfection, as long as this life goes on, cannot be certain, since even the wisest and most perfect men may go down into madness through bodily infirmities. Therefore beatitude cannot be had in this life.

a. *si beatitudo non posset esse in hac vita, nullus beatitudinem cognosceret, nisi qui de alia vita notitiam haberet*
b. Aristotle, *Ethics* I, ch. 7 (1097b14–16).

3. Further, beatitude is identified by all as the greatest good. But the greatest good is that which is thoroughly unmixed with evil. Since, therefore, regardless of how much someone is wise and perfect in virtue, this life cannot be without evils (as is manifestly apparent when one looks at the various accidents and misfortunes that befall man),[a] it seems that beatitude cannot be [had] in this life.

Response:

It should be said that in voluntary things appetite stands to an end—and things that are sought on account of an end stand to the attainment of the end—as in natural things motion stands to its terminus. And so, just as when a natural thing arrives at its terminus, its motion ceases, so too [with] the will: when it has what it seeks, its seeking desists, having been converted into love or delight.[b] Therefore, since it is the end to which all desires are referred, beatitude must be something such that, when one has it, nothing further remains to be desired.

[Qualities of beatitude.] Now, anyone naturally desires to exist, and to remain in the good that he has; and so beatitude is set down by everyone to be some such thing as has immobility and perpetuity.[c] But people have judged differently of the immobility and perpetuity of human beatitude.

[Opinion of Plato.] For some said that absolute perpetuity was not included in the *ratio* of human beatitude, but only a perpetuity with respect to man's life.[507] Nor yet in this perpetuity was considered the immobility that takes away potentiality for being changed, but only that which takes away the act of being changed. And this was the opinion of Plato, as is touched upon in *Ethics* I.[d] For he argued that that man is blessed in this life whose beatitude continued all the way to his death. But because the condition of a man, no matter how perfect, can be changed in this life, and we cannot have sure judgment of future contingents, therefore we cannot know of any man before his death whether his perfection would continue all the way to his death; but *at* the end of his life one would be able to know if it had been continued even to the end; and so, no one can be called blessed until his death.

[Opinion of Aristotle.] However, the Philosopher disproves this position,[e] because it is unfitting to argue that someone ought to be called

a. *ut manifeste apparet varios casus hominis intuendo*
b. "are sought": *appetuntur;* "seek": *quaerit;* and "seeking": *appetitus*
c. More loosely: "and so everyone identifies immovability and perpetuity as properties of beatitude."
d. Aristotle, *Ethics* I, ch. 10 (1100a10ff.).
e. Ibid.

blessed when he no longer exists and that he cannot be called blessed when he does exist. If therefore beatitude is in this life, if someone is blessed, he is blessed while he is alive; but when he is dead, he will not be blessed; and thus he is more able to be called blessed when alive than when dead. Hence the Philosopher in the same passage states a different opinion concerning beatitude or happiness—namely, as was said, that beatitude, in its perfect *ratio,* has absolute perpetuity and immobility. But according to its perfect *ratio,* it is impossible for beatitude to pertain[a] to man; what is possible is for a man to have some participation of it, however little, and owing to this participation, to be called blessed; and so, a blessed man need not be perpetually and immutably blessed, simply speaking,[b] but only according to the condition of human nature; hence he adds: "blessed, however, as men." Such immutability belongs to a man when the habits of virtues are firmly rooted in him, so that he cannot easily be deflected from acting virtuously.

[The truth of the matter.] But that position, too, does not seem to be reasonable. For it is commonly held by everyone that happiness, or beatitude, is a good of the rational or intellectual nature; and so where the rational or intellectual nature is found in its essence, and not only by participation, one must also posit beatitude in its essence, and not by participation. And so, since in man not only is there some overflow of intellect—as in the brute animals there is a certain overflow of reason inasmuch as they participate somewhat in prudence, as appears in their instincts[c]—but also there is in him reason or intellect in its essence, it must be posited that at some time he can attain true beatitude, and not merely a participation of beatitude; otherwise the natural appetite of the intellectual nature that is in man would be frustrated. Now true beatitude cannot be posited [to occur] in this life on account of the various inconstancies[d] to which man is subject; hence it is necessary for the beatitude that is the end of human life to be [had] *after* this life. And this, indeed, all philosophers conceded who posited the soul, which is the form of the human body, to be intellect in its essence; for they posited an immortal soul. Whereas those who posited the soul, which is the form of the human body, not to be intellect in its essence, but rather posited in it a reflection of an intellect that is separate, and one common to all, posit the soul, which is the form of the body, to be corruptible, and not to arrive at perfect beatitude, but only

a. *accidere*
b. Literally: "a blessed man need not be perpetual and immobile, simply speaking," etc.
c. *moribus*
d. *mutabilitates*

to arrive at a participation of beatitude, of such a sort as was spoken of above. But this opinion is absurd, as was demonstrated in Book II, Distinction 17, question 2, article 1. And therefore we concede that man's true beatitude, simply speaking, is after this life. Nevertheless, we do not deny that there can be to some extent a participation of beatitude in this life, according as man is perfect in the goods of reason—chiefly of speculative reason, secondarily of practical reason; and it is about this [earthly] happiness that the Philosopher determines in the book of *Ethics*, neither asserting nor denying another [happiness] that is after this life.

Replies to objections:

1. To the first, therefore, it should be said, as was said in Book III,[a] that the "beatitudes" in that passage designate acts of perfect virtues, according to which man is in a certain participation and likeness of future beatitude, which is true beatitude.

2. To the second, it should be said that those philosophers who, [though] speaking of beatitude, did not posit a future life were [accordingly] not speaking of true beatitude, but of a participation thereof, as was said.

3. To the third, it should be said that the end of human life surpasses the end of the life of other animals more than the one life surpasses the other life;[508] and from this the very life of man is nobler in that it is ordered to a nobler end. Hence human life need not include its ultimate end, as the life of other animals includes their end.

4. To the fourth, it should be said that, although man naturally desires the end, nevertheless he does not naturally desire those things that lead to the end; but he desires these by rational appetite, by deliberating about them and choosing them. Nor is it unfitting for something in itself worthy of hatred to be appetible with a view to an end, even as the amputation of bodily members is appetible on account of health [when it can be preserved only by that means]; and in this way death, from which everyone naturally flees, is appetible on account of beatitude, as is said in Philippians 1:23: "having a desire to be dissolved and to be with Christ."[509]

a. See *In III Sent.* d. 34, q. 1, a. 4.

ARTICLE 2   On beatitude as created and uncreated

SUBQUESTION 1ᵃ   Whether beatitude is
something uncreated

Objections:

Proceeding to the second. It seems that beatitude is something uncreated.

1. First of all, because of what Boethius says in *On the Consolation of Philosophy* III,ᵇ that beatitude is the godhead itself; whence he concludes that every blessed one is a god.

2. Further, that which is said by way of superabundance belongs to one alone. But God is the highest good, since he is the cause of all goodness; also, beatitude is the highest good, since it is desired by all as the ultimate end. Therefore beatitude is God himself alone.

3. Further, that which is desirable just on account of itself has the *ratio* of the enjoyable, as is evident from Augustine. But beatitude is appetible on account of itself, as is evident from the Philosopher in *Ethics* I.ᶜ Therefore beatitude is to be enjoyed. But God alone is to be enjoyed, as is evident from Augustine in *On Christian Doctrine* I.ᵈ Therefore God alone is beatitude.

4. Further, it belongs to the *ratio* of beatitude that there be sufficiency in it. But in God alone does the human appetite find sufficiency; hence Augustine says, in *Confessions:* "Our heart is restless until it comes unto thee."ᵉ Therefore God alone is beatitude itself.

5. Further, everything which is in us is in us either essentially or accidentally. But beatitude is not of the essence of man, for in that case, every man would be blessed, and all the time. Therefore if it is something in man, it will be an accident. But an accident cannot be the end of a substance, since substance is nobler than accident. Therefore it is impossible that beatitude be something in us; and so it will be something uncreated.

---

a. Parallel: *ST* I-II, q. 3, a. 1.

b. Boethius, *On the Consolation of Philosophy* III, Prose 10 (CCSL 94:54).

c. Aristotle, *Ethics* I, ch. 7 (1097a36).

d. Augustine, *On Christian Doctrine* I, ch. 5 (CCSL 32:9).

e. *Inquietum est cor nostrum donec perveniat ad te*—a slight misquotation of Augustine's famous sentence, which ends: *donec requiescat in te* (*Confessions* I, n. 1 [CCSL 27:1]). Aquinas gets the line right in five other places in his corpus where he quotes it, making it plausible that we are dealing here with a miscopy that a future critical edition will set to rights.

On the contrary:

1. As by the participation of justice men are called just, so by the participation of beatitude men are called blessed, as is evident from Boethius in *On the Consolation of Philosophy* III.[a] But justice is something created in us; hence so too is beatitude.

2. Further, happiness with the addition of a number of goods is more choiceworthy [than happiness alone], as is evident from the Philosopher in *Ethics* I.[b] But God, with whatever additional things we add, is not more choiceworthy [than he is all by himself]. Therefore happiness is something other than God; and so it is something created in us.

Response:

It should be said that the good that all long for is being,[c] as is evident from Boethius in *On the Consolation of Philosophy*.[d] Hence the ultimate object of desire for all things is perfect being, to the extent that it is possible in their nature. Now, everything that has being from another has its perfection from another, since each one receives being the more perfectly, the more truly it is conjoined to the principle of its being. Hence, lower bodies, owing to their great distance from the first principle, have corruptible being, as is clear from *On Generation and Corruption* II.[e] And so the ultimate end of anything whatsoever that has being from another is twofold: one outside [itself], namely according to that which is the principle of the desired perfection; another within [itself], namely its very own perfection, which union to its principle brings about. Hence, since beatitude is man's ultimate end, beatitude will be twofold [in the way described]: one that is within man himself, namely that ultimate perfection of himself at which it is possible for him to arrive, and this is created beatitude; whereas the other is outside himself, through union with which the aforementioned beatitude is *caused* in him; and this is uncreated beatitude, which is God himself.

a. Boethius, *On the Consolation of Philosophy* III, Prose 10 (CCSL 94:54).
b. Aristotle, *Ethics* I, ch. 7 (1097b16–19). This passage of Aristotle could be interpreted—and with greater plausibility—to be saying the opposite of what St. Thomas says here. Cf. *Ethics* X, ch. 2 (1172b27–35) and *Magna Moralia* I, chs. 2–4.
c. *bonum quod omnia concupiscunt, est esse*
d. Boethius, *On the Consolation of Philosophy* III, Prose 11 (CCSL 94:58–59).
e. Aristotle, *On Generation and Corruption* II, ch. 10 (336b30).

Replies to objections:

1. To the first, therefore, it should be said that just as God himself is good by his essence, whereas all other things are goods by participation, as is said in the book *On the Hebdomads*,[a] so too, God himself alone is beatitude by his essence, whereas others are blessed by participation. Hence created beatitude is a certain participation and likeness of uncreated beatitude. Yet it is not beatitude essentially, as if making men blessed by *its* essence; and thus is to be understood the citation from Boethius.

2. To the second it should be said that created beatitude is not the highest good simply, but the highest good among human goods; but God is the highest good simply, and so the objection does not prove its point.

3. To the third it should be said that an object of love is of two kinds.[b] There is an object that is loved in the manner of benevolence, when we will the good for another on account of himself, as we love our friends, even if nothing should come to us from them. And there is an object that is loved by the love of concupiscence; and this is either a good that is within us, or because from it something is made to be a good for us, as we love pleasure, or wine inasmuch as it produces pleasure. Now whatever is loved with a love of concupiscence cannot be the ultimate object of love, since it is referred to the good of another (his, namely, who has concupiscence for it); but that which is loved by a love of benevolence can be the ultimate object of love.

Therefore the created beatitude that is within us is loved only by a love of concupiscence; hence the love of it we refer to ourselves, and consequently we refer it to God, since we ought to refer even ourselves to God; and thus, it cannot be the ultimate object of love. Nevertheless it is the ultimate object of concupiscence by the very fact that it is the greatest good that comes *to us* from union with God, and so it is said to be sought or desired on account of itself; for each[c] signifies something ultimate among the things that are loved with a love of concupiscence.

a. Boethius, *On the Hebdomads* (PL 64:1311–14).

b. *duplex est diligibile*

c. *et ideo dicitur esse propter se quaesitum vel desideratum; utrumque enim importat aliquid ultimum in his quae diliguntur amore concupiscentiae.* The *utrumque* refers to *quaesitum vel desideratum* taken together with the prepositional clause, thus: *propter se quaesitum* or *propter se desideratum.* Thomas is making a point about the way we speak and why we speak that way. In the order of goods loved with concupiscence, that is, for the lover's good, there is some ultimate, and this is not pursued for any other good beyond itself—in its own order.

For although God [himself] is desired,ᵃ it is the same to desire God and to desire the greatest of goods that come to us from God, just as it is the same to desire wine and to desire the effect of wine in us, say, pleasure.⁵¹⁰

4. To the fourth it should be said that in God alone is found sufficiency as in the principle of all good, which the appetite seeks; but by the divine gift a sufficiency for themselves is found, in those to whom it is granted by God that they should possess all goods sufficiently.

5. To the fifth it should be said that, although every accident *as such* is less noble than a substance, nevertheless an accident, from some vantage, can be worthier than a substance. For an accident may be considered in two ways. In one way, as it inheres in a subject, from which it derives the *ratio* of being an accident; and from this vantage, every accident is less worthy than a substance. In another way, it may be considered in its order to something outside [the subject]; and from this vantage, some accident can be nobler than a substance, inasmuch as through it a substance is joined to something nobler than itself; and in this way created beatitude, and grace, and other such things, are something nobler than the nature of the soul in which they inhere. There is also another consideration according to which an accident is nobler, namely inasmuch as a substance is compared to an accident inhering in it as potency to act.

SUBQUESTION 2ᵇ   Whether happiness is an actᶜ

Objections:

Moreover, it seems that happiness is not an act.

1. For, according to Boethius in *On the Consolation of Philosophy* III,ᵈ beatitude is a state made perfect by the gathering together of all goods. But "state" does not name an act. Therefore beatitude is not an act.

2. Further, we are the cause of our own acts. If therefore beatitude consisted in an act of ours, we ourselves would be the cause of our own beatitude, which is absurd. [Therefore beatitude cannot be an act.]

3. Further, if anything in us is the ultimate end, this will be espe-

a. "desired" and "desire": *concupiscatur* and *concupiscere*

b. Parallels: *ST* I-II, q. 3, a. 2 and q. 55, a. 2, ad 3; *SCG* I, ch. 100; *Sent. Eth.* I, lec. 10; *In Metaphys.* IX, ch. 8.

c. The terms used are *felicitas* and *actus*. For the latter, one might translate "activity," but this would be awkward since Thomas also speaks in the same article of *operatio*, which better deserves that translation.

d. Boethius, *On the Consolation of Philosophy* III, Prose 2 (CCSL 94:38).

cially that which is never sought on account of anything else. But delight is not sought on account of another, but only on account of itself. Therefore beatitude consists most of all in delight. But delight is not an act, but a passion. Therefore happiness is not an act.

4. Further, there can be diverse acts arising from one agent and according to a single habit. If therefore beatitude were an act, there would be diverse beatitudes of the same blessed [person], which is absurd.

5. Further, the beatitude of the wayfaring state is a certain likeness of the beatitude of the fatherland. But the beatitude of the wayfaring state cannot be called an act, for if that were so, those who are sleeping would lose their beatitude. Therefore the beatitude of the fatherland is not an act.

On the contrary:

1. The Philosopher says in *Ethics* I that happiness is an activity according to perfect virtue.[a]

2. Further, that for the sake of which a thing exists is its ultimate end. But every thing exists for the sake of its own activity, as is said in *On the Heavens* II.[b] Therefore the activity proper to man is his ultimate end; and so his beatitude is a certain act.

3. Further, a man is blessed through maximally arriving at likeness to God. But man is maximally likened to God through being actually in act, because in this way he is maximally in act [and] remote from potentiality [as is God]. Therefore man's beatitude consists in an activity of his.

Response:

It should be said that, as is evident from what was said before, a thing's ultimate end, as taken in the thing itself, is that through which a thing is joined to its end outside, which is the principle of its perfection. Now to God, who is their ultimate end, things can be joined in two ways. In one way, by way of likening, so that a thing is said to be most of all *joined* to God when it is most of all *like* unto God; and according to this, it is necessary for each thing's ultimate end to be that according to which it is maximally likened to God. But each thing approaches likeness to God just insofar as it is in act, whereas it departs [from that likeness] insofar as it is in potency; and [so] that through

a. Aristotle, *Ethics* I, ch. 7 (1098a16–18) and ch. 13 (1102a5).
b. The text Thomas probably has in mind is *On the Heavens* II, ch. 3 (286a8): "Everything which has a function exists for its function."

which a thing is maximally in act is its ultimate end. In another way, [things can be joined to God] by reaching God himself—a union that, in fact, is possible only to the rational creature, which is able to be joined to God himself by knowledge and by love, precisely because God is the object of its activity but is not the object of any other [non-rational] creature's activity.

Now in whichever manner one considers man's ultimate perfection, which is his end, it must be located in the genus of act. For if we consider the manner of union with God that is common to all creatures, since a thing is more in act insofar as it is *acting* than insofar as it is [merely] capable of acting,[a] the ultimate perfection of each and every thing will be its perfect activity; hence a thing is said to exist on account of its activity. Likewise, if we consider the union proper to the rational creature, man's ultimate perfection consists in activity, for a habit is not united to its object except as mediated by an act; and therefore beatitude must be located in the genus of act. Nevertheless, this second consideration bears upon the consideration of beatitude more closely than the first, since beatitude belongs only to the rational creature.

Replies to objections:

1. To the first, therefore, it should be said that in any order whatsoever, all things that are toward an end work together for the ultimate end; hence, since the perfect activity of man is his ultimate end (as is the case with every single thing), all human goods work together for his perfect activity, as the habits by which his acts are informed work together for the perfect activity of man in this life; and other natural goods [work together for the end] as principles of acts, and external goods as instrumentally necessary for perfect activity. Thus, therefore, the gathering together of all goods is set down as beatitude insofar as all goods gathered together offer their support to the most perfect activity of man, which is essentially beatitude itself. All the aforesaid goods, too, are ordered to the beatitude of the fatherland, inasmuch as we merit through their [charitable] use; and while not all of them, in themselves, remain in beatitude, nevertheless they remain in those [perfections] that succeed to them, just as a sufficiency of eternal goods succeeds to faith.

2. To the second, it should be said that in an act two things are to be considered: the substance of the act, and its form, from which an

---

a. *cum res magis sit in actu secundum quod est operans, quam secundum quod est potens operari*

act has perfection. Therefore, as regards the substance of an act, its principle is a natural potency; but as regards its form, its principle is the habit [from which the act proceeds]. If therefore that habit be an acquired one, we will be entirely the cause of our act; if, on the contrary, that habit be an infused one, [we will be the cause of only the substance of the act, whereas] its perfection will be from the exterior cause that causes the habit. Now, an act of ours is not held to be our beatitude save by reason of its perfection, due to which it is most nobly joined to the end outside; and thus not we, but God, is the cause of our beatitude.

3. To the third, it should be said that delight is twofold. One is that which precedes the attainment of an end; and this is capable of being ordered to something else, for it can be ordered to perfect activity, insofar as we undertake more diligently that in which we delight. The other delight is that which follows upon the attainment of an end; and this is brought about by the activity that joins the agent to an end. Thus this latter delight is not beatitude itself, but a certain perfection and form of beatitude,[a] as was said above.

4. To the fourth, it should be said that a multitude of acts proceeding from the same habit with respect to the same object is caused only by the interruptions of time; and so in perfect beatitude, where there will be no interruptions but a continuous activity, there will be only a single beatitude.

5. To the fifth, it should be said, as was said above, that the beatitude of the wayfaring state is not perfect beatitude but a certain participation thereof; and so it is not always in act, but sometimes is [merely] in habit. Hence a sleeping person can be called blessed, not as regards that which he has right at that moment, but only insofar as the activity itself is in him habitually. For in the way in which effects are present in their causes, so activities are present in their habits.

SUBQUESTION 3[b] Whether man's beatitude is the same thing as eternal life

Objections:

Moreover, it seems that man's beatitude is not the same thing as eternal life.

a. *quaedam beatitudinis perfectio, et forma*—"a form of beatitude" in the sense of something completive, something that fills or rounds out the good of beatitude the essence of which consists, absolutely speaking, in a higher act of a nobler power.

b. Parallels: cf. *ST* I, q. 18, a. 2, esp. ad 2; *In II Sent.* d. 38, a. 2, ad 3 (above).

1. For as is said in *On the Soul* II, "for living things, to live is to be."[a] But beatitude, according to the Philosopher, does not consist in being [alone], but in activity. Therefore man's beatitude is not a *life.*

2. Further, the *ratio* of life consists in motion, as is evident from the Commentator on the *Book of Causes.* But beatitude includes in its *ratio* unchangeability. Therefore beatitude is not the same thing as eternal life.

3. Further, beatitude is something communicable to man. But eternity of life is not something that can be communicated to him, since what is made in time is not capable of being eternal. Therefore eternal life is not the same thing as beatitude.

4. Further, whatsoever endures perpetually participates, in a way, in eternal life, if "eternal" be taken in a broad sense to mean "perpetual." But the damned endure perpetually, sent into eternal fire, as is evident from Matthew 25:41. However, they have not beatitude, but the highest misery. Therefore beatitude and eternal life are not the same thing.

On the contrary:

1. That which is the end of human life is beatitude. But eternal life is the end of human life, as is evident from Romans 6:22: "You have your fruit unto sanctification, and the end, eternal life." Therefore, [beatitude and eternal life are the same thing].

2. Further, man's ultimate beatitude consists in the vision of God, as is evident from what was said above. But in this [vision] eternal life consists, as is evident from John 17:3: "This is eternal life, that they may know you, the one true God, and him whom you have sent, Jesus Christ." Therefore beatitude is the same thing as eternal life.

Response:

It should be said that "life" may be said in two ways. In one way, as the very being of living things; since, as is said in *On the Soul* II, "for living things, to live is to be."[b] Now, something is said to be alive from the fact that it is able to move itself according to some action; hence plants are said to live from the fact that they move themselves in regard to increase; and animals still more, in that they move themselves in regard to place and move themselves to sensing; and in man yet more, in that he is able to move himself to willing and to understanding. Now, the perfection of any power is its act; hence, second, the name "life"

a. Aristotle, *On the Soul* II, ch. 4 (415b13).
b. Ibid.

is carried over to signify an activity to which something moves itself, as sensing is called animal life, and understanding is called human life; and according to this way [of speaking], every single thing esteems as its life that activity which it maximally intends, as if its entire being were ordered to that activity (it is in keeping with this way of speaking that people say: "so-and-so leads such-and-such a life"); and thus it was that the Epicureans held beatitude to be a life of pleasures.[a] Now activity is not subject to the measure of time except insofar as it is bound up with motion; hence activities that are not bound up with motion but bear instead on the terminus of motion are not measured by time but in an instant, as is evident with illumination.[511] And so, if there is an activity that altogether transcends motion, such an activity will be measured not by time but by a measure above time. Now, the vision of God, which is held to be man's beatitude, cannot be an action measured by time in and of itself, since it is not successive; nor can it be measured by time on the part of the seer or on the part of the seen, since both are outside motion; hence it can be measured neither by time nor by the instant, which is the terminus of time. It cannot even be measured by an age, for an age,[b] insofar as it is distinguished from eternity, pertains to immutable creatures, whereas this vision exceeds the natural power of the creature, since no creature by its natural endowments is capable of arriving at it; hence its proper measure is eternity itself. And so, the vision of God, which is beatitude itself, is eternal life itself.

Replies to objections:

1. To the first, therefore, the response is evident from what has been said.

2. To the second, it should be said that although life is first recognized by motion, since it is through motion that the living are first distinguished from the non-living, nevertheless the name "life" is extended further to all activities that are not [merely] from some external mover, as willing, understanding, and other such things; hence, the name "motion," too, gets carried over to such activities, as when we call understanding a "movement of the intellect" or willing a "movement of the will."

3. To the third, it should be said that eternity is not communicable to man in such a way that it becomes an adequate measure of him, or of something within him, as the argument brought forward proves.

a. *vitam voluptuosam*
b. *aevo . . . aevum*

Still, it can be communicated to man according to a certain participation—so that, just as man is made a partaker of divine activity in seeing God, so he is made a partaker of eternity, by which the divine activity is measured; and it is thus that man's very activity can be called eternal life.

4. To the fourth, it should be said that the eternal life the saints will have is spoken of according to a participation of eternity, not merely with regard to lacking an end[a] (in which manner even the punishment of the damned is called "eternal"), but further with regard to the removal of all change, not only in act, which an "age" too excludes, but even in potency. For the saints, through clinging to God, will obtain such stability from the divine gift that they cannot be changed—a stability God has by his nature, by reason of which he is eternal.

SUBQUESTION 4[b]   Whether beatitude is the same thing as peace

Objections:

Moreover, it seems that beatitude is the same thing as peace.

1. First of all, because of what is said in Psalm 147:14: "who has placed peace in your borders [*fines*]."[c] But the end [*finis*] of the city of God, which is being spoken of there, is beatitude. Therefore beatitude is the same thing as peace.

2. Further, Augustine says, in *On the City of God* XIX: "We may say that the end of our goods is peace, just as we may say that it is eternal life."[d] But eternal life is the same thing as beatitude. Therefore so is peace.

3. Further, that which is naturally desired by all and for the sake of which other things are done would seem to be man's beatitude. But all desire peace, and do whatever they do for its sake, as Augustine says,[e] and Dionysius.[f] Therefore peace is beatitude itself.

a. *ad defectum finis*, i.e., being endless in duration.

b. There are several texts on peace that could be listed as partial parallels, e.g., *ST* II-II, q. 29, a. 2, ad 4; *Super Ioan.* 14, lec. 7; *Super Phil.* 4, lec. 1.

c. Ps. 147:3 iuxta Vulg. The Psalmist's mention of *fines* (borders, boundaries) allows for reading the verse to be saying: God has established peace as the "end" of the city. Since the end is already known to be beatitude, peace must be referring to the same thing.

d. Augustine, *On the City of God* XIX, ch. 11 (CCSL 48:674).

e. As there are many places where Augustine says that all things desire peace, it is by no means clear if Thomas has a specific text in mind.

f. See Pseudo-Dionysius, *On the Divine Names*, ch. 11 (PG 3:947ff.).

4. Further, peace signifies a certain resting. But the end of every change is rest, as can be shown, for example, among natural things. Therefore peace is the end of the whole of our changeable life; and so peace is the same thing as beatitude.

On the contrary:

1. According to the Philosopher, beatitude is a certain activity.[a] But peace does not name an act, but only immobility. Therefore peace is not the same thing as beatitude.

2. Further, peace refers most of all to appetite or the will, because it is a certain resting thereof. But beatitude consists especially in intellect, as was said above. Therefore beatitude is not the same thing as peace.

Response:

It should be said, as Augustine says in Book XIX of *On the City of God*, that "the peace of all things is the tranquillity of order"[b]—from which it is evident that the *ratio* of peace is taken from the fact that something is not impeded from right order; for tranquillity excludes the disturbance of an impediment. Now, peace especially bears upon that order by which the will is ordered to something; hence we say that a man has peace only when there is nothing that impedes the order of his will to something [he wants]; and in like manner, we say that a city has peace when there is nothing that disturbs the city's right order, which is from the will of the city's governor; and to the extent that even inanimate things are said to have natural appetite, we hold that every single thing has peace when it is not impeded from [following] the inclination that it has to its end, which it naturally desires.

Now, the activity in which beatitude consists must be an unimpeded activity; for any impediment would detract from its perfection. Hence delight, too, which follows upon perfect activity, is caused by an unimpeded activity, as is said in *Ethics* VII;[c] and thus peace is required for beatitude—not that it is the very essence of beatitude, but it is like a removal of whatever could impede beatitude. Now from the very fact that one desires something, one's appetite shuns its contrary; and for all naturally to shun these impediments is for them naturally to desire peace.

a. Aristotle, *Ethics* I, ch. 7 (1098a16–18) and ch. 13 (1102a5).
b. Augustine, *On the City of God* XIX, ch. 13 (CCSL 48:679).
c. Aristotle, *Ethics* VII, ch. 12 (1153a13–15).

Replies to objections:

1. To the first, therefore, it should be said that peace is said to be the end of the city of God in the sense of being the nearest disposition to the end, which is simultaneous with that very end, and not as if it were the end *per se.*

2. The second deserves a like response.

3. To the third it should be said that all desire peace, not as an end, but as that without which an end cannot be possessed.

4. To the fourth it should be said that a thing's ultimate end is not rest but activity, and this activity cannot be perfect unless the thing itself *be* perfect.[a] Motion, however, is an imperfect act; and accordingly, rest, in which motion terminates, is nearer the end than motion itself. And thus, motion is ordered to rest as to an end.

SUBQUESTION 5[b] Whether beatitude is the
same thing as the kingdom of God

Objections:

Moreover, it seems that beatitude is not the same thing as the kingdom of God.

1. For "kingdom," which is named in reference to the rule exercised by a king, seems to pertain to the governing that exercises providence.[c] But providence consists in the coordination of things that are *directed* toward the end itself [and so, does not bear upon the end as such]. Therefore "kingdom of God" does not seem to pertain to beatitude, which is the ultimate end.

2. Further, Dionysius says that "the kingdom is the distribution of every end and law and order."[d] But this distribution pertains not only to men but also to all creatures to which God distributes the aforesaid things, whereas beatitude belongs solely to rational creatures. Therefore beatitude is not the same thing as the kingdom of God.

3. Further, the only perfection that "kingdom" signifies is that of

---

a. *ultimus finis rei non est quies, sed operatio rei, cujus perfectio non potest esse nisi re perfecta existente*

b. There is no exact parallel to this subquestion. There are, of course, many discussions in Thomas's writings of the political concepts he employs here.

c. *Regnum enim, quod dicitur a regendo, ad gubernationem providentiae pertinere videtur*

d. Pseudo-Dionysius, *On the Divine Names,* ch. 12, n. 2 (PG 3:970).

the one who sits at the head.[a] But there is only one who stands at the head in the ruling of a kingdom, as is evident from the Philosopher in *Ethics* VIII.[b] Therefore the kingdom of God does not bespeak any perfection except in God himself. But beatitude bespeaks a perfection not only in God but in all the blessed. Therefore beatitude is not the same thing as the kingdom of God.

4. Further, beatitude does not suffer the admixture of any evil. But in the kingdom of God there can be some evils; hence it is said in Matthew 13:41 that at the end of the world the angels will gather up all scandals from the kingdom of God. Therefore the kingdom of God is not beatitude itself.

On the contrary:

1. Stands the statement of Augustine, who says in Sermon 22 to the Fathers in the Desert, that the first three petitions in the Lord's Prayer pertain to future beatitude.[c] Now, one of these is "Thy kingdom come." Therefore the kingdom of God pertains to beatitude.

2. Further, beatitude is what is promised to the saints as their reward. But the kingdom of God is so promised, as is clear from Matthew 5:10: "Blessed are they who suffer persecution for righteousness' sake, for theirs is the kingdom of heaven." Therefore the kingdom of heaven is beatitude itself.

Response:

It should be said that the name "kingdom" is named in reference to the rule exercised by a king. But ruling is an act of providence; hence someone is said to have a kingdom when he has others under his providence; and thus, men are said to be "in the kingdom of God" when they are perfectly subject to his providence. Now, it belongs to providence to order things to an end. But to an end are ordered both the things that stand at some distance from the end, inasmuch as they are led to it, and the things that have already gained the end, inasmuch as they are preserved in its possession. And since the end is the rule[d] of providence, those are under providence perfectly who are already stationed in the very end; and hence in them nothing can be foreign to the order of providence. Others, however, who stand at some distance

a. *nisi in praesidente*

d. Aristotle, *Ethics* VIII, ch. 10 (1160b1).

c. Pseudo-Augustine, *Sermons to the Fathers in the Desert,* Serm. 22 (PL 40:1272); cf. Augustine, *On the Sermon on the Mount* II, ch. 10 (CCSL 35:126).

d. *regula*

from the end are under divine providence more or less perfectly to the extent that they are nearer or further from the end;[a] and those are nearest to the end who are on the way to the end.[b] Now the way of arriving at the end is "faith working through love."[c] Hence "kingdom of God" is said, as if by antonomasia, in two ways: at times to mean the congregation of those who walk [toward heaven] by faith, and in this way the church militant is called the kingdom of God; at other times to mean the company[d] of those who are already established in the end, and in this way the church triumphant is called the kingdom of God. And in this latter way of speaking, to be in the kingdom of God is the same thing as to be in beatitude. Nor is there any difference between the kingdom of God and beatitude [in this latter sense], except as the common good of the whole multitude is distinguished from the singular good of each and every member thereof.[512]

Replies to objections:

1. To the first, therefore, it should be said that beatitude is under providence not as if it were ordered by providence to something as to an end but because other things are ordered by providence to it [viz., beatitude].[e]

2. To the second, it should be said that Dionysius sufficiently touches on the things that are required for a kingdom in the sense of a multitude governed by providence. For this activity, three things are required: namely an end, order to an end, and a rule[f] of order—which last indeed is twofold: one in the person ordering (and this is law, from which the rectitude of order proceeds); the other in the one who is ordered, through which he is made not to depart from the rectitude of order (and it is this rule that causes ordering to an end, whether the rule in question be a form, a virtue, or something else of the sort; and this is what Dionysius terms "adornment"). But although these four can pertain to all creatures, since all things are ordered by God to an end according to the law of eternal wisdom, and to all things are given powers[g] by which they tend to an end, still, in a special way, they pertain to rational creatures, who are fitted to arrive at the ultimate end

a. *magis et minus a fine elongantur*
b. *propinquissimi sunt fini qui sunt in via ad finem*
c. An indirect citation of Gal. 5:6.
d. *collegium*
e. *beatitudo non subest providentiae quasi ad finem ordinata, sed quia ad ipsam alia ordinantur*
f. *regula*
g. *virtutes*

itself in the most noble manner and who know the *ratio* of order and of end.

3. To the third, it should be said that kingdom implies perfection, both in the one who sits at the head and in the one who is subject; but in the one who sits at the head as the principle of perfection, who places his rectitude upon others; while in the subject as one receiving perfection from another. But the saints who are in the fatherland are subject to divine providence in this [somewhat different] way: they are made providers for themselves and for others, too, inasmuch as all other things will be subject to them. And so they pertain to the kingdom of God not only as being *under* a king but also as *being* kings, who will yet be under the one supreme king; and thus it is said in Revelation 5:10: "You have made us a kingdom and priests to our God, and we shall reign over the earth."

4. To the fourth, it should be said that in this passage "kingdom of God" refers to the church militant, not to the church triumphant.

ARTICLE 3   On appetite for beatitude

SUBQUESTION 1[a]   Whether all have appetite for beatitude[b]

Objections:

Proceeding to the third. It seems that not all have appetite for beatitude.

1. For no one wills that of which he is ignorant, as is evident from Augustine in *On the Trinity*,[c] and from the Philosopher, who says in *On the Soul* III that the object of will is the apprehended appetible.[d] But not

a. Parallel: *ST* I-II, q. 5, a. 8.

b. I have chosen to render *appetunt* as "have appetite for," in spite of the inelegancy, because it will not do to substitute systematically "desire" or "seek" or some other verb that has its own solid Latin equivalent (*desiderunt, concupiscunt, quaerunt*, etc.) when there is a metaphysical issue at stake, namely the understanding of *appetitus* as such, and not merely *desiderium* or *concupiscentia*. Also, the very awkwardness of "to have appetite for *x*" as a locution forces a reader to ask the question: "What does Aquinas mean by this phrase?," whereas a different formula, such as "to desire *x*," suggests false associations—for example, that we are dealing here with emotions. Hence, when Thomas asks in subarticle 2 "whether someone can have appetite for misery," he is not asking whether someone can want to feel miserable (the answer being an obvious yes), but whether rational appetite, as such, can be directed to the condition of misery.

c. Augustine, *On the Trinity* VIII, ch. 4 (CCSL 50:275).

d. Aristotle, *On the Soul* III, ch. 10 (433b10).

all know beatitude, since many have gone astray in regard to beatitude [insofar as they take as their end something that is not truly such]. Therefore not all have appetite for beatitude.

2. Further, whoever has appetite for beatitude has appetite for that which is essentially beatitude itself. But beatitude itself is the vision of God, for which not all have appetite. Therefore not all have appetite for beatitude.

3. Further, that which cannot be apprehended cannot be desired. But that two contraries should exist at the same time cannot be apprehended, as is evident from *Metaphysics* IV.[a] Therefore contraries cannot at the same time be objects of appetite. But some have appetite for things contrary to beatitude, such as those who have appetite for sins. Therefore not all have appetite for beatitude.

4. Further, it is a sin to cling to changeable things, despising the unchangeable good. But beatitude is an unchangeable good. Therefore he who sins despises it; and thus, not all have appetite for beatitude.

On the contrary:

1. Stands that which Boethius proves in *On the Consolation of Philosophy* III: longing for the true good is placed within the minds of all men.[b] But the true good is beatitude. Therefore all have appetite for beatitude.

2. Further, to each thing its own end is appetible. But beatitude is the ultimate end of human life. Therefore all men have appetite for beatitude.

Response:

It should be said that in every order of mobiles and movers, the secondary movers must be ordered to the end of the first mover through a disposition impressed into them by the first mover, as is evident when the soul moves the hand and the hand moves a stick, and the stick strikes, which is the end intended by the soul: the stick and the hand tend to an end intended by the soul owing to the fact that the soul impresses [a disposition] into them mediately or immediately. But there is this difference between natural motions and violent motions: in violent motions the impression left by the first mover in the secondary movers is beside their nature, and so the activity consequent upon such an impression is difficult and laborious for them, whereas in nat-

a. Aristotle, *Metaphysics* IV, ch. 3 (1005b29).
b. In this instance the reference is indeed to the whole of Book III of Boethius's *On the Consolation of Philosophy* (CCSL 94:37ff.).

ural motions, the impression left by the first mover in secondary movers is in them a natural cause, and so the activity consequent upon this impression is suitable and sweet (and so it is said in Wisdom 8:1 that "God disposes all things sweetly"), because every single thing, by the nature divinely implanted within it,[a] tends to that to which it is ordered by divine providence, according to the demands of the impression received. And since all things proceed from God inasmuch as he is good, as Augustine says,[b] and also Dionysius,[c] therefore all creatures, according to an impression received from the Creator, are, each according to its own mode, inclined by appetite to the good, so that a certain circular pattern is found in things: for, having gone forth from the good, they tend toward the good. But this circular pattern is brought to perfection in certain creatures, whereas in others it remains imperfect. For those creatures that are not ordered so as to attain the first good itself from which they proceeded, but are ordered merely to acquire some sort of likeness thereof, do not perfectly exhibit this circular pattern; [it is exhibited] only by those creatures that are able to attain, in some way, the first principle itself, and this belongs solely to rational creatures, which are able to gain God himself through knowledge and love—in which gaining their beatitude consists, as is evident from what has been said. And therefore just as any other thing naturally has appetite for its own good, so any rational creature naturally has appetite for its own beatitude.

Replies to objections:

1. To the first, therefore, it should be said that as the visible is twofold—*per se*, e.g., color, and *per accidens*, e.g., a man [who, having some color, is thus visible]—so too the appetible, which is the object of will, can be taken in two ways: *per se* and *per accidens*. The *per se* object of will is the good; but the *per accidens* object is this or that good. And as the good taken generally is the *per se* object of will, so the highest good [as such] is the ultimate end of the will, speaking *per se*; but this or that good is designated as the ultimate end of the will and its chief object as though *per accidens*. Therefore, beatitude is known to all insofar as the chief *per se* object of the will lies in it, but it is not known to all as regards what is accidental to the *per se* object [of the will]. For all know the "perfect good" and have appetite for it, when they have appetite for beatitude; but that this perfect good be pleasure or riches, virtue or

a. *ex natura sibi divinitus indita*
b. Augustine, *On Christian Doctrine* I, ch. 32 (CCSL 32:26).
c. Pseudo-Dionysius, *On the Divine Names,* ch. 4 (PG 3:694ff.).

something else of that kind, is *per accidens*; and so it is not unfitting for there to be many errors concerning this matter.[513]

2. To the second, it should be said that although the vision of God is beatitude itself, nevertheless it does not follow that whoever has appetite for beatitude has appetite for the vision of God, since beatitude, as such, implies the *per se* object of will, but not the very vision of God, just as someone may have appetite for something sweet, yet not have appetite for honey.

3. To the third, it should be said that although some have appetite for things contrary to beatitude as far as the truth of things is concerned, still, in their own estimation, these things are not contrary to it but [rather] lead to it.

4. To the fourth, it should be said that he who sins by clinging to changeable goods as [his] end takes the very changeable things as if they were the foremost appetible and the perfect good; and thus he clings to them out of appetite for beatitude. For as it does not follow that someone, in having appetite for beatitude, has appetite for that which is beatitude according to the truth of things; so too it does not follow that someone, in despising that which is beatitude according to the truth of things, despises beatitude; just as it does not follow that one who does not recognize a man does not recognize white, although a man be white.

SUBQUESTION 2[a] Whether someone can have appetite for misery

Objections:

Moreover, it seems that someone can have appetite for misery.

1. For every rational power extends to opposites. But the will is a rational power. Therefore it extends to opposites. Now, misery is what is opposed to beatitude. Therefore, if someone is able to have appetite for beatitude, he can also have appetite for misery.

2. Further, if someone is not able to want misery, it is impossible for him to want it. Therefore it is necessary for him not to want it. But necessity implies coercion or prohibition, as Anselm says. Therefore the will would be coerced, which is repugnant to its freedom.

3. Further, as beatitude is appetible to all, so is being. But certain

---

a. Parallels: The principle that no one can turn away willingly from beatitude, or willingly desire misery, is invoked numerous times by St. Thomas. In the *Scriptum* itself, see *In II Sent.* d. 7, q. 1, a. 1, ad 1; *In II Sent.* d. 25, a. 2.

people want not to be, as is evident in those who kill themselves. Therefore certain people are also able to want misery.

4. Further, the will is concerned with the end, as is said in *Ethics* III.[a] But the end is the good or the apparent good, as is said in *Physics* II.[b] Therefore not only the good but also the apparent good can be desired. But that which is evil can be an apparent good. Therefore misery, no matter how evil it may be, could still be willed by someone.

On the contrary:

1. Stands Augustine's proof in *On Free Choice of the Will* that no man is capable of wanting to be miserable.[c]

2. Further, as the intellect stands to the first intelligible, so the will stands to the first appetible. But the intellect is incapable of assenting to the contrary of the first intelligible, which is that an affirmation and a denial [of the same thing in the same respect] cannot be true at the same time, as is proved in *Metaphysics* IV.[d] Therefore the will is incapable of assenting to misery, which is contrary to its first appetible.

Response:

It should be said that the activity of a secondary cause is always founded upon the activity of the first cause, and presupposes it; and so every activity of the soul must proceed on the supposition of that which is implanted in the soul from the impression of the first agent, namely of God; and thus we see, on the side of the intellect, that the soul cannot proceed to understand anything except on the supposition of those things the knowledge of which is innate to it; and on account of this it cannot assent to something that is contrary to these principles that it naturally knows. And something similar must be the case on the side of the will. Hence, since from the impression of the first cause, namely of God, it is inserted into the soul that it should will the good, and it has appetite for the perfect good as ultimate end, it is impossible that the contrary thereof should enter into its appetite; and therefore no one is capable of wanting misery, or evil, except *per accidens*, which does happen whenever he has appetite for something evil that he apprehends as a good.

a. Aristotle, *Ethics* III, ch. 2 (1111b26).
b. Aristotle, *Physics* II, ch. 3 (195a25).
c. See Augustine, *On Free Choice of the Will* I, ch. 14 (CCSL 29:231–32), where we are given not so much a proof as a defense or explanation of the point.
d. See Aristotle, *Metaphysics* IV, chs. 4–8.

Replies to objections:

1. To the first, therefore, it should be said that a rational power extends to opposites as far as things beneath it are concerned, and such things are those that are determined by the power itself. It cannot, however, [extend] to the opposites of those things that are determined for it by another; and so the will cannot [extend] to the opposite of that which is determined [for it] by divine impression, namely to the opposite of the ultimate end. However, it *can* [extend] to opposites in regard to things it determines for itself, as are things ordered to the ultimate end, the choice of which pertains to the will.

2. To the second, it should be said that coercion, since it implies violence, and likewise prohibition do not pertain to that necessity which is attendant upon a thing's nature, since everything violent is contrary to nature; and so, since the will is *naturally* borne, of necessity, to beatitude, this [necessity] does not imply coercion in it, nor any diminishment of freedom.

3. To the third, it should be said that nothing prevents something that is appetible in itself from being non-appetible when something else is added on to it. Hence, even being, which is desired by all, and is good in itself, is rendered evil and worthy of hatred due to something added on to it, such as being in sorrow or misery; and so, *per accidens*, non-being is desired—not indeed, insofar as it lacks being, but insofar as it takes away that evil which was rendering being hateful. Now, to be lacking an evil is itself a good; and so he who has appetite for non-being has appetite for it as a good. But misery can never be taken as a good, because "misery" names the *ratio* of complete evil; and therefore no one can want to be miserable. In contrast, "non-being" does not name the very *ratio* of evil, but [only] that which is evil; and so, something added to it that has the *ratio* of good can make it appetible, as is evident from the Philosopher in *Ethics* IX,[a] and from Jerome in the gloss on Jeremiah 20, verses 14–18.[b] But what Augustine says—that no one has appetite for non-being—is to be understood as speaking *per se.*

4. To the fourth, it should be said that one is incapable of judging that white is black, although one could judge that that which is white, say a man, is black; and similarly one can judge that that which is good is an evil, but one is incapable of judging that goodness itself is badness, or that badness is goodness. And since misery implies in itself the

a. Aristotle, *Ethics* IX, ch. 4 (1166b11–13).

b. Jerome, *Commentary on Jeremiah,* Bk. IV, n. 28 (CCSL 74:194–95).

ratio of an evil, therefore one is incapable of judging it to be a good, and on this account one is incapable of having appetite for it.

SUBQUESTION 3ᵃ   Whether one merits
by having appetite for beatitude

Objections:

Moreover, it seems that no one merits by having appetite for beatitude.

1. For by natural endowments we do not merit. But the appetite for beatitude is natural to man, otherwise it would not be common to all. Therefore no one merits by having appetite for beatitude.

2. Further, since merit and demerit concern the same thing, no one merits in regard to what he is incapable of avoiding, just as neither does he sin [in that situation], as Augustine says.ᵇ But man is not capable of not having appetite for beatitude. Therefore no one merits by having [such an] appetite.

3. Further, no one can merit eternal life by his own powers, as Pelagius held. But man *can* have appetite for beatitude through his own powers. Therefore he does not merit by having appetite for beatitude.

On the contrary:

1. Someone desires beatitude and God in the same way. If therefore no one merits by desiring beatitude, no one will merit by desiring God—which is absurd.

2. Further, charity is the principle of meriting. But charity has reference chiefly to the end. Therefore by the motion of the will toward the ultimate end we merit the most; and so [we merit] in having appetite for beatitude.⁵¹⁴

Response:

It should be said that the good, which is the will's object, is in things, as the Philosopher says in *Metaphysics* VI;ᶜ and so the will's mo-

a. The principle used to solve the problem—namely that, since appetite for beatitude involves not only the general inclination of natural appetite but also a determinate act of rational appetite, it is therefore an act for which man is responsible and so can be a meritorious act—is a principle of frequent occurrence in St. Thomas. It is, in some sense, reducible to the claim that whoever acts from charity gains merit, owing to the power of the divine gift already possessed in the will.

b. Augustine, *On Free Choice of the Will* III, ch. 18, n. 50 (CCSL 29:304).

c. Implicitly in Aristotle, *Metaphysics* VI, ch. 4 (1027b24–26); cf. *Metaphysics* IV,

tion must have its term in a thing existing outside the soul. Now, although a thing, so far as it is in the soul, may be considered according to a common *ratio* prescinding from a particular *ratio*, a thing outside the soul cannot exist according to a common *ratio* alone without the addition of a proper *ratio*; and thus, however much the will is borne to the good, it must be borne to some determinate good; and likewise, however much it is borne to the highest good, it must be borne to the highest good under this or that *ratio*.

Now, although it belongs to the will by its natural inclination to be borne to beatitude according to a common *ratio*, yet to be borne to such-and-such a beatitude is not by its natural inclination but by the discernment of reason,[a] which discovers that the highest good of man consists in this thing or in that; and so whenever someone has appetite for beatitude, natural appetite and rational appetite are actually joined in that [appetite for beatitude]. And on the part of natural appetite there is always rectitude, while on the part of the rational appetite sometimes there is rectitude (namely, when appetite is had for beatitude where it truly exists) and sometimes there is perversity (when appetite is had for it where it does not truly exist); and thus, in having appetite for beatitude, someone can either merit (presupposing grace) or demerit, according as his appetite is either right or perverse.

Replies to objections:

1. To the first, therefore, it should be said that in the appetite for beatitude, together with that which is natural, there is always, in addition, something voluntary and not [merely] natural; and it is in this way that the *ratio* of merit or demerit can find a place there.

2. To the second, it should be said that, although no one can avoid having appetite for beatitude in some way, still he can avoid having appetite for it in the way in which it is supposed to be an object of appetite; and thus he can merit or demerit.

3. To the third, it should be said that man by his own powers is insufficient when it comes to having appetite for beatitude with a *perfect* appetite, such as would suffice for meriting; but he has this [sufficiency] from the gift of divine grace, as is evident from 2 Corinthians 5:5: "he who makes us for this very thing is God," that is (according to the gloss), he who makes us have appetite for true glory.[515]

---

ch. 4 (1008b3–31) and V, ch. 1 (1013a17–22); *On the Soul* III, ch. 10 (433a15–21, 433a26–31, 433b15–18).

a. *per discretionem rationis*

SUBQUESTION 4[a]   Whether everything is willed
for the sake of beatitude

Objections:

Moreover, it seems that not everything that a person wills is willed
for the sake of beatitude.

1. For no one wants pleasure for the sake of anything else, as is said
in *Ethics* VII.[b] But pleasure is not beatitude itself, as is evident from
what was said above. Therefore not everything that someone wills[c]
does he will for the sake of beatitude.

2. Further, that which can be desired for the sake of beatitude is
ordainable to beatitude. But many want some things that are not ordainable to beatitude, indeed, that turn one away from it, as is the
case with sinners. Therefore, not everything that someone wills does
he will for the sake of beatitude.

3. Further, that which has no appearance of good[d] in itself cannot
be desired with a view to beatitude. But at times something is desired
that has no appearance of good, as is evident from Augustine in *Confessions*, where he says: "I stole what I already had enough of, and indeed of better quality; nor did I want to enjoy the thing that I sought
by theft, but I sought to enjoy the very theft and sin. . . . And so I look
for what delighted me in the theft; and behold, there is no appearance
[of anything delightful.]"[e] Therefore something can be desired which is
not desired for the sake of beatitude.[f]

4. Further, death cannot be ordered to beatitude in any way, except
perhaps with hope of a life to be gained after death, since beatitude belongs only to the living. But certain people have willed to suffer death,
whether at their own hand or from another, without any hope of a future life. Therefore not everything that is willed is willed for the sake
of beatitude.

5. Further, man's will is revealed to be right by the fact that it is ordered to the right end. If therefore whatever is desired is desired for the
sake of beatitude, every human will is right—which is false. [There-

a. Parallels: *ST* I-II, q. 1, a. 6; *ST* I, q. 60, a. 2; *SCG* I, chs. 100–101.

b. Aristotle expressly makes this point at *Ethics* X, ch. 2 (1172b20–23); perhaps Thomas confused this text with *Ethics* VII, ch. 12 (1153a8–12), where it is
stated that some pleasures are simply ends.

c. *non quidquid aliquis vult*

d. *speciem boni*

e. Augustine, *Confessions* II, ch. 4 and ch. 6 (CCSL 27:22–23).

f. *Ergo aliquid desideratur non propter beatitudinem*

fore, beatitude is not that for the sake of which everything is willed.]

6. Further, that for the sake of which someone actually wills something must be actually thought about.[a] If therefore whatever someone wills he wills for the sake of beatitude, in every desire it will be necessary for beatitude to be actually thought about—which seems to be false. Therefore the same conclusion follows as before.

On the contrary:

1. In that which is desired for its own sake, and never for the sake of another, the motion of desire comes to a halt. But that in which the motion of desire comes to a halt is the ultimate end. If therefore something other than beatitude were desired for its own sake, and never for the sake of something else, something else than beatitude would be the ultimate end, which cannot be so. Therefore, every other desideratum has reference to the desire for beatitude, whether mediately or immediately.

2. Further, Dionysius says that all things desire peace and do whatever they do for its sake.[b] But peace is ordered to beatitude, as is evident from what was said before. Therefore whatever is desired is desired for the sake of beatitude.

Response:

It should be said that, according to the Philosopher in *Ethics* VII, in the order of appetible items, the end holds the rank that a principle holds in the order of intelligible items.[c] Now, since that which is first and maximum in any genus is the cause of those that are after it, so knowledge of the principles in speculative matters is the cause of the knowledge of all other such matters; and likewise, appetite for the end is the cause of having appetite for all other things that are toward the end. Hence, since beatitude is the end of human life, whatever the will has appetite to bring about, is ordered to beatitude. This is clear also from experience; for whoever has appetite for something, has appetite for it insofar as it is judged a good. But by the very fact that someone has something that he judges good, he reckons himself nearer to beatitude, since the addition of a good to a good makes one approach nearer to the perfect good, which is beatitude itself. And therefore any and every appetite is ordered to beatitude.

---

a. *propter quod aliquis vult aliquid actu, oportet actu esse cogitatum*
b. See Pseudo-Dionysius, *On the Divine Names,* ch. 11 (PG 3:947ff.).
c. Aristotle, *Ethics* VII, ch. 8 (1151a16–17).

Replies to objections:

1. To the first, therefore, it should be said that pleasure is among those things that are required for beatitude, since it is in beatitude; and so someone's very appetite for pleasure is ordered to beatitude, insofar as the pleasure itself is some likeness, whether near or remote, of that delight that perfects beatitude.[a]

2. To the second, it should be said that something may be ordered to beatitude through desire in two ways. In one way, as that which is sought so that through it a man may arrive at beatitude, as someone wants to undertake works of virtue so that through this, he may merit beatitude. In another way, when someone has appetite for something owing to the very fact that it has some likeness to beatitude. For the result of the will's having appetite for something[516] is that it also desires that in which the thing's likeness is found, even if it cannot have the chief desideratum; and in this way all who have appetite for sins are [still] striving for beatitude and toward an imitation of God, as Augustine says in *Confessions* II, speaking thus: "Pride imitates your loftiness, since you, O exalted God, are the one above all; ambition, what does it seek except honor and glory, while you are deserving of honor before all";[b] and he brings in the other vices in like manner.

3. To the third, it should be said that in that thievery, as Augustine says in the same place, there was something having an appearance of good, in which a certain shadow of freedom appeared; hence he says: "What, therefore, did I love in that thievery, and how was I imitating you, my God, [though] viciously and perversely?" And he answers, saying: "Or was it not pleasing to act against the law at least by trickery, since I could not do so by power, in order that I, being a slave, might imitate freedom by doing with impunity what was unlawful, in a dark likeness of omnipotence?"[c]

4. To the fourth, it should be said that people who expose themselves to death without hope of a future life do so in two different ways. In one way, for the sake of the activity of virtue, as those who willingly chose[d] to undergo death in order to save their fatherland or to shun an unworthy deed; and according to their judgment, they did in-

---

a. "Pleasure" and "delight" in this sentence are both *delectatio*, but modern English usage makes it odd to speak of the "pleasure" of eternal life.

b. Augustine, *Confessions* II, ch. 6, n. 13 (CCSL 27:23).

c. Ibid., n. 14 (CCSL 27:24).

d. *praeelegerunt*. It is true that choice is already an act of will, but "willingly chose" brings out perhaps the emphasis in the verb.

deed order this to beatitude—not a beatitude to be gained after death, but one that was to be achieved *then,* in the very work, because to do a perfect work of virtue, which was done by enduring death, was the thing desired most of all by them, the thing in which they placed their beatitude. In another way, [people expose themselves to death] on account of the weariness of the misery that they endure, which they reckon they can evade by death. Now, to evade misery and to have appetite for beatitude come to the same thing.[a] And so it stands that the desire of those who want to undergo death is ordered to beatitude.

5. To the fifth, it should be said that, for the will to be right, two things are required. One is that it be aimed at a due end; the other, that that which is ordered to the end be proportioned to the end. Now, although every desire has reference to beatitude, still it happens, in this or that way, that desire is perverse, since the very appetite for beatitude can be perverse when beatitude is sought where it does not exist, as is clear from what was said before; and even if it be sought where it truly exists, it can [also] happen that that for which one has appetite on account of the end is not proportioned to the end, as when someone wants to steal in order to give alms, through which [he intends] to merit beatitude.

6. To the sixth, it should be said that just as in intelligible items the first principles need not be employed in all consequent demonstrations by being actually thought about, but only by being present in power, so long as the demonstration is constructed out of items that have credibility from the first principles;[b] so, too, although every desire has reference to beatitude, it is not necessary that in every desire one should be actually thinking about beatitude, but the desire for beatitude is present by its power in all other desires, as a cause is present in its effects.

ARTICLE 4   On participation in beatitude

SUBQUESTION 1[c]   Whether the beatitude of the saints is going
to be greater after the last judgment than it was before

Objections:

Proceeding to the fourth. It seems that the beatitude of the saints is not going to be greater after the [last] judgment than it was before.

a. *in idem coincidunt*

b. *sic in intelligibilibus non oportet ut in omnibus consequentibus demonstrationibus prima principia essentialiter ingrediantur quasi actualiter cogitata, sed virtute tantum, dum demonstratio conficitur ex his quae per prima principia fidem habent*

c. This is the first text included in our translation that has its "parallel" (q. 93, a.

1. For the more something approaches to the divine likeness, the more perfectly it participates in beatitude. But the soul separated from the body is more like to God than the soul joined to its body. Therefore its beatitude is greater before the resumption of the body than afterwards.

2. Further, a united power is more powerful than a diversified one.[a] But the soul outside the body is more united than when it is joined to the body. Therefore its power is greater for acting; and so the more perfectly does it participate in beatitude, which consists in act.

3. Further, beatitude consists in an act of the speculative intellect, as is evident from what was said above. But the intellect in its act does not employ a bodily organ; and so, the body resumed will not bring it about that the soul understands more perfectly. Therefore the beatitude of the soul will not be greater after the resurrection.

4. Further, there cannot be anything greater than the infinite; and so, the infinite to which something finite is added is no greater than the infinite itself. But the blessed soul before the resumption of the body has beatitude owing to the fact that it rejoices in the infinite good, namely in God; and after the resumption of the body it will still not have joy in anything else, except perhaps the glory of the body, which is a certain finite good. Therefore their joy after the resumption of the body will not be greater than it was before.

On the contrary:

1. The Gloss, commenting on Revelation 8 where it says "I saw under the altar the souls of them that were slain for the word of God and for the testimony which they held,"[b] says: "Presently the souls of the saints are existing 'under,' that is, in a lesser dignity than will be [theirs] in the future." Therefore, [at some point] after death, their beatitude will be greater [than it is at first].[517]

2. Further, as beatitude is paid back to the good as a reward, so is misery paid back to the wicked. But the misery of the wicked after the

---

1) in the *Supplementum* of the *Summa theologiae,* compiled, as many have maintained, by Thomas's *socius* Reginald (see Torrell, *Person and Work,* 147, with n. 14). The text is freshly translated here from the Parma ed. For the most part, the compiler of the Supplement restrained himself to minor modifications, such as removing the cross-reference to "Distinction 44, above," and supplying Augustine for the closing *auctoritas* instead of Jerome. Interestingly, he excises qa. 2, skipping from qa. 1 to qa. 3—evidently aware that Thomas has already treated the contents of qa. 2 earlier in the *ST.*

a. *virtus unita . . . quam multiplicata*

b. Rightly Rev. 6:9. Cf. Strabo, *Glossa ordinaria* on this verse (PL 114:722); Haimo, *On the Apocalypse* II, on 6:9 (PL 117:1029).

resumption of their bodies will be greater than before, since they will be punished not only in soul but also in body. Therefore, too, the beatitude of the saints will be greater after the resurrection of the body than before it.

Response:

It should be said that it is indeed manifest that the beatitude of the saints after the resurrection will increase as regards its *extension,* since then beatitude will be not only in the soul but also in the body; and even the beatitude of the soul itself will be increased as regards extension, insofar as the soul will rejoice not only in its proper good, but also in the good of the body.

It can also be said that the beatitude of the soul itself will be increased as regards *intensity.* For man's body can be considered in two ways. In one way, as it is perfectible by the soul; in another way, as there is in it something that resists the soul in the soul's activities, as long as the body is not perfectly perfected by the soul. Now, according to the first way of considering the body, the union of body to soul adds a perfection to the soul, since every part [as such] is imperfect, and finds completion in the whole; hence the whole stands to the parts as form to matter, and hence the soul is more perfect in its natural being when it is in the whole—namely in man compounded of soul and body—than when it is separate by itself. But the union of the body according to the second way of considering it impedes the perfection of the soul; and thus it is said in Wisdom 9:15 that "the corruptible body weighs down the soul." If, therefore, from the body be taken away everything through which it resists the soul's action, then, simply speaking, the soul will be more perfect existing in such a body than separate by itself. But the more perfect something is in being, the more perfect it can be in acting; hence the activity of a soul united to such a body will be more perfect than the activity of a separated soul.

Now, a body of such a sort is the glorified body, which is altogether subject to the spirit, as was said above in Distinction 44. Hence, since beatitude consists in activity, the soul's beatitude will be more perfect after the resumption of the body than before. For as the soul separated from the corruptible body can act more perfectly than when it is united to it, so, after it shall have been united to a glorified body, its activity will be more perfect than when it was separated. Now, every imperfect thing thing has appetite for its own perfection; and so the separate soul naturally has appetite for conjunction with the body; and owing to this appetite proceeding from imperfection, its activity which is directed toward God is less intense; and this is what Jerome says: that due to appetite for the body, the soul is held back from passing into that highest good with its whole intention.[a]

Replies to objections:

1. To the first, therefore, it should be said that the soul united to the glorified body is more like unto God than when it is separated from such a body, insofar as the composite has being more perfectly. For the more perfectly something exists, the more like unto God it is, as the heart, since the perfection of its life consists in motion,[b] is more like to God when it is moving than when it rests, although God himself never moves.

2. To the second, it should be said that a power to which it belongs by its nature to be in matter is more powerful[c] when existing in matter than when separated from matter, although absolutely speaking a power that is separated from matter is more powerful [than a power existing in matter].

3. To the third, it should be said that, although the soul does not employ the body in the act of understanding, still the body's perfection will in a way cooperate unto the perfection of intellectual activity, inasmuch as the soul, from its union with the glorified body, will be more perfect in its nature, and consequently more effective in its activity; and in this respect the very good of the body will cooperate, as if instrumentally, unto that activity in which beatitude consists, even as the Philosopher states in *Ethics* I that external goods cooperate instrumentally unto happiness of life.[d]

4. To the fourth, it should be said that although a finite added to an infinite does not make a greater, still it makes more, because the infinite and the finite are two, since the finite, taken by itself, is one. Now, the extension of joy [spoken of] does not have reference to *greater*, but to *more*; hence joy will increase as regards extension, if one compares the joy taken in God and in the body's glory, to the joy that was taken in God [alone]. The body's glory will also contribute[e] to a more perfect activity by which the soul is borne into God. For the more perfect a

a. In the Editiones Paulinae text of the *ST*, the quotation is attributed rather to Augustine, with the editors supplying a reference to *On Genesis According to the Letter* XII, ch. 35 (PL 34:483).

b. Literally: "as the heart, the perfection of the life of which consists in motion," etc. For St. Thomas's thoughts about the crucial function of the heart's motion in the animal's life, see his opusculum *De motu cordis* (ed. Leon. 43:127–30).

c. "power . . . more powerful": *virtus . . . magis potens,* and below, *potentior.*

d. Aristotle, *Ethics* I, ch. 8 (1099a33) and ch. 9 (1099b27).

e. *operabitur*

suitable activity is, the greater will be the delight [in doing it], as is evident from what is said in *Ethics* X.[a]

SUBQUESTION 2[b]   Whether beatitude will
be equally participated in by all

Objections:

Moreover, it seems that beatitude will be equally participated in by all.

1. For it is said in Matthew 20:9 that "all shall receive a single denarius." Now the denarius there signifies something that all will have in common. But this is nothing other than beatitude. Therefore each one will have just as much of beatitude as any other.

2. Further, there is nothing beyond the ultimate. But beatitude is the ultimate of those things that can be desired by men. Therefore beyond the beatitude of any man there can be in no man something as if exceeding the other man's beatitude; and so the same conclusion follows as before.

3. Further, as a good is appetible to anyone, so a greater good is more appetible. If therefore someone were more blessed than another who was less blessed, the former's beatitude would be more appetible to the latter, according to a right appetite; yet he would not have it. Therefore he would not be blessed, since, as is said in the text, no one is called blessed unless he has all that he wants, and he wants nothing evil.

On the contrary:

1. It says in 1 Corinthians 15:41, "star differs from star in glory; thus it will be in the resurrection of the dead." Therefore among those who rise, one will have more glory than another.

2. Further, reward ought to correspond to merit. But certain ones have more excellent merits than others. Therefore, since beatitude is the reward of virtue, it seems that they will have a greater beatitude.

---

a. Aristotle, *Ethics* X, ch. 4 (1174b19).

b. Parallels: Among the many discussions of this question, see *In I Sent.* d. 44, a. 3, ad 5; *ST* I-II, q. 3, a. 2, ad 4; q. 5, a. 2; q. 112, a. 4, esp. ad 2; *SCG* III, ch. 58; *Super Ioan.* 14, lec. 14; *Super I Cor.* 3, lec. 2. As mentioned above, the compiler of the Supplement to the *ST* chose to omit this qa. in the "new" q. 93, aware that its subject-matter had already been treated.

Response:
It should be said that, since beatitude consists in activity, the level of beatitude is to be gauged according to the level of perfection in acting. Now, the perfection of activity in which happiness consists is evaluated on the basis of two factors: one on the side of the acting subject, the other on the side of the object.ᵃ Hence the Philosopher says in *Ethics* X that the most perfect activity is the one that is of the highest power perfected by the noblest habit (which is on the side of the acting subject) and with respect to the noblest object.ᵇ Now, the object of the activity in which beatitude consists is altogether one and the same, namely the divine essence, from the vision of which all will be blessed; hence on its side there will not be any level in beatitude. But on the side of the acting subject, the activity of beatitude will not be perfect in the same way, since insofar as the habit that brings to perfection the aforesaid activity, namely the light of glory, will be more perfect in one than in another, to that extent this activity will be more perfect, and the delight greater; and from this vantage, all the blessed will not be in the same level of beatitude.

Replies to objections:
1. To the first, therefore, it should be said that the denarius designates, on the part of the object of beatitude itself, the one who will be commonly rendered [to the blessed], since God will show his essence to all; but each one will gaze on it according to his own mode.

2. To the second, it should be said that, as fire is the most subtle kind of body and nevertheless one fire can be more subtle than another, so beatitude, considered according to its kind, is the ultimate of all things desirable to mankind; hence nothing prevents the beatitude of one from being more perfect than the beatitude of another. Moreover, the beatitude of each one is ultimate inasmuch as his appetite has its term wholly therein, even if it be not ultimate in the sense of existing in the ultimate degree of perfection.⁵¹⁸

3. To the third, it should be said that in the blessed there will be perfect charity; hence anyone there [in heaven] will love God more than himself, and so he will more want that which is more suited to God, than that which would be better for himself; and thus he will more want divine justice to be preserved by his having less, which is more

---

a. *ex parte operantis, et ex parte objecti*
b. See Aristotle, *Ethics* X, ch. 4 (1174b18–20) and ch. 7 (1177a12–21).

suited to God, than he will want to have more, which would be better for him.[a]

SUBQUESTION 3[b]   Whether the degrees of beatitude ought
to be called "dwelling places"[c]

Objections:

Moreover, it seems that these degrees of beatitude ought not to be called "dwelling places."

1. For beatitude carries with it the *ratio* of reward. But "dwelling place" signifies nothing that pertains to reward. Therefore different degrees of beatitude ought not to be called dwelling places.

2. Further, "dwelling place" seems to signify a place. But the place wherein the saints will be made blessed is not bodily but spiritual, namely God, who is one. Therefore there is only one dwelling place; and so different degrees of beatitude cannot be called dwelling places.

3. Further, as in the fatherland there will be men of diverse merits, so now there are such in purgatory, and there were such in the limbo of the fathers of old. But in purgatory and limbo, no dwelling places are distinguished one from another. Therefore, neither in the fatherland ought dwelling places to be distinguished one from another.

---

a. The Parma ed.: *et ideo magis volet divinam justitiam salvari in hoc quod ipse minus habeat, quod est deo convenientius, quam in hoc quod plus habeat, quod esset sibi melius.* We are reading the *in* of *in hoc quod plus habeat* as a mistake caused by unconciously making this clause correspond with the previous one. The content of the text makes little sense if one interprets the grammar as it stands. The reason why his having less is more suited to God, is precisely that the divine justice is thereby preserved. If the divine justice were preserved in his having more, there would be nothing more suited to God about his having less—none mentioned in the text, that is.

b. This qa. is brought over to *Supplementum* q. 93, a. 2, with no modification. A parallel, in some respects, is *ST* 1-2, q. 5, a. 2, esp. ad 1.

c. "Dwelling places" translates *mansiones*. The King James and Douay-Rheims simply say "mansions," while the RSV has "rooms" and the New American Bible, "dwelling places." Any of these, it seems, would be acceptable translations, but since "mansion" in contemporary English refers only to an oversized domicile of the wealthy class, it seems odd to use this word, whereas etymologically "dwelling places" is closer to the root of *mansio.*

On the contrary:

1. Stands what is said in John 14:2: "In the house of my father there are many dwelling places"—which Augustine expounds of the various dignities of the rewards.[a]

2. Further, in any city there is an orderly distinction of dwelling places. But the heavenly fatherland is compared to a city, as is clear from Revelation 21. Therefore different dwelling places must be distinguished there, according to diverse degrees of beatitude.

Response:

It should be said that since local motion is prior to all other motions, thus, according to the Philosopher, the names "motion" and "distance" and everything of the kind are carried over from local motion to all other motions.[b] Now the end of local motion is a place,[c] where something remains at rest once it has arrived,[d] and is preserved therein; and so, in any motion, we call "station"[e] or "dwelling" the very being-at-rest in the end of the motion; and therefore, since the name of motion is carried over all the way to the act of appetite and of will, the very gaining of the end of appetitive motion is called a dwelling place, or station, in the end. And hence different ways of obtaining the ultimate end are called different dwelling places, such that the unity of house corresponds to the unity of beatitude, which is on the side of the object, while the plurality of dwellings places corresponds to the differences that are found in beatitude on the side of the blessed—as we also see, in natural things, that it is the same place up above to which all light things tend, but each one arrives nearer to that place to the extent that it is lighter; and thus they have diverse dwelling places according to differences in lightness.

a. See Augustine, *On the Gospel of John* 14:1–3, tract. 67, n. 2 (CCSL 36:495–96).

b. Aristotle, *Physics* VIII, ch. 9 (265b17).

c. This works better in Latin: *finis motus localis est locus.*

d. *ad quem cum aliquod pervenerit, ibi manet quiescens*

e. The term is *collocatio.* The meaning here basically refers to something being at rest or stable due to its position vis-à-vis other things, or the place itself in which it is at rest: station, resting place. Thomas seems to be almost equivocating on the usage of *collocatio* and *mansio* when referring to the being at rest (standing, dwelling) and the usage when referring to the place in which something is at rest (station, dwelling place).

Replies to objections:

1. To the first, therefore, it should be said that "dwelling place" does imply the *ratio* of end, as is evident from what was said, and so consequently implies the *ratio* of reward, which is the end of merit.

2. To the second, it should be said that although there is one spiritual place, still, diverse are the steps for approaching to that place; and according to this are established diverse dwelling places.

3. To the third, it should be said that those who were in limbo or who are now in purgatory have not yet [or had not then] come to their end; and so in purgatory or in limbo dwelling places are not distinguished, one from the other; but this is done only in paradise and in hell, where there is the *end* of the good and of the wicked.

SUBQUESTION 4[a]   Whether diversity of dwelling places
follows upon different degrees of charity

Objections:

Moreover, it seems that different dwelling places are not distinguished according to different degrees of charity.

1. For it says in Matthew 25:15: "He gave to each one according to each one's own power." But the power proper to anything whatsoever is its natural force. Therefore gifts of both grace and glory are distributed according to different degrees of natural power.[b]

2. Further, in Psalm 62:12 it is said: "You will render to every man according to his works." But that which is rendered is the measure of beatitude. Therefore the degrees of beatitude are distinguished according to a diversity of works, and not according to a diversity of charity.

3. Further, the reward is owed to act, and not to habit; hence it is not the strongest who are crowned, but the ones who struggle the most, as is clear from *Ethics* I;[c] and in 2 Timothy 2:5: "He will not be crowned unless he strive lawfully." But beatitude is the reward. Therefore different degrees of beatitude are not according to different degrees of charity [which is a habit, but according to different degrees of active striving].

a. Parallels: This qa. is brought over to *Supplementum* q. 93, a. 3, with no modification; cf. *ST* I, q. 12, a. 6 and q. 62, a. 9. The more general point that a saint's subjective participation in God's blessedness corresponds to his capacity or receptivity, which was co-determined by God's grace and the saint's exercise of charity *in via*, is a commonplace in Thomas's works.
b. "Power": *virtus*; "force": *vis*   c. Aristotle, *Ethics* I, ch. 8 (1099a4).

On the contrary:

1. On the contrary is the fact that the more joined someone will be to God, the more he will be blessed. But the mode of union with God follows the mode of charity. There will therefore be differences in beatitude according to differences in charity.

2. Further, as one thing taken simply follows upon another taken simply, so a greater degree of the one follows upon a greater degree of the other. But having beatitude follows upon having charity. Therefore having *more* beatitude follows upon having *more* charity.

Response:

It should be said that the principle distinctive of heavenly dwelling places or degrees of beatitude is twofold: proximate and remote. The proximate principle is a diversity of disposition that will be found in the blessed, out of which there arises among them a diversity of perfection in the activity of beatitude; but the remote principle is the merit by which they attained such beatitude. Now, in the first way, the dwelling places are distinguished according to the charity of the fatherland—the more perfect it is in someone, the more it will render him receptive of the divine glory, according to which increase the perfection of divine vision will be increased. By contrast, in the second way the dwelling places are distinguished according to the charity of the wayfaring state. For our act [of charity in this life] does not possess the quality of being meritorious from the very substance of the act, but solely from the habit of virtue by which it is informed. But the power of meriting[a] is in every virtue owing to charity, which has the ultimate end as its object; and so, any difference in meriting comes down completely to a difference in charity. And in this manner, the charity of the wayfaring state will, by way of merit, differentiate heavenly dwelling places.

Replies to objections:

1. To the first, therefore, it should be said that "power" here [in this verse] is to be taken not solely for natural capacity but for natural capacity simultaneous with an effort toward having grace; and then power, so taken, will be a quasi-material disposition vis-à-vis the measure of grace and glory received. But charity is formally completive of merit ordered to glory; and therefore a distinction of degrees in glory is taken according to grades of charity rather than according to grades in the aforesaid power [i.e., natural capacity and effort].

a. *vis merendi*

2. To the second, it should be said that works do not have it in them that a recompense of glory should be rendered for them, except insofar as they are informed by charity; and so there will be different grades in glory according to different grades of charity.

3. To the third, it should be said that, while the habit of charity (or of any virtue) is not the merit to which a reward is owed, nevertheless the habit of charity is the principle and the whole *ratio* of meriting in any act; and so diverse rewards are distinguished according to its diversity—although one could also consider a grade in meriting by reason of the very genus of a certain act a grade not with respect to the essential reward, which is rejoicing in God, but with respect to accidental reward, which is rejoicing over a created good.

APPENDIX I

SCRIPTUM AND *ST* PARALLELS ON LOVE
AND CHARITY IN GENERAL

Scriptum texts corresponding to *Summa theologiae* I-II, qq. 26–28

Love in itself		
	ST	*Scriptum*
Whether love is in the concupiscible	I-II, 26, 1	*In III Sent.* d. 26, q. 1, a. 2; d. 27, q. 1, a. 2
Whether love is a passion	I-II, 26, 2	Cf. *In III Sent.* d. 27, q. 2, a. 1
Whether love is the same as rational love [*dilectio*]	I-II, 26, 3	*In I Sent.* d. 10, exp. text.; *In III Sent.* d. 27, q. 2, a. 1
Whether love is suitably divided into love of friendship and love of concupiscence	I-II, 26, 4	*In II Sent.* d. 3, q. 4; *In III Sent.* d. 29, a. 3; *In IV Sent.* d. 49, q. 1, a. 2, qa. 1, ad 3

Love's cause		
	ST	*Scriptum*
Whether the good is the sole cause of love	I-II, 27, 1	
Whether knowledge is a cause of love	I-II, 27, 2	*In I Sent.* d. 15, q. 4, a. 1, ad 3
Whether likeness is a cause of love	I-II, 27, 3	*In III Sent.* d. 27, q. 1, a. 1, ad 3
Whether any other passion of the soul is a cause of love	I-II, 27, 4	

Love's effects		
	ST	*Scriptum*
Whether union is an effect of love	I-II, 28, 1	*In III Sent.* d. 27, q. 1, a. 1
Whether mutual inherence is an effect of love	I-II, 28, 2	*In III Sent.* d. 27, q. 1, a. 1, ad 4
Whether ecstasy is an effect of love	I-II, 28, 3	*In III Sent.* d. 27, q. 1, a. 1, ad 4
Whether zeal is an effect of love	I-II, 28, 4	*In III Sent.* d. 27, q. 1, a. 1, ad 3

Love's effects *(cont.)*

	ST	*Scriptum*
Whether love is a passion that wounds the lover	I-II, 28, 5	*In III Sent.* d. 27, q. 1, a. 1, ad 4
Whether love is the cause of all the lover does	I-II, 28, 6	*In III Sent.* d. 27, q. 1, a. 1

Scriptum texts corresponding to *ST* II-II, qq. 23–27

Charity in itself		
	ST	*Scriptum*
Whether charity is friendship	II-II, 23, 1	*In III Sent.* d. 27, q. 2, a. 1
Whether charity is something created in the soul	II-II, 23, 2	*In I Sent.* (Paris version) d. 17, q. 1, a. 1; *In I Sent.* (Roman revision) d. 17, q. 1, a. 2
Whether charity is a virtue	II-II, 23, 3	*In III Sent.* d. 27, q. 2, a. 2
Whether charity is a special virtue	II-II, 23, 4	*In III Sent.* d. 27, q. 2, a. 4, qa. 2
Whether charity is one virtue	II-II, 23, 5	*In III Sent.* d. 27, q. 2, a. 4, qa. 1
Whether charity is the most excellent virtue	II-II, 23, 6	
Whether without charity there can be any true virtue	II-II, 23, 7	*In III Sent.* d. 27, q. 2, a. 4, qa. 3, ad 2
Whether charity is the form of the virtues	II-II, 23, 8	*In II Sent.* d. 26, a. 4, ad 5; *In III Sent.* d. 23, q. 3, a. 1, qa. 1; d. 27, q. 2, a. 4, qa. 3

Charity's subject		
	ST	*Scriptum*
Whether the will is the subject of charity	II-II, 24, 1	*In III Sent.* d. 27, q. 2, a. 3
Whether charity is caused in us by infusion	II-II, 24, 2	*In I Sent.* (Roman revision) d. 17, q. 1, aa. 1–2
Whether charity is infused in proportion to a sum of natural endowments	II-II, 24, 3	*In I Sent.* d. 17, q. 1, a. 3; *In II Sent.* d. 3, exp. text.; *In III Sent.* d. 31, q. 1, a. 4, qa. 1

Charity's subject *(cont.)*

	ST	*Scriptum*
Whether charity can increase	II-II, 24, 4	*In I Sent.* (Paris version) d. 17, q. 2, a. 1; *In I Sent.* (Roman revision) d. 17, q. 2, a. 1
Whether charity increases by addition	II-II, 24, 5	*In I Sent.* (Paris version) d. 17, q. 2, a. 2; *In I Sent.* (Roman revision) d. 17, q. 2, a. 3
Whether charity increases by every act of charity	II-II, 24, 6	*In I Sent.* d. 17, q. 2, a. 3; *In II Sent.* d. 27, a. 5, ad 2
Whether charity admits of indefinite increase	II-II, 24, 7	*In I Sent.* d. 27, q. 2, a. 4; *In III Sent.* d. 29, a. 8, qa. 1, ad 2
Whether a wayfarer's charity can be perfect	II-II, 24, 8	*In III Sent.* d. 27, q. 3, a. 4
Whether three degrees of charity are fittingly distinguished—beginning, progressing, and perfect	II-II, 24, 9	*In III Sent.* d. 29, a. 8, qa. 1
Whether charity can decrease	II-II, 24, 10	*In I Sent.* d. 17, q. 2, a. 5
Whether charity, once had, can be lost	II-II, 24, 11	*In III Sent.* d. 31, q. 1, a. 1
Whether charity is lost through one mortal sin	II-II, 24, 12	*In I Sent.* d. 17, q. 2, a. 5; *In III Sent.* d. 31, q. 1, a. 1

Charity's object

	ST	*Scriptum*
Whether the love of charity stops at God, or extends itself also to the neighbor	II-II, 25, 1	*In III Sent.* d. 27, q. 2, a. 4, qa. 1, ad 1–3
Whether charity should be loved from charity	II-II, 25, 2	*In I Sent.* d. 17, q. 1, a. 5
Whether irrational creatures also should be loved from charity	II-II, 25, 3	*In III Sent.* d. 28, a. 2
Whether a man ought to love himself from charity	II-II, 25, 4	*In III Sent.* d. 28, a. 6
Whether a man ought to love his body from charity	II-II, 25, 5	*In III Sent.* d. 28, a. 7
Whether sinners should be loved from charity	II-II, 25, 6	*In II Sent.* d. 7, q. 3, a. 2, ad 2; *In III Sent.* d. 28, a. 4

Charity's object *(cont.)*

	ST	Scriptum
Whether sinners love themselves	II-II, 25, 7	*In II Sent.* d. 42, q. 2, a. 2, qa. 2, ad 2; *In III Sent.* d. 27, exp. text.
Whether charity obliges us to love enemies	II-II, 25, 8	*In III Sent.* d. 30, a. 1
Whether charity obliges us to show signs and deeds of love to our enemies	II-II, 25, 9	*In III Sent.* d. 30, a. 2
Whether we ought to love angels from charity	II-II, 25, 10	*In III Sent.* d. 28, a. 3
Whether we ought to love demons from charity	II-II, 25, 11	*In III Sent.* d. 28, a. 5
Whether four things are fittingly reckoned as to be loved from charity, namely: God, our neighbor, our body, and ourselves	II-II, 25, 12	*In III Sent.* d. 28, a. 7

Charity's order

	ST	Scriptum
Whether there is an order in charity	II-II, 26, 1	*In III Sent.* d. 29, a. 1
Whether God should be loved more than one's neighbor	II-II, 26, 2	*In III Sent.* d. 29, a. 3, ad 5; d. 30, a. 4
Whether from charity a man ought to love God more than himself	II-II, 26, 3	*In III Sent.* d. 29, a. 3
Whether from charity a man ought to love himself more than his neighbor	II-II, 26, 4	*In III Sent.* d. 29, a. 5
Whether from charity a man ought to love a neighbor more than his own body	II-II, 26, 5	*In III Sent.* d. 29, a. 5
Whether one neighbor should be loved more than another	II-II, 26, 6	*In III Sent.* d. 29, a. 2
Whether we ought to love more those who are better than those who are joined to us	II-II, 26, 7	Cf. *In III Sent.* d. 29, a. 6 and d. 31, q. 2, a. 3, qa. 2
Whether the one most to be loved is he who is joined to us by way of fleshly origin	II-II, 26, 8	*In III Sent.* d. 29, a. 6
Whether from charity a man ought to love his son more than his father	II-II, 26, 9	*In III Sent.* d. 29, a. 7
Whether a man ought to love his mother more than his father	II-II, 26, 10	*In III Sent.* d. 29, a. 7, ad 4 & 5
Whether a man ought to love his wife more than his father and mother	II-II, 26, 11	*In III Sent.* d. 29, a. 7, ad 3

Charity's order *(cont.)*

	ST	*Scriptum*
Whether a man ought to love his benefactor more than the one he himself benefits	II-II, 26, 12	*In III Sent.* d. 29, a. 7, ad 2
Whether the order of charity remains in the fatherland	II-II, 26, 13	*In III Sent.* d. 31, q. 2, a. 3, qaa. 1 & 2

Charity's principal act, which is love

	ST	*Scriptum*
Whether it is more proper to charity to be loved or to love	II-II, 27, 1	[none]
Whether to love, considered as an act of charity, is the same as benevolence	II-II, 27, 2	Cf. *In III Sent.* d. 27, q. 2, a. 1
Whether from charity God should be loved on account of himself	II-II, 27, 3	*In III Sent.* d. 29, a. 4
Whether God can be loved immediately in this life	II-II, 27, 4	*In III Sent.* d. 27, q. 3, a. 1
Whether God can be totally loved	II-II, 27, 5	*In III Sent.* d. 27, q. 3, a. 2
Whether any measure should be observed in loving God	II-II, 27, 6	*In III Sent.* d. 27, q. 3, a. 3
Whether it is more meritorious to love an enemy than to love a friend	II-II, 27, 7	*In III Sent.* d. 30, a. 3; a. 4, ad 3
Whether it is more meritorious to love a neighbor than to love God	II-II, 27, 8	*In III Sent.* d. 30, a. 4

Scattered points of contact

	ST	*Scriptum*
Whether someone can have hatred for himself	I-II, 29, 4	*In II Sent.* d. 42, q. 2, a. 2, qa. 2, ad 2; *In III Sent.* d. 27, exp. text.
Whether pleasure differs from joy	I-II, 31, 3	*In III Sent.* d. 26, q. 1, a. 3; d. 27, q. 1, a. 2, ad 3; *In IV Sent.* d. 49, q. 3, a. 1, qa. 4
Whether hope and memory are causes of pleasure	I-II, 32, 3	*In III Sent.* d. 26, q. 1, a. 1, ad 3
Whether sadness should be fled more than pleasure should be pursued	I-II, 35, 6	*In III Sent.* d. 27, q. 1, a. 3, ad 3; *In IV Sent.* d. 49, q. 3, a. 3, qa. 3

Scattered points of contact *(cont.)*

	ST	*Scriptum*
Whether moral virtues can exist without charity	I-II, 65, 2	*In III Sent.* d. 27, q. 2, a. 4, qa. 3, ad 2 and d. 36, a. 2
Whether peace is the same as concord	II-II, 29, 1	*In III Sent.* d. 27, q. 2, a. 1, ad 6
Whether beneficence is an act of charity	II-II, 31, 1	*In III Sent.* d. 27, q. 2, a. 1; cf. d. 29, aa. 2 & 5
Whether we should bestow benefits more on those who are more joined to us	II-II, 31, 3	*In III Sent.* d. 29, a. 6, ad 3 & 5
Whether it was fittingly commanded that God be loved with one's whole heart	II-II, 44, 4	*In III Sent.* d. 27, exp. text.; cf. *In III Sent.* d. 27, q. 3, a. 4
Whether, in addition to the words "Love the Lord your God with all your heart," it was fittingly added, "and with all your mind and with all your strength"	II-II, 44, 5	*In III Sent.* d. 27, exp. text.
Whether this precept concerning the love of God can be fulfilled in the wayfaring state	II-II, 44, 6	*In III Sent.* d. 27, q. 3, a. 4
Whether the order of charity falls within the precept	II-II, 44, 8	*In III Sent.* d. 29, a. 1, ad 5

APPENDIX II

ENGLISH TRANSLATIONS OF

THE *SCRIPTUM*

It is clear that a translation of the entire *Scriptum* into English would be a daunting task, but there is no question it is a goal both possible and desirable for the near future. To the Dominicans of Bologna goes credit for the first complete translation of the *Scriptum* into any language: they have published a bilingual edition in ten volumes, with Italian and Latin on facing pages (*Commento alle Sentenze di Pietro Lombardo e testo integrale di Pietro Lombardo* [Bologna: Edizioni Studio Domenicano, 2001]), whose utility consists entirely in the translation, since the Latin text reproduced is not the semi-critical edition of Mandonnet and Moos but a reprinting of the Parma edition. A Spanish translation is currently under way.

Relatively few translations into English of sizeable passages from the *Scriptum* have been published. To my knowledge, the most significant are, listed in order of the layout of the *Sentences*:

Topic and citation	Publication data
Theology and theological method (*In I Sent.*, Prologue and q. 1)	Two translations: (1) *Thomas Aquinas: Selected Writings*, trans. Ralph McInerny (London/New York: Penguin, 1998), 50–66. By a serious typographical error, the text that immediately follows, from Book II, is not identified as a separate item in the collection or its table of contents. It has been listed below in due order. (2) Trans. Hugh McDonald, e-text at www.vaxxine.com/hyoomik/aquinas/sent1.html.
The unity of the divine essence; man's knowledge of God (*In I Sent.* d. 2, q. 1, a. 1; d. 3, q. 1, aa. 1–4)	Trans. John Laumakis, e-text at http://www4.desales.edu/~philtheo/loughlin/ATP/index.html
The multiplicity of names for God (*In I Sent.* d. 2, q. 1, a. 3)	*Aquinas: Selected Philosophical Writings*, trans. Timothy McDermott (Oxford: Oxford University Press, 1993), 230–40.
The divine essence (*In I Sent.* d. 8)	*Thomas Aquinas's Earliest Treatment of the Divine Essence*, trans. E. M. Macierowski (Binghamton: Global Publications, 1997), 22–131; includes the Latin text of Mandonnet on facing pages.

Topic and citation	Publication data
Whether God is entirely simple (*In I Sent.* d. 8, q. 4, a. 1)	Trans. John Laumakis, e-text at http://www4.desales.edu/~philtheo/loughlin/ATP/index.html
The Holy Spirit as Love (*In I Sent.* d. 10)	Trans. Peter A. Kwasniewski and Thomas Bolin, O.S.B., e-text at http://www4.desales.edu/~philtheo/loughlin/ATP/index.html
God's existence in things and his omnipresence (*In I Sent.* d. 37, q. 1, aa. 1–2; q. 2, aa. 1–3)	Trans. John Laumakis, e-text at http://www4.desales.edu/~philtheo/loughlin/ATP/index.html
Creation (*In II Sent.* d. 1, q. 1)	*Aquinas on Creation,* trans. Steven E. Baldner and William E. Carroll (Toronto: Pontifical Institute of Mediaeval Studies, 1997), 63–109, with a translation of the prologue of Book II on pp. 129–32.
The work of the six days of creation (*In II Sent.* d. 12)	McInerny, *Selected Writings,* 85–104.
The creation of man (*In II Sent.* d. 17)	McInerny, *Selected Writings,* 67–84 (note that this text is not listed in the book's table of contents).
The sin against the Holy Spirit (*In II Sent.* d. 43, q. 1)	Trans. Stephen Loughlin, e-text at http://www4.desales.edu/~philtheo/loughlin/ATP/index.html
Christian obedience to secular powers (*In II Sent.* d. 44, q. 2, a. 2) and the relationship between spiritual and temporal power (*In II Sent.* d. 44, q. 3, a. 4)	Several translations: (1) *Aquinas, Selected Political Writings,* ed. A. P. D'Entrèves, trans. J. G. Dawson (Totowa, NJ: Barnes & Noble, 1981), 91–94; (2) *Aquinas, Political Writings,* ed. R. W. Dyson (Cambridge: Cambridge University Press, 2002), 72–75 and 277–78; (3) the former text, in part, as Appendix II, text 6, in *On Kingship, to the King of Cyprus,* trans. Gerald B. Phelan, rev. I. Th. Eschmann (Toronto: Pontifical Institute of Mediaeval Studies, 1982), 103–5; (4) a larger portion of *In II Sent.* d. 44 seems to be translated in Michael P. Molloy's *Civil Authority in Medieval Philosophy: Lombard, Aquinas and Bonaventure* (Lanham, MD: University Press of America, 1985) on pp. 143–73, but unfortunately I have not been able to locate this volume.
The hypostatic union (*In III Sent.,* d. 5, q. 1, aa. 2–3 and d. 6, q. 2, aa. 1–2)	Trans. J. L. A. West, e-text at http://www4.desales.edu/~philtheo/loughlin/ATP/index.html
On the Eucharist (*In IV Sent.* d. 8, q. 1)	Trans. Peter A. Kwasniewski and Joseph Bolin, e-text at http://www4.desales.edu/~philtheo/loughlin/ATP/index.html
On fasting (*In IV Sent.* d. 15, q. 3)	Trans. Stephen Loughlin, e-text at http://www4.desales.edu/~philtheo/loughlin/ATP/index.html

Topic and citation	Publication data
Prayer (*In IV Sent.* d. 15, q. 4)	*Albert and Thomas, Selected Writings,* trans. Simon Tugwell (New York: Paulist Press, 1988), 363–418.
Happiness as the goal of human life (*In IV Sent.* d. 49, q. 1)	McDermott, *Philosophical Writings,* 315–41. Note that this same question is also translated in full in the present volume.

Of course, a good many articles on sacraments and on the Last Things were borrowed from Book IV of the *Scriptum* in order to "complete" the *Summa theologiae* after Thomas's death, making up the so-called *Supplementum* to the *Tertia pars,* and this portion of a (modified) *Scriptum* has long been available in the translation of the *Summa* made by the Fathers of the English Dominican Province (London: Burns, Oates & Washbourne, 1912–36; repr. in 5 vols., Westminster, MD: Christian Classics, 1981). Generally, the *Supplementum* shows a conservative editorial approach, with the main difference being some snipping away of less essential objections and replies. In the present volume, a small part of this overlapping *Scriptum-Supplementum* material, freshly translated, has been restored to its proper context in the *Scriptum* (cf. *In IV Sent.* d. 49, q. 1).

Finally, mention should be made of collections of Thomistic texts that contain topical snippets from the *Scriptum,* such as *An Aquinas Reader,* ed. Mary T. Clark (New York: Fordham University Press, 1988; rev. ed. 2000) (for texts from the *Scriptum,* see, in the ed. of 1988, pp. 44–48, 97–98, 196–98, 260–72 [a potpourri of texts on love and charity mainly from Book III, d. 27, but mistakenly identified as Book I, d. 27], 341–42, 411–12; and in the rev. ed. of 2000, 41–43, 61, 69, 89–90, 91, 93–94 [a text on 179–81 is mistakenly attributed to the *Scriptum*], 212–22 [the texts from *In III Sent.* d. 27 are rather chopped up; oddly, pages 212–17 are attributed to the commentary on *De anima*], 282–84, 346–47), and *St. Thomas Aquinas, Theological Texts,* ed. Thomas Gilby (London: Oxford University Press, 1955).

INDEX OF NAMES

Entries preceded by "s" refer to pages in the Full Introduction and Webnotes contained in the web-based Supplement to this volume. *Nota bene:* Because Aristotle, "the Philosopher," is cited on nearly every page, he has no separate entry in this index.

INDEX OF
SCRIPTURAL CITATIONS

Entries preceded by "s" refer to pages in the Full Introduction and
Webnotes contained in the web-based Supplement to this volume.

On Love and Charity: Readings from the "Commentary on the Sentences of Peter Lombard" was designed and typeset in Meridien by Kachergis Book Design of Pittsboro, North Carolina. It was printed on 60-pound Natures Natural and bound by Thomson-Shore of Dexter, Michigan.